The
Princeton
Review

Cracking the
TOEFL*
iBT

2010 Edition

Douglas Pierce and Sean Kinsell
Updated by Vanessa Coggshall

PrincetonReview.com

Random House, Inc. New York

ESL
428.24
TOEFL = Princeton Review

The Princeton Review, Inc.
2315 Broadway
New York, NY 10024
E-mail: editorialsupport@review.com

ISBN: 978-0-375-42920-0
ISSN: 1941-2029

Editor: Heather Brady
Production Editor: Meave Shelton
Production Coordinator: Kim Howie

TOEFL® is a registered trademark of Educational Testing Service.

10 9 8 7 6 5 4 3 2 1

2010 Edition

John Katzman, Chairman, Founder
Michael J. Perik, President, CEO
Stephen Richards, COO, CFO
Rob Franek, VP Test Prep Books, Publisher

Editorial
Seamus Mullarkey, Associate Publisher
Laura Braswell, Senior Editor
Rebecca Lessem, Senior Editor
Selena Coppock, Editor
Heather Brady, Editor

Production Services
Scott Harris, Executive Director, Production Services
Kim Howie, Senior Graphic Designer

Production Editorial
Meave Shelton, Production Editor
Emma Parker, Production Editor

Random House Publishing Team
Tom Russell, Publisher
Nicole Benhabib, Publishing Manager
Ellen L. Reed, Production Manager
Alison Stoltzfus, Associate Managing Editor
Elham Shabahat, Publishing Assistant

Acknowledgments

Thanks to Heather Brady, Meave Shelton, Kim Howie, and the staff and students of The Princeton Review. Thanks also to Vanessa Coggshall for her thorough review and to Michael Bagnulo for his updates to this edition.

Special thanks to Adam Robinson, who conceived of and perfected the Joe Bloggs approach to standardized tests and many of the other successful techniques used by The Princeton Review.

Contents

Part III:
Cracking
Each Section
of the TOEFL

Part IV:
Taking a Practice
Test

Part I
Orientation

1 Introduction

Chapter 1
Introduction

WELCOME!

Welcome to The Princeton Review's thorough test preparation guide for the Test of English as a Foreign Language (TOEFL). In this book, you will find everything you need to prepare for the TOEFL—information on the test format, test-taking strategies, drills, and, of course, a full-length practice exam.

Part I of this book gives a brief outline of how the test is organized. Part II helps you familiarize yourself with the basic concepts tested on the TOEFL. Part III presents you with strategies and tips for the questions and tasks on the test. Part IV provides you with a full-length practice exam with answers and explanations.

WHAT IS THE TOEFL?

The TOEFL is a test that assesses your proficiency in the type of English used in an academic environment. The test is administered on the Internet, which we'll explain in more detail on page 6.

The exam takes about four hours to complete and integrates four essential skills—reading, listening, writing, and speaking. This means that any given question or task may require you to use one or more of these skills. For example, before attempting a writing task on the TOEFL, you may have to first read a passage and listen to a lecture on the topic.

Fortunately, the TOEFL is not as daunting as it may seem because it tests each of the four skills in a fairly specific way. By working through this book in its entirety, you'll become comfortable with the type of writing, speaking, reading, and listening skills that are required to get a good score on the exam.

The Structure of the Test

The TOEFL is broken down into four distinct sections, one each for the skills listed. However, each section may require you to use more than one of the above four skills. The structure of the test is as follows:

- One **Reading** section, consisting of three to five passages that are roughly 700 words each. Each passage will be followed by 12 to 14 multiple-choice questions about the content of the passage. Most of these questions will be worth one point each, though a few toward the end of the section may be worth more. You will have 60 to 100 minutes to complete the entire section.
- One **Listening** section, consisting of six to nine audio selections, each of which are three to five minutes long. The selections will be either academic lectures or casual conversations. After each selection, there will be five to six multiple-choice questions about the content of the lecture or conversation. You will have 60 to 90 minutes to complete the entire section.
- One **Speaking** section, consisting of approximately six speaking tasks. Most speaking tasks will also require some listening and some reading. You will have to speak for 45 or 60 seconds, depending on the task, and you will have 20 minutes to complete the entire section.
- One **Writing** section, consisting of two writing assignments. As with the speaking section, the writing section also requires listening and reading. You will have 50 minutes to complete the entire section.

How the Test Is Scored

After finishing the TOEFL, you will receive a score from 0 to 30 for each of the four sections. You will also receive a total score on a 0 to 120 scale. Each score corresponds to a percentile ranking. This number shows how your score compares with the scores of other test takers. For example, a total score of 100 would put you in the 89th percentile, meaning that you scored higher than 89 out of 100 test takers, whereas a score of 50 would put you in the 26th percentile. The average TOEFL score is around 68.

Notice that the 0 to 30 scores are *scaled* scores, meaning that the 0 to 30 number doesn't represent how many questions you answered correctly or how many points your essay was awarded. For example, the Reading and Listening sections each contain roughly 40 questions. You will get a point for each correct answer (some Reading section questions will be worth two points) and a penalty for each incorrect answer. At the end of the section, your *raw* score, which represents how many points you've earned, is tallied and converted to a number on the 0 to 30 scale.

The Writing and Speaking sections are scored somewhat differently. Each writing sample receives a score between 0 and 5. These raw scores are then converted to the 0 to 30 scale. Similarly, each speaking task receives a score from 0 to 4. The scores from all six speaking tasks are averaged and converted to the 0 to 30 scale.

For help finding the right college for you, go online to PrincetonReview.com!

How Are the Scores Used?

Colleges and universities will look at your TOEFL score when considering your application. Of course, your TOEFL score is not the only factor that affects your chance of admission. Colleges and universities also look at your academic performance, letters of recommendation, application essays, and scores on other standardized tests. Although a high TOEFL score will not guarantee admission to a particular program, a low test score could jeopardize your chances.

Some schools and programs may require students with TOEFL scores below a certain cutoff score to take supplemental English classes. Others may only accept applicants who score better than a particular cutoff score. Make sure you check with the programs to which you are applying for specific information.

The Computer-Based Format Used for Internet-Based Testing (iBT)

The TOEFL is a computer-based test that is delivered to testing centers via the Internet. Therefore, the TOEFL can be offered at locations throughout the world. The test is administered by Educational Testing Service (ETS), the same testing organization that administers the GRE, SAT, and other standardized tests. According to ETS, Internet-based testing (iBT) is an easier and fairer way to capture speech and score responses. It also makes it possible for them to greatly expand access to test centers.

The iBT format will be new to the untrained eye and may be intimidating, especially if you have never taken a test on a computer. A brief tutorial is offered at the beginning of the TOEFL to allow you time to familiarize yourself with the format. Still, the iBT presents some challenges. For example, when working on a reading passage, you will see something like this:

TOEFL Reading

REVIEW   HELP   BACK   NEXT
   ?   →

PAUSE   SECTION
TEST   EXIT

Question 3 of 12

HIDE TIME   00:08:45

More Available

The Exoskeleton of the Arthropod

There are more arthropods alive on Earth than there are members of any other phylum of animals. Given that not only insects and spiders but also shrimp, crabs, centipedes, and their numerous relatives are arthropods, this fact should not occasion surprise. For all their diversity, arthropods of any type share two defining characteristics: jointed legs (from which the phylum takes its name) and an exoskeleton (the recognizable hard outer shell).

Though the shell itself is made of dead tissue like that of human hair and fingernails, it is dotted with sensory cells. These give the arthropod information about its surroundings, much as the nerve endings in human skin do. Also like human skin, the shell protects fragile internal organs from potentially hazardous contact with the environment. It seals in precious moisture that would otherwise evaporate but permits the exchange of gases.

Its primary component is chitin, a natural polymer that contains calcium and is very similar in structure to the cellulose in wood. Chitin and proteins are secreted in the epidermis, the living tissue just below the shell, after which they bond to form a thin sheet. Each new sheet is produced so that its chitin fibers are not parallel with those directly above, which increases their combined strength.

The result is the endocuticle, a mesh of molecules that forms the lowest layer of the shell. The endocuticle is not quite tough enough for daily wear and tear. Over time, however, its molecules continue to lock together. As the endocuticle is pushed upward by the formation of new sheets by

TOEFL Reading

PAUSE TEST   SECTION EXIT

REVIEW   HELP ?   BACK   NEXT

Question 3 of 12

HIDE TIME   00:08:45

More Available

the epidermis, it becomes the middle shell layer called the exocuticle. With its molecules bonded so tightly, the exocuticle is very durable. There are points on the body where it does not form, since flexibility is needed around joints. This arrangement allows supple movement but provides armor-like protection.

Though strong, the chitin and protein exocuticle itself would provide a poor barrier against moisture loss. Therefore, it must be coated with lipids, which are also secreted by the epidermis. These lipids, mostly fatty acids and waxes, form the third, outermost layer of the shell. They spread over the cuticles to form a waterproof seal even in dry weather. This lipid layer gives many arthropods their distinctive luster.

Combined, the endocuticle, exocuticle, and lipid coating form a shell that provides formidable protection. The external shell has other advantages. One is that, because it has far more surface area than the internal skeleton found in vertebrates, it provides more points at which muscles can be attached. This increased number of muscles permits many arthropods to be stronger and more agile for their body size than birds or mammals. The coloration and markings of the exoskeleton can be beneficial as well. Many species of scorpion, for instance, have cuticles that contain hyaline. The hyaline is excited by ultraviolet radiation, so these scorpions glow blue-green when a black light is flashed on them. Scientists are not sure why scorpions have evolved to fluoresce this way, but the reason may be that their glow attracts insects that they can capture and eat.

Adaptive as their shell is, it leaves arthropods with at least one distinct disadvantage: The

More Available

cuticle cannot expand to accommodate growth. As the animal increases in size, therefore, it must occasionally molt. The existing cuticle separates from newer, more flexible layers being secreted beneath it, gradually splits open, and can be shaken or slipped off. The new chitin and protein will harden and be provided with a fresh lipid coating, but this process can take hours or days after molting occurs. The arthropod must first take in extra air or water to swell its body to greater than its normal size. After the shell has hardened in its expanded form, the arthropod expels the air or water. It then has room for growth. But until it hardens, the new coat is tender and easily penetrated. Accordingly, the arthropod must remain in hiding. Otherwise, it risks being snapped up by a predator clever enough to take advantage of its lowered defenses.

Clearly, you cannot approach a computer-based TOEFL reading passage the same way you would approach a paper-based test. For one thing, you won't be able to underline, circle, or otherwise make marks on the text (well, you could, but the testing center probably wouldn't be happy if you ruined its computer screens!).

Also, on the computer-based TOEFL, you'll have to take each portion of the test in its entirety. Therefore, you cannot skip part of the Reading section, go to the Listening section, and return to the Reading section. However, you can skip questions *within* some sections of the Reading section.

The audio portions of the test are also computer-based, and the speaking portion will ask you to speak into a recording device.

Even though this book contains paper-based drills and questions, all of the strategies in this book are geared toward preparing you for a computer-based test. To get a feel for taking the test on a computer, you should practice at the TOEFL website: **http://toeflpractice.ets.org.**

Registering for the TOEFL

Make sure to register early!

The easiest way to register for the TOEFL is online, at **www.ets.org/toefl/index .html.** Because the test is Internet-based, many testing times are available, although this isn't necessarily true overseas. Make sure you register early so that you receive a testing time and location with which you are comfortable.

You may take the TOEFL as many times as you like. Many programs will simply take your best score, but don't forget to check for specific information with admissions counselors from the schools to which you are applying.

WHAT IS THE PRINCETON REVIEW?

The Princeton Review is *the* premier test-preparation company that prepares tens of thousands of students each year for tests such as the TOEFL, SAT, GMAT, GRE, LSAT, and MCAT. At The Princeton Review, we spend countless hours researching tests and figuring out exactly how to crack them. We offer students proven, high-powered strategies and techniques to help them beat the tests and achieve their best scores.

In addition to our books, we offer both live classroom instruction and online courses. If you would like more information about our programs, visit us at **PrincetonReview.com.**

If you are looking for information on Princeton Review courses offered outside the United States, go to www.princetonreview.com/international-locations.aspx.

WHAT'S IN THIS BOOK

Cracking the TOEFL iBT contains four parts.

1. **Orientation:** What you're reading now.
2. **Core Concepts:** The basic skills necessary to successfully complete the exam. By working through the exercises in this section, you will have a greater understanding of how the integrated tasks on the TOEFL fit together.
3. **Cracking:** The appropriate strategies to crack each question type on the TOEFL. Questions in the Listening, Speaking and Writing sections are accompanied by audio tracks on a CD.
4. **Full-Length Practice Test:** After you've worked through all the exercises and drills in the previous two sections, you'll get a chance to practice under real testing conditions. The practice exam includes detailed explanations for every question, as well as sample speaking and writing responses. In addition, the CD includes samples of the types of conversations and lectures that you will hear on the test to give you a good idea of what to expect and help you develop your listening skills.

Note: The CD that accompanies this book contains audio tracks in MP3 format. This CD will play in a computer that uses a Windows-based or Mac® operating system, or any device that will play MP3 files (some CD players and DVD players will also play MP3 files).

WHAT'S *NOT* IN THIS BOOK

This book is primarily designed to aid you in preparing to take the TOEFL. It docs not provide a comprehensive grammar guide or extensive English vocabulary lessons. By working through the book, you'll be able to pick up new vocabulary and some grammar rules, but if you need more help with the basics, there are a number of resources available.

- The Princeton Review's *Grammar Smart, Word Smart* and our new *TOEFL: Word Smart* books (available wherever you purchased this book, including online retailers) provide extensive help with grammar and vocabulary.
- Magazines such as *Time, Discover, Entertainment Weekly, Sports Illustrated,* and newspapers such as *USA Today* will help your comprehension and vocabulary.
- Television and radio are enjoyable ways to learn the language. Almost any show or program will be helpful.
- A quick search on the Internet will turn up a number of helpful web-sites devoted to helping people learn English.

This book is more useful if you are comfortable with the English language. If you are still having trouble with English, build up your confidence with the language first, then work through this book.

HOW TO USE THIS BOOK

The material in *Cracking the TOEFL iBT* is provided to help students of all levels achieve higher scores on the test. Ideally, all students should work through the sections of the book in the order in which they are presented. Even students who are fairly comfortable speaking, reading, and writing in English will benefit from the information in the Core Concepts section (Part II).

Of course, if you feel that you have a strong grasp of the material, you are free to skip ahead to the Cracking section (Part III) to start working on TOEFL questions. If you find you are not progressing as you'd hoped, return to Part II and work through it first.

The best way to prepare for the TOEFL is to practice as much as possible, and this book gives you the chance to work through more than 200 sample questions. However, to get maximum value from this book, you must use the strategies and techniques we present, even if you feel our approach to the TOEFL sometimes feels awkward or inefficient. You must trust that our techniques and strategies *do* work, and you should practice them accordingly.

CAN I REALLY IMPROVE MY SCORE?

Yes. Doing well on the TOEFL is a skill, and as with any skill, it can be learned. This book provides the tools necessary to do better on the TOEFL, but it is up to you to apply them. Work through the book at a comfortable pace. Take time to understand the strategies and techniques and *use* them. Look back at the questions you've answered: both the ones you answered correctly and the ones you got wrong. Figure out what your strengths and weaknesses are on the test. Many test takers find that if they fail to use the strategies we offer, their scores don't change. However, test takers who *do* master our techniques and strategies will improve their scores.

Before We Begin

Before we discuss the TOEFL, there are a few basic principles to keep in mind for any standardized, multiple-choice test.

Wrong Answers

One of the advantages of a multiple-choice test is that the answer to every question is right there on the screen! To minimize this advantage, test writers have to make the wrong answers *seem* correct; often, the wrong answers are particularly appealing, and test takers fall into the trap of picking answers that seem too good to be true.

Learning to recognize and avoid these trap answers is one of the keys to your success on the TOEFL. For each question in this book, be sure to review both the right and wrong answers so you have an idea of what both good and bad answers look like. Also, pay close attention to our discussion of common trap answers in the Reading and Listening sections.

Increase Your Odds

Identifying wrong answers greatly improves your chances of getting a question correct. On the TOEFL, each multiple-choice question has four answer choices, which means you have a 25 percent (1 in 4) chance of guessing correctly. However, by using Process of Elimination (POE) to cross off wrong answers, you greatly increase your odds. (We discuss POE thoroughly in the Cracking the Reading Section chapter later in this book.) Finding and eliminating just *one* wrong answer means you have a 33 percent (1 in 3) chance of guessing correctly, and eliminating *two* answers raises your odds of guessing correctly to 50 percent (1 in 2)! This is an important fact to remember. Although you will not be able to answer every question on the TOEFL correctly, you can increase your score simply by increasing your odds when guessing.

TAKING THE TOEFL iBT

Read the advice below before taking the TOEFL iBT.

Computer Practice

The TOEFL iBT is only offered online, so make sure you're comfortable with basic computer functions. No specialized knowledge is required, but you should know how to use a keyboard and mouse. Some basic typing skills will also be helpful on the Writing section.

The Week Before the Test

You should allow yourself about four to six weeks of preparation before you take the TOEFL. You cannot cram for the TOEFL, but there are some things you can do in the final week before the test.

1. **Review strategies:** Look back over the strategies in this book. Make sure you are comfortable with them.
2. **Review tasks:** Before the test, review the four different tasks on the TOEFL (Reading, Listening, Speaking, and Writing). Familiarize yourself with the format and the question types you'll see on test day.
3. **Know the directions:** Don't waste time on test day reading the directions for each task. Learn the directions ahead of time.
4. **Warm-up questions:** Look back at the questions you've completed. Review how you approached each one. Note any trap answers and question types that were particularly difficult for you.
5. **Have a plan:** Make sure you know the format for your speaking and writing tasks. Review the structure of your responses.

Test Day

On the night before the test, put your practice materials aside and give yourself a break. Make sure you know where your test center is, and plan to arrive at least 30 minutes before your scheduled test time. Be sure to dress comfortably and bring a valid photo ID, such as a passport, to the test center. You should also bring two pencils to take notes, although many centers will provide pencils. You may not take anything into the testing center, so do not bring food, backpacks, suitcases, cell phones, or laptops.

Part II
Core Concepts

Chapter 2
Core Concept:
Reading

The TOEFL is an integrated exam, which means that each task may measure more than one skill. But the TOEFL is also a standardized test, which means that it consists of definite patterns. Your goal when taking the TOEFL is to make sure your responses conform to the patterns present on the test.

The reading selections in this chapter will form the foundation for your listening and writing goals. Likewise, the skills needed to perform well in listening, speaking, and writing are closely intertwined. You'll find that mastering the core concepts of one section will also help you on other sections of the test.

READING ON THE TOEFL

There are three to five reading passages on the TOEFL, each around 700 words. Although the TOEFL test writers *attempt* to simulate the type of reading you will do at a school or graduate program, the reading skills required on the test are very different from the skills used in an academic environment. Let's take a look at a passage.

> Scientists at Michigan State University are asking a most challenging question. Can a computer program be considered alive? The members of the Digital Evolution Laboratory say yes. Computer scientists at the laboratory have created a program called Avida that has intrigued not only scientists and engineers but biologists and philosophers as well.

> The Avida project began in the late 1990s, when Chris Adami, a physicist, sought to create computer programs that could evolve to do simple addition problems and reproduce inside a digital environment. Adami called these programs "digital organisms." Whenever a digital organism replicates, it has a chance to alter the program of the newly created offspring. In this way, the programs mutate and evolve. The goal of the Avida program is to create a model that could simulate the evolutionary process.

> Initially, the digital creations were unable to process numbers in any way. But Adami designed Avida to reward digital organisms that were able to work with the numbers in some way. The digital organisms that could process numbers were allowed to reproduce in higher numbers. In only six short months, the primitive program had evolved a number of mechanisms to perform addition. And, most surprisingly, not all of the digital creatures performed addition in the same way.

> The Avida program now resides at Michigan State University, where it has been growing and changing for years. The digital creatures number in the billions and have colonized more than two hundred computers. The organisms compete with one another for resources, and the most successful ones are able to make more copies of themselves. Just like living creatures, the digital entities also undergo mutations. Mutations that are beneficial ensure

greater reproduction; harmful mutations have the opposite effect.

As a model for studying evolution, the Avida project has been a great success. Adami's digital organisms have suggested solutions to some of evolution's biggest mysteries. For example, Avida has helped disprove the theory of "irreducible complexity." Opponents of evolutionary theory have suggested that some structures, such as the eye, are too complex to have been created in piecemeal stages. The evolution of Avida's digital organisms proves that even extremely complex structures can be developed in stages over time.

The Avida program's success has also raised some unintentional philosophical dilemmas. Does Avida just simulate evolution? Or are digital organisms a new form of life? According to the director of the Avida project, the processes undergone by the digital creatures are the same as those experienced by biological organisms. The only difference is that biological entities are based on strings of DNA, whereas the digital creations from Avida are based on strings of ones and zeros. In a living creature, different sequences of DNA instruct cells to create certain proteins. In one of the Avida creations, different sequences of computer code instruct the program to perform certain functions. In both cases, the reproduction of the organisms is subject to forces such as competition and mutation.

Now, some biologists are maintaining that the programs in the Avida project are alive. The programs live, die, reproduce, compete, cooperate, and evolve—activities that many biologists consider the hallmarks of life. One prominent biologist says, "They don't have a metabolism—at least not yet. But otherwise, they're alive."

Of course, not everyone agrees that the program's creations are alive. One difficulty is that biologists do not even agree on the definition of life. The diversity of life on Earth constantly surprises scientists, and there are simply too many characteristics and qualities to provide one simple definition of life.

Despite these misgivings, the directors of the Avida program remain optimistic that their program, even if not considered alive, is leading to a greater understanding of life in all its forms. It may even facilitate future searches for life on other planets. According to one member of the Avida team, "The problem that we have now is that we are focused on looking for DNA-based life. But there may be other kinds of life out there that we have never dreamed of." The Avida program may provide biologists with another avenue to explore.

This passage is typical of the passages on the TOEFL. It's about 700 words long, and it discusses an academic topic. It contains some challenging vocabulary words and requires you to read about a topic in which you may have no interest or knowledge. Although you may end up reading passages such as this at a university or graduate program, your approach for the TOEFL should be very different. For example, in a college course, you would need to read this passage very carefully, paying close attention to the details and facts presented in it. However, that type of close reading is neither possible nor necessary on the TOEFL.

Working on Active Reading

You will have to face many challenges in the Reading section. You've already seen an example of the level of content and vocabulary you may encounter. Perhaps the greatest challenge, however, is to attempt to both read the passages and answer the questions in the limited time provided. You have only about a minute and a half per question, and that's without allowing any time for actually reading the passage!

It is clear, then, that the reading skills necessary for the TOEFL really are different from other types of reading that you do. Therefore, to do well on the TOEFL, you have to work on *active reading*.

Instead of attempting to retain all of the information in the passage, we are going to focus on the big picture. Active reading accomplishes three major tasks:

1.   **Finding the purpose:** This involves figuring out why the author wrote the piece.
2.   **Understanding the structure:** Mapping the passage to find out where key information is.
3.   **Finding the main idea:** Stating what the passage is about.

By mastering the skill of active reading, you'll be able to not only find the most important information in a passage but also effectively answer the questions that follow. After all, you gain no points on the TOEFL for simply *reading the passages*; you only get points for *answering the questions*.

Step 1: Find the Purpose

Writers write for many reasons. Some write to entertain, whereas others write to inform. If you know the **purpose** of a passage, then you know what the writer is trying to accomplish, and you can determine what is important and unimportant about the piece.

The majority of passages on the TOEFL will do one of the following:

- **Explain:** The purpose of these passages is to present you with information on specific topics, and they contain mostly facts.
- **Resolve:** The purpose of these passages is to find solutions for some sort of dilemma. There is usually a debate or question that needs an answer.
- **Convince:** The purpose of these passages is to try to argue the validity of a certain viewpoint or idea. They give opinions and support them with evidence.

To find the purpose of the passage, we'll start with the introduction or the first paragraph.

The Introduction Paragraph

Let's return to the sample passage in this chapter. Here's the first paragraph again.

> Scientists at Michigan State University are asking a most challenging question. Can a computer program be considered alive? The members of the Digital Evolution Laboratory say yes. Computer scientists at the laboratory have created a program called Avida that has intrigued not only scientists and engineers but biologists and philosophers as well.

The introduction paragraph is one of the most important paragraphs in the passage—it should give you a pretty good idea of what the author wants to accomplish. Let's look at it sentence by sentence and identify clues that will help us find the purpose.

First, we have the opening sentence.

> Scientists at Michigan State University are asking a most challenging question.

Now, let's focus on the important stuff. We do this by asking ourselves *what* and *why*.

The first question is: What are we reading about? This is the *subject* of the sentence. Write down the subject. _____

Now we ask ourselves: What is the author writing about this? Write down what you think the author wants us to know about. _____

So far, we are reading about the scientists. And why are we reading about them? Because they are asking a question. If you are still unsure about this information after reading the first sentence, then continue to the second sentence.

In the second sentence we have

> Can a computer program be considered alive?

This clarifies the first sentence. Now we know that the passage is about scientists and a computer program that may be considered alive. Try to predict why the author wrote this passage—to inform, to resolve, or to argue—and write it down.

_____

Now let's move on to the body paragraphs.

The Body Paragraphs

When looking for the purpose, don't get bogged down in the details. Read the first sentence or two of each paragraph. Here are the first four body paragraphs.

The Avida project began in the late 1990s, when Chris Adami, a physicist, sought to create computer programs that could evolve to do simple addition problems and reproduce inside a digital environment. Adami called these programs "digital organisms." Whenever a digital organism replicates, it has a chance to alter the program of the newly created offspring. In this way, the programs mutate and evolve. The goal of the Avida program is to create a model that could simulate the evolutionary process.

Initially, the digital creations were unable to process numbers in any way. But Adami designed Avida to reward digital organisms that were able to work with the numbers in some way. The digital organisms that could process numbers were allowed to reproduce in higher numbers. In only six short months, the primitive program had evolved a number of mechanisms to perform addition. And, most surprisingly, not all of the digital creatures performed addition in the same way.

The Avida program now resides at Michigan State University, where it has been growing and changing for years. The digital creatures number in the billions and have colonized more than two hundred computers. The organisms compete with one another for resources, and the most successful ones are able to make more copies of themselves. Just like living creatures, the digital entities also undergo mutations. Mutations that are beneficial ensure greater reproduction; harmful mutations have the opposite effect.

As a model for studying evolution, the Avida project has been a great success. Adami's digital organisms have suggested solutions to some of evolution's biggest mysteries. For example, Avida has helped disprove the theory of "irreducible complexity." Opponents of evolutionary theory have suggested that some structures, such as the eye, are too complex to have been created in piecemeal stages. The evolution of Avida's digital organisms proves that even extremely complex structures can be developed in stages over time.

Now, we are going to read only the first sentence of each paragraph and ask *what* and *why*. Look only at the first sentence of the first body paragraph. Write down *what* the author's subject is and *what* you think the author is telling us about it.

What?_____

What about it? _____

Do the same for the other three paragraphs.

What?_____

What about it? _____

What? _____

What about it? _____

What? _____

What about it? _____

Your answers should look something like this.

What? _Avida project_____

What about it? _To tell us how it began_____

What? _Avida program_____

What about it? _It's been changing_____

What? _Digital creatures_____

What about it? _They are similar to biological creatures_____

What? _Studying evolution_____

What about it? _They can help scientists learn more about evolution_____

Check back on the prediction you made earlier. Does this new information change it? Let's look at the remaining body paragraphs.

The Avida program's success has also raised some unintentional philosophical dilemmas. Does Avida just simulate evolution? Or are digital organisms a new form of life? According to the director of the Avida project, the processes undergone by the digital creatures are the same as those experienced by biological organisms. The only difference is that biological entities are based on strings of DNA, whereas the digital creations from Avida are based on strings of ones and zeros. In a living creature, different sequences of DNA instruct cells to create certain proteins. In one of the Avida creations, different sequences of computer code instruct the program to perform certain functions. In both cases, the reproduction of the organisms is subject to forces such as competition and mutation.

Now, some biologists are maintaining that the programs in the Avida project are alive. The programs live, die, reproduce, compete, cooperate, and evolve—activities that many biologists consider the hallmarks of life. One prominent biologist says, "They don't have a metabolism—at least not yet. But otherwise, they're alive."

Of course, not everyone agrees that the program's creations are alive. One difficulty is that biologists do not even agree on the definition of life. The diversity of life on Earth constantly surprises scientists, and there are simply too many characteristics and qualities to provide one simple definition of life.

Again, read only the first sentence of each paragraph and answer the questions.

What?_____

What about it? _____

What?_____

What about it? _____

What?_____

What about it? _____

Take a look at your responses. Do they match the following?

What? <u>Are digital organisms a form of life?</u>

What about it? <u>The digital creatures meet many of the criteria for life</u>

What? <u>Biologists</u>

What about it? <u>They think the program is alive</u>

What? <u>Other people</u>

What about it? <u>They don't agree with the biologists</u>

By now, we should have a pretty good idea of why the author has written this passage. Write down *your* reason here. _____

We'll check our final prediction in a moment, but before we do so, we have one more paragraph to review.

The Conclusion

Here's the final paragraph, but for this paragraph, let's read the first and last sentence.

> Despite these misgivings, the directors of the Avida program remain optimistic that their program, even if not considered alive, is leading to a greater understanding of life in all its forms. It may even facilitate future searches for life on other planets. According to one member of the Avida team, "The problem that we have now is that we are focused on looking for DNA-based life. But there may be other kinds of life out there that we have never dreamed of." The Avida program may provide biologists with another avenue to explore.

Now we'll answer our questions.

What?_____

What about it? _____

What?_____

What about it? _____

Here are our answers.

What? <u>Directors of the program</u>

What about it? <u>The program is helping people understand life</u>

What? <u>The Avida program</u>

What about it? <u>The program gives biologists something to explore</u>

Putting It All Together

Look back at what you've written. Based on only the six or seven sentences you've read, does it seem as if the author is trying to argue a point, resolve a dilemma, or simply provide you with information?

The purpose of this passage is to provide us with information—to explain something. It introduces the scientists and their Avida program. Next, it describes the beginning of the project and the current state of the Avida program. After that, the author talks about how the director of the project and other people view the project. Finally, the author indicates that scientists hope Avida will lead to new avenues of exploration. Thus, we could write down the following for the purpose:

Purpose: <u>To give us a brief overview of the Avida computer program and its implications</u>

Remember, you won't have time to read and comprehend every single word and sentence on the TOEFL. Therefore, with *active reading*, you'll read fewer sentences, and your comprehension will increase because you'll read only the important parts.

YOUR TURN: DRILL #1—FIND THE PURPOSE

Apply the techniques we've just learned to each of the passages that follow. Check your answers at the end of the drill.

Passage A

After a seven-year journey, the Cassini spacecraft approached the planet Saturn in June 2004. The spacecraft's successful entry into orbit around the world represented the culmination of a vision that took more than 20 years to realize. Launched amid controversy in October 1997, the Cassini spacecraft traveled more than one billion miles in its journey. Despite all the public and technological challenges, the Cassini mission has been more successful than even its planners imagined.

The Cassini mission resulted from the joint efforts of NASA (National Aeronautics and Space Administration), the European Space Agency, and the Italian Space Agency. The Cassini spacecraft actually consisted of two parts; the first is the Cassini orbiter itself, designed to explore the moons, rings, and atmosphere of Saturn. The second is the Huygens probe. Named after Christiaan Huygens, the discoverer of Saturn's rings, the Huygens probe was built to plunge into the atmosphere of Saturn's largest moon, Titan. Hundreds of engineers and scientists from more than 30 countries contributed to the Cassini-Huygens project.

Mission designers set highly ambitious goals for the project. After Cassini reached Saturn, scientists hoped the craft would help provide answers to some great astronomical mysteries. Most intriguing to many scientists was the nature of Saturn's awesome ring system. Other scientists hoped to learn the composition and geological features of some of Saturn's many moons. And not a few scientists waited eagerly for information on Titan, the only known moon with an atmosphere. Some believe that Titan has a chemical composition resembling that of early Earth and so it may hold important clues about Earth's formation.

The Cassini spacecraft itself is a marvel of engineering. Measuring 22 feet high and 13 feet wide, the Cassini orbiter weighs more than 4,000 pounds. With the Huygens probe attached and fuel added, the total weight of the craft is more than 12,000 pounds. The orbiter holds a variety of scientific instruments, including a cosmic dust analyzer, a magnetometer, and infrared and ultraviolet cameras. All told, the craft has 18 different scientific instruments designed to carry out 27 different scientific experiments.

One of the greatest challenges faced by engineers working on the Cassini project involved getting the spacecraft to Saturn. Saturn lies almost 800 million miles away from Earth, an immense distance. The amount of fuel needed to send Cassini on a direct route to the planet would be prohibitive. Therefore, mission strategists had to come up with a plan to get the craft to Saturn using a minimum amount. The solution was to use a technique called *gravity assist*, in which the craft uses the gravitational pull of a planet to "slingshot" it into deep space. Mission planners sent Cassini on a route that passed by the planet Venus twice and back toward Earth for a final push. This circuitous route added more than 200 million miles to the craft's journey.

Another challenge to the Cassini mission came from a most unexpected source. Because of Saturn's great distance from the Sun, solar panels would not be able to provide sufficient energy to power the orbiter. To solve this problem, engineers decided to use nuclear power, placing a 72-pound chunk of plutonium in the craft. This strategy immediately incurred criticism from environmentalists and others who were worried that, were an accident to occur, the radioactive material could harm people on Earth.

Fortunately, the launch of Cassini went off without a problem. For seven years, the spacecraft traveled through the void of space. Upon reaching Saturn, Cassini's instruments awoke from their long slumber and began transmitting data. After several months of orbiting, the Huygens probe began its descent towards the surface of Titan. The probe relayed data from its 25-hour descent before reaching the surface and shutting down, while Cassini continued its scheduled four-year orbit. It sent back startling images of Saturn's surface, including photographs of a giant hurricane system more than 500 miles across. Yet the mission is not over. On Earth, scientists continue analyzing all the new information they've received, hoping for answers to the mysteries of the solar system.

Paragraph 1

What?_____

What about it? _____

Paragraph 2

What?_____

What about it? _____

Paragraph 3

What?_____

What about it? _____

Paragraph 4

What?_____

What about it? _____

Paragraph 5

What?_____

What about it? _____

Paragraph 6

What?_____

What about it? _____

Paragraph 7

What?_____

What about it? _____

Purpose?_____

Passage B

Sometimes it appears that the human mark on this planet is indelible. In only a blink of geological time, 200 years or so, human construction and expansion has resulted in the destruction of more than one-fifth of the world's forests, the recession of the polar icecaps, and the creation of a huge hole in the ozone layer. Additionally, industrial activity has damaged rivers and oceans, as well as groundwater supplies. Environmental scientists and activists warn that if Earth's future is not taken into account, humankind could very well destroy the planet.

However, Earth is an amazingly resilient place. In its 4.5-billion-year lifespan, Earth has endured bombardment by cosmic rays and meteors, violent earthquakes, volcanism, and frigid ice ages. In light of all these catastrophic events, many geologists and ecologists say that Earth could recover from any damage caused by human actions.

The author Alan Weisman has gone so far as to predict exactly what would happen on Earth if all humans were to disappear. Without upkeep, the concrete jungles of the world's greatest cities would be slowly reclaimed by the wilderness around them. Harsh temperatures would cause pavement to crack. Plants would return to areas covered by streets and sidewalks.

Different fates would await humankind's other creations. Litter and leaf matter would accumulate, and it would take only one chance lightning strike to start a raging fire. Many structures would burn to the ground. The steel foundations supporting larger buildings and bridges would corrode and buckle, especially with the rise in groundwater that would accompany the clogging of sewer systems.

Without human interference, many of the threatened or endangered fauna would reclaim their ecological niches. Unfortunately, household pets would suffer. In addition, the rat, one of the greatest pests in large cities, would not have the waste of humankind to feed off of and would be hunted mercilessly by growing populations of hawks and falcons. And the cockroach, which to many a city dweller seems to symbolize invincibility, would disappear from all but the warmest climes without artificial heat to sustain it.

Within 500 years, again barely a heartbeat in geological time, most of humankind's monuments would be gone, covered over by plants and trees. It's happened before; the Mayan civilization in Northern Guatemala survived for 2,000 years but was swallowed up by the jungle at its end. And after a few thousand years, if earthquakes and volcanic eruptions have not obliterated everything made by humans, the glaciers would come, sweeping down from the mountains, slowly and inexorably destroying everything in their path. Several times in its history, Earth has been swept clean by these giant sheets of ice. The legacy of humankind would be wiped from Earth.

Of course, not every man-made artifact would be reclaimed by nature. Plastic is a synthetic material that does not occur in nature. The strong bonds that hold plastic together are virtually impervious to natural erosion. Long after concrete and glass have turned back into sand and all processed metals have rusted away, plastics will still be cycling through the Earth's ecosystem, resilient to even most destructive of natural forces. Some scientists believe that plastic molecules may eventually break down entirely, but there is no reliable data on just how long complete re-assimilation into the environment might take. Furthermore, it is impossible to predict just what sort of resources Mother Nature might develop in the distant future. There is always the possibility that, given enough time, some microbe or bacteria may evolve the capability to digest plastic. If nature somehow evolved a way to process plastics, then even humanity's most enduring artifacts might vanish in the space of a few hundred years.

The question of plastics, aside, there is some evidence that Weisman's view may be true. Since 1953, a 150-mile-long tract of land separating North and South Korea has been declared a no-man's-land. After only a little more than 50 years, there is almost no trace of the rice paddies that farmers had created and used for almost 5,000 years. Even more spectacular are the flocks of red-crowned cranes that now inhabit the zone. These birds are the second rarest of all birds, but they have flourished in this area, free from human interference of all kinds.

Paragraph 1

What? _____

What about it? _____

Paragraph 2

What? _____

What about it? _____

Paragraph 3

What? _____

What about it? _____

Paragraph 4

What? _____

What about it? _____

Paragraph 5

What? _____

What about it? _____

Paragraph 6

What? _____

What about it? _____

Paragraph 7

What? _____

What about it? _____

Purpose? _____

Paragraph 8

What? _____

What about it? _____

Purpose? _____

Passage C

What causes hallucinations, vivid perceptions of unreal sights or sounds that appear quite real to the person experiencing them? These mystical experiences have long fascinated psychologists, neuroscientists, and anthropologists alike. In many cultures, shamans, prophets, and seers are marked by their susceptibility to hallucinations. Are hallucinations caused by ghosts or spirits? Are they messages from another world? Although researchers don't have all the answers, there is some intriguing information on the topic.

According to surveys, anywhere from 10 to 25 percent of the population has experienced at least one hallucination. Most often, the hallucination comes in the form of some visual experience, but some people report hearing a sound or even voices. Even rarer, but not unheard of, is a hallucination of a particular smell or aroma. It is not known exactly what causes hallucinations, although one commonly accepted theory is that hallucinations occur when the external stimulus received by the senses no longer matches the level of activity occurring in the brain. Sensory deprivation is one of the surest ways to elicit hallucinations.

Hallucinations can also be elicited in a number of other ways. Some of the most common experiences of hallucinations happen when a person is in the throes of an epileptic fit or suffering from a high fever. Other methods of bringing about a hallucination include fasting or sleeplessness. Admiral Richard Byrd reported having hallucinations after spending several months alone in the Antarctic. Hallucinations can be so powerful that members of many cultures seek them out, undertaking "vision quests" in the hopes of having a hallucinatory experience. Usually the participants who go on these quests journey out into the elements without food or shelter.

Not all hallucinations are the product of extreme physical conditions. Some very complex hallucinations can be triggered by nothing more unusual than everyday memories. People who have lost limbs often report that they continue to feel physical sensations as if the limb were still there. These "phantom limbs" are most likely the result of the brain interpreting signals it receives from severed nerve endings in the context of its memories of the missing limb. An even stranger phenomenon involves hallucinations produced by the memories of recently departed loved ones. Called grief hallucinations, these vivid visions can be simple visual hallucinations or more complex fantasy interactions. In one reported case, a woman reported receiving multiple visits from her departed children. The woman claimed that she and her "ghosts" regularly held long and involved conversations. Neuroscientists theorize that grief hallucinations may be the product of vivid memories that last in the mind long after a loved one has passed away. As bizarre as grief hallucinations may sound, the experience is quite common. Some researchers estimate that up to 80 percent of people will experience some form of grief hallucination in their lifetime.

Although neuroscientists may not be sure of the exact mechanism in the brain that causes hallucinations, they have isolated activity in the left temporal lobe of the brain that appears to play a part in the phenomenon. Certain drugs that affect this region of the brain are known for their ability to cause hallucinations. Drugs such as LSD, psilocybin, and mescaline gained popularity with the 1960s Western youth culture for their ability to provide vivid hallucinatory experiences.

It is also suspected that the brain has its own chemicals designed to produce hallucinations. For example, some patients suffer from *delirium tremens,* a violent period of hallucinations accompanied by sweating, an increase in heart rate, and a rise in body temperature. Through experience treating episodes such as this, it is also known that certain chemicals can stop hallucinations. The drug Thorazine is often used to treat patients suffering from psychotic disorders that involve hallucinations.

Regardless of the causes of hallucinations, the effects they have on their subjects are very real. Hallucinations can cause the aforementioned change in heart rate and body temperature, and they can also lead a person to act on the hallucination. Psychologists have found that the memories created by a hallucination are processed by the same part of the brain that handles normal memories. Thus, for the subject of a hallucination, the experience is as real as any other.

Paragraph 1

What?_____

What about it? _____

Paragraph 2

What?_____

What about it? _____

Paragraph 3

What?_____

What about it? _____

Paragraph 4

What?_____

What about it? _____

Paragraph 5

What?_____

What about it? _____

Paragraph 6

What?_____

What about it? _____

Purpose?_____

Paragraph 7

What?_____

What about it? _____

Purpose?_____

Passage D

In the Arctic tundra, temperatures are below freezing for nine months out of the year. Soil in the Arctic, called permafrost, remains permanently frozen, making agriculture impossible. Travel over the land, whether covered in snow and ice in the winter or in boggy marshes during the summer, is extremely difficult. And perhaps most distressing of all, the sun shines for only six months out of the year. Yet this foreboding landscape has been inhabited for more than 12,000 years, longer than any other part of North America.

Natives of this frozen land benefited from the ample food provided by the marine animals of the region. Indeed, one reason people settled in the Arctic was the almost continuous availability of seals. And although the Arctic is above the tree line, meaning that no trees can grow there, the summer months brought a rich growth of lichen (a form of plant composed of fungi and algae) and other plants. Herds of caribou would migrate north to feed on these plants, providing more food to the Arctic peoples.

Inhabitants of the Arctic and sub-Arctic regions cleverly used the environment to their advantage. The constant wind drove the snow into compact masses that in some ways resembled stone. Since they had no wood or rock from which to build structures, inhabitants built their homes from the snow itself. Using knives and tools made from the antlers of caribou, a native of the Arctic could build a home that was both elegant and warm.

The harsh terrain demanded much of its inhabitants. Many residents of the tundra were nomadic, moving about in small bands, following the migrations of caribou, seals, and whales. Cooperation among groups was essential for survival in this land, and the cultures developed elaborate rituals of reciprocity. Groups of hunters often waited patiently at the various breathing holes used by seals. If one hunter caught a seal, all would eat of it. Bravery was also rewarded, as evidenced by the Inupiaq people, who risked death by wandering far across sea ice to hunt seals.

To survive the brutal cold, Arctic dwellers devised special clothing. Most people wore parkas made of double layers of caribou hide, with boots and pants also made of the same material. The natives fashioned the coats so that caribou hair on the inner layer faced outward, while that on the outer layer faced inward. This provided a high degree of insulation and allowed a hunter to remain outside all day.

Among the many other innovations of the people living in the Arctic were the seal-oil lamps, to compensate for the lack of natural sunlight, and snow goggles, to prevent snow blindness. These remarkable people also developed snowshoes, kayaks, and harpoons with detachable heads. Such resourcefulness was necessary to thrive in the unforgiving conditions of the tundra.

The Arctic inhabitants also developed a body of knowledge adapted to their unique living conditions. When American and European explorers first began long-term expeditions in the Arctic, they ignored the knowledge and survival skills of the Arctic's native inhabitants at their own peril. For example, some animals suited to frozen climates process nutrients from their food differently than animals in more hospitable environments. One of the notable differences is the concentration of vitamin A in the livers of Arctic mammals. In small doses, vitamin A is an essential nutrient. In large doses, it can be toxic. Vitamin A poisoning causes hair loss, brittle bones, skin lesions, nausea, and the build up of potentially fatal pressure on the brain. Arctic hunters had long ago learned to avoid eating the liver of certain animals. The newly arrived explorers rarely trusted native folklore and did not benefit from their wisdom. Famed explorers Douglas Mawson and Xavier Mertz both suffered from vitamin A poisoning. Only Mawson survived the experience.

Later arrivals to the Arctic region required the use of advanced technology to make a living in the region. But the native inhabitants of the tundra existed there for generations without the need for guns, steel knives, vehicles, or modern clothing. Rather than struggling against the harsh environment around them, the original inhabitants found ways to live in harmony with it. The Arctic offers an abundance of riches, and these people, through their resourcefulness, were able to harvest them.

Paragraph 1

What?_____

What about it? _____

Paragraph 2

What?_____

What about it? _____

Paragraph 3

What?_____

What about it? _____

Paragraph 4

What?_____

What about it? _____

Paragraph 5

What?_____

What about it? _____

Paragraph 6

What?_____

What about it? _____

Paragraph 7

What?_____

What about it? _____

Purpose?_____

Paragraph 8

What?_____

What about it? _____

Purpose?_____

Passage E

Alexis de Tocqueville's *Democracy in America* studies the interplay between political power and society. The treatise was the first of its kind and was revolutionary for its use of empirical methods, which were more common in the "hard" sciences—chemistry, biology, and physics—than in the social sciences. Tocqueville distinguished himself from his colleagues by viewing democracy not as a system based on freedom but as one based on power. In fact, Tocqueville argues that democracy is a form of government with more power than any other governmental system.

Born in France in 1805, Tocqueville had a conflicted relationship with his reformist ideals. His grandfather, a liberal aristocrat, lawyer, and politician, was a powerful force for social reforms prior to and during the French Revolution. Despite this, he was condemned as a counterrevolutionary and executed along with several members of his family. Tocqueville adopted his grandfather's liberal ideals, but never lost a profound distrust for the potentially violent extremes to which the drive for democracy can push a nation. Tocqueville's famous study of the United States was the product of a nine-month trip to the young republic, beginning in 1831. Tocqueville had traveled to the United States to produce a study of America's prisons. That initial study was published in 1833, a year after he returned to France. He then labored another nine years over *Democracy in America*. The book itself was written in two distinct volumes. The first volume focused specifically on Tocqueville's observations of American culture. He stressed the growth of social equality promoted by a stable social order, an issue that was close to his heart given France's repeated violent efforts to establish a lasting democracy. The second volume, written four years after the first had been completed, was more abstract. Tocqueville turned his attention to the conflict of individuality and centrality in democratic cultures.

Tocqueville ascribes the power of a democracy to its tendency to centralize power. In a democracy, there are no guilds, estates, or sharply defined social classes. These institutions, in earlier times, represented a check on the powers of kings and tyrants. But in their absence, the government holds the ultimate authority. According to Tocqueville, it is the lower classes that primarily drive the centralization of power in a democracy.

One reason the lower classes prefer a centralization of power relates to the historical role of the aristocratic class. In many class-based societies, the lower classes were subject to the rule of classes above them. Local affairs were overseen by aristocrats, who often acted like petty tyrants. Only by surrendering authority to a central government could the lower classes achieve equality.

Another connection between the lower classes and the centralization of power is literacy, or more accurately, illiteracy. In aristocratic societies, widespread illiteracy did not result in the consolidation of power because the social structure was so segmented. But in an egalitarian society, the intermediate agencies vanish. Without these agencies acting on behalf of the less-informed citizenry, the responsibility falls to the government. Centralization is therefore necessary to aid and provide for citizens who may otherwise have nowhere else to turn to for assistance.

But perhaps the most profound effect the lower classes can have on the centralization of power in a democracy concerns the nature of the democratic leader. In an aristocracy or a monarchy, the ruler was always viewed as a person apart from the lower classes, a person whose birth made him (or her) superior to his subjects. In a democracy, the lower classes can identify more closely with a leader whom they can view as one of them and thus are willing to rally around him (or her) more readily.

Of course, other factors increase the centralization of a democracy. Tocqueville points out that war is an important agent of centralization. To succeed in war, contends Tocqueville, a nation must be able to focus its resources around a single point. Countries with a centralization of power are far more able to accomplish this task than are countries with fragmented power structures. But it is interesting how Tocqueville sees democracy as a vehicle not for freedom but for power, driven by the very people the democracy is designed to empower.

Paragraph 1

What?_____

What about it? _____

Paragraph 2

What?_____

What about it? _____

Paragraph 3

What?_____

What about it? _____

Paragraph 4

What?_____

What about it? _____

Paragraph 5

What?_____

What about it? _____

Paragraph 6

What?_____

What about it? _____

Purpose?_____

Paragraph 7

What?_____

What about it? _____

Purpose?_____

Answers to Drill #1

Passage A

The purpose of this passage is *to provide information about the goals and challenges of the Cassini mission.* Take a look at the first paragraph. It starts by describing Cassini's arrival on Saturn. Next, it states that this event was the final part of a long mission. After reading these two sentences, you should have an idea of what the passage will be about: the Cassini mission.

Now skim through the remaining paragraphs, again looking only at the first line of each one. The second paragraph begins by mentioning the agencies involved in the project, and the third paragraph introduces some of the goals of the mission. The third paragraph mentions the engineering of the spaceship, and the next two paragraphs describe challenges to the mission. Remember, for the final paragraph, read the first and last line. The first line of the last paragraph states that the mission began successfully. The last line indicates that scientists are now working with the data from the mission.

Passage B

The purpose of passage #2 is *to convince the reader of the outcome of a situation.* The first paragraph states that humans have made a mark on the planet. But notice how the second paragraph starts.

> However, Earth is an amazingly resilient place.

The use of the word *however* indicates that the author is now going to discuss the *opposite* of the idea that humans have left their mark on the planet. Each of the next paragraphs then mentions what the theorist thinks will happen if people were to disappear. The final paragraph states there may be evidence for the view, and it ends by repeating the idea of a world free from human interference.

Passage C

The purpose of this passage is *to answer questions about the nature of hallucinations.* The introduction begins with a brief description of hallucinations. We also learn that hallucinations are related to supernatural experiences. The topic sentences of the next two body paragraphs tell us that many people experience hallucinations and mentions how they are caused. Next, the passage mentions the causes of hallucinations and the area of the brain where hallucinations occur. The passage ends by stating that the subjects of hallucinations perceive them as real.

Passage D

The purpose of this passage is *to explain how people survived in the Arctic.* The introduction only provides us with information on the Arctic. So if you weren't sure exactly why the author is writing about this topic, that's okay. Once we get to the next paragraph, we have a clearer idea of the author's direction. The first body paragraph talks about the available food, and the next one mentions clever use of the environment. After that, there is another mention of the harsh terrain and a paragraph about the clothes that natives wore. The final body paragraph talks of the peoples' other inventions, and the conclusion contrasts the resourcefulness of the native inhabitants of the land with modern inhabitants.

Passage E

The purpose of this passage is *to describe one person's view of a government system.* Right away, we know we are reading about someone's book. That's the "what." The "why" requires a little more reading, but once again, the body paragraphs help us figure out why the author wrote the passage. Each one mentions something about the centralization of power in a democracy. The passage ends by again mentioning centralization of power and that Tocqueville's view of democracy is "interesting."

Notice how in each case, we were able to take a 700-word passage and condense it into a brief description. The key point is to *ignore the details*! All we need to worry about (at first) is the big picture.

Summary: How to Find the Purpose

1. **Read the first two lines of the first paragraph.** Note *what* the topic is and *what* the author is writing *about it.*
2. **Read the first line of each body paragraph.** Again, note *what* the topic is and *why* the author introduces it.
3. **Read the first and last line of the final paragraph.** Pay particular attention to *how* the author ends the passage.
4. **Look back at your notes.** What's the common idea? Is the author presenting facts? Examining different views? Answering questions?

Step 2: Understand the Structure

Once we've found the purpose, we'll have a better idea of the *structure* of the passage. The structure refers to the organization or layout of the passage. On the TOEFL, different types of questions will address different parts of the passage. If you are familiar with the types of structures on the TOEFL, you'll know where to look to find the information you need.

What Is the Structure of a TOEFL Passage?

On the TOEFL, the passages will all follow a very similar structure, which will look like the following:

1. An **introduction** paragraph that contains the basic topic of the passage.
2. Four or five **body** paragraphs that provide more information about the topic.
3. A **conclusion** that brings the passage to a close with a final statement.

Let's look at the structure of each of these paragraphs in detail.

What Is the Structure of the Introduction?

Here's the introduction of a passage you've already read.

(1) Sometimes it appears that the human mark on this planet is indelible. (2) In only a blink of geological time, 200 years or so, human construction and expansion has resulted in the destruction of more than one-fifth of the world's forests, the recession of the polar icecaps, and the creation of a huge hole in the ozone layer. (3) Additionally, industrial activity has damaged rivers and oceans, as well as groundwater supplies. (4) Environmental scientists and activists warn that if Earth's future is not taken into account, humankind could very well destroy the planet.

Now let's look at this very same paragraph in terms of its structure or what each sentence contributes to the passage.

(1)   This sentence introduces the topic about which the author is writing.
(2)   This sentence provides information to support the first sentence.
(3)   This sentence also provides information to support the first sentence.
(4)   This sentence uses the information in sentences 1, 2, and 3 to make a point.

As you can see, stripping down the paragraph in terms of its structure makes it easier to comprehend. Many of the passages on the TOEFL will conform to this basic structure. That means for our purposes, when reading the introduction you should

1.   **Read the first sentence—and sometimes the second, if the first doesn't provide enough information—and the last sentence very carefully.** They will most likely contain key information about the passage.
2.   **Skim through the sentences in the middle.** They typically contain background information that merely supports the author's first or last sentence.

Reading the introduction is helpful for answering questions about the *main idea* or the *primary purpose* of the passage. The introduction may also contain background information about the topic. However, introduction paragraphs rarely contain important details; you'll find most of the details in the body paragraphs.

YOUR TURN: DRILL #2—ANALYZE THE STRUCTURE

For each of the following introduction paragraphs, write down what role each sentence plays in the paragraph. Check your answers at the end.

Introduction A

(1) Scientists at Michigan State University are asking a most challenging question. (2) Can a computer program be considered alive? (3) The members of the Digital Evolution Laboratory say yes. (4) Computer scientists at the laboratory have created a program called Avida that has intrigued not only scientists and engineers but biologists and philosophers as well.

(1)_____

(2) _____

(3) _____

(4) _____

Introduction B

(1) After a seven-year journey, the Cassini spacecraft approached the planet Saturn in June 2004. (2) The spacecraft's successful entry into orbit around the world represented the culmination of a vision that took more than 20 years to realize. (3) Launched amid controversy in October 1997, the Cassini spacecraft traveled more than one billion miles in its journey. (4) Despite all the public and technological challenges, the Cassini mission has been more successful than even its planners imagined.

(1)_____

(2) _____

(3) _____

(4) _____

Introduction C

(1) What causes hallucinations, vivid perceptions of sights or sounds that appear quite real to the person experiencing them? (2) These mystical experiences have long fascinated psychologists, neuroscientists, and anthropologists alike. (3) In many cultures, shamans, prophets, and seers are marked by their susceptibility to hallucinations. (4) Are hallucinations caused by ghosts or spirits? (5) Are they messages from another world? (6) Although researchers don't have all the answers, there is some intriguing information on the topic.

(1)_____

(2) _____

(3) _____

(4) _____

(5) _____

(6) _____

Introduction D

(1) In the Arctic tundra, temperatures are below freezing for nine months out of the year. (2) Soil in the Arctic, called permafrost, remains permanently frozen, making agriculture impossible. (3) Travel over the land, whether covered in snow and ice in the winter or in boggy marshes during the summer, is extremely difficult. (4) And perhaps most distressing of all, the sun shines for only six months out of the year. (5) Yet this foreboding landscape has been inhabited for more than 12,000 years, longer than any other part of North America.

(1)_____

(2) _____

(3) _____

(4) _____

Introduction E

(1) Alexis de Tocqueville's *Democracy in America* studies the interplay between political power and society. (2) The treatise was the first of its kind and was revolutionary for its use of empirical methods, which were more common in the "hard" sciences—chemistry, biology, and physics—than in the social sciences. (3) Tocqueville distinguished himself from his colleagues by viewing democracy not as a system based on freedom but as one based on power. (4) In fact, Tocqueville argues that democracy is a form of government with more power than any other governmental system.

(1)_____

(2) _____

(3) _____

(4) _____

Answers to Drill #2

Introduction A

(1)   This sentence introduces the main question of the passage.

(2)   This sentence states what the question is.

(3)   This sentence gives an answer to the question.

(4)   This sentence states what type of program the scientists think is alive.

Introduction B

(1)   This sentence introduces the topic of the passage.

(2)   This sentence provides background about the topic.

(3)   This sentence provides more background about the topic.

(4)   This sentence states that the project has been successful.

Introduction C

(1)   This sentence asks a question about the topic.

(2)   This sentence states who is interested in the topic.

(3)   This sentence provides more information about the topic.

(4)   This sentence asks another question about the topic.

(5)   This sentence asks another question about the topic.

(6)   This sentence states that some answers will be provided about the topic.

Introduction D

(1)   This sentence introduces the topic.

(2)   This sentence gives more support for sentence 1.

(3)   This sentence gives more support for sentence 1.

(4)   This sentence gives more support for sentence 1.

(5)   This sentence indicates a contrast to the previous sentences.

Introduction E

(1)   This sentence introduces the topic.

(2)   This sentence explains why the topic is important.

(3)   This sentence indicates why the topic is different.

(4)   This sentence states a viewpoint.

You should notice that these paragraphs all have similar structures. The important stuff is at the beginning and the end, which is typical: The TOEFL is a standardized test and therefore uses the same types of passages and questions repeatedly. So you should expect to see a similar structure on your test.

What Is the Structure of a Body Paragraph?

Body paragraphs, just like introduction paragraphs, also share a similar structure. Here's an example of a typical body paragraph.

(1) One of the greatest challenges faced by engineers working on the Cassini project involved getting the spacecraft to Saturn. (2) Saturn lies almost 800 million miles away from Earth, an immense distance. (3) The amount of fuel needed to send Cassini on a direct route to the planet would be prohibitive. (4) Therefore, mission strategists had to come up with a plan to get the craft to Saturn using a minimum amount. (5) The solution was to use a technique called *gravity assist*, in which the craft uses the gravitational pull of a planet to "slingshot" it into deep space. (6) Mission planners sent Cassini on a route that passed by the planet Venus twice and back toward Earth for a final push. (7) This circuitous route added more than 200 million miles to the craft's journey.

Now we'll look at this paragraph in terms of its structure.

(1)   This sentence states the specific topic discussed (in this case, a challenge).
(2)   This sentence gives specific details about the challenge.
(3)   This sentence gives more specific details about the challenge.
(4)   This sentence explains what the specific challenge is.
(5)   This sentence gives a solution to the challenge.
(6)   This sentence gives more detail on the solution.
(7)   This sentence gives more detail on the solution.

Looking at the paragraph this way, it's clear that these body paragraphs are all about details. Of course, these details are all closely related to the topic sentence. This means that when dealing with body paragraphs on the TOEFL, you should

1.   **Read the topic sentence carefully.** Make sure you are looking in the right paragraph for the information you need.
2.   **Sort through the specific details until you find what you need.** It is easy to get distracted by all the information in a body paragraph. Stay focused on the information you need.

Reading the body paragraphs will help you answer *detail* and *inference* questions. When answering *main idea* or *primary purpose* questions, do not read more than the first sentence of the body paragraphs. The information found in the body paragraphs is too narrow. We'll cover these question types more thoroughly in Chapter 6.

Types of Body Paragraphs

The body paragraph above *supports* the author's views. Most body paragraphs on the TOEFL will be of this type. However, some passages have body paragraphs that present an *opposing* point of view. Usually, these show up in passages that try to resolve a dilemma or convince the reader of something.

You usually can tell when you are reading a body paragraph that *contradicts* the author by reading the first sentence. The first sentence may have a transition word that indicates the author is now discussing an opposing point of view. Here's an example of such a paragraph:

(1) Of course, not everyone agrees that the program's creations are alive. (2) One difficulty is that biologists do not even agree on the definition of life. (3) The diversity of life on Earth constantly surprises scientists, and there are simply too many characteristics and qualities to provide one simple definition of life.

Again, here's the structure of the paragraph.

(1)   This sentence presents an opposite point of view.
(2)   This sentence explains why some biologists disagree with the author's position.
(3)   This sentence supports sentence 2.

The first line states: "Of course, not everyone agrees…" This line indicates that this paragraph will contradict the author. It is important to recognize these types of paragraphs, especially when answering *main idea* or *primary purpose* questions on the TOEFL.

YOUR TURN: DRILL #3—ANALYZING BODY PARAGRAPHS

State the role of each sentence in the following paragraphs. Also note whether the paragraph appears to support or contradict the passage.

Body Paragraph A

(1) The harsh terrain demanded much of its inhabitants. (2) Many residents of the tundra were nomadic, moving about in small bands, following the migrations of caribou, seals, and whales. (3) Cooperation among groups was essential for survival in this land, and the cultures developed elaborate rituals of reciprocity. (4) Groups of hunters often waited patiently at the various breathing holes used by seals. (5) If one hunter caught a seal, all would eat of it. (6) Bravery was also rewarded, as evidenced by the Inupiaq people, who risked death by wandering far across sea ice to hunt seals.

(1)_____

(2) _____

(3) _____

(4) _____

(5) _____

(6) _____

Supports or contradicts? _____

Body Paragraph B

(1) Without human interference, many of the threatened or endangered fauna would reclaim their ecological niches. (2) Unfortunately, household pets would suffer. (3) In addition, the rat, one of the greatest pests in large cities, would not have the waste of humankind to feed off of and would be hunted mercilessly by growing populations of hawks and falcons. (4) And the cockroach, which to many a city dweller seems to symbolize invincibility, would disappear from all but the warmest climes without artificial heat to sustain it.

(1)_____

(2) _____

(3) _____

(4) _____

Supports or contradicts? _____

Body Paragraph C

(1) According to surveys, anywhere from 10 to 25 percent of the population has experienced at least one hallucination. (2) Most often, the hallucination comes in the form of some visual experience, but some people report hearing a sound or even voices. (3) Even rarer, but not unheard of, is a hallucination of a particular smell or aroma. (4) It is not known exactly what causes hallucinations, although one commonly accepted theory is that hallucinations occur when the external stimulus received by the senses no longer matches the level of activity occurring in the brain. (5) Sensory deprivation is one of the surest ways to elicit hallucinations.

(1)_____

(2)_____

(3)_____

(4)_____

(5)_____

Supports or contradicts?_____

Body Paragraph D

(1) Another connection between the lower classes and the centralization of power is literacy, or more accurately, illiteracy. (2) In aristocratic societies, widespread illiteracy did not result in the consolidation of power because the social structure was so segmented. (3) But in an egalitarian society, the intermediate agencies vanish. (4) Without these agencies acting on behalf of the less-informed citizenry, the responsibility falls to the government. (5) Centralization is therefore necessary to aid and provide for citizens who may otherwise have nowhere else to turn to for assistance.

(1)_____

(2)_____

(3)_____

(4)_____

(5)_____

Supports or contradicts?_____

Answers to Drill #3

Body Paragraph A

(1) This sentence states that much is demanded of people.

(2) This sentence gives an example of something demanded.

(3) This sentence gives an example of how the people adapted.

(4) This sentence provides a detail related to sentence 3.

(5) This sentence provides an additional detail related to sentence 3.

(6) This sentence gives an example of something else demanded.

This paragraph *supports* the passage.

Body Paragraph B

(1) This sentence gives a consequence of a situation.

(2) This sentence gives an exception to sentence 1.

(3) This sentence gives another exception to sentence 1.

(4) This sentence gives another exception to sentence 1.

This paragraph *contradicts* the passage.

Body Paragraph C

(1) This sentence gives a fact about the topic.

(2) This sentence provides more information related to sentence 1.

(3) This sentence provides more information related to sentence 1.

(4) This sentence provides another fact about the topic.

(5) This sentence provides more information related to sentence 4.

This paragraph *supports* the passage.

Body Paragraph D

(1) This sentence introduces another connection.

(2) This sentence provides a detail related to sentence 1.

(3) This sentence explains sentences 1 and 2 more fully.

(4) This sentence also explains sentences 1 and 2 more fully.

(5) This sentence summarizes the other sentences.

This paragraph *supports* the passage.

As you can see, body paragraphs start off with a narrow topic followed by details that are closely related to that narrow topic. Sometimes, as in paragraph C, there are two topics, but most body paragraphs deal with only one topic. Most times, the body paragraphs support the author, but occasionally they are used to present contradictory information.

What Is the Structure of a Conclusion Paragraph?

Many of the passages on the TOEFL are edited versions of longer passages. Thus, the last paragraph will usually provide some additional details and a final wrap-up of the topic.

Let's revisit a conclusion paragraph.

> (1) Of course, other factors increase the centralization of a democracy. (2) Tocqueville points out that war is an important agent of centralization. (3) To succeed in war, contends Tocqueville, a nation must be able to focus its resources around a single point. (4) Countries with a centralization of power are far more able to accomplish this task than are countries with fragmented power structures. (5) But it is interesting how Tocqueville sees democracy as a vehicle not for freedom but for power, driven by the very people the democracy is designed to empower.

Again, here's the structure of the conclusion.

(1) This sentence provides a detail that contrasts with the main point of the passage.
(2) This sentence provides more information on sentence 1.
(3) This sentence provides a detail related to sentence 1.
(4) This sentence provides a detail related to sentence 1.
(5) This sentence states the author's final point.

As you can see, the conclusion paragraph offers some specific details similar to a body paragraph. However, it also contains an important final statement that should apply to the passage as a whole. Therefore, when reading a conclusion paragraph, you should

1. **Read the first sentence.** If the topic sentences introduce more details, skim through them.
2. **Read the very last sentence.** Try to figure out what the author's final message or point is.

Conclusion paragraphs can be very useful for *primary purpose* questions. They also usually contain some specific details as well.

YOUR TURN: DRILL #4—ANALYZING CONCLUSIONS

For each of the following conclusion paragraphs, specify the role each sentence plays. Also, write down the author's final point or message.

Conclusion Paragraph A

(1) Despite these misgivings, the directors of the Avida program remain optimistic that their program, even if not considered alive, is leading to a greater understanding of life in all its forms. (2) It may even facilitate future searches for life on other planets. (3) According to one member of the Avida team, "The problem that we have now is that we are focused on looking for DNA-based life. (4) But there may be other kinds of life out there that we have never dreamed of." (5) The Avida program may provide biologists with another avenue to explore.

(1)_____

(2) _____

(3) _____

(4) _____

Final point: _____

Conclusion Paragraph B

(1) Newcomers to the Arctic region required the use of advanced technology to make a living in the region. (2) But the native inhabitants of the tundra existed there for generations without the need for guns, steel knives, vehicles, or modern clothing. (3) Rather than struggling against the harsh environment around them, the original inhabitants found ways to live in harmony with it. (4) The Arctic offers an abundance of riches, and these people, through their resourcefulness, were able to harvest them.

(1)_____

(2) _____

(3) _____

Final point: _____

Conclusion Paragraph C

(1) The question of plastics aside, there is some evidence that Weisman's view may be true. (2) Since 1953, a 150-mile-long tract of land separating North and South Korea has been declared a no-man's-land. (3) After only a little more than 50 years, there is almost no trace of the rice paddies that farmers had created and used for almost 5,000 years. (4) Even more spectacular are the flocks of red-crowned cranes that now inhabit the zone. (5) These birds are the second rarest of all birds, but they have flourished in this area, free from human interference of all kinds.

(1)_____

(2) _____

(3) _____

(4) _____

Final point: _____

Conclusion Paragraph D

(1) Regardless of the causes of hallucinations, the effects they have on their subjects are very real. (2) Hallucinations can cause the aforementioned change in heart rate and body temperature, and they can also lead a person to act on the hallucination. (3) Psychologists have found that the memories created by a hallucination are processed by the same part of the brain that handles normal memories. (4) Thus, for the subject of a hallucination, the experience is as real as any other.

(1)_____

(2) _____

(3) _____

Final point: _____

Answers to Drill #4

Conclusion Paragraph A

(1) This sentence provides information on the future of the topic.

(2) This sentence provides more information related to sentence 1.

(3) This sentence presents a quote to support sentence 2.

(4) This sentence supports sentence 2.

Final point: The Avida program is providing biologists with new things to explore.

Conclusion Paragraph B

(1) This sentence introduces new information about the topic.

(2) This sentence contrasts the two subjects.

(3) This sentence contrasts the two subjects.

Final point: The inhabitants of the Arctic are able to use its many resources.

Conclusion Paragraph C

(1) This sentence introduces evidence to support a view.

(2) This sentence provides details about the evidence.

(3) This sentence provides more details about the evidence.

(4) This sentence presents a new piece of evidence.

Final point: Without human interference, the land and animals can flourish.

Conclusion Paragraph D

(1) This sentence introduces another point about the main topic.

(2) This sentence provides a detail related to sentence 1.

(3) This sentence provides a detail related to sentence 1.

Final point: Hallucinations are experienced as real.

Following the Direction of the Passage

Based on our analysis of passages so far, you should begin to see that each passage is broken down into pieces, each with a main topic and supporting details. The key to active reading is to focus only on the larger topics and not be distracted by details.

Our next step when analyzing structure is to pay attention to the *direction* of the passage. We've already seen paragraphs that either support or contradict an author's position. We say a passage is going in the *same direction* if the information or paragraph supports the author. If a paragraph contradicts the author, we say that it is going in the *opposite direction*.

Read the passage below, and circle the changes in direction.

Art has always occupied a special place in society. Many people consider artists to be the ultimate authorities on aesthetics, the nature and expression of beauty. For much of history, the practice of art was inscrutable, and artists were viewed as being somewhat strange and often mad. Even the word most commonly associated with artists—inspiration—has its own magical overtones. Literally, "inspiration" is the breathing in of a spirit. Artists were thought of as people who were divinely inspired to create.

Of course, artists contributed to this mythology. Many artists ascribed their talents to the presence of some supernatural agent or "muse." Whole movements of art have centered on the supposedly otherworldly nature of art. For example, the Romantic poets believed that art was the search for the sublime, a term for them that meant an ultimate expression of beauty and truth. The search for this ideal led them to explore both natural and supernatural themes in their works.

Another persistent view of art regarded its divorce from rationality. Reason and logic were the province of scientists and philosophers, whereas creativity and intuition were the domain of the artists. The two separate spheres of the mind were supposed to remain distinct.

But in 1704, a major transgression occurred. Sir Isaac Newton, mathematician and physicist extraordinaire, published his study of light, *Opticks*. One of Newton's major discoveries was on the nature of color. Using a prism, Newton found that white light is actually composed of all the colors of the rainbow. He even provided a scientific explanation for the presence of rainbows. The artistic community was shocked. A scientist had taken a beautiful and magical experience and reduced it to the simple refraction of beams of light through the prism of a raindrop. A scientist had intruded into their sacred territory.

More than a hundred years later, John Keats, one of the most famous Romantic poets, accused Newton of diminishing beauty by "unweaving the rainbow." His colleague, Samuel Taylor Coleridge, famously remarked that the souls of five hundred Newtons would be needed to make one Shakespeare. And yet, from another perspective, Newton did not diminish the beauty of the rainbow; he enhanced it. In his quest to uncover the secrets of the rainbow, Newton demonstrated the wonder, creativity, and inspiration of an artist. He also gave the world another opportunity to experience the sublime. Newton's discovery paved the way for the development of the science of spectroscopy, a way of analyzing the chemical makeup of light. Now scientists can look at the stars and discern their composition. The sense of wonder this ability creates is not much different from the wonder the poet or artist feels when gazing at those same stars.

Here's the passage again, with the direction changes indicated. To make it easier to tell them apart, in this passage the same-direction words are **bolded**, whereas the opposite-direction words are underlined.

Art has always occupied a special place in society. Many people consider artists to be the ultimate authorities on aesthetics, the nature and expression of beauty. **For** much of history, the practice of art was inscrutable, and artists were viewed as being somewhat strange and often mad. **Even** the word most commonly associated with artists—*inspiration*—has its own magical overtones. Literally, "inspiration" is the breathing in of a spirit. Artists were thought of as people who were divinely inspired to create.

Of course, artists contributed to this mythology. Many artists ascribed their talents to the presence of some supernatural agent or "muse." **Whole** movements of art have centered on the supposedly otherworldly nature of art. **For example,** the Romantic poets believed that art was the search for the sublime, a term for them that meant an ultimate expression of beauty and truth. The search for this ideal led them to explore both natural and supernatural themes in their works.

Another persistent view of art regarded its divorce from rationality. Reason and logic were the province of scientists and philosophers, whereas creativity and intuition were the domain of the artists. The two separate spheres of the mind were supposed to remain distinct.

But in 1704, a major transgression occurred. Sir Isaac Newton, mathematician and physicist extraordinaire, published his study of light, *Opticks*. One of Newton's major discoveries was on the nature of color. Using a prism, Newton found that white light is actually composed of all the colors of the rainbow. He **even** provided a scientific explanation for the presence of rainbows. The artistic community was shocked. A scientist had taken a beautiful and magical experience and reduced it to the simple refraction of beams of light through the prism of a raindrop. A scientist had intruded into their sacred territory.

More than a hundred years later, John Keats, one of the most famous Romantic poets, accused Newton of diminishing beauty by "unweaving the rainbow." His colleague, Samuel Taylor Coleridge, famously remarked that the souls of five hundred Newtons would be needed to make one Shakespeare. And yet, from another perspective, Newton did not diminish the beauty of the rainbow; he enhanced it. In his quest to uncover the secrets of the rainbow, Newton demonstrated the wonder, creativity, and inspiration of an artist. He also gave the world another opportunity to experience the sublime. Newton's discovery paved the way for the development of the science of spectroscopy, a way of analyzing the chemical makeup of light. Now scientists can look at the stars and discern their composition. The sense of wonder this ability creates is not much different from the wonder the poet or artist feels when gazing at those same stars.

When reading actively, use direction words to help you organize the information. Same-direction markers mean that the information you are about to read supports the topic. Once you notice this, you can often skim through this information. However, pay particular attention to changes of direction in a passage. These indicate an important shift in the author's purpose.

Look for the following common direction words:

Same Direction	Opposite Direction
And	Although
Because	However
Even	Yet
Therefore	Despite
Another	But
For example	In contrast to
One reason	On the other hand
Due to	Rather

YOUR TURN: DRILL #5—FINDING DIRECTIONS

Read each paragraph, circle the direction markers, and identify whether they are same-direction or opposite-direction words.

Direction Paragraph A

Hallucinations can also be elicited in a number of other ways. Some of the most common experiences of hallucinations happen when a person is in the throes of an epileptic fit or suffering from a high fever. Other methods of bringing about a hallucination include fasting or sleeplessness. Admiral Richard Byrd reported having hallucinations after spending several months alone in the Antarctic. Hallucinations can be so powerful that members of many cultures seek them out, undertaking "vision quests" in the hopes of having a hallucinatory experience. Usually, the participants who go on these quests journey out into the elements without food or shelter.

Direction Paragraph B

Another connection between the lower classes and the centralization of power is literacy, or more accurately, illiteracy. In aristocratic societies, widespread illiteracy did not result in the consolidation of power because the social structure was so segmented. But in an egalitarian society, the intermediate agencies vanish. Without these agencies acting on behalf of the less-informed citizenry, the responsibility falls to the government. Centralization is therefore necessary to aid and provide for citizens who may otherwise have nowhere else to turn to for assistance.

Direction Paragraph C

It is also suspected that the brain has its own chemicals designed to produce hallucinations. For example, some patients suffer from *delirium tremens,* a violent period of hallucinations accompanied by sweating, an increase in heart rate, and a rise in body temperature. Through experience treating episodes such as this, it is also known that certain chemicals can stop hallucinations. The drug Thorazine is often used to treat patients suffering from psychotic disorders that involve hallucinations.

Direction Paragraph D

The career of Phillip Johnson, one of America's foremost architects, was a study in contrasts. Initially, Johnson was a staunch proponent of the Modernist school of architecture, and he achieved his early fame by working in this style. After a time, however, Johnson apparently became bored with Modernism, even though he claimed that he loved the experience of the new above all things. Johnson decided to move from Modernism to Classicism, a style that he explored thoroughly. He soon tired of the Classical school as well and moved back toward Modernism, although his later works still incorporate classical elements.

Answers to Drill #5

Direction Paragraph A

Hallucinations can **also** *(same direction)* be elicited in a number of other ways. Some of the most common experiences of hallucinations happen when a person is in the throes of an epileptic fit or suffering from a high fever. **Other** *(same direction)* methods of bringing about a hallucination include fasting or sleeplessness. Admiral Richard Byrd reported having hallucinations after spending several months alone in the Antarctic. Hallucinations can be so powerful that members of many cultures seek them out, undertaking "vision quests" in the hopes of having a hallucinatory experience. Usually, the participants who go on these quests journey out into the elements without food or shelter.

Direction Paragraph B

Another *(same direction)* connection between the lower classes and the centralization of power is literacy, or more accurately, illiteracy. In aristocratic societies, widespread illiteracy did not result in the consolidation of power **because** *(same direction)* the social structure was so segmented. <u>But</u> *(opposite direction)* in an egalitarian society, the intermediate agencies vanish. Without these agencies acting on behalf of the less-informed citizenry, the responsibility falls to the government. Centralization is **therefore** *(same direction)* necessary to aid and provide for citizens who may otherwise have nowhere else to turn to for assistance.

Direction Paragraph C

It is **also** *(same direction)* suspected that the brain has its own chemicals designed to produce hallucinations. **For example** *(same direction),* some patients suffer from *delirium tremens,* a violent period of hallucinations accompanied by sweating, an increase in heart rate, and a rise in body temperature. Through experience treating episodes such as this, it is **also** *(same direction)* known that certain chemicals can stop hallucinations. The drug Thorazine is often used to treat patients suffering from psychotic disorders that involve hallucinations.

Direction Paragraph D

The career of Phillip Johnson, one of America's foremost architects, was a study in contrasts. **Initially** *(same direction),* Johnson was a staunch proponent of the Modernist school of architecture, and he achieved his early fame by working in this style. After a time, <u>however</u>, Johnson apparently became bored with Modernism, <u>even though</u> *(opposite direction)* he claimed that he loved the experience of the new above all things. Johnson decided to move from Modernism to Classicism, a style that he explored thoroughly. He soon tired of the Classical school as well and moved back toward Modernism, <u>although</u> *(opposite direction)* his later works still incorporate classical elements.

Summary: Understanding Structure

1. **Identify the structure of the passage** because this knowledge will help you to find information quickly.
2. **Remember, TOEFL passages are made up of the following paragraph types:** introduction, body, and conclusion. Know what type of information is usually found in each paragraph.
3. **Use the first sentence of the paragraph as a guide** to the information contained in the rest of the paragraph.
4. Keep in mind that the **remaining sentences provide details about the topic.**
5. **Pay attention to direction markers.** Same-direction markers indicate the author is continuing the discussion. Opposite-direction markers highlight contrasting ideas.

Step 3: State the Main Idea

All passages on the TOEFL have a main idea. The main idea is the central message or point of the passage. When we looked for the primary purpose, we asked ourselves two questions: What is the author writing about, and why is the author writing about that topic? The main idea is the "what" part, whereas the primary purpose is the "why" part.

Let's return to a prior passage and look at how the main idea is different from the primary purpose.

Sometimes it appears that the human mark on this planet is indelible. In only a blink of geological time, 200 years or so, human construction and expansion has resulted in the destruction of more than one-fifth of the world's forests, the recession of the polar icecaps, and the creation of a huge hole in the ozone layer. Additionally, industrial activity has damaged rivers and oceans, as well as groundwater supplies. Environmental scientists and activists warn that if Earth's future is not taken into account, humankind could very well destroy the planet.

However, Earth is an amazingly resilient place. In its 4.5-billion-year lifespan, Earth has endured bombardment by cosmic rays and meteors, violent earthquakes, volcanism, and frigid ice ages. In light of all these catastrophic events, many geologists and ecologists say that Earth could recover from any damage caused by human actions.

The author Alan Weisman has gone so far as to predict exactly what would happen on Earth if all humans were to disappear. Without upkeep, the concrete jungles of the world's largest cities would be slowly reclaimed by the wilderness around them. Harsh temperatures would cause pavement to crack. Plants would return to areas covered by streets and sidewalks.

Different fates would await humankind's other creations. Litter and leaf matter would accumulate, and it would take only one chance lightning strike to start a raging fire. Many structures would burn to the ground. The steel foundations supporting larger buildings and bridges would corrode and buckle, especially with the rise in groundwater that would accompany the clogging of sewer systems.

Without human interference, many of the threatened or endangered fauna would reclaim their ecological niches. Unfortunately, household pets would suffer. In addition, the rat, one of the greatest pests in large cities, would not have the waste of humankind to feed off of and would be hunted mercilessly by growing populations of hawks and falcons. And the cockroach, which to many a city dweller seems to symbolize invincibility, would disappear from all but the warmest climes without artificial heat to sustain it.

Within 500 years, again barely a heartbeat in geological time, most of humankind's monuments would be gone, covered over by plants and trees. It's happened before; the Mayan civilization in Northern Guatemala survived for 2,000 years but was swallowed up by the jungle at its end. And after a few thousand years, if earthquakes and volcanic eruptions have not obliterated everything made by humans, the glaciers would come, sweeping down from the mountains, slowly and inexorably destroying everything in their path. Several times in its history, Earth has been swept clean by these giant sheets of ice. The legacy of humankind would be wiped from Earth.

Of course, not every man-made artifact would be reclaimed by nature. Plastic is a synthetic material that does not occur in nature. The strong bonds that hold plastic together are virtually impervious to natural erosion. Long after concrete and glass have turned back into sand and all processed metals have rusted away, plastics will still be cycling through the Earth's ecosystem, resilient to even most destructive of natural forces. Some scientists believe that plastic molecules may eventually break down entirely, but there is no reliable data on just how long complete re-assimilation into the environment might take. Furthermore, it is impossible to predict just what sort of resources Mother Nature might develop in the distant future. There is always the possibility that, given enough time, some microbe or bacteria may evolve the capability to digest plastic. If nature somehow evolved a way to process plastics, then even humanity's most enduring artifacts might vanish in the space of a few hundred years.

The question of plastics aside, there is some evidence that Weisman's view may be true. Since 1953, a 150-mile-long tract of land separating North and South Korea has been declared a no-man's-land. After only a little more than 50 years, there is almost no trace of the rice paddies that farmers had created and used for almost 5,000 years. Even more spectacular are the flocks of red-crowned cranes that now inhabit the zone. These birds are the second rarest of all birds, but they have flourished in this area, free from human interference of all kinds.

Remember that the primary purpose of this passage is *to convince the reader of the outcome of a situation.* To find the main idea we'll proceed in much the same way as we did to find the primary purpose. Read the first sentence or two of the introduction, the first sentence of each body paragraph, and the first and last sentence of the conclusion.

After reading each sentence again ask yourself, "What is the author writing about?" Let's gather up the first sentences of each paragraph and the last sentence of the conclusion to see what we have.

Paragraph 1	Sometimes it appears that the human mark on this planet is indelible.
Paragraph 2	However, Earth is an amazingly resilient place.
Paragraph 3	The author Alan Weisman has gone so far as to predict exactly what would happen on Earth if all humans were to disappear.
Paragraph 4	Different fates would await humankind's other creations.
Paragraph 5	Without human interference, many of the threatened or endangered fauna would reclaim their ecological niches.
Paragraph 6	Within 500 years, again barely a heartbeat in geological time, most of humankind's monuments would be gone, covered over by plants and trees.
Paragraph 7	Of course, not every man-made artifact would be reclaimed by nature.
Paragraph 8	The question of plastics aside, there is some evidence that Weisman's view may be true.
Last sentence	These birds are the second rarest of all birds, but they have flourished in this area, free from human interference of all kinds.

When stating the main idea, we must try to tie together all of these topics. Take a look at the sentences above and write down what you think the main idea is.

_____

_____

_____

A good answer to this question might be

If humans were to disappear, plants and animals would soon take over Earth again.

Notice how this sentence brings together all of the elements. The sentences from paragraphs one, three, and four all mention people; the sentence from paragraph two talks about Earth; and the sentences from paragraphs five, six, seven and eight mention both.

Let's try it one more time. Try to find the main idea of the following passage. Write your answer in the space provided after the passage.

Scientists at Michigan State University are asking a most challenging question. Can a computer program be considered alive? The members of the Digital Evolution Laboratory say yes. Computer scientists at the laboratory have created a program called Avida that has intrigued not only scientists and engineers but biologists and philosophers as well.

The Avida project began in the late 1990s, when Chris Adami, a physicist, sought to create computer programs that could evolve to do simple addition problems and reproduce inside a digital environment. Adami called these programs "digital organisms." Whenever a digital organism replicates, it has a chance to alter the program of the newly created offspring. In this way, the programs mutate and evolve. The goal of the Avida program is to create a model that could simulate the evolutionary process.

Initially, the digital creations were unable to process numbers in any way. But Adami designed Avida to reward digital organisms that were able to work with the numbers in some way. The digital organisms that could process numbers were allowed to reproduce in higher numbers. In only six short months, the primitive program had evolved a number of mechanisms to perform addition. And, most surprisingly, not all of the digital creatures performed addition in the same way.

The Avida program now resides at Michigan State University, where it has been growing and changing for years. The digital creatures number in the billions and have colonized more than two hundred computers. The organisms compete with one another for resources, and the most successful ones are able to make more copies of themselves. Just like living creatures, the digital entities also undergo mutations. Mutations that are beneficial ensure greater reproduction; harmful mutations have the opposite effect.

As a model for studying evolution, the Avida project has been a great success. Adami's digital organisms have suggested solutions to some of evolution's biggest mysteries. For example, Avida has helped disprove the theory of "irreducible complexity." Opponents of evolutionary theory have suggested that some structures, such as the eye, are too complex to have been created in piecemeal stages. The evolution of Avida's digital organisms proves that even extremely complex structures can be developed in stages over time.

The Avida program's success has also raised some unintentional philosophical dilemmas. Does Avida just simulate evolution? Or are digital organisms a new form of life? According to the director of the Avida project, the processes undergone by the digital creatures are the same as those experienced by biological organisms. The only difference is that biological entities are based on strings of DNA, whereas the digital creations from Avida are based on strings of ones and zeros. In a living creature, different sequences of DNA instruct cells to create certain proteins. In one of the Avida creations, different sequences of computer code instruct the program to perform certain functions. In both cases, the reproduction of the organisms is subject to forces such as competition and mutation.

Now, some biologists are maintaining that the programs in the Avida project are alive. The programs live, die, reproduce, compete, cooperate, and evolve—activities that many biologists consider the hallmarks of life. One prominent biologist says, "They don't have a metabolism—at least not yet. But otherwise, they're alive."

Of course, not everyone agrees that the program's creations are alive. One difficulty is that biologists do not even agree on the definition of life. The diversity of life on Earth constantly surprises scientists, and there are simply too many characteristics and qualities to provide one simple definition of life.

Despite these misgivings, the directors of the Avida program remain optimistic that their program, even if not considered alive, is leading to a greater understanding of life in all its forms. It may even facilitate future searches for life on other planets. According to one member of the Avida team, "The problem that we have now is that we are focused on looking for DNA-based life. But there may be other kinds of life out there that we have never dreamed of." The Avida program may provide biologists with another avenue to explore.

Write down what you think the main idea is. _____

_____

_____

Here are the first sentences of each paragraph and the last sentence of the conclusion.

Paragraph 1	Scientists at Michigan State University are asking a most challenging question.
Paragraph 2	The Avida project began in the late 1990s, when Chris Adami, a physicist, sought to create a computer program that could evolve to do simple addition problems and reproduce inside a digital environment.
Paragraph 3	Initially, the digital creations were unable to process numbers in any way.
Paragraph 4	The Avida program now resides at Michigan State University, where it has been growing and changing for years.
Paragraph 5	As a model for studying evolution, the Avida project has been a great success.
Paragraph 6	The Avida program's success has raised some unintentional philosophical dilemmas.
Paragraph 7	Now, some biologists are maintaining that the programs in the Avida project are alive.
Paragraph 8	Of course, not everyone agrees that the program's creations are alive.
Paragraph 9	Despite these misgivings, the directors of the Avida program remain optimistic that their program, even if not considered alive, is leading to a greater understanding of life in all its forms.
Last sentence	The Avida program may provide biologists with another avenue to explore.

We could state our main idea as follows:

The features of the Avida computer program have led some biologists to consider the program alive.

Because the Avida program is mentioned in sentences from paragraphs 2, 4, 5, 6, 7, 8, and 9 we definitely need it in our main idea. The sentences from paragraphs 2 and 4 talk about the program "evolving," "changing," and "growing." Later, the program is described as "alive" and likened to a "biological organism." So we need to put this concept into our main idea.

Main Idea: Paying Attention to Direction Markers

When finding the main idea, pay close attention to direction markers. Some passages introduce an idea or a topic, but they go on to discuss the opposite of it.

Here's an example.

Art has always occupied a special place in society. Many people consider artists to be the ultimate authorities on aesthetics, the nature and expression of beauty. For much of history, the practice of art was inscrutable, and artists were viewed as being somewhat strange and often mad. Even the word most commonly associated with artists—*inspiration*—has its own magical overtones. Literally, "inspiration" is the breathing in of a spirit. Artists were thought of as people who were divinely inspired to create.

Of course, artists contributed to this mythology. Many artists ascribed their talents to the presence of some supernatural agent or "muse." Whole movements of art have centered on the supposedly otherworldly nature of art. For example, the Romantic poets believed that art was the search for the sublime, a term for them that meant an ultimate expression of beauty and truth. The search for this ideal led them to explore both natural and supernatural themes in their works.

Another persistent view of art regarded its divorce from rationality. Reason and logic were the province of scientists and philosophers, whereas creativity and intuition were the domain of the artists. The two separate spheres of the mind were supposed to remain distinct.

But in 1704, a major transgression occurred. Sir Isaac Newton, mathematician and physicist extraordinaire, published his study of light, *Opticks*. One of Newton's major discoveries was on the nature of color. Using a prism, Newton found that white light is actually composed of all the colors of the rainbow. He even provided a scientific explanation for the presence of rainbows. The artistic community was shocked. A scientist had taken a beautiful and magical experience and reduced it to the simple refraction of beams of light through the prism of a raindrop. A scientist had intruded into their sacred territory.

More than a hundred years later, John Keats, one of the most famous Romantic poets, accused Newton of diminishing beauty by "unweaving the rainbow." His colleague, Samuel Taylor Coleridge, famously remarked that the souls of five hundred Newtons would be needed to make one Shakespeare. And yet, from another perspective, Newton did not diminish the beauty of the rainbow; he enhanced it. In his quest to uncover the secrets of the rainbow, Newton demonstrated the wonder, creativity, and inspiration of an artist. He also gave the world another opportunity to experience the sublime. Newton's discovery paved the way for the development of the science of spectroscopy, a way of analyzing the chemical makeup of light. Now scientists can look at the stars and discern their composition. The sense of wonder this ability creates is not much different from the wonder the poet or artist feels when gazing at those same stars.

Take a look at the topic sentences from the first three paragraphs.

Paragraph 1   Art has always occupied a special place in society.

Paragraph 2   Of course, artists contributed to this mythology.

Paragraph 3   Another persistent view of art regarded its divorce from rationality.

At this point, you may predict that the main idea of the passage will be about views of art and artists. But look at the remaining topic sentences.

Paragraph 4   But in 1704, a major transgression occurred.

Paragraph 5   More than a hundred years later, John Keats, one of the most famous Romantic poets, accused Newton of diminishing beauty by "unweaving the rainbow."

Last sentence   The sense of wonder this ability creates is not much different from the wonder the poet or artist feels when gazing at those same stars.

The sentence from paragraph 4 is an important one because it contains the direction marker "but." The author is introducing an important new idea contrary to the prior topics. We should figure out what this new idea is. In paragraph 4, the author discusses science's relationship to art. We need to make sure this idea is part of our main idea.

Look through the passage again. Do you see any other direction markers that may clue us in to the main idea?

You may have noticed the following sentence in the last paragraph:

And yet, from another perspective, Newton did not diminish the beauty of the rainbow; he enhanced it.

See if you can come up with a main idea that incorporates these elements. Write down what you think the main idea is.

_____

_____

_____

Your answer should look something like this:

Science does not diminish art but instead provides another source of wonder.

Thus, it is important to incorporate all parts of the passage. The first part of this passage establishes the view of art, whereas the second discusses the intersection of art and science.

YOUR TURN: DRILL #6—STATE THE MAIN IDEA

For each of the following passages, try to find the main idea. Read the topic sentences of each paragraph and paraphrase them. Then, try to state the main idea. Be on the lookout for direction markers!

Main Idea Passage A

Plants reproduce by seeding. The seed of the plant contains all the necessary genetic information to create a new plant, and more important, it is designed to start growing only when the surrounding conditions are perfect. For example, the seed of a plant growing in a temperate area will "wait" until the cold winter passes before growing. When spring arrives, the seed responds to environmental triggers such as water intake, rising air temperature, humidity levels, and amount of sunlight. Some seeds are programmed in such a way that they will not grow until they've passed through a period of cold weather.

A germinating seed will first display tiny leaves, called *cotyledons*. Plants are either monocotyledons, producing just a single leaf, or dicotyledons, producing two leaves. These tiny leaves quickly grow into a mature leaf system, which then begins gathering energy for the young plant. Plants gather the light of the sun and transform it into energy in a process called photosynthesis. This process allows the plant to produce glucose, which the plant then uses to both further its growth and to produce cellulose and starch, two compounds essential to a plant. Cellulose is a strong, fibrous material that gives shape and structure to the cell walls. Starch is stored in the cells and used for energy.

Beneath the surface, the plant's root system grows and provides not only an anchor for the plant but a constant supply of food as well. Some plants possess what is called a taproot system, in which there is one main root. Others have a more dispersed root system, which lacks a main root. In either case, the roots of the plant are covered with microscopic hairs, which spread into the surrounding soil. These hairs greatly increase the surface area of the root system and allow the plant to absorb water and essential nutrients from the soil.

Water drawn in through the roots undergoes a process called *transpiration*. During this process, minerals are carried up to the leaves of the plant, while oxygen and water vapor escape through tiny pores, called *stomata,* on the surface of the leaves. Interestingly, the movement of water through the plant is also responsible for keeping the plant upright; a plant that lacks water will wilt and may die. Too much water may also harm the plant by saturating the soil and preventing the roots from absorbing oxygen.

Once a plant reaches full maturity, its energy is devoted to reproduction. The plant forms flowers and fruits, the structures essential to reproduction. The flowers of a plant are typically hermaphrodites, meaning that they contain both male and female reproductive organs. Thus, many plants are able to fertilize themselves. The flowers of some plants are unisexual, being all male or all female. These plants require another plant for fertilization. Some plants are polygamous, meaning they have both hermaphrodite and unisexual flowers. Fruits are created from the ovaries of flowering plants. The main purpose of the fruit is to protect the seed, but many fruits aid in the seed's dispersal as well. For example, a soft, fleshy fruit attracts animals, which eat the fruit and thus spread the seeds. Or a pod or capsule will split open and scatter its seeds. Some of the seeds distributed in this manner will take hold in favorable soil, and the entire process begins anew.

Paragraph 1 _____

Paragraph 2 _____

Paragraph 3 _____

Paragraph 4 _____

Paragraph 5 _____

Last sentence _____

Did you find any direction markers?

List them _____

_____

Main idea _____

_____

Main Idea Passage B

The business practices of the Intel Corporation, a technology company best known for the production of microprocessors for computers, illustrate the importance of brand marketing. Intel was able to achieve a more than 1,500 percent increase in sales, moving from $1.2 billion in sales to more than $33 billion, in a little more than 10 years. Although the explosion of the home-computer market certainly accounted for some of this dramatic increase, the brilliance of its branding strategy also played a significant role.

Intel became a major producer of microprocessor chips in 1978, when its 8086 chip was selected by IBM for use in its line of home computers. The 8086 chip and its successors soon became the industry standard, even as Intel's competitors sought to break into this potentially lucrative market. Intel's main problem in facing its competitors was its lack of trademark protection for its series of microchips. Competitors were able to exploit this lack by introducing clone products with similar-sounding names, severely inhibiting Intel's ability to create a brand identity.

In an effort to save its market share, Intel embarked on an ambitious branding program in 1991. The corporation's decision to invest more than $100 million in this program was greeted with skepticism and controversy. Many within the company argued that the money could be better spent researching and developing new products, while others argued that a company that operated within such a narrow consumer niche had little need for such an aggressive branding campaign. Despite these misgivings, Intel went ahead with its strategy, which in a short time became a resounding success.

One of the keys to the success of Intel's new branding initiative was its close partnership with computer manufacturers. Intel involved the manufacturers in its plan by first offering them a rebate on the purchase of an Intel microprocessor. The money saved on the purchase of microprocessors was redirected into advertising, with Intel offering to pay fully half of manufacturers' advertising costs, provided their computers prominently featured the Intel brand logo. In an even more effective strategy, Intel also required computer manufacturers to produce products using competitors' chips. These products noticeably lacked the prominent Intel logo, which had a negative effect on consumers, who had come to expect to see Intel's brand on the computer.

Intel's successful branding campaign led to two important developments. The first was Intel's positioning of itself as the leader in microprocessors, recognized for creating products that were both reliable and ubiquitous, appearing in many different computer brands. This occurred despite the public's general lack of understanding of exactly what a microprocessor was or how Intel's processor was better than its competitors' chips. Second, Intel's campaign led to a boom in computer advertising. Prior to Intel's branding initiative, many advertisers avoided the computer industry, which generally spent far more of its money on research and development. But the success of Intel's branding program led to a new and eminently profitable relationship between computer manufacturers and advertisers.

Ironically, the success of Intel's branding strategy led to a marketing dilemma for the company. In 1992, Intel was prepared to unveil its new line of microprocessors. However, the company faced a difficult decision: release the new product under the current brand logo and risk consumer apathy or give the product a new name and brand and risk undoing all the work put into the branding strategy. In the end, Intel decided to move forward with a new brand identity. It was a testament to the strength of Intel's earlier branding efforts that the new product line was seamlessly integrated into the public consciousness.

Paragraph 1 _____

Paragraph 2 _____

Paragraph 3 _____

Paragraph 4 _____

Paragraph 5 _____

Paragraph 6 _____

Last sentence _____

Did you find any direction markers?

List them _____

_____

Main idea _____

_____

Main Idea Passage C

On December 18, 1912, an amateur geologist named Charles Dawson and paleontologist Arthur Smith Woodward presented a stunning finding to the Geological Society of London. One year earlier, Dawson had found a piece of a human cranium in a gravel pit near Piltdown Common, Sussex. Further searching by Dawson uncovered remnants of what appeared to be flint tools and the remains of prehistoric animals. Excited by his discovery, Dawson took the fossils to Woodward at the British Museum, and the two men returned to the gravel pit for a systematic excavation.

In the summer of 1912, Dawson and Woodward made the discoveries that would later shock the assembled scientists at the Geological Society. Among the animal bones and primitive tools, the two men found another skull and an almost entirely intact jawbone. The geologic and biologic evidence dated the site to the Pleistocene era, and the bones were clearly of a creature that resembled no other known at that time. Although the skull resembled those of other finds, including the famous ape-men of Java, the jaw appeared to come from some type of heretofore unknown species of ape. Startlingly, however, the teeth were worn down in a human fashion.

Dawson and Woodward's announcement of the so-called Missing Link between man and apes, which they called Piltdown Man, set off an immediate firestorm. Across the Atlantic, *The New York Times* reported the story with the dramatic headline "Paleolithic Skull Is a Missing Link." The ensuing controversy over human origins eventually led the *Times* to publish an editorial that cautioned readers from seeing Piltdown Man as *the* missing link; instead, the editors advised readers to see Piltdown Man as a link to man's prehistoric past, but not necessarily proof of evolution.

Similar editorials sprang up across the United States, and the American public was divided over the issue of human origins. Although no fossil could conclusively prove evolution, scientists had amassed a huge collection of fossils in the early twentieth century. These fossils seemed to indicate a pattern of evolution and demanded attention. In the United States during the 1920s, a movement sprang up to counter the theory of evolution. This movement culminated in one of the most famous trials in history, the Scopes "Monkey" Trial.

John T. Scopes was a biology teacher in a Tennessee school. The textbook he used in his class contained a chapter on evolution and natural selection, a violation of Tennessee law. Scopes was brought to trial for the offense, and the ensuing confrontation riveted the American public. Scopes was defended by Clarence Darrow, a noted lawyer, and William Jennings Bryan, a former secretary of state, worked for the prosecution. After a confrontational trial, which even included Darrow calling Bryan as a witness, Scopes was ultimately found guilty.

Although Scopes's conviction was later overturned, the precedent set by the case endured. It wasn't until 1967 that Tennessee repealed its law forbidding the teaching of evolution. And even today, the reverberations of the trial are still visible. One school district in Georgia recently began placing stickers on its biology textbooks disavowing the validity of evolution. The Supreme Court eventually decided that the stickers were unconstitutional, but a cultural battle over the validity of evolution still rages in the United States.

Paragraph 1 _____

Paragraph 2 _____

Paragraph 3 _____

Paragraph 4 _____

Paragraph 5 _____

Paragraph 6 _____

Last sentence _____

Did you find any direction markers?

List them _____

_____

Main idea _____

_____

Main Idea Passage D

One of the most commonplace instructional strategies in elementary and middle schools is that of oral reading. Virtually all teachers, at some point in the school day, engage in this activity, whether by reading aloud to the class or by having the students read to one another. Although some recent educational theorists have challenged the efficacy of oral reading, its popularity in schools and classrooms is unchallenged.

The history of oral reading in the classroom is inextricably linked with the history of the culture that engendered it. Prior to the development of computers, television, and radio, reading was the predominant form of family entertainment. However, printed books were often scarce, and literacy rates were often low. Thus, families would gather around and listen to a book being read to them. Early classrooms were modeled after this phenomenon, and oral reading was such a part of academic life that schools were sometimes called *blab* schools. In these schools, students often read their lessons aloud simultaneously, even when the students had different lessons. At other times, all students read the same text aloud.

With the increasing availability of books, schools began using textbooks to teach reading in the classroom. By the nineteenth century, the focus had moved to teaching students "eloquent reading." Students were expected to recite stories, poems, and prayers for the class, and the teacher graded them on their articulation and pronunciation, as well as their abilities to recall what they had just read. This method persisted into the twentieth century and became known as the story method of instruction. Oral reading was such a focal point of instruction that philosopher William James stated "...the teacher's success or failure in teaching reading is based...upon the oral reading method."

However, as the twentieth century progressed, the effectiveness of oral reading was called into question. Educational scholars in both Europe and the United States wondered exactly what oral reading was teaching students. With oral reading focusing excessively on pronunciation and dynamics, educators doubted that students were even able to comprehend what they were saying. One scholar quoted a study that claimed that eleven-twelfths of students did not understand what they were reciting when they read orally. Friedrich Froebel, a German education specialist, argued that oral reading inappropriately placed emphasis on expression, when the emphasis should be placed on process.

Also at this time, science was gaining increasing prominence, and across all fields researchers were placing a premium on empirical studies. Many long-standing beliefs and views were challenged, and educational theories were no exception. Behavioral scientists studied reading practices and determined that oral reading was no longer in fashion. In fact, they concluded that the only time students read orally was in school. Most individuals read silently, and this finding led many schools to change their methods to reflect this change.

The new preponderance of written texts also played a role in the history of oral reading. With the amount of printed material rapidly expanding, silent reading, which was more efficient, became the reading model of choice. For a number of years, oral reading was absent from many a classroom. But in time, new research and studies brought oral reading back to the forefront of education. Pressley's and Afflerbach's influential book *Verbal Protocols of Reading* emphasizes the importance of oral reading, tracing its history back to the methods of Aristotle and Plato. In many ways, however, the new research reiterates what most teachers already know. For them, the necessity and effectiveness of oral reading was never in doubt.

Paragraph 1 _____

Paragraph 2 _____

Paragraph 3 _____

Paragraph 4 _____

Paragraph 5 _____

Paragraph 6 _____

Last sentence _____

Did you find any direction markers?

List them _____

_____

Main idea _____

_____

Answers to Drill #6

Main Idea Passage A

Paragraph 1: "Plants reproduce by seeding." For short sentences like this one, don't worry about paraphrasing. Keep things simple.

Paragraph 2: "Seed first has tiny leaves." When finding the main idea, don't worry about strange or difficult vocabulary words (*cotyledons*). They are not important to the main idea.

Paragraph 3: "Plants have a root system that helps growth." When paraphrasing, you don't necessarily have to note the exact functions of the root system. Details are not important. All we need to know is that the root system is helpful to the plant.

Paragraph 4: "Water comes through the roots." Again, ignore the fancy term *transpiration*.

Paragraph 5: "After maturity, plants focus on reproduction."

Last sentence: "Process starts all over again." Pay attention to the last sentence. Look for the author's final word. Is there a definite conclusion? The author wraps up things nicely, but some passages may end with a question or a call for more information or research on the topic.

Direction Markers

(Remember, we use **boldface** for same-direction markers and <u>underline</u> opposite-direction markers.)

> **For example,** the seed of a plant growing in a temperate area will "wait" until the cold winter passes before growing.

> **During this process,** minerals are carried up to the leaves of the plant, <u>while</u> oxygen and water vapor escape through tiny pores, called *stomata*, on the surface of the leaves.

> **The main purpose** of the fruit is to protect the seed, <u>but</u> many fruits aid in the seed's dispersal as well.

> **For example,** a soft, fleshy fruit attracts animals, which eat the fruit and **thus** spread the seeds.

You may have spotted some others, but the key thing about this passage is that the information is all going in the same direction. The purpose of this passage is to inform the reader, and all the details provide an explanation of a process.

Main idea: "A plant reproduces with a seed, which grows from a tiny leaf into a mature plant capable of making its own seeds." Each of our topic sentences discusses reproduction and the steps. Notice we left out the root system. That's because the root system is mentioned as a part of the growth process. We don't need to explicitly mention each detail when stating the main idea, especially if the author is not introducing any contrasting ideas.

Main Idea Passage B

Paragraph 1: "Intel is an example of good brand marketing." By reading the first sentence, we may be able to predict what's coming in the passage. It looks as if we're going to read a description of this company's business practices.

Paragraph 2: "Intel became a major producer in 1978." In addition to direction markers, time markers are also helpful. We know that we're going to read some of the background story.

Paragraph 3: "To save its market share, Intel started a new program." This sentence supports the introduction paragraph.

Paragraph 4: "One key to Intel's success." When the author presents an example, don't worry too much about what the example is. We don't need to know exactly what the details are for the main idea; it's enough to know that this paragraph will describe it.

Paragraph 5: "Two important developments from the program." Again, don't worry too much about what the developments are. The important thing is that the author is giving the results of the program.

Paragraph 6: "Success led to a problem." The author introduces a problem, but we should note that it is the last paragraph. Therefore, we may think the problem isn't a main focus of the passage.

Last sentence: "New product introduced with no problems." This last sentence indicates that everything ended well. The earlier problem was mentioned only to show how good the company's strategy was. Even the problem fits into the overall direction of the passage.

Direction Markers
(Again, we use **boldface** for same-direction markers and <u>underline</u> opposite-direction markers.)

> <u>Although</u> the explosion of the home-computer market certainly accounted for some of this dramatic increase, the brilliance of its branding strategy also played a significant role.

> <u>Despite</u> these misgivings, Intel went ahead with its strategy, which in a short time became a resounding success.

> In an **even more** effective strategy, Intel **also** required computer manufacturers to produce products using competitors' chips.

> <u>But</u> the success of Intel's branding program led to a new and eminently profitable relationship between computer manufacturers and advertisers.

> <u>However</u>, the company faced a difficult decision: release the new product under the current brand logo and risk consumer apathy or give the product a new name and brand and risk undoing all the work put into the branding strategy.

This passage contains a few opposite-direction markers. Notice how each one serves to indicate how successful Intel's branding campaign was.

Main idea: "Intel's branding strategy was important to its success and also led to some important developments in the market." As we predicted from the first sentence, we were going to read about a successful business strategy. We also brought in the developments mentioned later in the passage. The problem mentioned in the final paragraph doesn't need special mention because it again illustrates how successful Intel's campaign was.

Main Idea Passage C

Paragraph 1: "Two scientists made a stunning finding." This is a good "teaser" introduction: The author doesn't tell us right away what the topic is. In this case, you may want to read another sentence or two to figure out what the finding is.

Paragraph 2: "The discoveries were made in 1912." This is another reference to the shocking discovery.

Paragraph 3: "The announcement set off controversy." If you are not sure what the word *firestorm* means, keep reading! You'll find hints in the next two sentences.

Paragraph 4: "The public was divided over human origins." Now the author is adding another dimension to the discussion. Often, a passage will introduce a controversy or problem, as is the case here.

Paragraph 5: "Scopes was a teacher." This sentence appears to be off the topic. We should read another sentence to discover why the author brings up Scopes.

Paragraph 6: "Lasting effects from the case." Don't be thrown off by the vocabulary! If you are not sure of some of the words in the sentence, read another line or two. The passage makes it clear that the situation lasted for many years.

Last sentence: "A battle still rages over the subject." The passage ends without a nice resolution; the author indicates that the situation is ongoing.

Direction Markers
(Again, we use **boldface** for same-direction markers and <u>underline</u> opposite-direction markers.)

<u>Although</u> the skull resembled those of other finds, including the famous ape-men of Java, the jaw appeared to come from some type of heretofore unknown species of ape.

The ensuing controversy over human origins eventually led the *Times* to publish an editorial that cautioned readers from seeing Piltdown Man as the missing link; **instead,** the editors advised readers to see Piltdown Man as a link to man's prehistoric past, <u>but</u> not necessarily proof of evolution.

<u>Although</u> no fossil could conclusively prove evolution, scientists had amassed a huge collection of fossils in the early twentieth century.

And even today, the reverberations of the trial are still visible.

This passage is presenting a rather controversial topic. There are two sides to the discussion, and the author indicates them by using the direction markers highlighted above.

Main idea: "The discovery of fossils that supported evolution led to a battle over the theory of evolution, which continues to this day." This passage is neatly divided into three large areas. The first two paragraphs talk about the discovery, the next two talk about the controversy, and the final two talk about the court case and its effects. Our main idea should touch on each of these topics.

Main Idea Passage D

Paragraph 1: "Oral reading is used a lot in schools." This sentence prepares us to read about an educational topic. Remember to try to keep in mind the author's purpose—why the author is writing. The author may want to support oral reading, attack it, or just give a history of it. Did you spot any clues that indicate what this passage will do?

Paragraph 2: "The history of oral reading is linked to culture." This paragraph discusses the history of oral reading.

Paragraph 3: "Schools started to use textbooks to teach reading." This continues the history and indicates a change in the way reading was taught.

Paragraph 4: "The usefulness of oral reading is questioned." The author introduces a problem.

Paragraph 5: "Changes in research and science." If you're not sure how this sentence fits into the rest of the passage, read another sentence or two. It appears that new research was against oral reading.

Paragraph 6: "Written books played a role in oral reading." Check the following sentence to see how this fits into the discussion. The author states that silent reading was taking over.

Last sentence: "Good things about oral reading were never in doubt." This final sentence seems to go against what we've been reading. The last three paragraphs all discussed negative aspects of oral reading. But the author ends on a positive note. To understand this ending, let's check our direction markers.

Direction Markers
(Again, we use **boldface** for same-direction markers and <u>underline</u> opposite-direction markers.)

> <u>Although</u> some recent educational theorists have challenged the efficacy of oral reading, its popularity in schools and classrooms is unchallenged.

However, printed books were often scarce, and literacy rates were often low. **Thus,** families would gather around and listen to a book being read to them.

In fact, they concluded that the only time students read orally was in school.

For a number of years, oral reading was absent from many a classroom. But in time, new research and studies brought oral reading back to the forefront of education.

By looking at these direction markers, the author's purpose and main idea become much clearer. The author wishes to show how oral reading has persisted despite challenges. This explains why three paragraphs discuss negative aspects, but the final sentence is positive.

Main idea: "Despite challenges to its usefulness, oral reading remains an important educational technique." If your main idea isn't similar to the one above, you may have missed some of the direction markers. This passage isn't presenting oral reading in a negative manner, but rather supporting it. The last sentence of the first paragraph is a very important one.

Summary: Stating the Main Idea

1. **Read the first sentence of each paragraph.** State what topic the author is writing about.
2. **Skim the rest of the paragraph for direction markers.** Pay particular attention to opposite-direction markers.
3. **Remember to read both the first sentence of each paragraph in the passage and last sentence of the conclusion.** The last sentence will contain the author's final point.
4. **The main idea should connect all the ideas found in the first sentences of the paragraphs and the last sentence of the conclusion.** If you're having trouble connecting all of the topics, ask yourself what the purpose of the passage is to help you put all the pieces together.

DEALING WITH DIFFICULT PASSAGES

One of the greatest challenges of the TOEFL is dealing with passages that are written for native speakers. Because the TOEFL is designed to measure your ability to perform at an academic institution, you can expect to see passages that contain some difficult vocabulary and complicated structures. Don't be intimidated by them! Keep in mind that even native English speakers often have difficulties with the types of passages found on standardized tests such as the TOEFL.

If you find yourself struggling with a passage on the TOEFL, use the following helpful strategies.

Tip #1: Skim, Don't Read!

Now that you've practiced finding the main idea and purpose of a passage, you have seen how little of the passage you actually have to read to understand what an author is writing about. If you find yourself getting lost as you are reading, move on to another part of the passage. Often, you can still figure out the main idea even if you're not sure what one or two paragraphs are about. Focus on the big picture!

Tip #2: Trim the Fat!

A sentence is a simple thing. All it requires is a subject, usually a noun (for example, a person, place, or thing) and a verb (an action). However, writers like to make sentences more complicated by adding all sorts of words to this basic formula. Let's look at two sample sentences.

> Joe ran.
>
> Joe, a competitive runner for nearly 20 years, ran perhaps the best race of his entire life last week when he narrowly defeated his arch rival in a stunning showdown.

These two sentences have the same subject (Joe) and the same verb (ran). The second sentence has a lot more information in it, but they are basically telling us the same thing.

One way to increase your comprehension is to ignore all the extra words in a sentence—trim the fat. When faced with a difficult sentence, look for the following three basic parts:

> 1. **Subject.** Find out who or what is performing the action.
> 2. **Verb.** This is the action being performed.
> 3. **Object.** This receives the action of the verb.

Here's another example.

> Scientists using NASA's Spitzer Space Telescope have found a new class of stellar object, miniature stars too small to initiate fusion but large enough to have their own planets orbiting them.

That's quite a mouthful, but if we trim the fat, the sentence basically says

> Scientists...have found a new...object.

That's it! All of the other words provide some useful details, but the really important stuff is the subject, verb, and object. Let's try this a few more times.

DRILL #7—TRIM THE FAT

For each of the following sentences, find the subject, verb, and object. Write down a simpler version of each sentence. Check your answers at the end of the drill.

1. Wild horses, which once roamed freely over the grasslands of Europe, Asia, and Africa, are found only in isolated patches of Southeastern Africa and Eastern Asia now.

Simple version: _____

2. In a digital camera, light entering the camera is focused on a charged coupled device, or CCD, which converts light energy into a charged electron.

Simple version: _____

3. A major stumbling block in the development of a viable hydrogen-fueled car is the expectation of many drivers that the vehicle will travel at least 300 miles before needing to refuel.

Simple version: _____

4. Prior to the development of germ theory, John Snow, a London physician, was able to halt an outbreak of cholera by restricting access to a water pump that he suspected was contributing to the spread of the disease.

Simple version: _____

5. Cores of ice, drilled from glaciers in Greenland and the Antarctic, provide climatologists with valuable data on Earth's prehistoric climate, including changes in the concentration of greenhouse gases in the atmosphere.

Simple version: _____

6. In 1899, Nikola Tesla, famed inventor of the alternating current electrical system, shocked an assembled audience at a conference by operating a six-foot radio-controlled electric boat.

Simple version: _____

7. Fainting, which can be a sign of a serious ailment such as heart failure or a result of something as harmless as standing up too quickly, results from an insufficient supply of oxygen to the brain.

Simple version: _____

8. One of the main provisions of the Taft-Hartley Labor Act was the government's ability to prevent a strike by any workers it considered essential to the nation's health or safety.

Simple version: _____

9. After spending nearly 26 years in jail, South African statesman Nelson Mandela was elected president of South Africa in that country's first multiracial election in 1994.

Simple version: _____

10. On Shrove Tuesday in 217 A.D., soldiers in Derby, England celebrated a victory over Roman soldiers by playing the first recorded soccer match, starting an annual event that lasted for almost 1,000 years.

Simple version: _____

Answers to Drill #7

Important information is in **bold**.

1. **Wild horses,** which once roamed freely over the grasslands of Europe, Asia, and Africa, **are found** only **in** isolated **patches of** Southeastern **Africa and** Eastern **Asia** now.

Simple version: <u>Wild horses are found in patches of Africa and Asia.</u>

Watch out for phrases that begin with the word *which*. These phrases are not essential to the sentence and can be ignored.

2. In a digital camera, **light** entering the camera **is focused on a** charged coupled **device,** or CCD, which converts light energy into a charged electron.

Simple version: <u>Light is focused onto a device.</u>

Fancy technical terms are always good candidates for trimming. Ignore them whenever possible.

3. **A** major stumbling **block** in the development of a viable hydrogen-fueled car **is the expectation** of many drivers **that the vehicle will travel** at least **300 miles** before needing to refuel.

Simple version: <u>A block is the expectation that the vehicle will travel 300 miles.</u>

This sentence contains numerous prepositional phrases. These are little phrases that start with words like *in, of,* and *at*. When you see these words, you can cut their phrases out of the sentence.

4. Prior to the development of germ theory, **John Snow,** a London physician, **was able to halt an outbreak** of cholera by restricting access to a water pump that he suspected was contributing to the spread of the disease.

Simple version: <u>John Snow was able to halt an outbreak.</u>

Often, a phrase in the beginning of a sentence that is set off with a comma ("Prior to the development of germ theory,") can be trimmed away.

5. **Cores of ice,** drilled from glaciers in Greenland and the Antarctic, **provide** climatologists with **valuable data** on Earth's prehistoric climate, including changes in the concentration of greenhouse gases in the atmosphere.

Simple version: <u>Cores of ice provide valuable data.</u>

Similarly, phrases at the end of a sentence that are set off with a comma ("including changes in…atmosphere") can be removed as well.

6. In 1899, **Nikola Tesla,** famed inventor of the alternating current electrical system, **shocked an** assembled **audience** at a conference by operating a six-foot radio-controlled electric boat.

Simple version: <u>Nikola Tesla shocked an audience.</u>

When trimming the fat, a good strategy is to locate the subject first. Then find the verb. Once you do that, you can cut out everything in between them.

7. **Fainting,** which can be a sign of a serious ailment such as heart failure or a result of something as harmless as standing up too quickly, **results from an insufficient supply of oxygen** to the brain.

Simple version: <u>Fainting results from an insufficient supply of oxygen.</u>

Once again, we have another phrase using the word *which*. Get rid of it.

8. **One** of the main **provisions** of the Taft-Hartley Labor Act **was the government's ability to prevent a strike** by any workers it considered essential to the nation's health or safety.

Simple version: <u>One provision was the government's ability to prevent a strike.</u>

This sentence has a bunch of prepositional phrases: "of the main...," "of the Taft-Hartley Labor Act...," "by any workers...," and "to the nation's health or safety." These can all be trimmed away.

9. After spending nearly 26 years in jail, South African statesman **Nelson Mandela was elected president** of South Africa in that country's first multiracial election in 1994.

Simple version: <u>Nelson Mandela was elected president.</u>

You can also eliminate any words that provide descriptions, such as "South African statesman" and "first multiracial." Although these words provide more details, they are not essential to the sentence.

10. On Shrove Tuesday in 217 A.D., **soldiers** in Derby, England **celebrated** a victory over Roman soldiers **by playing** the first recorded **soccer** match, starting an annual event that lasted for almost 1,000 years.

Simple version: <u>Soldiers celebrated by playing soccer.</u>

There are many phrases that can be trimmed here. As you can see, most of the words in this sentence are only there to provide more details. Ignore them and focus on the important stuff.

Tip #3: Dealing with Difficult Vocabulary

Passages on the TOEFL may contain a number of difficult or unfamiliar words. It's easy to become frustrated with these words and lose track of what you've read. Fortunately, you often do not need to understand these words to determine the passage's main idea. As we just saw, trimming the fat eliminates many of the words in a sentence because they are not crucial to understanding it.

Let's look at some examples of sentences with difficult vocabulary words.

> Despite the <u>preponderance</u> of evidence <u>debunking</u> this outdated notion, many people continue to <u>vigorously</u> defend it.

First, let's trim the fat. Remember, we said that phrases at the beginning of a sentence that are set off with commas can be cut. That eliminates two of the difficult words, leaving us with

> Many people continue to <u>vigorously</u> defend it.

Now the sentence isn't so complicated. Let's just focus on the subject, verb, and object. Our sentence now reads

> People continue to defend it.

The other words are just modifiers. They add detail, but they're not essential to understanding the basic idea.

In some cases, the difficult vocabulary word is the subject or the verb. In these cases, trimming the fat won't be too helpful. Here's an example.

> The <u>gentility</u> of Victorian England viewed work as the domain of men and often limited women's access to various jobs and professions.

Need more review of prepositional phrases? Pick up The Princeton Review's *Grammar Smart*.

Let's trim away some of the unnecessary phrases. Start by eliminating some of the prepositional phrases (those phrases beginning with words such as *on, of, in,* and so forth) and modifiers.

That leaves us with

> The <u>gentility</u> viewed work as the domain of men and often limited women's access to jobs and professions.

Our first verb is *viewed,* and our subject is a difficult vocabulary word. However, to understand this sentence, we don't need to know exactly what gentility means. Instead, let's just replace gentility with

> Some people viewed work as the domain of men.

This is good enough for understanding the author's general idea. This even works when the difficult vocabulary takes the form of a verb. Here's an example.

> In time, the Scythians were able to subjugate the Slavs, a people who throughout their history suffered under the dominion of many foreign rulers.

Using the same "trimming" process, we can reduce this sentence to the following:

> The Scythians were able to subjugate the Slavs.

Then we can replace our difficult word with a simple phrase.

> The Scythians were able to do something to the Slavs.

Most likely, you'll find some information in another part of the passage that will help you figure out what the difficult word means. But when you are looking for the main idea or purpose, don't focus on what you don't know—work with what you *do* know.

DRILL #8—DIFFICULT VOCABULARY

The following sentences contain one or more difficult vocabulary words. Paraphrase each sentence, avoiding difficult words or replacing them with more familiar ones whenever possible.

1. The authorship of *The Art of War*, an influential treatise on war, tactics, and espionage, is often attributed to Sun Tzu, but the tome was more likely penned by a number of writers.

Paraphrase:_____

2. One of the more controversial incidents of government intervention into the private sector occurred when, during the early 1970s, the government imposed a cap on wages to combat inflation.

Paraphrase:_____

3. Saccharin, a white crystalline compound that tastes more than 100 times sweeter than sugar, was discovered by accident in 1879.

Paraphrase:_____

4. The writ of *habeas corpus* functions not to ascertain a detainee's guilt or innocence, but to determine if the prisoner has been accorded due process.

Paraphrase:_____

5. Theodor Adorno, Walter Benjamin, and Herbert Marcuse, distinguished philosophers of the Frankfurt School, were instrumental in formulating seminal critical theories on capitalism.

Paraphrase:_____

6. Based on his observations of the Andromeda galaxy and others like it, Walter Baade inferred the existence of ancient stars in the Milky Way that were formed from primordial hydrogen and helium.

Paraphrase:_____

7. Most critics consider *Dracula* the archetypal horror novel, the one from which all other macabre stories originate.

Paraphrase:_____

8. Archaeologists usually employ two types of dating methods; one that attempts to determine the temporal order of a sequence of events and one that strives to date an object or event in terms of absolute calendar years.

Paraphrase:_____

9. A modem operates by converting discrete digital data into an analog signal that varies continuously in reference to a standard reference point.

Paraphrase:_____

10. Abstract expressionism emerged from the turbulent 1940s New York City art scene and quickly captivated critics with its stylistic diversity and nonrepresentational framework.

Paraphrase:_____

Answers to Drill #8

Many of these examples are similar to the exercises in Drill #7. The important information is in **bold**.

1. **The authorship** of *The Art of War,* an influential treatise on war, tactics, and espionage, is **often attributed to Sun Tzu, but** the tome was more likely penned **by a number of writers.**

Words such as *treatise, espionage,* and *tome* are not important to the general idea of this sentence.

2. One of the more **controversial incidents** of government intervention into the private sector **occurred when**, during the early 1970s, the **government** imposed a cap on wages to combat inflation.

In this sentence, it is necessary to realize that a controversial incident occurred. Thus, it is not important what words such as *intervention* and *sector* mean. If you are unsure of what *imposed* means, you can still get the basic idea.

3. **Saccharin**, a white crystalline compound that tastes more than 100 times sweeter than sugar, **was discovered by accident** in 1879.

In this example, one of our difficult words—*saccharin*—is the subject. But don't dwell on it. The sentence's message is that it was discovered by accident.

4. The writ of *habeas corpus* **functions** not to ascertain a detainee's guilt or innocence, but **to determine** if the prisoner has been accorded **due process**.

Some passages may contain *jargon*, which is specialized terminology relating to a particular field of study. Ignore it. In this sentence, we can cut out *writ of habeas corpus* and *due process* and read the sentence as "This thing functions to determine one thing."

5. Theodor Adorno, Walter Benjamin, and Herbert Marcuse, distinguished philosophers of the Frankfurt School, **were instrumental** in formulating seminal critical **theories** on capitalism.

This sentence has a lot of information packed into it. But we can avoid a lot of trouble by simply paraphrasing it as, "Some guys were doing something with theories." That will be enough to help you find the main idea of a passage.

6. Based on his observations of the Andromeda galaxy and others like it, Walter Baade inferred the **existence of ancient stars in the Milky Way** that were formed from primordial hydrogen and helium.

Inferred and *primordial* do not affect the meaning of this sentence in a major way.

7. Most **critics consider *Dracula*** the archetypal horror novel, the one from which **all other** macabre stories **originate**.

Many times, an author will provide clues as to the meaning of a word in the rest of the sentence. In this case, *archetypal* is defined as something from which other things originate. Even so, the meaning of the word is not important to the sentence. *Macabre* is also not necessary.

8. **Archaeologists** usually **employ two types** of dating **methods**; one that attempts to determine the temporal order of a sequence of events and one that strives to date an object or event in terms of absolute calendar years.

Once again, the important stuff is surrounded by lots of extra information. Don't worry about words such as *temporal* or *strive*.

9. A modem **operates** by **converting** discrete digital data into an analog signal that varies continuously in reference to a standard reference point.

There a few parts of this sentence that may be difficult to understand. Let's simplify it: "A thing operates by changing one type of thing into another." That's much easier to understand.

10. Abstract expressionism **emerged** from the turbulent 1940s New York City **art scene** and quickly **captivated critics** with its stylistic diversity and nonrepresentational framework.

Sometimes the entire sentence is filled with difficult vocabulary or jargon. If you encounter this, move on. No single sentence will be absolutely essential to understanding an author's main idea, so look for your information elsewhere. For this sentence, we need to know that "something emerged from an art scene and did something to critics."

FINAL EXAM

Now it's time to try out all the strategies you've learned. For the following passage, identify the main idea, structure, and author's primary purpose in writing it. Briefly paraphrase each paragraph after you read it. Check your answers at the end of the exercise.

Since 1979, there has been a consensus that a doubling of carbon dioxide would raise global temperatures 1.5 to 4.5 degrees Celsius. Emissions of methane, nitrous gases, and other gases that absorb infrared radiation could speed this process further. Although attention has been given to strategies intended to limit global warming, most climatologists feel an average temperature increase of one to two degrees Celsius is inevitable.

A potentially hazardous consequence of even a slight increase in worldwide temperature was identified in the early 1970s. Scientists predicted a nearly 20-foot rise in global sea levels as a result of the Antarctic ice sheet melting. Although this prediction has since been discredited by new research that shows such an occurrence would take place over a span of roughly 500 years, more recent studies have identified several sites, including smaller glaciers and large parts of the ice sheet in Greenland, that are more susceptible to rapid thawing. Based on data compiled from researchers, a seven-foot rise in sea level is possible by the year 2100.

Even a small rise in sea level, an average of two feet worldwide, would result in inundation, erosion, flooding, and saltwater intrusion. Coastal areas of the United States would lose a significant amount of land: Scientists predict a 50- to 100-foot loss in New Jersey, and up to 1,000 feet of shore areas flooded in Florida. According to some studies, the rise in water levels could contribute to a loss of 50 to 90 percent of U.S. wetlands.

Currently, two major policy approaches are being considered by coastal communities. The first, known as the no-protection approach, is based on a philosophy of nonintervention. Communities in coastal regions simply zone areas they anticipate losing land to erosion within the next 30 to 60 years. No new buildings are permitted to be built in zones likely to be lost to flooding or erosion, and the current structures are left to their fates. Communities that take a no-protection approach acknowledge the coming danger, but they are often unwilling or unable to incur the financial losses associated with condemning and removing beachfront property. However, it should be noted that communities that elect a no-protection approach place the financial burden on the federal government, which compensates home owners for homes lost to floods or storms.

The second option, and certainly the more appealing one, involves raising the land level along the shore. This approach, although a far costlier one, offers several advantages. First, it does not require the removal or demolition of buildings. Instead, the entire land mass is raised to protect it from the ocean. Second, the federal government does not have to intervene in the form of land buys or flood insurance. Despite these benefits, many communities choose not to raise the land due to the great cost and large amount of labor involved. To raise the land, sand must be pumped onto the beach (including the underwater part of the beach) until the land level gradually rises. In addition, roads, houses, and other structures must be gradually raised again. The size of this undertaking prevents many communities from considering it.

One of the major hurdles facing policy makers is the lack of urgency surrounding the onset of global warming and rising sea levels. Many communities do not see the need to take action in response to effects that will not materialize for 100 years. However, considering the possible consequences of inaction, community leaders would be wise to begin serious discussions about their preferred strategy.

Purpose:

_____

_____

How is the passage structured?

_____

_____

_____

_____

Paragraph 1: _____

_____

Paragraph 2: _____

_____

Paragraph 3: _____

_____

Paragraph 4: _____

_____

Paragraph 5: _____

_____

Paragraph 6: _____

_____

Main idea: _____

_____

Answers to Final Exam

Purpose: The purpose of this passage is *to provide a possible solution to a problem*. The first paragraph introduces a situation that would cause Earth's temperature to rise. The next two paragraphs reveal consequences of the warming. After that, the author discusses two possible solutions. Finally, the author states that leaders need to act soon.

How is the passage structured? Because the purpose of the passage is to provide a solution to a problem, the passage predictably contains information on the problem and the solutions. The first three paragraphs all deal with the nature of the problem, and the next three deal with the possible solutions.

Paragraph 1: This paragraph indicates that a doubling of carbon dioxide leads to an increase in temperature. The "although" near the end of the passage should be noted. The sentence states that the warming seems inevitable.

Paragraph 2: The author gives information on the consequence: a rise in sea levels. Remember, you don't need to pay too much attention to the details.

Paragraph 3: This paragraph continues the discussion of results of the rise in sea level. Note the word "even." This is a direction word.

Paragraph 4: Now the author introduces two major approaches to solving the problem. The first possible solution is the no-protection approach. Did you find the direction word at the end of the paragraph? Note that this approach places a financial burden on the government.

Paragraph 5: This is the second option, and it is important to note that the author favors it ("more appealing"). The second option involves raising the land level. There are quite a few direction markers in this paragraph.

Paragraph 6: The author ends with a "hurdle," or obstacle, to solving the problem. The author thinks people should decide on the best solution soon and act on it.

What is the main idea?

There are two main approaches to dealing with rising sea levels caused by global warming, and communities should give thought to which strategy they will use.

The Last Word on Reading

We've spent a lot of time working with passages, but the time has been well spent. The elements of reading we've reviewed in this chapter form the core of the skills required to do well on the TOEFL.

Reading skills will also prove invaluable on two other sections of the TOEFL—speaking and writing. But first, let's look at the core concepts you'll need to master the next section—listening.

Summary

There are a few Core Concepts to keep in mind when tackling Reading passages on the TOEFL.

- **Find the purpose:** Why did the author write the passage? Was it to explain, resolve, or convince?

- **Understand the structure:** Familiarize yourself with the typical layout of a Reading passage (introduction, several body paragraphs, and a conclusion) and the organization within each part.

- **State the main idea:** Use the first sentence of each paragraph, the last sentence of the conclusion, and direction markers throughout the passage to help you find the main idea.

When dealing with more difficult passages, don't forget to skim, trim the fat, and replace challenging vocabulary words with simpler substitutes.

Chapter 3
Core Concept:
Listening

The Listening section can seem like one of the most intimidating sections on the TOEFL. The tasks in the Listening section require you to sort through lectures and conversations that are filled with distracting pauses and brief digressions—a very frustrating experience, but a very realistic scenario. Don't be discouraged! The Listening section does follow some common patterns. The key to getting a good score is to find these patterns; this chapter is going to teach you how to do exactly that.

LISTENING ON THE TOEFL

In this section, you'll be asked to listen to *lectures* and *conversations*. These listening tasks will have a definite structure, which is similar to the reading passages we just studied. There will be an introduction, supporting details or examples, and a conclusion.

Let's take a closer look at the structure of these lectures and conversations.

In a *lecture,* you can expect to hear the following:

1. **Opening:** The teacher or professor will greet the class and announce the topic of the lecture.
2. **Purpose of the lecture:** After stating the topic, the speaker will usually mention the focus of this particular lecture.
3. **Details and/or examples:** The lecture will usually include several supporting details and/or examples.
4. **Conclusion:** Conclusions in the lectures will not always be obvious. Some lectures or talks will end rather abruptly.

Additionally, an academic lecture or talk on the TOEFL is also likely to contain:

5. **Questions and/or comments:** During the lecture, a student will often ask a question or make a comment. The answers to these questions typically reinforce the speaker's purpose.

In a *conversation,* you can expect to hear the following:

1. **Greeting:** The two people talking will first exchange greetings.
2. **Statement of problem/issue:** Conversations on the TOEFL typically revolve around a problem or an issue faced by one of the speakers.
3. **Response:** After the problem or issue is raised, one of the speakers will respond, usually by making a suggestion to the other.
4. **Resolution:** The conversation will end with some sort of closing or resolution to the problem.

Your challenge in the Listening section is similar to your challenge in the Reading section of the TOEFL. When listening to a conversation or lecture, you need to do the following:

1.   Identify *what* the topic is.
2.   Figure out *why* the topic is being addressed.
3.   Note the supporting *examples*.

You've practiced identifying these parts in the previous chapter. Now the challenge is to apply what you've learned to the Listening section. There are some things, however, that make the listening tasks especially difficult.

CHALLENGES IN THE LISTENING SECTION

In the Speaking and Writing sections (which you'll learn about as you move through this book), you will be required to listen to lectures and respond, just like you will in the Listening section. However, there is a difference between that these tasks in other sections and those in the Listening section.

The difference is that the tasks in the Listening section have intentional distractions. These distractions are pauses, interruptions, and interjections that disrupt the flow of the speaker's talk. Interestingly, if you were to respond on the Speaking section in the same way the speakers talk on the Listening section, you would receive a fairly low score.

For example, you may hear something like the three brief statements that follow, which include common distractions (try reading them aloud, or ask a friend to read them to you).

   "Okay, so, uh…today we're going to discuss the hunting practices of the umm…Trobriand Islanders. As you remember, we uh…last week, last week we talked about their social structure, now we're moving into their day-to-day activities."

   "So let's take our example of...what did we say? Right, our example is the proposed flat tax rate. Now this example isn't a perfect one because, well…it's only a hypothetical example, but it'll do for this discussion."

   "Therefore—and this is an important point—the New Historicism Movement—didn't um, didn't come out of nowhere. It was a product of its time. Okay?"

Another characteristic that makes the Listening section different from the others is that you will have to follow conversations between multiple speakers. It can be difficult to identify the purpose or the supporting details of a conversation when the speaker changes.

TAKING NOTES

You are allowed to take notes on the TOEFL. Of course, you must balance your note-taking with your ability to comprehend the speech or lecture. A common mistake is to try to write too much; this often causes you to miss hearing some important information. Therefore, keep your note-taking to a minimum and focus only on major points.

Here's a suggestion on how to organize your notes.

```
  I.    What? _____
  II.   Why? _____
  III.  Reasons/examples _____
        1. _____
        2. _____
        3. _____
  IV.   Conclusion _____
```

Whether or not you take notes, you will need to listen actively to do well on this part of the TOEFL.

ACTIVE LISTENING

Active listening strategies are similar to the *active reading* strategies on which we worked in the previous chapter, Core Concept: Reading. Of course, active listening is more difficult than active reading. However, by familiarizing yourself with the overall structure of the lectures and conversations, you'll have an easier time understanding the main points.

When listening actively, pay attention to the following:

1. **Purpose:** The speaker will usually state the purpose of the lecture or conversation within the first few lines of the talk.
2. **Reasons/examples:** The rest of the conversation or lecture will contain reasons or examples related to the purpose.

The next sections provide you with some practice in listening actively to lectures and conversations. Let's start with lectures.

Listening to Lectures

Track 1 on the CD that accompanies this book is a lecture in a sociology class. As you listen to the lecture, try to identify the purpose and the reasons or examples. How is this lecture similar to the reading passages we've looked at? How is it different?

Play Track 1 on the accompanying CD. A transcript of the lecture can be found at the end of the chapter.

Purpose: _____

Examples: _____

_____

_____

_____

Lecture Analysis

Lectures typically follow the format of reading passages. The speaker will provide an introduction, supporting reasons and examples, and some sort of conclusion. Of course, as you're listening to the lecture, you won't be aware of when a paragraph ends, but you should still know what to expect based on the part of the lecture to which you're listening.

Here's the introduction of the lecture, broken down piece by piece.

(1) Okay, class, let's get started. (2) Today, um, today we're going to talk about the ah...structural functionalist theory in sociology. (3) You guys remember last week we discussed the interactionist perspective, right? (4) Now that theory, the interactionist theory, focused on how people get along with one another and, uh, the way that interactions um...create behaviors.

Now, let's analyze what's going on in this first part of the introduction.

1. **Introduction.** On the TOEFL, the lectures and conversations usually start with a greeting of some sort. This greeting is not important to the lecture.
2. **Topic.** At some point early in the lecture, the professor will probably state what the class is going to talk about "today," or "in this class." This is very important. Note the topic on your scrap paper.
3. **Background.** Usually, the professor will refer to a prior lecture or topic. The professor will state that the class talked about this topic "last time," "last class," or something along those lines. This information may be important to the lecture or it may be a distraction; it depends on what the purpose of the lecture is.
4. **More background.** This line provides more background information.

Here's the second part of the introduction.

> (1) This theory...the structural functionalist theory...I'm just going to call it the functionalist theory...is very different. (2) Now, we'll talk about the historical context of this theory a little bit later, (3) but first I would like to just...um, go over the main tenets of the theory.

Let's analyze what's going on in this second part of the introduction.

1. **Transition:** Speeches and lectures tend to have more transitions. These transitions don't add any new information.
2. **Digression:** You will also notice a digression or two during the lectures. Usually, the professor will refer to something that will be "discussed later" or "at another time." Sometimes the professor will say, "I'm not going to get into this now." This information is unimportant.
3. **Purpose:** Listen for the statement of purpose early on in the lecture. If you figure out the purpose, write it down on your scrap paper.

This is the next part of the lecture.

> (1) The basic view of functionalism is that our behaviors and actions can be best explained with...explained by the role...or function, if you will...that they perform for the society as a whole. (2) Now, that may be a little vague. (3) What do I mean by that? (4) Well, let's look at some different behaviors and, uh, see how a functionalist would explain them.

Let's analyze what's happening in this part of the lecture.

1. **Definition/explanation:** The purpose of many of the lectures is to define or explain a term.
2., 3. **Digression:** Both lines 2 and 3 don't add anything to the lecture. As you're listening, try to focus on the topic and the examples given to support/explain it.
4. **Transition:** Here's another transition. Note how the speaker is about to discuss examples. Typically, the lecturer will say something such as, "Now, let's look at..." or "Now, I want to talk about..." These words let you know that examples are coming.

Here's the next section.

> (1) A good example would be the, uh, drug use. (2) A functionalist wouldn't really um...judge a drug user as a deviant, a bad person. Instead, the functionalist would try to ah...figure out what role the drug user, the person, fills in society. (3) This seems a little strange at first but bear with me. (4) Think about what role a drug user fills in society. (5) You may automatically think that the role, um, the PD role is always negative—crime, the cost of treatment, maybe more jails—but the functionalist tries to see the positives as well.

And here's the analysis of this section.

1. **Example:** Once the lecturer begins discussing examples, the structure is very similar to a reading passage. There will be an example followed by specific details.
2. **Detail:** Many of the questions will ask about details, so try to note some of them.
3., 4. **Digression:** These two lines address the class. They emphasize the lecturer's example, but they are relatively unimportant.
5. **Detail:** This is similar to line 2. Don't try to write down or memorize everything the lecturer says. You won't have time.

Here is the next part of the lecture.

(1) I bet you're thinking that drug use doesn't have too many positives, right? (2) Well, here's what a functionalist would say. (3) While a drug user may be harming himself or herself, to be fair, he is also benefiting society. Having drug users means we need to have more police, which means obviously, more jobs.

And also...if you think about it...more doctors, nurses, and social workers. Even drug counselors. All these people would be out of work, probably, if we didn't have a drug problem. Let's keep going...without drug users, we wouldn't need the entire Drug Enforcement Agency, that bureau employs thousands of people, you know, and there's also the border patrol, customs agents, and so on, and so on.

And here's what's happening in this section.

1. **Transition:** This line acts as a bridge from one paragraph (which describes negative factors) to the next sentences (which describe positive factors).
2. **Detail:** This line brings the discussion back to the topic.
3. **Detail:** The rest of the lines all give details about the topic. Again, you can't possibly note every single part, so just try to note down one or two important points.

Finally, here is the last part of the lecture.

(1) So I think our example has given you a pretty good idea of how a functionalist views behaviors. (2) Again, the important thing is that they don't really judge behaviors as good or bad...they only view them based on their role or function in society.

And I think we can probably guess then, that to a functionalist, all behaviors...no matter how good or bad you may think they are... are necessary to society. (3) It's really a, uh, pretty interesting viewpoint, if you think about it.

Here's what's going on in this last part.

1. **Conclusion:** Listen for the conclusion of the lecture. The speaker may say something such as, "So…" or "Thus…" or "And so…"
2. **Summary:** Some lectures will end with a brief summary of the important points.
3. **Digression:** This line contains no new or important information.

As this exercise shows, many of the parts of the lecture are similar to the reading passages. While you listen to the sample lectures, think about their purpose and structure, just as you would with a reading passage.

Summary: Lectures

Try to identify the main parts of the lecture. Listen for the following:

1. **Topic:** This should appear early in the lecture, after the greeting.
2. **Purpose:** Shortly after the topic is introduced, the purpose of the lecture will be stated.
3. **Examples:** The majority of the lecture will be examples and details. Don't try to write down or memorize every single one.
4. **Conclusion:** Note any final points or summaries.

Listening to Conversations

Now let's listen to a conversation similar to what you'll hear on the TOEFL and see how this form works.

Play Track 2 on the accompanying CD. A transcript can be found at the end of the chapter.

Conversation Analysis

Conversations have the basic elements of reading passages. There should be some basic purpose to the conversation and reasons or examples related to that purpose. Here is a breakdown of the conversation you just heard.

Computer Lab Monitor: Hi. Do you need help with something?

Student: Yes. I'm supposed to use this program for my statistics class, but I'm not sure how.

Conversations also start with a greeting. Usually, the purpose will appear right at the beginning. Note this purpose on your scrap paper. Let's see what's next.

CLM: Okay. Do you have the program with you?

S: Sure, here it is.

CLM: Okay, let's bring this over to a computer and see how it works.

S: I think there's something wrong with the program. When I tried to run it on my computer, nothing happened.

These lines provide a detail about the problem the student is having. The questions will often ask about this type of detail, so be sure to note it.

CLM: Hmm. That's interesting. Well, let's see what happens here. It looks like its running fine on this computer.

S: Weird. My computer freezes every time I try to open the program.

CLM: You mean the entire computer locks up? Have you had this type of problem before?

S: Yeah, I guess. Sometimes when I try to use certain programs, they just don't seem to work correctly. I don't know why though.

More specific details are provided about the problem. Note that in a conversation, you'll have to pay attention to the roles of the speakers. In this case, one speaker is describing a problem, and the other is trying to help find a solution.

CLM: You can always use the computers here in the lab, you know. That way you won't have to worry about it.

S: I know. But I'd rather figure out what the problem is with my computer. The computer lab can be busy, and I need to work on this project often. It's going to be one-third of our grade.

CLM: What class is this for?

S: It's for Statistics 101, with Professor Lee.

CLM: And this program is required for the course?

S: Yep. Professor Lee even got the campus bookstore to stock a bunch of copies. That's where I bought it.

CLM: Do you use your computer for a lot of things? Maybe you should clear up some memory before you run the program.

> S: Yeah, I've tried that actually. I do have a lot of programs on my computer, but I should have enough memory to run this program.

Here, the lab monitor proposes a solution. This is an important part of the conversation, so make sure to note it. Also note the student's response to the solution. Many of the other details, such as the course or the professor's name, are not important. Focus only on details that relate back to the purpose. Let's see how the conversation wraps up.

> CLM: Well, I'm not quite sure what the problem could be. But you're welcome to use the program here.
>
> S: Okay.
>
> CLM: And you should definitely come back later and talk to my supervisor. She's a computer whiz. I bet she can solve your problem.

Conversations should have a fairly definite conclusion. You want to pay attention to how the conversation ends. Has the purpose been achieved? Note this on your scrap paper.

Summary: Conversations

Conversations have a definite structure. When listening to a conversation, pay attention to the following:

1. **Purpose:** What do the people in the conversation hope to achieve? Why are the people having this conversation?
2. **Details:** What specific details or examples are offered? How do these examples relate back to the purpose?
3. **Conclusion:** Is there any resolution? Do the people achieve their purpose?

TRANSCRIPTS

Track 1

Professor: Okay, class, let's get started. Today, um, today we're going to talk about the ah... structural functionalist theory in sociology. You guys remember last week we discussed the interactionist perspective, right? Now that theory, the interactionist theory, focused on how people get along with one another and, uh, the way that interactions um...create behaviors.

This theory...the structural functionalist theory...I'm just going to call it the functionalist theory...is very different. Now, we'll talk about the historical context of this theory a little bit later, but first I would like to just...um, go over the main tenets of the theory.

The basic view of functionalism is that our behaviors and actions can be best explained with...explained by the role...or function, if you will...that they perform for the society as a whole. Now, that may be a little vague. What do I mean by that? Well, let's look at some different behaviors and uh, see how a functionalist would explain them.

A good example would be the, uh, drug use. A functionalist wouldn't really um... judge a drug user as a deviant, a bad person. Instead, the functionalist would try to uh...figure out what role the drug user, the person, fills in society. This seems a little strange at first but bear with me. Think about what role a drug user fills in society. You may automatically think that the role, um the role is always negative— crime, the cost of treatment, maybe more jails—but the functionalist tries to see the positives as well.

I bet you're thinking that drug use doesn't have too many positives, right? Well, here's what a functionalist would say. While a drug user may be harming himself... or herself, to be fair...he is also benefiting society. Having drug users means we need to have more police, which means obviously, more jobs.

And also...if you think about it...more doctors, nurses, and social workers. Even drug counselors. All these people would be out of work, probably, if we didn't have a drug problem. Let's keep going...without drug users, we wouldn't need the entire Drug Enforcement Agency...that bureau employs thousands of people, you know...and there's also the border patrol, customs agents, and so on, and so on.

So I think our example has given you a pretty good idea of how a functionalist views behaviors. Again, the important thing is that they don't really judge behaviors as good or bad...they only view them based on their role or function in society.

And I think we can probably guess then, that to a functionalist, all behaviors...no matter how good or bad you may think they are...are necessary to society. It's really a, uh, pretty interesting viewpoint, if you think about it.

Track 2

Computer Lab Monitor: Hi. Do you need help with something?

Student: Yes. I'm supposed to use this program for my statistics class, but I'm not sure how.

CLM: Okay. Do you have the program with you?

S: Sure, here it is.

CLM: Okay, let's bring this over to a computer and see how it works.

S: I think there's something wrong with the program. When I tried to run it on my computer, nothing happened.

CLM: Hmm. That's interesting. Well, let's see what happens here. It looks like its running fine on this computer.

S: Weird. My computer freezes every time I try to open the program.

CLM: You mean the entire computer locks up? Have you had this type of problem before?

S: Yeah, I guess. Sometimes when I try to use certain programs, they just don't seem to work correctly. I don't know why though.

CLM: You can always use the computers here in the lab, you know. That way you won't have to worry about it.

S: I know. But I'd rather figure out what the problem is with my computer. The computer lab can be busy, and I need to work on this project often. It's going to be one-third of our grade.

CLM: What class is this for?

S: It's for Statistics 101, with Professor Lee.

CLM: And this program is required for the course?

S: Yep. Professor Lee even got the campus bookstore to stock a bunch of copies. That's where I bought it.

CLM: Do you use your computer for a lot of things? Maybe you should clear up some memory before you run the program.

S: Yeah, I've tried that actually. I do have a lot of programs on my computer, but I should have enough memory to run this program.

CLM: Well, I'm not quite sure what the problem could be, but you're welcome to use the program here.

S: Okay.

CLM: And you should definitely come back later and talk to my supervisor. She's a computer whiz. I bet she can solve your problem.

Chapter 4
Core Concept:
Speaking

As mentioned earlier, the TOEFL is an integrated exam which means that each individual section will measure several abilities. You'll be learning speaking skills that will remind you of the Reading and Listening chapters you just read. You will also be able to apply some of those speaking skills to elements in the final Core Concepts chapter, Writing.

SCORING FOR THE SPEAKING SECTION

Although the Speaking section is different from the Writing section in some ways, many of the guidelines for scoring it are similar. The Speaking section is graded on a scale of 0 to 4, while the Writing section is 0 to 5. In both Speaking and Writing, a score of 0 is reserved for a response that simply repeats the prompt, is in a foreign language, or is left blank, whereas a score of 4 on the Speaking section is judged to have accomplished the following:

- The response fulfills the demands of the task.
- The response presents a clear progression of ideas.
- The response includes appropriate details.

These standards conform to our three basic Core Concept Reading skills: *purpose, main idea,* and *structure.*

The main difference on the Speaking section is that the graders will also consider the quality of your speech. While they don't expect perfect English, they expect a top response to

- use speech that is clear, fluid, and sustained, although it may contain minor lapses in pronunciation or intonation. Pace may vary at times, but overall intelligibility remains high.
- demonstrate good control of basic and complex grammatical structures and contain generally effective word choice. Minor errors or imprecise use may be noticeable, but they neither require listener effort nor do they obscure meaning.

The best way to make sure you meet these guidelines is to *practice.* We'll give you suggestions and tips on how to achieve these goals, but there's no substitute for continued repetition.

PART 1: STATING YOUR PURPOSE

You remember that you needed to find a purpose in Reading passages and listen for a purpose in lectures on the listening section. Well, the best way to succeed on the Speaking section of the TOEFL is to use those skills you've learned in the reading and listening exercises.

Purpose and the Speaking Section

The speaking tasks on the TOEFL usually require you to do one of the following:

- Present your opinion on an issue.
- Explain facts presented in a lecture or reading.
- Summarize someone else's position.
- Describe something of importance to you.

Your speech on the TOEFL will need an introduction, just as you've observed in reading passages. Let's look at some ways to come up with an effective introduction.

Clearly Expressing Purpose on the Speaking Section

Let's look at a sample speaking task.

> Describe a job that you've held, and explain why it was important.

Now, here are the steps to follow.

Step 1: Decide What Your Purpose Is

Make sure you take a moment to decide what your purpose is; otherwise, you will not be able to communicate it effectively. As you have seen in the previous bullet points, there are four different types of tasks that you may encounter on the Speaking section of the TOEFL.

Step 2: State the Topic

For speaking tasks that ask you to present your opinion or to describe something personal to you, use the following introductory phrases:

I believe	*I think*	*I feel*
My view is	*My opinion is*	*My preference is*

After each of these statements, you'll need to mention the topic and whatever example you're going to use. For the sample task about a job you've held, your first sentence could be

I think that the most important job I've had was working at a library.
(introductory statement)   *(topic)*   *(specific example)*

State your topic in a clear, direct way. Also, note that on opinion questions, there is no right or wrong answer. Your purpose is to convince the listener that your position is correct, whatever your position may be.

For speaking tasks that require you to summarize someone else's opinion or to explain facts, the following introductions are appropriate:

This person believes that	*This person holds that*	*This person argues that*
This person's view is that	*This person's point is that*	*The lecture stated*
The reading stated	*The reading presented*	*The lecture offered*

After each statement, fill in what the topic or position is. For example, a TOEFL task may ask you to summarize facts from a reading. Your introduction may sound like this:

The reading presented facts on...(topic)

Step 3: State *What* or *Why*

For speaking tasks that ask your opinion, you will have to state *why* you believe something. For speaking tasks that require you to summarize facts or someone else's position, you'll have to say *what* his or her reasons are. Use the following words to indicate *what* and *why*:

Because	*The reason*	*Due to*	*For*

Once you put it all together, your speech may look like the following:

I think that the most important job I've had was working at a library. The reason I believe this is the number of interesting people I met at this job.

Spoken responses on the TOEFL are only 45 or 60 seconds, so most of your time will be used presenting details or examples. Therefore, your introduction should be brief and to the point.

YOUR TURN: DRILL #1—PRACTICE SPEAKING AN INTRODUCTION TO A SPEECH

Practice speaking introductions for each of the following tasks. If possible, record yourself and later review and evaluate your responses.

1. If you could have any job in the world, which job would you choose?
2. Describe a person you admire, and explain why you admire him or her.
3. A university has recently received a large sum of money. The university desperately needs to improve housing on campus, but students have also complained that the library needs to be fixed. Do you think that the money should be spent on housing or the library? Provide examples and reasons for your choice.
4. Read the following short passage:

The cane toad, a poisonous species of toad, is causing problems in Australia. The cane toad was brought to Australia in 1935 to help control the population of greyback beetles. Unfortunately, the toads did nothing to reduce the beetle population. Now, however, cane toads number in the millions and are threatening native animal populations.

The cane toad has two poisonous sacs located near its head and is so toxic that dingoes, snakes, and even crocodiles die within fifteen minutes of eating a cane toad. Now, conservationists are forced to transport some endangered species of animals to islands free from cane toads so that the endangered species can breed in safety.

The passage above describes a problem. Explain what the problem is and what steps are being taken to fix it.

5. Read the following conversation between two coworkers:

Employee A: I'm really swamped at work. I don't know if I'm going to be able to finish all of my projects by the deadline.

Employee B: I know. We really need to hire some more people around here. What are you going to do?

Employee A: I don't know. My boss said I have to finish the budget analysis by Friday, but he just gave me a new project that he needs completed right away.

Employee B: Well, if I were you, I'd tell your boss that there's no way you can finish both in time. I'd ask for more time.

Employee A: Yeah, I guess I could do that.

Employee B: Or maybe you can ask your boss to assign the project to someone else. That way you can focus on the budget analysis.

Employee B offers two possible solutions to Employee A's problems. Describe the problem, and state which of the two solutions you prefer. Explain why.

Sample Responses to Drill #1

Read the following responses, and practice speaking them aloud:

1. If I could have any job, I think that I would like to be an ambassador. I think this because I enjoy visiting other countries and meeting and interacting with other people.

2. One person whom I admire very much is Mohandas Gandhi. I admire him for many reasons, especially his strong sense of justice and rightness.

3. In my opinion, the university should spend its money on the library. I think this because a university should be an institution of learning, and a good library is essential to that.

4. The passage states that the problem is the poisonous cane toad. The toad is threatening many of the species in Australia.

5. The problem the employee has is that he or she cannot finish his or her work on time. In my opinion, the better solution is to ask the boss to assign the project to someone else. I think this because it is better to get the work done on time than to extend the deadline.

Summary: Stating Your Purpose

Your introduction is the first chance you have to make a good impression on your reader—so make it solid. Since you won't have much time to give your spoken response, make your introduction quick and concise.

The three points you need to convey in your introduction are

- **Purpose**: Your task.
- **Thesis**: Your topic. The thesis is basically a statement of your position or belief on a topic or your main idea. It will be slightly different based on what you are trying to accomplish in your spoken response.
- **Why**: After introducing the topic, state why you are discussing it. The answer to this *why* question should relate back to the purpose.

In your Introduction, don't go into specific details about your examples. You'll get to those later in the body of your speech. Also, avoid repeating the prompt word-for-word.

PART 2: ORGANIZING YOUR IDEAS

Before you begin speaking, take a few seconds to think about how you will organize your response. Make sure to follow the same guidelines that you saw in the Reading passages. You should include these parts in every spoken response:

- **Introduction**: State your purpose, which is what we practiced earlier.
- **Body**: Take the majority of your time to give examples and details which refer back to your purpose. (We will focus next on the body of your response.)
- **Conclusion**: Finally, summarize your thoughts. We will take a look at conclusions toward the end of this chapter.

Developing Body Paragraphs When Speaking

Everything you learned about body paragraphs in the Reading section applies to speaking. Body paragraphs are the place where the author, or speaker, develops his or her ideas. While the introduction states the purpose, the body paragraphs provide specific details to support that purpose.

Note that your responses on the Speaking section will only be 45 or 60 seconds, which means you will have a limited amount of time to develop your body paragraphs.

Articulating Your Body Paragraph

As we've seen from the reading exercises, the body paragraphs are where an author attempts to accomplish his or her purpose by presenting facts, arguments, and evidence.

A good body paragraph contains the following elements:

- A **topic sentence** that introduces the main point of the paragraph.
- **Examples, facts, and evidence** that help the author achieve his or her purpose.

Step 1: Provide a Topic Sentence

A good topic sentence does two things: It provides a transition between ideas and clearly states that main idea of the paragraph.

Let's look back at the introduction we established before:

> "I think the most important job I've had was working at a library. The reason I believe this is the number of interesting people I met at this job."

Now, each spoken body paragraph should begin with a topic sentence that supports your introduction.

Therefore, a good topic sentence for the first body paragraph might be:

"Working at the library was my most important job because I met Professor Martin, who has become my advisor this semester."

The topic sentence is introducing your idea (the job was important because you met Professor Martin), and then the rest of your body paragraph will give details that support your example. Perhaps Professor Martin convinced you to change your major, suggested you submit an article to the school's literary magazine, or hinted at a promotion on the library staff. These are all details that support your topic sentence.

Another good topic sentence is one that indicates a progression of ideas by using the phrase "One reason..."

In this instance, a good topic sentence might be:

"One reason that my job at the library was important is that I met Professor Martin, who has become my advisor this semester."

Other phrases that accomplish this progression are as follows:

Another reason	*Additionally*	*First*	*Moreover*
Second	*Third*	*Furthermore*	

These are transition statements that help you move from one idea to the next. Each succeeding topic sentence should a transition statement and connect back to the thesis.

The topic sentence for our next body paragraph might use the following transition:

"Another reason that my job at the library was important is that I met Dr. Lucas, who asked me to edit the book he was writing."

And then the rest of your body paragraph will provide details that support this example.

By writing topic sentences that connect ideas in this way, your response will sound well structured and will be easy to follow.

Step 2: Make Your Case with Examples

To support your thesis statement, you will want to provide details or information, usually in the form of facts or reasons.

Your examples should be:

- **Specific:** They should not be vague or too general.
- **Explained:** Make sure you give details to support your examples.

Use the following template to articulate your examples:

> Statement 1: State your example and tie it back to your thesis.
> Statement 2: Give one reason why your example is relevant to your thesis.
> Statement 3: Add detail to reason #1.
> Statement 4: Give another reason why your example is relevant to your thesis.
> Statement 5: Add detail to reason #2.
> Statement 6 (optional): Provide a summary of your reasons and relate them to your thesis.

Step 2

Your Turn: Drill #2—Practice Speaking With Examples

For each task, speak aloud using two examples to support your point. Use the template above as a guide while you articulate your thoughts.

Record your answers so you can review and evaluate your responses based on our sample answers.

1. Do you agree or disagree with the following statement?

It is better for students to gain real-world experience than to spend their time in a classroom.

2. Describe an influential person, and explain why you feel this person is a positive role model.
3. Some schools require first-year students to take the same courses, whereas other schools allow students to select the classes they want. Which policy do you think is better for first-year students and why?
4. Do you agree or disagree with the following statement?

The most important education occurs not during adulthood but during childhood.

5. Read the following passage about insect behavior:

Many insects are social creatures, living in large groups containing literally millions of individuals. Social insects, which include ants, termites, bees, and wasps, are the prime example of unselfish behavior in animals.

In any insect social system, each insect performs a specialized duty that is necessary for the survival of the hive as a whole. For example, among ants, there are certain types of ants that are soldiers—large, fearsome creatures with terrible jaws. Other ants, called drones, do not reproduce, instead devoting their time to taking care of the hive and the young of the queen. Each ant selflessly performs its role, not for its own benefit, but for the benefit of all the other ants.

Now entomologists have found an interesting case of this sort of cooperation in a nonsocial insect, the cricket. Crickets are a prime example of a "selfish" insect, leading a very isolated existence. They typically interact with other crickets only when mating or fighting over territory. But scientists have observed a species of cricket that undergoes periodic mass migrations. Every so often, the crickets set off to find more favorable living areas. When these migrations occur, the crickets band together into a huge caravan. Surely at a time like this, the crickets realize there is safety in numbers and put aside their selfish instinct for the good of all members.

Now read the following lecture on the same subject:

Professor: One of the biggest misconceptions in biology is the belief that organisms act out of concern for the "greater good" of the species. It is somewhat amazing how people assume that an ant or a mouse has enough sense to figure out how its actions impact all the members of its species!

Still, it is understandable why many people might believe this erroneous view. Many actions can be misinterpreted as being for the "good of the species." A classic example found in many early biology textbooks discussed the behavior of the stag. During mating season, a stag typically battles with other males, and the winner of these contests gains access to the females, while the loser walks away. Some people believed that the loser realizes that his offspring will be weaker, so the defeated stag "allows" the winner to mate to ensure the survival of the stag species.

This couldn't be further from the truth. The defeated stag wants to mate just as much as the winner does; the only problem is that he doesn't want to risk his life for the chance to mate. The stag is better off looking for other females to mate with. Thus, both stags—the winner and the loser—are acting not for the good of the species, but for their own selfish reasons.

Another good example of this is a recent study on the behavior of crickets. Scientists noted that crickets occasionally band together, traveling in huge swarms from location to location. The easy assumption was that the crickets believed in strength in numbers. But a researcher showed this is not the case. He attached tags to a sampling of crickets. Some of the tagged crickets were allowed to travel with the group. But some of them were separated from the rest. All the crickets that were separated were eaten by birds or rodents, whereas the tagged crickets in the group survived.

Apparently, there is safety in numbers, but the crickets aren't looking to help their fellow travelers. They want to avoid being eaten, and what better way is there than to disappear into a group of thousands of other tasty morsels?

Summarize the points in the professor's lecture, and explain how the points cast doubt on the reading.

Sample Responses To Drill #2

See how your responses compared to the suggested answers below. When you review the answers, read them aloud for more practice speaking.

1. Real-world experience is usually better than time spent in a classroom. I believe this because experience is the best teacher.

   One example of a way in which real world experience is valuable is that students studying auto mechanics cannot just read about an engine. Instead, they have to practice taking that engine apart piece by piece and then put it back together. Only then will students understand the concept.

   A second example of a way in which real world experience is valuable can be applied to learning a foreign language. If students in a classroom never have a chance to practice the language, they may forget the skills they were taught. In this instance, it would also be helpful to practice their skills in a real-world environment.

2. I believe that Mikhail Gorbachev is both an influential person and a positive role model.

   One reason Mikhail Gorbachev is a role model is because he is willing to work for change. Many people are content to have things stay the same, but he worked hard to change the Communist system. Even though his reforms were not as helpful as he would have liked, his willingness for change makes him a good role model.

   Another reason that Mikhail Gorbachev is a positive role model is because of his devotion to ideals that are larger than himself. For instance, he reached out to Ronald Reagan when he wanted to end the Cold War, instead of just following the in footsteps of Soviet leaders who came before him. Ensuring the future success of the Soviet Union was more important than simply concentrating on his personal power.

3. I would support mandatory classes for freshman instead of allowing the students to pick whatever classes they want.

   First, this will ensure a certain quality of education. With standardized classes, universities can make sure that all of their students are familiar with important intellectual works. That way, all students will have a basic educational level.

   Moreover, required classes will serve to increase the camaraderie of students. Universities are good places for students to meet each other and make connections that will help them later in life. Freshman can sometimes have difficulty fitting in, so required classes will help them make friends.

4. I agree that the most important education happens when one is a child.

   One reason why I agree with this statement is that younger children are very open to ideas and perceptions. A young child is very impressionable, so the lessons learned at this age can have a great impact.

Furthermore, childhood is a time when education focuses on the essentials of our society. Although children may not be learning advanced skills, they are learning basic life lessons. At this age, children learn important lessons, such as the difference between right and wrong and how to treat other people.

5. *The points made in the professor's lecture cast doubt on the reading.*

   The first point the professor makes that casts doubt on the reading is his point about the behavior of stags. For example, some people interpret the stag's action as being for the "good of the species," but the professor shows that the stag is actually acting in self-interest. Likewise, the professor talks about how crickets act only in self-interest, which does not support the example in the reading.

   The second point the professor makes that casts doubt on the reading is his point about the intelligence of animals and insects. He states that it would require a lot of intelligence for an animal or insect to evaluate how its behavior will affect an entire species. Therefore, his argument is that the cricket is only acting out of self-preservation, which again casts doubt on the reading.

Summary: Choosing Examples and Developing Body Paragraphs When Speaking

Good examples are important for your responses. Make sure your examples and your structure are organized.

Remember to do the following:

- **State** the example.
- **Explain** how the example supports your position.
- **Transitions:** Provide a topic sentence or transition statement to move from one example to the next.
- **Details:** Support each example with details.

Focus on stating just a few examples and explaining their significance. Always provide specific details for each example, and articulate the ways in which your examples relate to your purpose.

PUTTING IT ALL TOGETHER

Now take what you learned about organizing your ideas, stating your purpose, providing topic sentences, and making your case with examples to articulate both an introduction and a full body paragraph for each of the following tasks.

Your Turn: Drill #3—Practice Speaking an Introduction and Body Paragraph

Speak a body paragraph for each of the following tasks. It may help to repeat your introduction statement first. If possible, record your responses and evaluate them when you are finished.

1.   If you could have any job in the world, which job would you choose?
2.   Describe a person you admire, and explain why you admire him or her.
3.   A university has recently received a large sum of money. The university desperately needs to improve housing on campus, but students have complained that the library needs to be fixed. Do you think that the money should be spent on housing or the library? Provide reasons and examples for your choice.
4.   Read the following short passage:

The cane toad, a poisonous species of toad, is causing problems in Australia. The cane toad was brought to Australia in 1935 to help control the population of greyback beetles. Unfortunately, the toads did nothing to reduce the beetle population. Now, however, cane toads number in the millions and are threatening native animal populations.

The cane toad has two poisonous sacs located near its head and is so toxic that dingoes, snakes, and even crocodiles die within fifteen minutes of eating a cane toad. Now, conservationists are forced to transport some endangered species of animals to islands free from cane toads so that the endangered species can breed in safety.

The passage above describes a problem. Explain what the problem is and what steps are being taken to fix it.

5.   Read the following conversation between two coworkers:

Employee A: I'm really swamped at work. I don't know if I'm going to be able to finish all of my projects by the deadline.

Employee B: I know. We really need to hire some more people around here. What are you going to do?

Employee A: I don't know. My boss said I have to finish the budget analysis by Friday, but he just gave me a new project that he needs completed right away.

Employee B: Well, if I were you, I'd tell your boss that there's no way you can finish both in time. I'd ask for more time.

Employee A: Yeah, I guess I could do that.

Employee B: Or maybe you can ask your boss to assign the project to someone else. That way you can focus on the budget analysis.

Employee B offers two possible solutions to Employee A's problems. Describe the problem, and state which of the two solutions you prefer. Explain why.

Sample Responses to Drill #3

Read the following responses aloud, and practice speaking them until you're comfortable. Pay attention to the use of transitions and direction markers.

1. (*Introduction*) If I could have any job, I think that I would like to be an ambassador. I think this because I enjoy visiting other countries and meeting and interacting with other people.

   (*Body*) The primary role of an ambassador is to travel to other countries. I would enjoy doing this very much because I love learning about new cultures. I have traveled to many countries already, and I would like the opportunity to visit more.

   (*Body*) Another reason that I would like to be an ambassador is to have the opportunity to meet and interact with new people. An ambassador's job is to represent his or her country to other people, and I think this would be an exciting role.

2. (*Introduction*) One person whom I admire very much is Mohandas Gandhi. I admire him for many reasons, especially his strong sense of justice and rightness.

   (*Body*) The main reason I admire Gandhi is his commitment to his ideas. Gandhi was convinced that his country should be free and devoted his life to that goal. He went on a hunger strike and led many protests.

   (*Body*) A second reason I admire Gandhi is for his use of nonviolent protest. Even though Gandhi was devoted to his ideas, he realized that there was a right way of achieving them. He rejected violence as a method, and I admire this very much.

3. (*Introduction*) In my opinion, the university should spend its money on the library. I think this because a university should be an institution of learning, and a good library is important for that.

   (*Body*) The first reason I would spend money on the library is to benefit the students. It would be a disservice to students if they couldn't perform the type of research required for their classes. To do well in school, students need a good library.

   (*Body*) Furthermore, I think it is a good idea to spend money on a library to help the reputation of the school. If a university has a top library, it can attract more students. This will bring more money to the university.

4. (*Introduction*) The passage states that the problem is the poisonous cane toad. The toad is threatening many of the species in Australia.

   (*Body*) According to the passage, the problem is that the cane toad is very poisonous. The cane toad can kill animals that eat it. This is making it very dangerous for many species in Australia.

   (*Body*) To fix the problem, conservationists have decided to move some animals to other islands. They think this will allow the animals to breed in safety.

5. (*Introduction*) The problem the employee has is that he or she cannot finish his or her work on time. In my opinion, the better solution is to ask the boss to assign the project to someone else. I think this because it is better to get the work done on time than to extend the deadline.

(*Body*) I believe the employee should ask the boss to assign the project to someone else for two reasons. First, it is more important that the job get done on time and correctly. If the employee doesn't have enough time, the job may be finished late or the work may not be of good quality.

(*Body*) Second, I believe that an employee who can admit when he or she has too much work to do is a very responsible employee. It is better to be honest with your boss about what you can do instead of making him or her think you can do everything.

WRAPPING THINGS UP: THE CONCLUSION

The conclusion is essential to a well-organized speech or essay. Without a conclusion, it will seem to end abruptly, or worse yet, trail off. Fortunately, the conclusion is probably the easiest part to create. A conclusion has to do one thing and one thing only.

* **Restate** your thesis.

The conclusion is your last chance to make your point to the reader. You want to remind the reader that you accomplished your purpose. As with body paragraphs, conclusions still need to have good transitions. Here are some good words and phrases to use for your final paragraph.

And so	*In conclusion*	*Finally*	*Thus*
Ultimately	*As I've stated*	*Clearly*	*To sum up*
	As this essay has demonstrated		

Here's a sample conclusion from our practice prompt:

In conclusion, if I could have any job, I would choose to be an ambassador. As I mentioned before, I feel this would be a perfect fit for my skill set because I love traveling to other countries and meeting new people.

Your Turn: Drill #4—Develop Conclusions for Speaking

Practice conclusions for your speeches, on the same topics we've practiced before.

1. If you could have any job in the world, which job would you choose?
2. Describe a person you admire, and explain why you admire him or her.
3. A university has recently received a large sum of money. The university desperately needs to improve housing on campus, but students have complained that the library needs to be fixed as well. Do you think that the money should be spent on housing or the library? Provide reasons and examples for your choice.
4. Read the following short passage:

The cane toad, a poisonous species of toad, is causing problems in Australia. The cane toad was brought to Australia in 1935 to help control the population of greyback beetles. Unfortunately, the toads did nothing to reduce the beetle population. Now, however, cane toads number in the millions and are threatening native animal populations.

The cane toad has two poisonous sacs located near its head and is so toxic that dingoes, snakes, and even crocodiles die within fifteen minutes of eating a cane toad. Now, conservationists are forced to transport some endangered species of animals to islands free from cane toads so that the endangered species can breed in safety.

The passage above describes a problem. Explain what the problem is and what steps are being taken to fix it.

5. Read the following conversation between two coworkers:

Employee A: I'm really swamped at work. I don't know if I'm going to be able to finish all of my projects by the deadline.

Employee B: I know. We really need to hire some more people around here. What are you going to do?

Employee A: I don't know. My boss said I have to finish the budget analysis by Friday, but he just gave me a new project that he needs completed right away.

Employee B: Well, if I were you, I'd tell your boss that there's no way you can finish both in time. I'd ask for more time.

Employee A: Yeah, I guess I could do that.

Employee B: Or maybe you can ask your boss to assign the project to someone else. That way you can focus on the budget analysis.

Employee B offers two possible solutions to Employee A's problems. Describe the problem, and state which of the two solutions you prefer. Explain why.

Sample Responses to Drill #4

Read the following responses aloud, and practice speaking them until you're comfortable:

1. For all the reasons I have stated, I feel that being an ambassador would be my dream job. I think that it is the perfect match for my interests and skills.

2. As I have stated, there are many reasons that I admire Gandhi. His values and ideas are things that I find very important in a person.

3. So, to conclude, it is my opinion that the money would be best spent on a library. Spending money on a library is the right thing to do for an academic institution.

4. In conclusion, the conservationists think the best solution to the problem of the cane toad is to move the animals to a different place.

5. Ultimately, I believe the best solution is to ask the boss to reassign the project. This is best for the company and is what a responsible employee would do.

Summary: Concluding Your Response

Because you only have 45 or 60 seconds for a spoken response, you won't have a lot of time to wrap up your thoughts. But you always need a concluding sentence so make it short and simply restate your thesis.

One important point to remember is: Don't introduce any new ideas or examples. It will leave your listener or reader feeling as though you should have explained those new examples in more detail.

Now you have all the tools you need to give great spoken responses on the TOEFL!

Chapter 5
Core Concept:
Writing

In the "real" world, speaking and writing are two very different skills. But on the TOEFL, the basic skills you'll be graded on are very similar. Many of the constructions that you used in your speaking can easily be transferred to your writing. Similarly, many of the forms you use when writing can also be used when speaking.

SCORING FOR THE WRITING SECTION

By examining the scoring guidelines for the Writing section, we can gain a better understanding of what our goals should be for this section.

The writing responses will be graded on a scale of 0 to 5. On the TOEFL, according to ETS, an essay receiving a score of 5 has the following characteristics:

- It effectively addresses the topic and the task.
- It is well organized and well developed, using clearly appropriate explanations, exemplifications, and/or details.
- It displays unity, progression, and coherence.
- It displays consistent facility in the use of language, demonstrating syntactic variety, appropriate word choice, and idiomaticness, although it may have minor lexical or grammatical errors.

At the other end of the scoring scale, an essay receiving a score of 1 suffers from

- serious disorganization or underdevelopment
- little or no detail, irrelevant specifics, or questionable responsiveness to the task
- serious or frequent errors in sentence structure or usage

An essay receiving a score of 0 is blank, written in a foreign language, identical to the prompt, or consists of random keystrokes.

What the Writing Scoring Guidelines Mean

Each of the first three scoring guidelines relates to one of the topics we've already studied. Here's how.

- **The essay effectively addresses the topic and the task.** This guideline corresponds to the work we've done on *finding the purpose*. An effective written response accomplishes a specific purpose. On the TOEFL, this means responding to one of their prompts. A weak essay has no clear purpose or doesn't achieve its purpose.
- **The essay is well organized and well developed, using clearly appropriate explanations, exemplifications, and/or details.** This guideline matches with the exercises we completed on understanding the *structure*. Good essays demonstrate strong structure, whereas weak essays frequently lack well-developed examples.

- **The essay displays unity, progression, and coherence.** This guideline corresponds to the work we've done on *finding the main idea* of a reading passage. Each paragraph should be connected to the main theme of the passage and contribute to the development of the passage's ideas or argument. An essay receiving a score of 5 stays on topic, whereas an essay receiving a lower score goes off the topic.

The fourth and final guideline will be addressed later in this chapter. However, it is worth noting that on the TOEFL, you don't have to write in perfect English to get a 5. It's acceptable to have some spelling and grammar mistakes in your essay.

Similarities in the Writing and Speaking Guidelines

As you may have noticed, there are many similarities in what the TOEFL graders are looking for in your written and spoken responses. Both tasks require you to clearly address the topic given. Both tasks ask that your response be organized and coherent. And both tasks expect you to use specific details and examples to support your position. As we said earlier, many of the strategies you'll learn in this book will work for both the Writing and the Speaking sections. You can practice these strategies in both written and spoken forms. For example, practice speaking aloud what you've written. Or make a tape of your speech, and then write down what you said.

PART 1: EXPRESSING YOUR PURPOSE

Our first goal is to make sure your essays have a clear purpose. To do that, we need to look at the types of tasks the TOEFL will feature.

Purpose and the Writing Section

Most writing tasks on the TOEFL ask you to do one of the following:

- Present your opinion on an issue (a *value* essay).
- Evaluate the information on a topic (a *fact* essay).

You need to clearly express your purpose in your introductory paragraph. If you recall our earlier discussion of introduction paragraphs (in the Reading and Speaking chapters), you may already have a good idea of how to express your purpose. In general, your introduction needs to accomplish the following tasks:

1. Introduce the topic of your discussion.
2. Present your *thesis* statement.

Writing an Effective Introduction Paragraph

Here's an example of a writing task similar to one you may encounter on the TOEFL. You would be asked to write an essay explaining whether you agree or disagree with the following topic:

> Parents should select their children's friends carefully to make sure those friends reflect proper values.

Although there are many ways of writing an introduction paragraph, the following strategy will help you write an effective introduction regardless of the topic. Following this strategy will help you write *quickly*.

Step 1: Pick a Side

If the goal of your writing is to have a clear purpose, you must know what that purpose is before you start writing. Otherwise, your essay will lack focus and coherence. On opinion questions, there is no right or wrong answer, as discussed in Core Concept: Speaking. You will be evaluated only on how well you defend your position. Remember that **for an opinion essay, your purpose as an author is to convince the reader that your position is correct.**

Step 2: State Your Position

Once you've chosen your position, your first job is to state it. Here's an example of a typical first sentence for this type of response.

> I do not believe that parents should select their children's friends.

As on the Speaking section, it's best to make a clear, direct statement of your position. Try using some of the following phrases:

I believe	*I feel that*	*In my opinion*
In my view	*I think that*	*I do not believe*
I do not feel that	*My position is*	*It is my belief that*

Step 3: State the Reason for Your Opinion

Once you've stated your position, you've established for the reader *what* you believe. Now, you must explain *why* you believe your position is correct. Here's an example.

> I do not believe that parents should select their children's friends. It would be harmful to children if they were not allowed to choose their own friends. Parents should be interested in their children's friends, but they should let their children pick their own friends.

When stating why you believe your position, it may be helpful to use some of the following phrases:

> *I believe this because*   *I feel this way because*   *The reason I think this is*
>
> *This is because*   *Since*

YOUR TURN: DRILL #1—WRITE AN INTRODUCTION PARAGRAPH

Write an introduction paragraph explaining whether you agree or disagree with each of the following prompts. Remember to follow the three steps described on the previous page.

1. It is the teacher's responsibility to make a student learn the material.

   _____
   _____
   _____
   _____
   _____

2. Material on the Internet should be censored or controlled to protect the public.

   _____
   _____
   _____
   _____
   _____

3. Colleges and universities should offer more distance learning courses to accommodate the needs of students.

   _____
   _____
   _____
   _____
   _____

4. When choosing a career, financial gain should be the most important consideration.

   _____
   _____
   _____
   _____

5. Schools should have mandatory testing each year to prove they are meeting minimum educational standards.

   _____
   _____
   _____
   _____
   _____

SAMPLE RESPONSES TO DRILL #1

The following are sample introduction paragraphs for the prompts. Compare your paragraphs with the ones below, and see how well they match up. Phrases in bold are useful transitions that you can try out in your writing.

1. I believe that it is a teacher's responsibility to make a student learn the material. Many students are of a young age and do not realize the value of education. **Therefore**, it is up to the teacher to help them learn the lessons and realize the value of the material.

2. In my opinion, material on the Internet should not be censored. The Internet is a free zone and it would be wrong for this area to be controlled. **Plus**, what government or agency would be responsible for censoring the Internet, which is available worldwide?

3. In my view, colleges and universities should offer more distance learning courses. I believe this because in today's world, many people have a lot of demands on their time. Some students are parents or hold part-time jobs. This means that they don't have as much time for school. Distance learning courses would be a good solution to this problem.

4. I do not feel that financial considerations should be the most important ones when choosing a career. If a person is not happy in his or her job, then the money will not be important. A person's happiness should be the number-one consideration when choosing a career.

5. I feel that it would be wrong for schools to have mandatory testing each year. I think that each school should be allowed to decide how best to educate its students. Some schools do not focus as much on testing as other schools and use other ways of grading their students, such as projects and final papers. These schools should not be forced to have tests.

These examples are not perfect, and that's acceptable on the TOEFL. But each one is simple, direct, and clearly states the purpose. That's all that is required of an introductory paragraph.

Summary: Expressing Your Purpose

The introduction is your first impression, so make it a good one! To craft an effective introduction, follow these steps.

1. **Decide what your purpose is:** Know what your task is. Are you trying to convince or inform? Are you picking one option over another?
2. **State the thesis:** Always include a simple and direct statement of the topic.
3. **State why:** This is your connection between the task and topic.

For an effective introduction, remember these "don'ts."

- **Don't** go into detail about your examples in your introduction.
- **Don't** repeat the task or assignment word for word.

PART 2: ORGANIZING YOUR IDEAS

Now that we've taken care of the purpose, we need to focus on organization. Organization is one of the most important factors in your writing score. Disjointed or unfocused writing is easy for the graders to spot and will lead to a lower score.

On the TOEFL, each writing task should be organized as follows (this might look familiar from the Speaking chapter):

- **Introduction:** We've worked on this already. This is the part in which you state the topic and your purpose.
- **Body:** As with speaking, this is the part in which you should provide the details and examples important to your purpose. We'll examine body paragraphs next.
- **Conclusion:** This is the part in which you summarize your essay. We'll look at written conclusions later in this chapter.

Building the Body

The one major difference between the Writing and Speaking sections is the amount of time you have to create your response. Because spoken responses are only 45 or 60 seconds, you don't have to do as much explaining. However, in the Writing section, you will have 20 or 30 minutes to craft your response. This will require you to thoroughly provide support for your purpose.

Writing an Effective Body Paragraph

Good body paragraphs make your writing more effective and more organized, which are both good things on the TOEFL. The first step in creating a good body paragraph is to write a topic sentence.

Step 1: The Topic Sentence

A good topic sentence does two things: It provides a *transition* between ideas and clearly states the main idea of the paragraph. To refresh your memory on how to compose a topic sentence, flip back to Core Concept: Speaking. For writing, we are going to use the same method. A topic sentence should introduce the main point of the paragraph.

Let's continue to work with our previous topic.

> Parents should carefully select their children's friends to make sure those friends reflect proper values.

In our introduction, we stated what our position was and why we believe our opinion was correct. Now, in the body paragraphs, we have to support our position. Here's our introduction.

I do not believe that parents should select their children's friends. It would be harmful to children if they were not allowed to choose their own friends. Parents should be interested in their children's friends, but they should let their children pick their own friends.

To make a clear transition statement, use the topic or thesis of the previous paragraph as a starting point. Look at the following transition:

One reason I believe that **parents should let children pick their friends** is that children need to develop independence.

Notice how the bold portion repeats an idea found in the last sentence of the introduction. Using this technique makes your writing flow better and appear more organized.

Our next paragraph may say

Another reason I think **parents should let children pick their friends** is that children may resent a parent who picks their friends.

And our final paragraph may say

In addition to the *feelings of resentment* a child may have, a final reason **parents shouldn't pick their children's friends** is that the children may not get along very well.

This paragraph also uses a link to the main idea of the preceding paragraph. As with the Speaking section, topic sentences and transitions will help your essay appear organized.

Step 2: The Examples

For many of the assignments on the TOEFL, your main goal in the body paragraphs will be to support your opinions. On others, your task will be to report facts stated in either a reading passage or lecture.

In either case, your model is still the same.

- **state** the example or reason (what the example is)
- **explain** its significance (why the example is important)

Here's a body paragraph for our sample topic.

One reason I believe that parents should let children pick their friends is that children need to develop independence (**topic sentence**). It is very important for a child to become independent, and the early part of a child's life can affect the level of independence a child has (**statement of example**). For example, children who are not allowed to pick their friends may believe that their parents will always make important decisions for them (**explanation of significance**). This belief could make children dependent on their parents, which would have a negative effect on their development (**explanation of significance**).

That's all there is to it. Now, try to write some body paragraphs for the topics that follow.

YOUR TURN: DRILL #2—WRITE BODY PARAGRAPHS

For each of the following tasks, write a body paragraph (or two). You've already written introductions for these, so it may help to read over what you've written. Before you write, think of one or two examples that support your view.

1.   It is the teacher's responsibility to make a student learn the material.

    _____
    _____
    _____
    _____
    _____
    _____
    _____

2.   Material on the Internet should be censored or controlled to protect the public.

    _____
    _____
    _____
    _____
    _____
    _____
    _____

3.   Colleges and universities should offer more distance learning courses to accommodate the needs of students.

    _____
    _____
    _____
    _____
    _____
    _____
    _____

4.   When choosing a career, financial gain should be the most important consideration.

    _____
    _____
    _____
    _____
    _____
    _____
    _____

5.   Schools should have mandatory testing each year to prove they are meeting minimum educational standards.

   _____
   _____
   _____
   _____
   _____
   _____
   _____

SAMPLE RESPONSES TO DRILL #2

The following are sample responses. Check your paragraphs against these models. Make sure your body paragraph includes both a topic sentence and an example or reason.

1. One reason I believe it is a teacher's responsibility to help students learn is that many students are of a young age (**topic sentence**). A first- or second-grade teacher works with children who are only six or seven years old (**statement of example**). At this age, a student is too young to recognize the value of education (**explanation of example**). Therefore, it should be the teacher's job to make sure the children learn.

This body paragraph ends by restating the author's main point, which also helps the reader stay focused on the thesis.

2. First of all, material on the Internet should not be censored because the Internet is a free zone. The Internet is not owned by any one government or company. This means that no one should have the right to say what can or cannot be posted on it. Companies or governments can control what material shows up on their sites, but they cannot control what private citizens do.

   Second, technology makes it too difficult to censor material on the Internet (**topic sentence**). Every day, new computer programs are developed that make other programs obsolete (**statement of example**). As soon as someone figures out how to censor material on the Internet, someone else can figure out how to break the code (**explanation of example**). This means that a tremendous amount of money would have to be spent on developing new technology, and this expense would not be worth it (**explanation of example**).

This response includes two body paragraphs. Notice how the second paragraph logically connects to the first through the use of the transition word *second*. Try to make sure your body paragraphs are nicely connected both to the thesis and to each other.

3. One important reason that colleges should offer more distance learning courses is that people are busier (**topic sentence**). In addition to work and hobbies, there are more parents going to college these days (**statement of example**). All these things make it difficult to attend college (**explanation of example**). However, education is a valuable thing, and everyone should have access to it (**explanation of example**). If universities offered more distance learning courses, more people could find time for an education (**explanation of example**).

Try to use some of the direction marker words and transitions you learned in the reading exercises in Core Concept: Reading and Core Concept: Speaking. For example, this paragraph uses "however" to emphasize the importance of education and how distance learning courses will allow more people to get their education.

4. The most important thing in choosing a career should be the happiness it brings, not the money (**topic sentence**). There is an old saying that states, "You can't buy happiness," and this statement is very true (**statement of example**). Many people who have lots of money also have strained relationships with their spouses and children (**explanation of example**). Often, they feel they can't trust whether people like them or their money (**explanation of example**). These strains can make a person very unhappy, no matter how much money they have (**explanation of example**).

You should also try to use some emphasis markers in your writing. Stating something is the "most" important reason or something is "very true" gives your words more of an impact. However, don't overuse these words. Too many of them can distract the reader.

5. Schools should not have mandatory testing each year because tests are not always the best way of measuring education (**topic sentence**). Tests, especially standardized tests, can cover only a limited amount of skills (**statement of example**). There are some things in education that are not easy to test, such as writing and creative thinking (**explanation of example**). For this reason, schools should not be forced to have mandatory testing (**explanation of example**).

    In addition, not all students do well on tests (**topic sentence with statement of example**). Some students are better at writing essays or giving a speech (**explanation of example**). Not all students perform best on standardized tests (**explanation of example**). Therefore, it is unfair for those students to have to take these tests, and schools may not get an accurate view of how successful they are (**explanation of example**).

In the second paragraph, the topic sentence is combined with the statement of the example, which is fine.

Summary: Building the Body

The body provides the reader with the key points of your thesis. Build strong body paragraphs by doing the following:

1. **Begin with a topic sentence:** A good topic sentence references the subject you will discuss and also provides a transition to link your ideas together.
2. **Provide details:** The rest of the body should contain important details that help you achieve your purpose.

Build strong body paragraphs by avoiding the following:

- **Don't** try to discuss more than one example per paragraph.
- **Don't** present an example without providing specific details.

PART 3: USING EXAMPLES

You've learned how to incorporate examples into your spoken and written responses. Remember that the key to making good use of examples is to make sure each example is

- **specific**, not overly general or hypothetical
- **explained** in sufficient detail

Now let's look at three types of examples that will help make your essay more convincing: examples that *support* your main idea, examples that *summarize* your main idea, and examples that *evaluate* your main idea.

Supporting Examples

Supporting examples are the most familiar type of examples and perhaps the easiest to use. They are used to show the reader why you have a particular viewpoint or position. On the TOEFL, you may see similar tasks that ask the following:

1. Do you agree or disagree with the following statement? It is better for students to gain real-world experience than to spend their time in a classroom.
2. Describe a book you have read and why that book was important to you.
3. Some teachers prefer to lecture to students, whereas others prefer to engage students in a dialogue. Which teaching style do you think is better and why?

For each of these tasks, your mission is to convince your readers that your view is correct by presenting them with facts and evidence.

Summarizing Examples

Some tasks require you to explain or summarize someone else's opinion. For these tasks, you are not trying to *convince* the reader of anything; instead, your purpose is to *report* what you've read or heard. On the TOEFL, summarizing tasks look like the following:

1. The professor describes the controversy surrounding a new technique. Explain the technique and what the controversy is.

2. In the conversation above, the man presented his opinion on the new budget proposal. State his opinion and explain the reasons he gives for holding that opinion.

3. Using details and examples from the piece you just heard, explain how musicians have been influenced by cultural and intellectual movements.

Evaluating Examples

One of the more difficult tasks you may encounter on the TOEFL asks you to evaluate someone else's viewpoint. These tasks require you to judge how valid a position is. The purpose of your examples is to weaken the position. The following is an example of an evaluation task:

Explain how the points in the lecture you've just heard cast doubt on it.

Regardless of the type of example, the way you present your examples remains the same.

Effective Examples

As stated at the beginning of this chapter, you must provide details for each example and an explanation of the meaning or significance of each. The following is a sample response containing poorly used examples:

One reason I believe lecturing is a better teaching method is that teachers can control the content. Also, the teachers are able to organize things better. Finally, lectures let the students focus on only the important parts of the lesson.

This response contains several good ideas, but the problem is that the author failed to provide specific details for each example. You cannot assume that your reader understands exactly what point you are making and why; instead, you must explain each of your examples fully.

For each example you intend to use, ask yourself why the example is appropriate. What makes the example a convincing one?

Let's return to our previous examples and see how they can be made better. Here is the first example from the response above.

1. Lectures allow teachers to control the content.

Now, we need to ask why this example should convince a reader that lecturing is a better teaching method. Here are some reasons.

Example: Lectures allow teachers to control the content.

Why?

1.	The teacher is the only one speaking, so there are no digressions.
2.	The teacher can plan the lecture beforehand, ensuring all the important information is addressed.

Example: Lectures allow teachers to organize better.

Why?

1.	Speaking without planned notes can be difficult.
2.	The teacher can practice the lecture numerous times, ensuring it is well organized.

Example: Lectures help students focus on important information.

Why?

1.	The teacher can emphasize important information more effectively in a lecture.
2.	Students can pay attention to the teacher, not other students.

Now, let's rewrite our earlier paragraph, using the examples more effectively.

One reason I believe lecturing is a better teaching method is that teachers can control the content. When a teacher lectures, all the information presented is supplied by the teacher. There are no digressions because the students are not interrupting the lesson or distracting the teacher. Also, a teacher has the opportunity to plan the lecture beforehand, meaning that the teacher can ensure all the important information is discussed. In a conversation or dialogue, a teacher may never get to some important points because the students may ask too many questions about a certain topic.

Another reason I prefer lecturing to a conversation or a dialogue is that a lecture is much more organized. It can be very difficult to speak without notes or a plan. During a dialogue, the subjects can change very rapidly and can be hard to follow. But a lecture is planned beforehand, so the topics are easier to follow. Also, the teacher can practice the lecture repeatedly and fix any problems in organization.

The final advantage of a lecture is that it helps the students focus on only the most important information. Because the teacher has planned the talk in advance, he or she can let the students know when an important point is being made. This will help the students focus. Additionally, when the students are engaged in a dialogue, a student may pay too much attention to another student's remarks or become distracted by a question or response. In a lecture, this problem is avoided because the student has to pay attention only to the teacher.

Note that when we use examples effectively, we end up having to use more paragraphs. This is necessary to keep our responses organized.

The Example Template

When you use an example in an essay, try to follow this template.

Sentence 1: Introduce the example and tie it back to your thesis.
Sentence 2: State one reason why your example is important or relevant to your thesis.
Sentence 3: Add detail to reason #1.
Sentence 4: State another reason why your example is important or relevant to your thesis.
Sentence 5: Add detail to reason #2.
Sentence 6 (optional): Provide a summary of your reasons, and relate them back to your thesis.

Here's an example of the template in action.

Task: Describe a book you have read and why that book was important to you.

(1) One book that is extremely important to me is *The Suffrage of Elvira* by V. S. Naipaul. (2) One reason I enjoy this book so much is that I like its subject matter. (3) The book provides a humorous look at local politics, and I find politics a fascinating subject. (4) Naipaul is skilled at critically examining his topics, and I think his depiction of politics is very interesting. (5) In this book, he presents a satire of the political process that is both witty and insightful. (6) Because of my interest in politics, *The Suffrage of Elvira* is an important book.

YOUR TURN: DRILL #3—WRITE BODY PARAGRAPHS THAT USE EXAMPLES

These sample tasks may look familiar. Now that you've practiced them in the Speaking section, use the additional time allotted in the writing section to make your responses even better. Then read the sample responses at the end of the drill to see how your writing compares.

1.   Do you agree or disagree with the following statement?

It is better for students to gain real-world experience than to spend their time in a classroom.

Example #1: _____

Why example #1 is important: _____

_____

_____

_____

Example #2: _____

Why example #2 is important: _____

_____

_____

Body paragraph #1: _____

_____

_____

_____

_____

_____

_____

_____

Body paragraph #2: _____

_____

_____

_____

_____

_____

2.   Describe an influential person, and explain why you feel this person is a positive role model.

Example #1: _____

Why example #1 is important: _____

_____

_____

_____

Example #2: _____

Why example #2 is important: _____

_____

_____

Body paragraph #1: _____

_____

_____

_____

_____

_____

_____

Body paragraph #2: _____

_____

_____

_____

_____

_____

_____

3. Some schools require first-year students to take the same courses, whereas other schools allow students to select the classes they want. Which policy do you think is better for first-year students and why?

Example #1: _____

Why example #1 is important: _____

_____

_____

Example #2: _____

Why example #2 is important: _____

_____

_____

Body paragraph #1: _____

_____

_____

_____

_____

_____

_____

Body paragraph #2: _____

_____

_____

_____

_____

_____

_____

_____

4. Read the following announcement and the conversation that follows it.

Announcement: Due to recent budget cuts, the university will be forced to reduce the library hours. Effective immediately, the library will close at 8:00 P.M. on weekdays and 5:00 P.M. on weekends.

Student A: I can't believe this! Did you hear the announcement about the library?

Student B: Yes. This is terrible. These new hours are going to be a real problem for me.

Student A: What's the problem?

Student B: Well, I work on weekends from noon to 6:00 P.M. at the bookstore. That means I won't be able to get to the library to work on my research project.

Student A: What are you going to do?

Student B: I guess I'm going to have to wake up early and go to the library in the morning, but it's going to be tough. My schedule is so busy. Between the five classes I'm taking and my hours at the bookstore, I don't have much time. These new library hours are really going to hurt me.

Student B expresses her opinion about the announcement. State what her opinion is, and explain the reasons she gives for holding it.

Reason #1: _____

Why reason #1 is important: _____

_____

_____

_____

Reason #2: _____

Why reason #2 is important: _____

_____

_____

Body paragraph #1: _____

_____

_____

_____

_____

_____

Body paragraph #2: _____

_____

_____

_____

_____

_____

5.   Do you agree or disagree with the following statement?

The most important education occurs not during adulthood but during childhood.

   Example #1: _____

   Why example #1 is important: _____

   _____

   _____

   _____

   Example #2: _____

   Why example #2 is important: _____

   _____

   _____

   Body paragraph #1: _____

   _____

   _____

   _____

   _____

   _____

   Body paragraph #2: _____

   _____

_____

_____

_____

_____

_____

_____

6.   Read the following passage about insect behavior:

Many insects are social creatures, living in large groups containing literally millions of individuals. Social insects, which include ants, termites, bees, and wasps, are the prime example of unselfish behavior in animals.

In any insect social system, each insect performs a specialized duty that is necessary for the survival of the hive as a whole. For example, among ants, there are certain types of ants that are soldiers—large, fearsome creatures with terrible jaws. Other ants, called drones, do not reproduce, instead devoting their time to taking care of the hive and the young of the queen. Each ant selflessly performs its role, not for its own benefit, but for the benefit of all the other ants.

Now entomologists have found an interesting case of this sort of cooperation in a nonsocial insect, the cricket. Crickets are a prime example of a "selfish" insect, leading a very isolated existence. They typically interact with other crickets only when mating or fighting over territory. But scientists have observed a species of cricket that undergoes periodic mass migrations. Every so often, the crickets set off to find more favorable living areas. When these migrations occur, the crickets band together into a huge caravan. Surely at a time like this, the crickets realize there is safety in numbers and put aside their selfish instinct for the good of all members.

Now read the following lecture on the same subject:

Professor: One of the biggest misconceptions in biology is the belief that organisms act out of concern for the "greater good" of the species. It is somewhat amazing how people assume that an ant or a mouse has enough sense to figure out how its actions impact all the members of its species!

Still, it is understandable why many people might believe this erroneous view. Many actions can be misinterpreted as being for the "good of the species." A classic example found in many early biology textbooks discussed the behavior of the stag. During mating season, a stag typically battles with other males, and the winner of these contests gains access to the females, while the loser walks away. Some people believed that the loser realizes that his offspring will be weaker, so the defeated stag "allows" the winner to mate to ensure the survival of the stag species.

This couldn't be further from the truth. The defeated stag wants to mate just as much as the winner does; the only problem is that he doesn't want to risk his life for the chance to mate. The stag is better off looking for other females to mate with. Thus, both stags—the winner and the loser—are acting not for the good of the species, but for their own selfish reasons.

Another good example of this is a recent study on the behavior of crickets. Scientists noted that crickets occasionally band together, traveling in huge swarms from location to location. The easy assumption was that the crickets believed in strength in numbers.

But a researcher showed this is not the case. He attached tags to a sampling of crickets. Some of the tagged crickets were allowed to travel with the group. But some of them were separated from the rest. All the crickets that were separated were eaten by birds or rodents, whereas the tagged crickets in the group survived.

Apparently, there is safety in numbers, but the crickets aren't looking to help their fellow travelers. They want to avoid being eaten, and what better way is there than to disappear into a group of thousands of other tasty morsels?

Summarize the points in the professor's lecture, and explain how the points cast doubt on the reading.

Point #1: _____

Why point #1 casts doubt on the reading: _____

_____

_____

_____

Point #2: _____

Why point #2 casts doubt on the reading: _____

_____

_____

Body paragraph #1: _____

_____

_____

_____

_____

_____

Body paragraph #2: _____

_____

_____

_____

_____

_____

_____

SAMPLE RESPONSES TO DRILL #3

Use the following sample responses as a guide to judge your work. Did your response contain strong topic sentences? Did you relate your examples back to your thesis? Did you explain why your examples are relevant?

1.   Do you agree or disagree with the following statement?

It is better for students to gain real-world experience than to spend their time in a classroom.

Real-world experience is usually preferable to time spent in a classroom. I believe this because experience is the best teacher. Students will not be able to grasp difficult topics unless they are able to discover them on their own. For example, students who are studying auto mechanics cannot just read about an engine. Instead, for a student to really understand an engine, the student must take it apart piece by piece and put it back together again. Only then will a student truly understand the concept.

In addition, real-world experience gives a student a chance to apply knowledge. Many times, things learned in a classroom are quickly forgotten if a student does not have a chance to apply them. In some schools, students are required to learn a foreign language. But these classes rarely involve opportunities to apply the new language. If a student never uses the skills learned in class, the skills will quickly become useless. Thus, some real-world experience is necessary.

2.   Describe an influential person, and explain why you feel this person is a positive role model.

One reason I consider Mikhail Gorbachev a positive role model is his willingness to work for change. Many people are content with the status quo and are reluctant to change things. But Gorbachev saw that the Communist system was no longer viable. He worked hard to change the system, instituting new policies to increase the openness of the Soviet system. Even though his reforms were not as helpful as he wished them to be, his willingness to work for change makes him a good role model.

In addition to his willingness to work for change, I believe Gorbachev is a positive role model because of his devotion to ideals that are larger than himself. Gorbachev came to power at a very tense time in history, the Cold War. Whereas before him, Soviet and American leaders had perpetuated the Cold War, Gorbachev knew that peace was a greater ideal. He reached out to President Ronald Reagan and signed treaties to limit nuclear arms. His devotion to this ideal was so great that he dissolved the Communist Party, of which he was the head. The future success of the Soviet Union was more important than his personal power.

3.   Some schools require first-year students to take the same courses, whereas other schools allow students to select the classes they want. Which policy do you think is better for first-year students and why?

The first reason I would support mandatory classes for freshmen is to ensure a certain quality of education. Although standardized education is not desirable, a college degree should hold a certain value. It should be the duty of universities to make sure their students are familiar with important intellectual works. That way, all students will have a basic educational level.

Another reason I believe universities should have required classes for freshmen is that required classes will serve to increase the camaraderie of the students. In addition to being institutions of learning, universities also give students an opportunity to meet other people and make connections that may help them later in life. Required classes would make it easy for students to meet one another and interact. Freshmen can sometimes have a hard time fitting in at a school, and required classes would make it easier for them to adapt.

4. Student B expresses her opinion about the announcement. State what her opinion is, and explain the reasons she gives for holding it.

One reason Student B is upset about the new library hours is that she is concerned she won't be able to work on her research paper. Student B works at a bookstore, and her hours on the weekends are from noon to 6:00 P.M.; however, the library closes at 5:00 P.M. This means that she will no longer be able to go to the library after work.

Another reason Student B is upset is because her personal schedule makes it difficult for her to use the library. To go to the library on weekends, she will have to go early in the morning, but she finds that problematic. Student B is taking five classes and has a job, so she is very busy. The new library hours will makes things harder for her.

5. Do you agree or disagree with the following statement?

The most important education occurs not during adulthood but during childhood.

There are many reasons why I agree with the statement that the most important education occurs during childhood. One of the most important reasons is that younger children are very open to ideas and perceptions. At a young age, a child has not fully developed his or her personality, so education can have a very powerful effect. A child is very impressionable, and the lessons learned at this age can have a great impact.

Another reason why I believe that the most important education is during childhood is because childhood is a time when education focuses on the very essentials of our society. Although children may not be learning advanced skills or disciplines, they are learning valuable life skills. A child who learns the difference between right and wrong and how to treat other people has learned some of life's most important lessons.

6. Summarize the points in the professor's lecture, and explain how the points cast doubt on the reading.

The first point the professor makes that casts doubt on the reading is his point about the behavior of stags. The professor shows how the actions of an animal can be interpreted in different ways. For example, some people interpret the stag's actions as being for the "good of the species," but the professor shows that the stag is actually acting in self-interest. This casts doubt on the reading because it appears that the crickets' behavior can be interpreted as helping only individual crickets and not the group as a whole. The professor then talks about the results of the experiment, which seem to indicate the crickets are acting only in self-interest.

Another point the professor makes that casts doubt on the reading is his point about the intelligence of animals and insects. As he states, it would seem to require a lot of intelligence to evaluate how a behavior will affect an entire species. This makes the explanation in the reading seem less likely; a cricket is probably unable to think of the consequences of its actions. It is more likely that the cricket is only acting out of self-preservation, as the professor indicates.

Summary: Using Examples Effectively

Proper use of examples is important to your TOEFL score. When using examples, always remember to do the following:

1. **State** the example.
2. **Explain** how the example supports your position or achieves your purpose.

Avoid these common mistakes when using examples.

- **Don't** introduce an example without explaining how it relates to your purpose.
- **Don't** forget to provide specific details for each of your examples.
- **Don't** use more than one example per paragraph.

CONCLUDING YOUR RESPONSE

As you've seen in Core Concepts: Reading and Core Concepts: Speaking, a conclusion is essential to summarizing any argument. In this section, you are going to follow the same approach and simply restate your purpose.

Here's a sample conclusion from our practice prompt.

In conclusion, there are many reasons why parents should not pick friends for their children. Children who are allowed to pick their own friends will be more independent and will get along better with friends they've selected.

That's all there is to it. A conclusion has to be only two or three sentences long. After you restate your thesis, repeat your reasons or make a final statement about the correctness of your views.

YOUR TURN: DRILL #4—WRITE A CONCLUSION

For each of the following topics, write a conclusion. Check the sample responses afterward for more ideas on ending your essay.

1. It is the teacher's responsibility to make a student learn the material.

    _____
    _____
    _____
    _____
    _____

2. Material on the Internet should be censored or controlled to protect the public.

    _____
    _____
    _____
    _____
    _____

3. Colleges and universities should offer more distance learning courses to accommodate the needs of students.

    _____
    _____
    _____
    _____
    _____

4. When choosing a career, financial gain should be the most important consideration.

    _____
    _____
    _____
    _____
    _____

5. Schools should have mandatory testing each year to prove they are meeting minimum educational standards.

    _____
    _____
    _____
    _____
    _____

Sample Responses to Drill #4

1. Ultimately, it is the teacher's responsibility to make students learn the material. Education is too valuable to be left in the hands of students. A good teacher not only teaches the material but also gives students a love of learning.

This conclusion ends by making a general statement about the purpose. This is a good strategy if you don't want to repeat your examples or reasons again.

2. As this essay has demonstrated, material on the Internet should not be censored. The Internet is too big to be controlled, and the technology involved in censoring it would be too expensive.

This conclusion restates both the purpose and the examples.

3. In conclusion, it makes sense for colleges and universities to offer more distance learning courses. It is always better to make education more available, not less.

Here, we end with a strong statement about what we believe. The conclusion is a good time to emphasize a key point or idea, as the following examples show:

4. Clearly, there are many more important considerations than money when choosing a career. Happiness and family are much more important than money.

5. Thus, schools should not be required to have mandatory testing. Testing does not provide students with a fair assessment of their skills, and it makes schools focus more on the tests than on teaching important things.

Summary: Wrapping Things Up

The conclusion is essential to your responses on the TOEFL. It's easy to conclude an essay or speech. All you have to do is

*   **Restate:** Tell the reader once more what your purpose is and why you believe it.

Make sure to avoid the following:

*   **Don't** introduce new examples or ideas.
*   **Don't** leave out the thesis.

GRAMMAR REVIEW

This is a brief summary of the basics of English grammar. Get familiar with these terms so you can avoid common grammatical errors in your written and spoken responses.

Parts of speech:

- **Noun**: person, place, or thing
  Example: I just remembered that I need to call my *mother*.

- **Pronoun**: stands in the place of a noun
  Example: *She* asked for a call last night.

- **Verb**: action word
  Example: I *dial* her home phone number.

- **Adverb**: modifies a verb
  Example: *Eagerly,* I wait for her to answer.

- **Adjective**: modifies a noun
  Example: When she picks up, I can tell that she is *happy* to hear my voice.

- **Preposition**: links nouns or pronouns to other words
  Example: I excitedly share the details *of* my new job.

Tenses:

- **Present**: an action that is currently happening
  Example: I *walk* to work every day.

- **Past**: an action that already happened
  Example: I *decided* that walking is better than driving.

- **Future**: an action that has not happened yet
  Example: I *may change* my mind later.

Agreement:

- **Subject/Verb Agreement**: A singular subject needs a singular verb. A plural subject needs a plural verb.
  Example: The *window is* open.
  Example: The *windows are* closed.

- **Noun/Pronoun Agreement**: A singular noun takes a singular pronoun. A plural noun takes a plural pronoun.
  Example: The *student* wore *his/her* backpack.
  Example: The *students* wore *their* backpacks.

Parallelism:

- Items in a list must all have the same form.
  Example: The professor likes to *read books, grade papers,* and *play guitar.*

If you're interested in a more thorough review, The Princeton Review's *Grammar Smart* can be found in most bookstores or online at PrincetonReview.com.

For an intensive vocabulary review check out our new *Word Smart for the TOEFL*, published this spring.

Complete sentences versus fragments:

- A sentence must have a subject and a verb to be complete. An incomplete sentence is known as a fragment and should be avoided.

  Example of a complete sentence: Wearing a cap and gown, the *student attended* graduation.

  Example of a fragment (Avoid): Wearing a cap and gown, the *student* at graduation.

Summary of All Core Concepts: Reading, Writing, Speaking, and Listening

o   The TOEFL is a standardized test format that evaluates reading, writing, speaking, and listening. All the tasks on the TOEFL require you to work with and identify some basic features common to all of them. The more comfortable you are with these core concepts, the more comfortable you will be taking the TOEFL.

o   For each passage that you read, write on, speak about, or listen to on the TOEFL, you should focus on the purpose, examples, and conclusion. Practice identifying these parts in the sample drills in this book as well as other types of writing you encounter.

o   Now that you've become more familiar with the core concepts on the TOEFL, we will move on to Part III of the book. In Part III, we will see how to crack the specific types of questions and tasks on the TOEFL.

Part III
Cracking Each Section of the TOEFL

Chapter 6
Cracking the
Reading Section

The TOEFL Reading section consists of

> Three to five **passages**, each approximately 700 words long
>
> - Each passage is followed by about 12 to 14 questions
> - You will have 60 to 100 minutes to complete the entire section

As mentioned in the introduction, many of the questions are multiple choice and worth one point each, but some questions are worth two or more points. Typically, questions that are worth more appear at the end of the section.

Some of the words and phrases in the reading passages are underlined in blue on the screen; if you click on these phrases, a definition is provided. You can see what the screen will look like in the picture on the opposite page.

In this case, if you click on the words *uranium isotope* or *moniker*, you will see a definition of the word in question. You'll also notice that some of the words appear in gray boxes. These words have a special type of question associated with them, which we'll look at soon.

Remember, if you prefer, you are free to skip questions within this section; simply click on the "Next" button on the top right-hand side of the screen. You can return to questions you've skipped when you are ready. You can also click the "Review" button to see a display of all the questions you've answered and left blank. You can return to any question from this screen.

TOEFL Reading

Question 3 of 12

HIDE TIME   00:08:45

PAUSE TEST

SECTION EXIT

REVIEW   HELP ?   BACK   NEXT

More Available

➤Although Otto Hahn and Fritz Strassmann discovered the process of nuclear fission in 1938, it took another year for scientists to truly understand the process. During this process, a <u>uranium isotope</u> is split by firing neutrons at it. When the neutron strikes the isotope, it ejects neutrons of its own, which in turn strike other uranium atoms. This sets off a chain reaction, with each split atom causing another atom to break up as well. When controlled, this type of chain reaction can be harnessed to produce useful nuclear energy. But if the reaction is not controlled, the result is far more devastating: a nuclear explosion.

➤Shortly after the discovery of the potential destructiveness of nuclear power, President Franklin Roosevelt set up a committee to investigate the feasibility of a nuclear weapon. Although initial progress was slow, the program was reorganized in 1942 under the <u>moniker</u> the Manhattan Engineer District, or simply the Manhattan Project. The project was headed by Robert Oppenheimer and was authorized to call on the full resources of the government and military to achieve its goal.

CRACKING THE READING SECTION: BASIC PRINCIPLES

Basic Principle #1: It's in There!

The first and most important principle to the Reading section is a simple one.

> The answer to every single question is found in the passage!

That's right. The answer to each question is right there in front of you. This principle is simple enough, but it is one that is often either forgotten or misunderstood by test takers.

On the TOEFL Reading section, you are *not* expected to give your interpretation of what you've read. You are *not* required to analyze what you've read. All you're asked to do is simply *find the answer* to the question in the passage or, in some cases, infer what *must be true* based on information provided in the passage.

Of course, this is very different from what you are used to doing in a more academic setting. The Reading section can be difficult for test takers who think too much beyond what is written in the passage. When completing the reading exercises in this book, pay careful attention to the approach used and the explanation for why the correct answer is correct.

Basic Principle #2: The Two-Pass System

Time is one of the largest barriers to your success on the TOEFL Reading section. You have only 60 minutes to read three passages and answer 39 questions. And although the majority of the questions are worth one point each, the questions are *not* equally difficult. Some question types are inherently faster or easier, whereas others will take more time or are more difficult.

Because your only goal is to get as many points as possible, it makes no sense to spend time on difficult questions when an easier question may be a click away. When we discuss the question types later in this chapter, we'll let you know which types tend to be easier. In addition, as you practice, you'll get a feel for the types of questions you can do most quickly. Make sure to seek these questions out. *Do them first*, and save the killer questions for later.

Basic Principle #3: Process of Elimination

POE: Part I

Even though the right answer is found somewhere in the text, the TOEFL Reading section is still very difficult. Why? Because the other answer choices are often very tempting. Many questions include trap answers—answer choices that look correct but are actually incorrect.

To do well on the Reading section, you must use Process of Elimination, or POE. Simply put, POE involves comparing answer choices and finding reasons to eliminate one or more. POE requires you to be aggressive and get rid of many of the answer choices! Because the majority of the questions have only four choices, eliminating even one answer greatly increases your odds of getting a question correct if you are forced to guess. When using POE, make sure you examine each answer choice carefully. *Never* blindly pick the first answer that stands out or seems good, because it may be a trap!

Let's look at a sample question and see an example of how to use POE.

1. The word feasibility as used in the passage is closest in meaning to

   (A) appropriateness
   (B) reasonableness
   (C) possibility
   (D) viability

This question is based on an earlier reading passage, but that is actually not important right now. We are only concerned with the answer choices. When using POE, make a mark next to each answer, based on your impression of it. Some possibilities are listed below.

Symbol	Meaning
✓	Good or OK answer
~	Weak answer
?	Unknown answer
✓✓	Best answer
X	Bad answer

For the example on the previous page, we may mark our scrap paper in the following way:

1. The word feasibility as used in the passage is closest in meaning to

   X   (A)   appropriateness
   ~   (B)   reasonableness
   ✓   (C)   possibility
   ?   (D)   viability

So in this case, even if we can't decide which answer is the "best" one, we can see that one of the choices is definitely out. And because we like the third answer, we may as well eliminate the "weak" answer too. That leaves us with the third and fourth answer choices. In this case, the third choice looks OK, whereas the fourth choice is a bit of a mystery.

On the TOEFL, there will be times when you're unsure of a choice. The answer may contain difficult vocabulary words or be hard to follow. Never eliminate an answer just because you don't understand it. Instead, mark it as "unknown," and check the other choices. If the remaining choices are no good, then the "unknown" choice must be correct. If one of the other choices seems more likely, then go with that one.

We'll talk more about what to do when you are stuck or down to two choices when we look at the different question types.

POE: Part II

The second part of POE is the ability to recognize the types of wrong answers found on the TOEFL. The wrong answers have to be tempting enough for you to want to pick them, but not right enough to be the best answer. In general, the wrong answers on the TOEFL Reading section fall into one of the following categories:

- **Not mentioned:** This category consists of information that is not found in the passage. Often, the answer makes common sense or may be true in the real world. However, on the TOEFL, every correct answer must be found in the passage.
- **Extreme:** These answer choices use wording that is too strong or absolute. These choices usually include words such as *all, always, impossible, must, never,* or *none.* Correct answers on the TOEFL do not generally contain such strong language.
- **Right answer, wrong question:** These choices contain information that is mentioned in the passage; however, the information doesn't answer the question.
- **Verbatim:** Many wrong answers repeat parts of the passage word for word. Unfortunately, the choices use these words in the wrong context or incorrectly. These answers can be especially tempting.
- **Beyond the information:** Choices in this category are based on information in the passage, but they go beyond the given information. For example, if the passage states "some species of chimpanzees make crude tools out of branches," the answer choice may read "many

animals can make tools." This answer goes beyond the information by changing "some species of chimpanzees" to "many animals."

When you are preparing for the TOEFL, make sure you review all the questions, even the ones you've gotten right. Read each wrong answer choice, and see if you can figure out what makes it wrong. Becoming familiar with the wrong answers is almost as important as finding the right answers.

CRACKING THE READING SECTION: BASIC APPROACH

When approaching the Reading section of the TOEFL, follow these steps.

> 1. **Actively read the passage,** looking for the purpose, structure, and main idea.
> 2. **Attack the questions** based on question type.
> 3. **Find the answer** to the question in the passage.
> 4. **Use POE** to eliminate bad answers.

Let's look at each of these steps in greater detail.

Step 1: Actively Read the Passage

One of the biggest mistakes you can make on the TOEFL is to attempt to read and understand every single word of the passage. There are many problems with this approach. One is that you simply do not have enough time to read the entire passage and accurately answer all of the questions. A second problem is that there is far more information in the passage than you will ever need to know to answer the questions. The more of the passage that you read, the more likely you are to become confused or distracted. Finally, remember that you get points for answering questions, not reading passages. You want to spend your time answering questions and earning points, not reading.

Instead of reading the entire passage, use the active reading strategies described in Core Concept: Reading. Don't spend too much time on this step, and don't try to understand all the details in the passage. Read the passage, looking for the major points:

1. The purpose
2. The main idea
3. The structure

Here's a passage similar to one you would find on the TOEFL. It should look familiar to you. We used it to introduce you to the look of the test in Chapter 1. Take a few moments to actively read it.

More Available

The Exoskeleton of the Arthropod

There are more arthropods alive on Earth than there are members of any other phylum of animals. Given that not only insects and spiders but also shrimp, crabs, centipedes, and their numerous relatives are arthropods, this fact should not occasion surprise. For all their diversity, arthropods of any type share two defining characteristics: jointed legs (from which the phylum takes its name) and an exoskeleton (the recognizable hard outer shell).

➤Though the shell itself is made of dead tissue like that of human hair and fingernails, it is dotted with sensory cells. **These give the arthropod information about its surroundings, much as the nerve endings in human skin do.** Also like human skin, the shell protects fragile internal organs from potentially hazardous contact with the environment. It seals in precious moisture that would otherwise evaporate but permits the exchange of gases.

Its primary component is chitin, a natural polymer that contains calcium and is very similar in structure to the cellulose in wood. Chitin and proteins are secreted in the epidermis, the living tissue just below the shell, after which they bond to form a thin sheet. Each new sheet is produced so that its chitin fibers are not parallel with those directly above, which increases their combined strength.

The result is the endocuticle, a mesh of molecules that forms the lowest layer of the shell. The endocuticle is not quite tough enough for daily wear and tear. Over time, however, its molecules continue to lock together. As the endocuticle is pushed upward by the formation of new sheets by the epidermis, it becomes the middle shell layer called the exocuticle. With its

More Available

molecules bonded so tightly, the exocuticle is very durable. There are points on the body where it does not form, since flexibility is needed around joints. This arrangement allows supple movement but provides armor-like protection.

Though strong, the chitin and protein exocuticle itself would provide a poor barrier against moisture loss. Therefore, it must be coated with lipids, which are also secreted by the epidermis. These lipids, mostly fatty acids and waxes, form the third, outermost layer of the shell. They spread over the cuticles to form a waterproof seal even in dry weather. This lipid layer gives many arthropods their distinctive luster.

Combined, the endocuticle, exocuticle, and lipid coating form a shell that provides formidable protection. The external shell has other advantages. One is that, because it has far more surface area than the internal skeleton found in vertebrates, it provides more points at which muscles can be attached. This increased number of muscles permits many arthropods to be stronger and more agile for their body size than birds or mammals. The coloration and markings of the exoskeleton can be beneficial as well. Many species of scorpion, for instance, have cuticles that contain hyaline. The hyaline is excited by ultraviolet radiation, so these scorpions glow blue-green when a black light is flashed on them. Scientists are not sure why scorpions have evolved to fluoresce this way, but the reason may be that their glow attracts insects that they can capture and eat.

Adaptive as their shell is, it leaves arthropods with at least one distinct disadvantage: The cuticle cannot expand to accommodate growth. As the animal increases in size, therefore, it must

TOEFL Reading

PAUSE
TEST

SECTION
EXIT

Question 3 of 12

REVIEW

HELP
?

BACK

NEXT

HIDE TIME   00:08:45

More Available

occasionally molt. The existing cuticle separates from newer, more flexible layers being secreted beneath it, gradually splits open, and can be shaken or slipped off. The new chitin and protein will harden and be provided with a fresh lipid coating, but this process can take hours or days after molting occurs. The arthropod must first take in extra air or water to swell its body to greater than its normal size. After the shell has hardened in its expanded form, the arthropod expels the air or water. It then has room for growth. But until it hardens, the new coat is tender and easily penetrated. Accordingly, the arthropod must remain in hiding. Otherwise, it risks being snapped up by a predator clever enough to take advantage of its lowered defenses.

On the TOEFL, you will see that paragraphs referred to in the questions are marked by a ➤; this will help you quickly locate the paragraphs. You may see black squares ■ in the passage, and some of the words will be shaded in gray, whereas others will be boldfaced. Try not to be distracted by these symbols, words, and phrases—there will be questions about them later, but don't get bogged down by them while you're reading.

Now that you've had a minute to look over this passage, state the main idea. What is the author's purpose, and how is the passage structured?

Main idea: _____

_____

Structure: _____

_____

Purpose: _____

_____

For this passage, the main idea is "arthropods have a tough outer shell that protects them and provides them with other advantages." The structure is fairly typical, with each of the body paragraphs describing some aspect of the shell. The last paragraph presents a disadvantage of the shell. Putting this all together, the author's purpose is "to inform."

If you had trouble coming up with these answers, be sure to review the Core Concept: Reading chapter.

Step 2: Attack the Questions

After actively reading the passage, go to the questions. The questions on the TOEFL come in a few different varieties.

Most of the questions are multiple choice, as shown below.

10. Why is an arthropod vulnerable after molting?

(A)   It is far from sources of water.
(B)   It is more visible to predators.
(C)   Its shell is soft.
(D)   The loss of energy makes it weak.

On the test, you won't see the answer choices as letters, but we'll use them in this book to make the explanations clearer.

Other questions require you to click on part of the passage. These questions look like the following:

15. Look at the four squares [■] in the passage. Where would the following sentence best fit in the passage? Click on the [■] to add the sentence to the passage.

For these questions, you'll have to go back to the passage and click on one of the squares to answer it. Other questions of this variety may ask you to click on a word or phrase.

The final type of question is multiple-multiple-choice questions. These questions require you to choose several correct answers.

22. A brief summary of the passage is provided below. Click on the THREE sentences that best complete the summary. Some sentences are not part of the summary because they do not express the main idea. *This question is worth 2 points.*

These questions are followed by several sentences. Use the mouse to drag the sentences you select into the summary box. You can remove one of your choices by clicking on it again.

In general, the multiple-choice questions are the easiest. You should do them on your first pass. The summary questions—the multiple-multiple-choice ones—take the longest, so save them for last. (They usually turn up at the end anyway.) The passage-based questions fall somewhere in between these two.

Question Types

The questions on the Reading section of the TOEFL can be grouped into several different categories. Each question requires its own strategy, but remember that for each question, the answer is somewhere in the passage. Also, some questions are much more common than others, so you may not see all of the following types when you take the TOEFL.

The question types on the TOEFL are as follows:

1. **Vocabulary in context:** These are some of the most common questions on the TOEFL. You may be asked the meaning of a word or phrase. These questions are some of the easiest, so do them on your first pass.
2. **Reference:** These questions usually ask you what noun a pronoun connects to, though sometimes they may ask you about a noun, adverb, or adjective. Because these questions also direct you to a certain point in the passage, do these on your first pass.

3. **Lead words:** Some questions will refer to a word highlighted in gray in the passage. Other questions may ask about a specific word or phrase, even if there is nothing highlighted in the passage. Also do these on your first pass.

4. **Detail:** Often the easiest type of question, detail questions ask about specific facts from the passage. Again, get these questions done on your first pass.

5. **Paraphrase:** Paraphrase questions ask you to find the answer choice that means the same as a bolded sentence in the passage.

6. **Definition:** This type of question asks you to find the part of the passage that defines a certain word or phrase.

7. **Before/after:** These questions are rare. They ask you what kind of paragraph would likely precede or follow the passage.

8. **Sentence insertion:** For this type of question, you'll see four black squares [■] placed throughout the passage. Your job is to figure out in which of these spots a new sentence would best fit.

9. **EXCEPT/NOT/LEAST:** These questions can be some of the most difficult on the test so save them for the second pass. For these, you are looking for the answer that is *not* supported by the passage. EXCEPT/NOT/LEAST questions also tend to take longer to answer than most multiple-choice questions.

10. **Inference:** This popular question type can be one of the trickiest types; therefore, you'll want to save these questions for the second pass. Inference questions ask you to find the statement that is implied or suggested by the passage. Remember, the TOEFL uses a narrow interpretation of *inference*, and correct responses to these questions *must be true* based on the information provided in the passage.

11. **Summary:** Typically worth two points, these questions ask you to find main points and ideas from the passage. Because they require some knowledge of the passage, do them on your second pass after you have had a chance to become familiar with the material.

Familiarize yourself with this list. As you'll see, being able to recognize the question types will aid you in both your approach to finding the answer and your POE strategy.

Step 3 and Step 4: Find the Answer in the Passage and Use POE

We'll look at steps 3 and 4 together, because they are the two most important steps, and because as you successfully complete step 3, you'll naturally be able to complete step 4.

As we've stated before—and it cannot be emphasized enough—the correct answer to each question is *always* found in the passage. The trick on the TOEFL is, of course, finding that answer in an efficient manner. Fortunately, each question provides a clue, or hint, as to where we need to look for our answer.

Here is our general system for dealing with questions on the TOEFL.

1. **Read and rephrase the question.** You'll notice that many questions on the TOEFL are not written in a straightforward manner. Before you head back to the passage to find the answer, make sure you understand what the question is asking you to find.

2. **Go back to the passage and find the answer.** The question will direct you to the appropriate part of the passage. Go back to the passage and read enough lines (around 6–10) to get the context of the text. Never answer a question from memory alone because you're more likely to fall for a trap answer.

3. **Answer in your own words first.** This is the most important step of all. After returning to the passage and reading the appropriate part of it, you should be able to answer the question in your own words. If you can't, you may be reading the wrong part of the passage or you may need to read more lines.

4. **Use POE.** Once you have an idea of the type of answer for which you're looking, return to the question and use POE.

Make sure to practice this system on each question until it becomes automatic. The best way to approach the TOEFL is to have a clear, consistent plan of attack.

PUTTING IT ALL TOGETHER

Now, let's return to our earlier passage and work through the questions, one of each type. We'll go through the steps and talk about the best way to find the correct response. Then you can try the process on your own with the drills at the end of the chapter.

The Exoskeleton of the Arthropod

There are more arthropods alive on Earth than there are members of any other phylum of animals. Given that not only insects and spiders but also shrimp, crabs, centipedes, and their numerous relatives are arthropods, this fact should not occasion surprise. For all their diversity, arthropods of any type share two defining characteristics: jointed legs (from which the phylum takes its name) and an exoskeleton (the recognizable hard outer shell).

Though the shell itself is made of dead tissue like that of human hair and fingernails, it is dotted with sensory cells. **These give the arthropod information about its surroundings, much as the nerve endings in human skin do.** Also like human skin, the shell protects fragile internal organs from potentially hazardous contact with the environment. It seals in precious moisture that would otherwise evaporate but permits the exchange of gases.

Its primary component is chitin, a natural polymer that contains calcium and is very similar in structure to the cellulose in wood. Chitin and proteins are secreted in the epidermis, the living tissue just below the shell, after which they bond to form a thin sheet. Each new sheet is produced so that its chitin fibers are not parallel with those directly above, which increases their combined strength.

The result is the endocuticle, a mesh of molecules that forms the lowest layer of the shell. The endocuticle is not quite tough enough for daily wear and tear. Over time, however, its molecules continue to lock together. As the endocuticle is pushed upward by the formation of new sheets by the epidermis, it becomes the middle shell layer called the exocuticle. With its molecules bonded so tightly, the exocuticle is very durable. There are points on the body where it does not form, since flexibility is needed around joints. This arrangement allows supple movement but provides armor-like protection.

Though strong, the chitin and protein exocuticle itself would provide a poor barrier against moisture loss. Therefore, it must be coated with lipids, which are also secreted by the epidermis. These lipids, mostly fatty acids and waxes, form the third, outermost layer of the shell. They spread over the cuticles to form a waterproof seal even in dry weather. This lipid layer gives many arthropods their distinctive luster.

Combined, the endocuticle, exocuticle, and lipid coating form a shell that provides formidable protection. The external shell has other advantages. One is that, because it has far more surface area than the internal skeleton found in vertebrates, it provides more points at which muscles can be attached. This increased number of muscles permits many arthropods to be stronger and more agile for their body size than birds or mammals. The coloration and markings of the exoskeleton can be beneficial as well. **Many species of scorpion, for instance, have cuticles that contain hyaline.** The hyaline is excited by ultraviolet radiation, so these scorpions glow blue-green when a black light is flashed on them. Scientists are not sure why scorpions have evolved to fluoresce this way, but the reason may be that their glow attracts insects that they can capture and eat.

Adaptive as their shell is, it leaves arthropods with at least one distinct disadvantage: The cuticle cannot expand to accommodate growth. As the animal increases in size, therefore, it must occasionally molt. The existing cuticle separates from newer, more flexible layers being secreted beneath it, gradually splits open, and can be shaken or slipped off. The new chitin and protein will harden and be provided with a fresh lipid coating, but this process can take hours or days after molting occurs. The arthropod must first take in extra air or water to swell its body to greater than its normal size. After the shell has hardened in its expanded form, the arthropod expels the air or water. It then has room for growth. But until it hardens, the new coat is tender and easily penetrated. Accordingly, the arthropod must remain in hiding. Otherwise, it risks being snapped up by a predator clever enough to take advantage of its lowered defenses.

Remember, before going to the questions, take a moment to identify the main idea, purpose, and general structure. But don't spend too much time doing this (no more than two minutes)! If you're having trouble finding the main idea or purpose, go to the questions. Ready?

Question Type #1: Vocabulary in Context Questions

Here's our first question.

Don't forget to pick up your copy of *Wordsmart for the TOEFL* for extra vocabulary practice!

1. The word occasion in the passage is closest in meaning to

   (A) multiply
   (B) cause
   (C) demonstrate
   (D) limit

First, identify the question type. This is a **vocabulary in context** question, one of the most common and easy question types on the TOEFL. You can identify them because they ask for the meaning or definition of a word, typically shaded in gray, in the passage. Let's look at this type in more detail.

Now that we've identified what type of question it is, let's rephrase the question to make sure we know what it's asking. Generally, when rephrasing, try to rethink the question using the words *what* or *why*. For example, this question is basically asking us

> What does the word *occasion* mean in the passage?

You may want to jot down your rephrased version of the question on your scrap paper. Even if you don't, it is important to make sure you know exactly what it is you're looking for when you return to the passage.

For a vocabulary in context question, we'll first go back to the passage and read a few lines before and after the word in question:

> There are more arthropods alive on Earth than there are members of any other phylum of animals. Given that not only insects and spiders but also shrimp, crabs, centipedes, and their numerous relatives are arthropods, this fact should not occasion surprise. For all their diversity, arthropods of any type share two defining characteristics: jointed legs (from which the phylum takes its name) and an exoskeleton (the recognizable hard outer shell).

Next look at the word in question and try to replace it with your own word. Usually, the sentence itself or the surrounding sentences should give you a clue as to the meaning of the word. In this case, the line says that the "fact should not _____ surprise." Look at the first sentence, which tells us that there are "more arthropods alive...than there are members of any other phylum." And after that, the passage states that "given that...are arthropods."

The context clues are that there a lot of these arthropods and that we shouldn't be surprised. So when answering in your own words, you may think that *occasion* means to "cause" or "lead to." Once we've come up with our own answer, we can return to the choices and use POE. We need a word that means "lead to" or "cause."

1. The word occasion in the passage is closest in meaning to

    (A) multiply
    (B) cause
    (C) demonstrate
    (D) limit

Let's evaluate our choices.

- Does (A) mean "lead to" or "cause"? No. *Multiply* means to increase the amount of something. Cross it out.
- Choice (B) is *cause*, which is exactly what we're looking for. Keep it. Even though (B) looks good, we should check the other answer choices. On the TOEFL, it's better to be safe than sorry.
- Choice (C) doesn't look like a good fit—*demonstrate* means "to show" or "present."
- And (D) doesn't work either. *Limit* means "to confine" or "restrict."
- So it looks like (B) is the best answer.

Give it another shot with this next question.

8. The word excited in the passage is closest in meaning to

(A) stimulated
(B) attracted
(C) captured
(D) enthused

This question means "What does the word *excited* mean in the passage?" Go back to the passage, find the word *excited*, and read a few lines before and after it.

> The coloration and markings of the exoskeleton can be beneficial as well. **Many species of scorpion, for instance, have cuticles that contain hyaline.** The hyaline is excited by ultraviolet radiation, so these scorpions glow blue-green when a black light is flashed on them. Scientists are not sure why scorpions have evolved to fluoresce this way, but the reason may be that their glow attracts insects that they can capture and eat.

Remember, we must always try to answer in our own words first. Look at the sentences before and after and find the context. The sentence says "The hyaline is _____ by ultraviolet radiation, so these scorpions glow...." The next sentence also mentions the glow of the scorpion. In our own words, we may say that *excited* means "to make glow."

Now, let's go back to the answer choices.

• Choice (A) is *stimulated*. Could that mean "cause to glow"? Perhaps. Let's leave it for now.
• How about (B)—*attracted*? *Attracted* means "to be drawn to." Eliminate it.
• *Captured* means "to be seized or taken." So choice (C) is not what we're looking for.
• All we have left is (D). *Enthused* does mean "to be excited," but be careful! This is a trap answer. On many vocabulary in context questions, one of the wrong choices will be a dictionary definition of the word in question. Make sure the definition works in context. Remember, the right answer is always based on the passage. In context, it doesn't make sense to say that "hyaline is enthused by ultraviolet radiation." Therefore, eliminate (D).
• And keep (A) as our answer.

POE Strategies for Vocabulary in Context Questions

The previous questions may have been easy for you, or they may have been fairly difficult. If they were easy, chances are you were comfortable with the words. If you had a hard time, you probably didn't know all the words.

Even if you don't know all of the words in a vocabulary in context question, there are still some steps you can take to help increase your chances of getting the question correct. Let's look at the POE strategies we can use to answer this next question.

4. The word hazardous in the passage is closest in meaning to

(A) frequent
(B) perilous
(C) outer
(D) unpredictable

Here's the text from the passage.

> These give the arthropod information about its surroundings, much as the nerve endings in human skin do. Also like human skin, the shell protects fragile internal organs from potentially hazardous contact with the environment. It seals in precious moisture that would otherwise evaporate but permits the exchange of gases.

A few things may affect your ability to answer this question. First, you may have trouble making sense of the lines in the passage. Second, you may not be confident about each of the words in the answer choices.

In either of these cases, your strategy is the same. Pick a word from the answers with which you are familiar. Let's start with "frequent," which means "happening often." If this is the correct answer, there should be a word or phrase in these lines that means something similar to "happening often." However, none of the words in the passage has anything to do with "frequent" or "happening often." Therefore, we can eliminate (A).

You can repeat this strategy for the other words with which you are confident. As we've said before, the right answer is supported by the passage. You should be able to match your answer to a word or phrase from the passage. If you can't, it's not the right answer.

For this question, the correct answer is (B). The sentence tells us that the "shell protects...organs...." Therefore, "hazardous" must mean "something to protect against." Neither (C) nor (D) is close to this meaning.

Vocabulary in Context Questions Summary

For vocabulary in context questions, do the following:

1. **Go back to the passage** and read a few lines before and after the word in question.
2. **Come up with your own word** for the shaded word based on the clues in the sentences.

3. **Return to the answer choices and eliminate** any choices that
   - are not supported by any words or phrases from the passage
   - are dictionary definitions of the word, but are incorrect in the context of the passage

Question Type #2: Reference Questions

Now let's move on to the next type of question.

6. The phrase This arrangement in the passage refers to

   (A) the low number of joints on an arthropod
   (B) the absence of the exocuticle on certain parts of the body
   (C) the toughness of the exocuticle
   (D) the composition of the lipid coating

This question looks similar to a vocabulary in context question. The difference, however, is that this question asks us not what the phrase *means,* but what it *refers to.* If we rephrase the question, it would look something like this

What does the phrase *This arrangement* refer to?

This type of question is called a **reference** question. Our strategy for solving reference questions is similar to that for vocabulary in context questions. For reference questions, however, we want to focus on the lines *before* the phrase or word because the reference cannot be after the phrase.

Here are the lines we need to work with.

As the endocuticle is pushed upward by the formation of new sheets by the epidermis, it becomes the middle shell layer called the exocuticle. With its molecules bonded so tightly, the exocuticle is very durable. There are points on the body where it does not form, since flexibility is needed around joints. This arrangement allows supple movement but provides armor-like protection.

For a reference question, it is important to understand how authors use pronouns in writing. A pronoun is used to take the place of a noun. Therefore, the author must introduce the noun before using a pronoun. Otherwise, the reader will have no idea what the author is writing about.

Thus, for a reference question, find the noun that appears before the reference. Look at the sentence before the reference.

There are points on the body where it does not form, since flexibility is needed around joints.

The answer to our question should be found in this sentence. What's the noun in this sentence? The most specific one is *points on the body where it does not form.* This is probably the one for which we're looking. Let's return to the answer choices and use POE.

6. The phrase This arrangement in the passage refers to

   (A) the low number of joints on an arthropod
   (B) the absence of the exocuticle on certain parts of the body
   (C) the toughness of the exocuticle
   (D) the composition of the lipid coating

We're looking for an answer that is close to *points on the body where it does not form.* By the way, because we're using POE, we are not especially concerned about what "it" is. Nor are we going to worry about fancy terms such as *exocuticle.* So, let's look at the answer choices.

- Start with choice (A). This choice mentions the *low number of joints.* Not what we're looking for at all.
- Answer choice (B) seems to match. It mentions the *absence...on certain parts of the body.* Notice how that answer is very similar to "points on the *body* where it *does not form.*" Still, check the remaining choices as well.
- Answer choice (C) may seem tempting, but notice that the toughness is mentioned not in the sentence before the shaded phrase, but two sentences away. It is very rare for an author to place the referent so far away from the pronoun. Therefore, eliminate this choice.
- Finally we come to choice (D). Notice that (D) mentions the *lipid coating.* The lipids don't show up until after the phrase, so (D) cannot be correct.
- Therefore, (B) is the best answer.

POE Strategies for Reference Questions

Reference questions have clear POE guidelines. Eliminate answers that

- mention words or phrases that show up only *after* the reference
- use words or phrases that are not mentioned at all in the two or three sentences before the reference

As long as you follow these two guidelines, reference questions should be fairly easy.

Question Type #3: Lead Word Questions

Here is the next question type.

> 5. The layer of the shell called the exocuticle is strong because
>
>   (A) its molecules are closely bonded
>   (B) it is drier than the endocuticle
>   (C) its fibers are parallel
>   (D) it is water-resistant

Our first task is to rephrase the question. Remember to try to use "what" or "why." For this question, our rephrasing may say

> Why is the exocuticle strong?

We call this a **lead word** question. A question of this sort has a word or phrase that will *lead* you to the right answer. For lead words, pick the most specific part of the question. Your lead word should also be something that you will have an easy time spotting in the passage. For this question, our lead word should be *exocuticle*. It's easy to find in the passage, and it's the most specific part of the question. Once we find the lead word, we'll read a few lines before and after it.

Here's the text on which we need to focus.

> With its molecules bonded so tightly, the exocuticle is very durable. There are points on the body where it does not form, since flexibility is needed around joints. This arrangement allows supple movement but provides armor-like protection.

When looking for lead words, there are a couple of things to keep in mind. First, the questions are arranged in a rough chronological order. That means the early questions will refer to earlier parts of the passage, whereas later questions refer to later parts. Use the question number to give yourself a rough idea of where to look for the lead word. Second, when looking for lead words, always look for the first instance of the word. Some words may show up more than once in the passage. Start with the first word. If you are unable to answer the question in your own words, move on to the next mention of the lead word.

In this case, it looks like we're in the right section of the passage. Answer the question in your own words first. According to the passage, the exocuticle is "durable" because "its molecules" are "bonded so tightly." This appears to be what we need. Let's look at the question again.

5. The layer of the shell called the exocuticle is strong because

    (A) its molecules are closely bonded
    (B) it is drier than the endocuticle
    (C) its fibers are parallel
    (D) it is water-resistant

Now, let's consider each answer choice.

- (A) seems to match very nicely. Still, we should check the remaining choices.
- (B) states the reason the exocuticle is strong is because it is drier than the endocuticle. This is not stated in the passage, so it must be wrong.
- (C) states that the exocuticle's strength is due to parallel fibers. This is a trap answer. According to the passage, the *endo*cuticle has parallel fibers. If you fell for this choice, you probably tried to answer from memory. *Always* return to the passage to verify your answer.
- (D) The same reasoning applies to choice (D). According to the passage, it is the lipids that are water-resistant, not the exocuticle.

Thus, our answer is (A).

Let's try another one.

7. Why is the large surface area of the exoskeleton an advantage?

    (A) More water can be retained.
    (B) More detailed coloration and markings are possible.
    (C) It can accommodate a long period of growth.
    (D) Many muscles can be attached.

This question is phrased in a straightforward manner, so we don't need to rephrase it. We do, however, have to pick our lead word. Which word or words from this question do you think would be easiest to spot? You may be tempted to pick *exoskeleton*. However, this is where our initial active reading of the passage comes in handy. Because the entire passage is about the shell, we may find numerous references to the exoskeleton. So let's use even more specific lead words—*large surface area*. Of course, you can probably still get the question correct if you use *exoskeleton* as your lead word. Note that this is question 7, so we should look toward the end of the passage for our answer.

Did you find it? Here are the lines with which we need to work.

The external shell has other advantages. One is that, because it has far more surface area than the internal skeleton found in vertebrates, it provides more points at which muscles can be attached. This increased number of muscles permits many arthropods to be stronger and more agile for their body size than birds or mammals.

From these lines, it appears that the "large surface area...provides more points at which muscles can be attached." That looks like our answer. Let's use POE.

- (A) is not mentioned in these lines, so eliminate it.
- Choice (B) is mentioned, but the passage doesn't state that the large surface area is necessary for the colorations.
- Answer (C) is also not mentioned in these lines.
- We're left with choice (D), which says exactly what we want. Thus, (D) is our answer.

Question Type #4: Detail Questions

Now let's look at a question type that is fairly similar to the lead word questions.

3. According to paragraph 2 of the passage, an arthropod's shell is similar to human hair and fingernails in that

   (A) it contains few sensory cells
   (B) it has several distinct layers
   (C) it is made of dead tissue
   (D) it is mostly made of cellulose

This question is very similar to a lead word question. However, this question is actually a little easier because the question tells us exactly where to look. We call this a **detail** question. It asks us to retrieve a fact or detail from a specific part of the passage. Rephrase the question first.

How is the arthropod's shell similar to human hair and fingernails?

We know the answer is somewhere in paragraph 2, so all we have to do is read paragraph 2 until we find the answer to our question. Remember to know what you're looking for before you start to read; if the lines you're reading aren't about "human hair and fingernails," skim through them. Don't waste time reading if what you read won't answer the question!

Here are the lines that refer to "human hair and fingernails."

➤Though the shell itself is made of dead tissue like that of human hair and fingernails, it is dotted with sensory cells. **These give the arthropod information about its surroundings, much as the nerve endings in human skin do.** Also like human skin, the shell protects fragile internal organs from potentially hazardous contact with the environment.

If we answer in our own words, it looks as if the shell is "made of dead tissue like that of human hair and fingernails." This is the answer we need. Let's review the choices again.

- Answer (A) is a trap. If you read carefully, the passage doesn't say that human hair and fingernails have sensory cells; only the shell does.
- (B) is not mentioned in this part of the passage at all.
- Answer choice (C) matches our answer, so let's keep it.
- Finally, choice (D) is also not mentioned at all in this part of the passage.
- Choice (C) is the best answer.

POE Strategies for Lead Word and Detail Questions

You may have noticed that some of the wrong answers on lead word and detail questions contain words or phrases found throughout the passage. There are a couple of reasons for this. First, if you are trying to answer the question from memory, you are likely to pick one of these choices because it contains words or phrases you may remember having read. Second, on the TOEFL, it is actually a *disadvantage* to try to read and understand everything in the passage. But many students still try to comprehend everything. This makes them more likely to become confused about what they've read and choose one of these trap answers.

Thus, on lead word and detail questions, you should focus on only a small part of the passage, no more than six to eight lines. Try to match words or phrases from the answer choices with the lines that you are studying. Eliminate any choices that

- contain words or phrases not mentioned in the lines close to the lead word or detail
- mention words or phrases that show up in the passage, but are beyond the six- to eight-line range

On the TOEFL, the correct answers to lead word and detail questions are generally within four to six lines of the lead word or detail, so if you're stuck, these are safe guidelines to follow.

Quick Review: Vocabulary in Context, Reference, Lead Word, and Detail Questions

These questions tend to be easier than the others. Make sure you find and do all of these questions in your first pass. As you may have noticed, there is a pattern. In each case, the question referred us to a specific part of the passage. The answer to the question was found within four to five lines of the part of the passage referred to in the question. Thus, to summarize our strategy

1. Rephrase the question.
2. Use clues in the question to find the appropriate place in the passage.
3. Read a few lines before and after the lead word or reference.
4. State the answer to the question in your own words.

The wrong answers to these questions also follow a very similar pattern. Make sure to eliminate answers that are

- not mentioned in the passage at all
- mentioned in the passage, but beyond the specific lines needed to answer the question

Let's continue our discussion of question types. Here's our passage again.

The Exoskeleton of the Arthropod

There are more arthropods alive on Earth than there are members of any other phylum of animals. Given that not only insects and spiders but also shrimp, crabs, centipedes, and their numerous relatives are arthropods, this fact should not occasion surprise. For all their diversity, arthropods of any type share two defining characteristics: jointed legs (from which the phylum takes its name) and an exoskeleton (the recognizable hard outer shell).

Though the shell itself is made of dead tissue like that of human hair and fingernails, it is dotted with sensory cells. **These give the arthropod information about its surroundings, much as the nerve endings in human skin do.** Also like human skin, the shell protects fragile internal organs from potentially hazardous contact with the environment. It seals in precious moisture that would otherwise evaporate but permits the exchange of gases.

Its primary component is chitin, a natural polymer that contains calcium and is very similar in structure to the cellulose in wood. Chitin and proteins are secreted in the epidermis, the living tissue just below the shell, after which they bond to form a thin sheet. Each new sheet is produced so that its chitin fibers are not parallel with those directly above, which increases their combined strength.

The result is the endocuticle, a mesh of molecules that forms the lowest layer of the shell. The endocuticle is not quite tough enough for daily wear and tear. Over time, however, its molecules continue to lock together. As the endocuticle is pushed upward by the formation of new sheets by the epidermis, it becomes the middle shell layer called the exocuticle. With its molecules bonded so tightly, the exocuticle is very durable. There are points on the body where it does not form, since flexibility is needed around joints. This arrangement allows supple movement but provides armor-like protection.

Though strong, the chitin and protein exocuticle itself would provide a poor barrier against moisture loss. Therefore, it must be coated with lipids, which are also secreted by the epidermis. These lipids, mostly fatty acids and waxes, form the third, outermost layer of the shell. They spread over the cuticles to form a waterproof seal even in dry weather. This lipid layer gives many arthropods their distinctive luster.

Combined, the endocuticle, exocuticle, and lipid coating form a shell that provides formidable protection. The external shell has other advantages. One is that, because it has far more surface area than the internal skeleton found in vertebrates, it provides more points at which muscles can be attached. This increased number of muscles permits many arthropods to be stronger and more agile for their body size than birds or mammals. The coloration and markings of the exoskeleton can be beneficial as well. **Many species of scorpion, for instance, have cuticles that contain hyaline.** The hyaline is excited by ultraviolet radiation, so these scorpions glow blue-green when a black light is flashed on them. Scientists are not sure why scorpions have evolved to fluoresce this way, but the reason may be that their glow attracts insects that they can capture and eat.

Adaptive as their shell is, it leaves arthropods with at least one distinct disadvantage: The cuticle cannot expand to accommodate growth. As the animal increases in size, therefore, it must occasionally molt. The existing cuticle separates from newer, more flexible layers being secreted beneath it, gradually splits open, and can be shaken or slipped off. The new chitin and protein will harden and be provided with a fresh lipid coating, but this process can take hours or days after molting occurs. The arthropod must first take in extra air or water to swell its body to greater than its normal size. After the shell has hardened in its expanded form, the arthropod expels the air or water. It then has room for growth. But until it hardens, the new coat is tender and easily penetrated. Accordingly, the arthropod must remain in hiding. Otherwise, it risks being snapped up by a predator clever enough to take advantage of its lowered defenses.

Question Type #5: Paraphrase Questions

Our next group of questions deals with the passage and its structure. Here's one example.

10. Which of the following choices best expresses the essential meaning of the highlighted sentences in paragraph 7? Incorrect choices will change the meaning or leave out important details.

    (A) Arthropods are only vulnerable to predators during the period in which their shell is tender and easily penetrated.
    (B) Predators typically prefer to eat arthropods that are waiting for their new coats to harden.
    (C) While the arthropod's shell is hardening, the arthropod can not rely on its shell to protect it from predators.
    (D) When the arthropod's defenses are lowered, it will use many different strategies to avoid predators.

This type of question is a **paraphrase** question. We usually won't have to rephrase these questions. Instead, we have to worry more about rephrasing the shaded portion of the passage. Let's take a look at the lines in question.

> But until it hardens, the new coat is tender and easily penetrated. Accordingly, the arthropod must remain in hiding. Otherwise, it risks being snapped up by a predator clever enough to take advantage of its lowered defenses.

When paraphrasing, you need to *find the essential information*. Thus, trim the fat. Get rid of unnecessary modifiers and descriptive phrases. Look for the subject and the main verb of the sentence or sentences in question. For example, let's break down the sentences into their most basic parts.

1. ~~But until it hardens~~, the new coat is tender and easily penetrated.

The subject here is *new coat*, and the important thing about it is that it's *tender* and *easily penetrated*. Cut out the phrase *but until it hardens*, which is a modifier.

2. ~~Accordingly~~, the arthropod must remain in hiding.

The subject of this sentence is *arthropod*, and the verb is *remain in hiding*. Trim the rest.

3. ~~Otherwise~~, it risks being snapped up by a predator ~~clever enough to take advantage of its lowered defenses~~.

The important parts here are *it* (the arthropod) *risks being snapped up by a predator.*

Now, our job is to find the answer choice that contains these elements and these elements only. Here are the choices again.

(A) Arthropods are only vulnerable to predators during the period in which their shell is tender and easily penetrated.

(B) Predators typically prefer to eat arthropods that are waiting for their new coats to harden.

(C) While the arthropod's shell is hardening, the arthropod cannot rely on its shell to protect it from predators.

(D) When the arthropod's defenses are lowered, it will use many different strategies to avoid predators.

Let's consider each choice.

- Start with choice (A). It does mention *arthropods* and *predators*, which is good. However, we are missing some information. There is no mention of *hiding*, one of our key elements. Also, choice (A) states that arthropods are "only vulnerable...during this period." That is beyond the information in the passage. Eliminate (A).

- Answer (B) is problematic because it makes *predators* the subject. We should have something that talks about arthropods. Eliminate this choice.

- Now look at (C). It first mentions the weakened shell, which matches with sentence 1. Next, it says the arthropod "cannot rely on its shell." At first this doesn't seem to match, but sentence 2 stated that the creature "must remain in hiding"—this is an example of "not relying on its shell." Finally, the choice mentions the predators from sentence 3. Everything matches, so keep this choice.

- Choice (D) is close, but it has one big problem. It mentions "many different strategies," whereas the passage only mentions one. We don't want any choice that adds information, so eliminate (D).

- That leaves choice (C) as the best answer.

POE Strategies for Paraphrase Questions

If you're having trouble paraphrasing the sentence in question, the easiest POE strategy is to eliminate any answers that introduce new information. These choices will always be *wrong*. Another good strategy is to try to identify the subject of the sentence. One of the choices will usually have a different subject. Eliminate this choice.

Question Type #6: Definition Questions

Let's look at another type of question.

> 11. Click on the highlighted sentence in the passage in which the author gives a definition.

This is a **definition** question. Once again, we don't have to rephrase this type of question. Go to the passage and look for the four sentences in boldface. Here they are.

1. These give the arthropod information about its surroundings, much as the nerve endings in human skin do.
2. Its primary component is chitin, a natural polymer that contains calcium and is very similar in structure to the cellulose in wood.
3. Combined, the endocuticle, exocuticle, and lipid coating form a shell that provides formidable protection.
4. Many species of scorpion, for instance, have cuticles that contain hyaline.

We need to paraphrase each one, looking for the sentence that clarifies the meaning of a word or phrase. Unfortunately, these questions are mostly based on your comprehension. If you are comfortable with the words in the sentences, then go ahead and answer the question. If you are having trouble understanding the sentences, move on to another question.

In Core Concept: Reading, we discussed "trimming the fat"—cutting out the nonessential information from the sentence. In a definition question, the definition will usually turn up in the "fat" part of the sentence. Thus, we need to separate the sentence into its different parts and examine them. For definition questions, follow the procedure below:

1. Find the subject, verb, and object.
2. Look at the other parts of the sentence.
3. See if the remaining parts define or clarify the subject, verb, or object.

For example, in sentence 1, the subject is *These*, and the main verb is *give*. The object is *information*. So, the sentence basically reads

These give information.

Now, examine the remaining parts of the sentence. First, we have the phrase *the arthropod*—does this define anything from the basic sentence? No. It only clarifies what is receiving the information. The next phrase is *about its surroundings*. This is not a definition; it is a prepositional phrase. The final part is "much as the nerve endings in human skin do." Does this refer back to the main sentence, defining something from it? No, it does not. Instead, it makes a comparison. Eliminate this choice.

Do the same for the second sentence. The second sentence breaks down as

Its component is chitin.

The first word we cut out was *primary*. This is a modifier. It doesn't define anything. The rest of the sentence states "a natural polymer that contains calcium and is very similar in structure to the cellulose in wood." Could this define one of the terms from the main sentence? In fact, it does. It provides a definition of *chitin*. Thus, this is our answer.

POE Strategies for Definition Questions

As stated previously, your success on definition questions will be largely based on your comfort level with the sentences. If you're having a hard time figuring out the meaning of a sentence, keep the following in mind:

- Definitions frequently are introduced using the words *which, that,* or *means.* Look for sentences in which the author uses these words.
- Trim away prepositional phrases. These are phrases beginning with words such as *of, on,* and *in.* A definition will *not* be a prepositional phrase.
- Watch out for sentences that merely list or introduce examples. Remember, you need a phrase that tells you what a word or concept means, *not an example* of the word or concept.

Question Type #7: Before/After Questions

It's time to look at yet another type of question.

9. The paragraph following the passage would most logically continue with a discussion of

(A) different strategies used by predators to capture arthropods
(B) non-arthropods that have protective shells
(C) the defense mechanisms of other types of animals
(D) adaptations arthropods make to survive during molting

Some questions ask about a hypothetical paragraph before or after the passage; thus, we call these **before/after** questions (note that *before* questions are very rare on the TOEFL). First, rephrase the question.

What would a paragraph after the passage discuss?

To answer this type of question, we need to concern ourselves with only the last paragraph. Here it is again.

> Adaptive as their shell is, it leaves arthropods with at least one distinct disadvantage: the cuticle cannot expand to accommodate growth. As the animal increases in size, therefore, it must occasionally molt. The existing cuticle separates from newer, more flexible layers being secreted beneath it, gradually splits open, and can be shaken or slipped off. The new chitin and protein will harden and be provided with a fresh lipid coating, but this process can take hours or days after molting occurs. The arthropod must first take in extra air or water to swell its body to greater than its normal size. After the shell has hardened in its expanded form, the arthropod expels the air or water. It then has room for growth. But until it hardens, the new coat is tender and easily penetrated. Accordingly, the arthropod must remain in hiding. Otherwise, it risks being snapped up by a predator clever enough to take advantage of its lowered defenses.

Use active reading strategies to figure out the basic meaning of the paragraph. The first sentence tells us that we will discuss "disadvantages" of the shell. The body of the paragraph proceeds to give details about the disadvantages but, once again, we don't need to worry too much about these details. The author ends the paragraph by discussing how the arthropod is at a disadvantage while its "defenses are lowered."

The correct answer to a before/after question will be related to the *main idea* of the paragraph. In our own words, this final paragraph is about a disadvantage of the shell and the arthropod's vulnerability.

Now use POE on the answer choices.

- Choice (A) discusses the strategies of predators. But the final paragraph—in fact, the entire passage—is about arthropods. Thus, our answer should also be about arthropods. Eliminate this choice.
- (B) has the same problem; it discusses non-arthropods, but our paragraph is specifically about arthropods. Thus, (B) is wrong.
- (C) mentions defense mechanisms, but once again it discusses other animals, not arthropods. That means (C) is wrong as well.
- Finally, we're left with choice (D). This choice discusses both arthropods and their defenses when they lack shells ("adaptations…during molting"). That is exactly what we need. (D) is our answer.

Let's try it again.

13. Which of the following would most likely be the topic of the paragraph before this passage?

    (A) A brief discussion of the different phylum of animals
    (B) A scientific examination of human hair and nails
    (C) A description of various natural polymers
    (D) A listing of some common arthropods

This question asks about the paragraph before the passage, so we'll focus on the first paragraph. Look at the first paragraph, and state its general idea.

There are more arthropods alive on Earth than there are members of any other phylum of animals. Given that not only insects and spiders but also shrimp, crabs, centipedes, and their numerous relatives are arthropods, this fact should not occasion surprise. For all their diversity, arthropods of any type share two defining characteristics: jointed legs (from which the phylum takes its name) and an exoskeleton (the recognizable hard outer shell).

Here, the basic idea is that there are more arthropods than any other type of animal and that all arthropods share two common characteristics. Our answer should somehow lead into this discussion. Let's go through the answer choices and use POE.

- Answer choice (A) discusses different phylum of animals. This could be our answer because the first paragraph states that arthropods are more numerous than "any other phylum." (A) could be a good introduction to the topic. We'll leave this choice for now.
- Choice (B) talks about human hair and nails. This doesn't match very well with arthropods and their characteristics. Plus, you may have noticed that this topic appears in the second paragraph. It wouldn't make sense to place a paragraph about this subject before the first paragraph.
- Answer choice (C) is off topic. Our paragraph is about arthropods, not natural polymers. Eliminate this choice.
- Choice (D) is appealing, but there is one problem with it. The first paragraph already provides a listing of some common arthropods. Thus, it would be repetitive to have a paragraph about this topic preceding the passage.
- Choice (A) is the best answer.

POE Strategies for Before/After Questions

The key to these questions is to stay as close as possible to the main idea of the first or last paragraph, depending on whether you are doing a before or an after question. Eliminate answer choices that do the following:

- **Introduce new information:** The right answer will match the topic of the paragraph. Get rid of any choices that bring in information not mentioned in the paragraph.
- **Interrupt the structure:** Make sure the topic in the answer choice doesn't appear elsewhere in the passage. The ideas in the passage should follow a logical order—don't return to a topic that's been discussed previously.
- **Repeat information:** The correct answer will be based on the paragraph, but will not repeat information that has already been mentioned.

Question Type #8: Sentence Insertion Questions

Now we'll look at another structure-based question. Here's the passage again, but notice the placement of four black squares (■).

The Exoskeleton of the Arthropod

There are more arthropods alive on Earth than there are members of any other phylum of animals. Given that not only insects and spiders but also shrimp, crabs, centipedes, and their numerous relatives are arthropods, this fact should not occasion surprise. For all their diversity, arthropods of any type share two defining characteristics: jointed legs (from which the phylum takes its name) and an exoskeleton (the recognizable hard outer shell).

Though the shell itself is made of dead tissue like that of human hair and fingernails, it is dotted with sensory cells. **These give the arthropod information about its surroundings, much as the nerve endings in human skin do.** Also like human skin, the shell protects fragile internal organs from potentially hazardous contact with the environment. It seals in precious moisture that would otherwise evaporate but permits the exchange of gases.

Its primary component is chitin, a natural polymer that contains calcium and is very similar in structure to the cellulose in wood. Chitin and proteins are secreted in the epidermis, the living tissue just below the shell, after which they bond to form a thin sheet. Each new sheet is produced so that its chitin fibers are not parallel with those directly above, which increases their combined strength.

The result is the endocuticle, a mesh of molecules that forms the lowest layer of the shell. The endocuticle is not quite tough enough for daily wear and tear.■ Over time, however, its molecules continue to lock together.■ As the endocuticle is pushed upward by the formation of new sheets by the epidermis, it becomes the middle shell layer called the exocuticle.■ With its molecules bonded so tightly, the exocuticle is very durable.■ There are points on the body where it does not form, since flexibility is needed around joints. This arrangement allows supple movement but provides armor-like protection.

Though strong, the chitin and protein exocuticle itself would provide a poor barrier against moisture loss. Therefore, it must be coated with lipids, which are also secreted by the epidermis. These lipids, mostly fatty acids and waxes, form the third, outermost layer of the shell. They spread over the cuticles to form a waterproof seal even in dry weather. This lipid layer gives many arthropods their distinctive luster.

Combined, the endocuticle, exocuticle, and lipid coating form a shell that provides formidable protection. The external shell has other advantages. One is that, because it has far more surface area than the internal skeleton found in vertebrates, it provides more points at which muscles can be attached. This increased number of muscles permits many arthropods to be stronger and more agile for their body size than birds or mammals. The coloration and markings of the exoskeleton can be beneficial as well. Many species of scorpion, for instance, have cuticles that contain hyaline. The hyaline is excited by ultraviolet radiation, so these scorpions glow blue-green when a black light is flashed on them. Scientists are not sure why scorpions have evolved to fluoresce this way, but the reason may be that their glow attracts insects that they can capture and eat.

Adaptive as their shell is, it leaves arthropods with at least one distinct disadvantage: The cuticle cannot expand to accommodate growth. As the animal increases in size, therefore, it must occasionally molt. The existing cuticle separates from newer, more flexible layers being secreted beneath it, gradually splits open, and can be shaken or slipped off. The new chitin and protein will harden and be provided with a fresh lipid coating, but this process can take hours or days after molting occurs. The arthropod must first take in extra air or water to swell its body to greater than its normal size. After the shell has hardened in its expanded form, the arthropod expels the air or water. It then has room for growth. But until it hardens, the new coat is tender and easily penetrated. Accordingly, the arthropod must remain in hiding. Otherwise, it risks being snapped up by a predator clever enough to take advantage of its lowered defenses.

These black squares are used for **sentence insertion** questions. Here's an example.

14. Look at the four squares [■] that indicate where the following sentence could be added.

    While this process continues, the endocuticle is gradually shifted.

    Where would the sentence best fit?

To answer this type of question correctly, we need to look at the sentences before and after the black squares. The correct answer will join these two sentences together by mentioning an idea from each sentence. Here are the sentences before and after the first black square.

> The endocuticle is not quite tough enough for daily wear and tear. ■ Over time, however, its molecules continue to lock together.

Our task is to try to match the sentence in the question with the ideas in these two sentences. The answer choice mentions a "process." Does this match with anything in the two sentences? It doesn't appear to do so. Let's look at the rest of the sentence in the answer. It also states that the "endocuticle is gradually shifted." Does this match with the details in these two sentences? Although we can match the word *endocuticle*, neither of the sentences discusses a "shift." Therefore, we can't place the sentence here.

The second pair of sentences is

> Over time, however, its molecules continue to lock together. ■ As the endocuticle is pushed upward by the formation of new sheets by the epidermis, it becomes the middle shell layer called the exocuticle.

Now, we'll try to match our sentence with ideas from this pair of sentences. We need to find something that corresponds to "this process." The first sentence in the pair refers to "molecules...lock together." This seems like a process. Next, we want to match up the part of the sentence that talks about the endocuticle gradually shifting. The second sentence in the pair says "as the endocuticle is pushed upward..." This matches nicely with the "gradually shifting" part in the question. This looks like a likely place to add the new sentence.

Check the other two sentence pairs. Here's the third.

> As the endocuticle is pushed upward by the formation of new sheets by the epidermis, it becomes the middle shell layer called the exocuticle. ■ With its molecules bonded so tightly, the exocuticle is very durable.

As we've already seen, the first sentence in this pair is a good match for the sentence we have to add. However, the problem is the second sentence in the pair. This sentence mentions the *durability* of the exocuticle, which doesn't match with anything in the sentence we have to add. That makes this choice incorrect.

Finally, here's the fourth pair.

> With its molecules bonded so tightly, the exocuticle is very durable.
> ■ There are points on the body where it does not form, since flexibility is needed around joints.

In this case, it is clear that this pair of sentences does not match at all. The first sentence refers to the *exocuticle,* whereas the sentence we need to add is about the *endocuticle.* Furthermore, the second sentence in the pair is about places where there is no shell because flexibility is needed. These ideas are not part of the sentence we have to add. It looks as if the second black square is the best place to add the sentence, so your answer should look like this.

Over time, however, its molecules continue to lock together. While this process continues, the endocuticle is gradually shifted. As the endocuticle is pushed upward by the formation of new sheets by the epidermis, it becomes the middle shell layer called the exocuticle.

Keep in mind that when you click the black square on the TOEFL, the sentence will appear in the passage. This will make it easier to look for matches.

POE Strategies for Sentence Insertion Questions

Much like other questions in the Reading section of the TOEFL, these questions are all about matching information. The best answer is simply the one that is the closest match to the information in the passage. When doing a sentence insertion question, eliminate choices that don't match or are only half right.

- **Doesn't match:** The sentence you add should form a link between two sentences. If the ideas in the paragraph don't match the ideas in the added sentence, eliminate that choice.
- **Half-right:** Make sure the added sentence matches ideas with *both* the sentence before and after it. Wrong answers often are only partial matches.

We've looked at several different question types. Let's pause for a brief review before we continue.

Quick Review: Paraphrase, Definition, Before/After, and Sentence Insertion Questions

All of these question types refer you to a specific part of the passage, which is typically highlighted or marked. So there is no difficulty in figuring out where in the passage the answer lies. The difficulty lies in finding the right answer. In general, when answering questions of this type, focus on the following POE guidelines:

- **Doesn't match:** This is one of the easiest ways to eliminate an answer choice. If the information in the choice doesn't match the passage, it's wrong.
- **New information:** Be very suspicious of answer choices that introduce new information. These choices are usually wrong.
- **Half-right:** Read each choice carefully because wrong answers will typically match only half of the information in the passage or answer choice. Make sure *all* the information corresponds.

Questions of this type can be a little more challenging than the question types we've looked at already. Try these questions only after answering the vocabulary in context, reference, lead word, and detail questions.

Question Type #9: EXCEPT/NOT/LEAST Questions

This type of question tends to be one of the most difficult questions in the Reading section. Let's look at these questions and figure out how to crack them.

Once again, here's our practice passage for reference.

The Exoskeleton of the Arthropod

There are more arthropods alive on Earth than there are members of any other phylum of animals. Given that not only insects and spiders but also shrimp, crabs, centipedes, and their numerous relatives are arthropods, this fact should not occasion surprise. For all their diversity, arthropods of any type share two defining characteristics: jointed legs (from which the phylum takes its name) and an exoskeleton (the recognizable hard outer shell).

Though the shell itself is made of dead tissue like that of human hair and fingernails, it is dotted with sensory cells. **These give the arthropod information about its surroundings, much as the nerve endings in human skin do.** Also like human skin, the shell protects fragile internal organs from potentially hazardous contact with the environment. It seals in precious moisture that would otherwise evaporate but permits the exchange of gases.

Its primary component is chitin, a natural polymer that contains calcium and is very similar in structure to the cellulose in wood. Chitin and proteins are secreted in the epidermis, the living tissue just below the shell, after which they bond to form a thin sheet. Each new sheet is produced so that its chitin fibers are not parallel with those directly above, which increases their combined strength.

The result is the endocuticle, a mesh of molecules that forms the lowest layer of the shell. The endocuticle is not quite tough enough for daily wear and tear. Over time, however, its molecules continue to lock together. As the endocuticle is pushed upward by the formation of new sheets by the epidermis, it becomes the middle shell layer called the exocuticle. With its molecules bonded so tightly, the exocuticle is very durable. There are points on the body where it does not form, since flexibility is needed around joints. This arrangement allows supple movement but provides armor-like protection.

➤Though strong, the chitin and protein exocuticle itself would provide a poor barrier against moisture loss. Therefore, it must be coated with lipids, which are also secreted by the epidermis. These lipids, mostly fatty acids and waxes, form the third, outermost layer of the shell. They spread over the cuticles to form a waterproof seal even in dry weather. This lipid layer gives many arthropods their distinctive luster.

Combined, the endocuticle, exocuticle, and lipid coating form a shell that provides formidable protection. The external shell has other advantages. One is that, because it has far more surface area than the internal skeleton found in vertebrates, it provides more points at which muscles can be attached. This increased number of muscles permits many arthropods to be stronger and more agile for their body size than birds or mammals. The coloration and markings of the exoskeleton can be beneficial as well. Many species of scorpion, for instance, have cuticles that contain hyaline. The hyaline is excited by ultraviolet radiation, so these scorpions glow blue-green when a black light is flashed on them. Scientists are not sure why scorpions have evolved to fluoresce this way, but the reason may be that their glow attracts insects that they can capture and eat.

Adaptive as their shell is, it leaves arthropods with at least one distinct disadvantage: The cuticle cannot expand to accommodate growth. As the animal increases in size, therefore, it must occasionally molt. The existing cuticle separates from newer, more flexible layers being secreted beneath it, gradually splits open, and can be shaken or slipped off. The new chitin and protein will harden and be provided with a fresh lipid coating, but this process can take hours or days after molting occurs. The arthropod must first take in extra air or water to swell its body to greater than its normal size. After the shell has hardened in its expanded form, the arthropod expels the air or water. It then has room for growth. But until it hardens, the new coat is tender and easily penetrated. Accordingly, the arthropod must remain in hiding. Otherwise, it risks being snapped up by a predator clever enough to take advantage of its lowered defenses.

Now, take a look at a new type of question.

14. All of the following are mentioned as benefits of the exoskeleton EXCEPT:

    (A) protection against water loss
    (B) distinctive coloration and markings
    (C) ability to take in extra air or water
    (D) armor-like protection

You'll notice this question has the word EXCEPT written in capital letters. Yet, test takers still often look for the "right" answer. For EXCEPT/NOT/LEAST questions, your task is to find the answer that is *not* mentioned. Here's how:

1. Rephrase the question, eliminating the EXCEPT/NOT/LEAST part.
2. Use the answer choices like a checklist, returning to the passage to find each one.
3. Mark each answer choice as either TRUE or FALSE based on the passage.
4. Choose the answer that's different from the other three.

Here's how it works. First, we'll rephrase the question, removing the EXCEPT part. Our new question asks

What are the benefits of an exoskeleton?

Now, we'll go through each choice, looking for evidence in the passage. Think of each choice as a lead word—scan the passage for the word or phrase, and read a few lines before and after to see if it answers the questions.

- The first choice is "protection against water loss." Go back to the passage and try to find the part that talks about "water loss." This topic appears in paragraph 5. It states that the shell forms a "waterproof seal." This means that answer choice (A) is true. Mark that on your scratch paper.
  (A)   True
- Next, check choice (B). Our lead phrase for this choice is "coloration and markings." Scan through the passage. Where does it mention this topic? Paragraph 6 says that "coloration and markings of the exoskeleton can be beneficial..." So this answer is true as well. Mark it down on your scrap paper.
  (A)   True
  (B)   True
- The third choice is "ability to take in extra air or water." Let's look through the passage for these lead words. Find them? These words show up in the final paragraph, but that paragraph is about the *disadvantages* of the shell. So this choice is false. Note this on your scrap paper.
  (A)   True
  (B)   True
  (C)   False

- Finally, let's verify our answer by checking the fourth choice, which is "armor-like protection." A quick scan of our passage reveals this phrase in the fourth paragraph. This statement is true as well. Thus, we're left with the following:
  - (A)   True
  - (B)   True
  - (C)   False
  - (D)   True
- Now all we do is pick the answer choice that is different: choice (C). It is very important to check all of the choices when doing EXCEPT/NOT/LEAST questions. Many test takers go through the choices too quickly and end up picking the answer that *is* in the passage instead of the one that *isn't*.

POE Strategies for EXCEPT/NOT/LEAST Questions

These questions are similar to detail and lead word questions. However, they are the *opposites* because you are going to *eliminate* answers that are

- **Supported by the passage:** Remember, we want the choice that is *not* supported by the passage.

Additionally, the correct answer may

- **Contain information not mentioned:** Information not found in the passage makes a good answer for these questions.
- **Use extreme language:** Extreme language is usually bad; but for these questions, it's acceptable.

EXCEPT/NOT/LEAST questions can take a little more time to answer than other types of detail or lead word questions, so make sure to do them in your second pass.

Question Type #10: Inference Questions

Here's our next question type.

11.   It can be inferred from the passage that molting

    (A)   happens regularly during the life of the arthropod

    (B)   always takes days to complete

    (C)   leaves the arthropod without its normal defense

    (D)   causes the arthropod to grow larger

Inference questions ask for a very specific type of answer. An inference is a conclusion reached based on the available evidence. For example, if a friend of yours walks in and has wet hair, you may infer that it is raining outside. That inference may or may not be true. Perhaps your friend just washed his hair or was sprayed with a hose. However, on the TOEFL, the correct inference is the answer that *must be true* based on the information in the passage.

Our approach to these questions remains the same as many other types. First, restate the question.

> What does the passage suggest about molting?

Next, use a lead word to locate the appropriate part of the passage. For this question, we'll use the word *molting*. This word shows up in the final paragraph. As we've seen with detail and lead word questions, the correct answer should be within four or five lines of the reference. However, for inference questions, you should not attempt to answer in your own words first; this is because you can't be sure which inference will be the correct response, and the answer you predict may not be close to the answer choice.

Instead, we'll follow a process similar to the one we used for EXCEPT/NOT/LEAST questions. We'll look at each answer choice and see if it is true based on the lines about molting.

- Let's start with the first choice: Go back to the paragraph about molting, and look for any information regarding how regularly it takes place. Remember to read only the lines around our lead word. Because there is no information on the regularity of molting, choice (A) must be wrong. Eliminate it.
- Now move on to the next choice: Go back to the passage, and look for evidence that molting "always takes days to complete." There is some information about time, but make sure you read carefully. The passage states that "this process can take hours or days..." But that doesn't mean that molting "always" takes days. So, eliminate choice (B).
- For the third choice, there is some indication that it is true. If you read toward the end of the paragraph, it states that the "new coat is tender and easily penetrated. Accordingly, the arthropod must remain in hiding." It took a little searching, but this is the answer we need.
- Of course, we should still look at the final answer. The fourth choice suggests that molting "causes the arthropod to grow larger." Is there any evidence for this in the passage? Answer choice (D) is supported in the passage ("As the animal increases in size, therefore, it must occasionally molt."), but the passage doesn't say that molting *causes* growth.
- So choice (C) is the best answer.

POE Strategies for Inference Questions

Inference questions require a very careful reading of the passage because the wrong answers can be very attractive. It is important to look for the following when eliminating answers:

- **Could be true:** Some answers may be true. However, this is not good enough on the TOEFL. You must be able to support the truth of the answer with the passage.
- **Extreme:** The wrong answer on inference questions will often use extreme wording. Watch out for answers that contain the following words:

> *always   never   impossible   all   none   best   worst*

- **Beyond the information:** The wrong answer on an inference question may contain some information found in the passage but make a claim or connection that is not found in the passage.

Inference questions require careful reading of both the passage and the answer choices. The right answer is usually a clever paraphrase of information in the passage. Because these questions can be very tricky, you may want to do them during your second pass.

Question Type #11: Summary Questions

The final question type on the TOEFL is the **summary** question. These questions are typically worth two points and require you to find multiple correct answers.

Here's an example of one.

15. **Directions:** An introductory sentence for a brief summary of the passage is provided below. Complete the summary by selecting the THREE answer choices that express the most important ideas in the passage. Some sentences do not belong in the summary because they express ideas that are not presented in the passage or are minor ideas in the passage. *This question is worth 2 points.*

Animals in the phylum called arthropods have shells or exoskeletons with distinctive characteristics.

-
-
-

Answer Choices	
Insects, spiders, shrimp, crabs, and centipedes are all arthropods.	The chitin in the exoskeleton is similar in chemical composition to the cellulose in wood.
The shell has three layers that protect an arthropod from injury and water loss.	Because the shell is hard, it must be discarded and replaced as the arthropod grows.
The hyaline in a scorpion's shell glows under black light because it is excited by ultraviolet radiation.	The large surface area of the shell makes possible a high number of muscles and a variety of adaptive colorations.

For this type of question, you will click and drag answer choices to add them to the summary. Fortunately, these questions always show up at the end of the section, so by the time you attack a summary question, you should have a pretty good idea of the passage's main points.

Your main task for this question is to separate *details* from *main ideas*. Use your understanding of the structure of a passage to figure out which choice is a detail and which choice is a main point. In general, details will appear in the middle of paragraphs and are often mentioned only once. Main ideas will appear at the beginning or end of paragraphs and show up throughout the passage.

Let's go through each choice and decide if it's a detail or a main idea.

- The first choice is

    Insects, spiders, shrimp, crabs, and centipedes are
    all arthropods.

Is this one of the main ideas of the passage? It's certainly mentioned in the first paragraph, but what is the majority of the passage about? If you said the exoskeleton, you are correct. Our answers should be about the exoskeleton, so let's eliminate this choice.

- Here's the second choice.

    The shell has three layers that protect an arthropod
    from injury and water loss.

This choice is more in line with what we need. The passage described the shell, and this answer summarizes the structure of the shell. Let's add it to our summary.

  - The shell has three layers that protect an arthropod
    from injury and water loss.

  -

  -

- The next choice says

    The hyaline in a scorpion's shell glows under black
    light because it is excited by ultraviolet radiation.

Is this a main idea or a detail? Where does this fact appear in the passage? Notice how it shows up in a paragraph about the benefits of the shell. That means that this fact is likely just an example of a benefit. The passage even uses the phrase "for instance" when discussing this fact. Plus, the entire passage is not about scorpions. Thus, it's a detail, not a main idea.

- Here's the next choice.

    The chitin in the exoskeleton is similar in chemical
    composition to the cellulose in wood.

Although it does talk about the exoskeleton, this choice provides a *very specific* detail about the chitin. We're looking for a *more general* description. Let's look at the other choices and see if they are better answers.

- The next choice reads

    > Because the shell is hard, it must be discarded and replaced as the arthropod grows.

This choice talks about the shell as well. It gives a good summary of the final paragraph of the passage, which talked about the disadvantages of the exoskeleton. Because the entire passage gave information on the benefits and disadvantages of the exoskeleton, we should add this choice to our list.

- The shell has three layers that protect an arthropod from injury and water loss.

- Because the shell is hard, it must be discarded and replaced as the arthropod grows.

- Here's our final option.

    > The large surface area of the shell makes possible a high number of muscles and a variety of adaptive colorations.

This choice is also part of the main idea. Notice how it differs from the previous choice about the scorpion's markings. This choice mentions two benefits, not just one. And it doesn't mention just one type of arthropod. Therefore, it belongs in the summary.

- Here are our final choices.

- The shell has three layers that protect an arthropod from injury and water loss.

- Because the shell is hard, it must be discarded and replaced as the arthropod grows.

- The large surface area of the shell makes possible a high number of muscles and a variety of adaptive colorations.

Notice how this summary matches the summaries we practiced in Core Concept: Reading. We've mentioned each of the important points from the topic sentences of the passage.

POE Strategies for Summary Questions

For these questions, eliminate answers that don't show up as key points during your initial reading of the passage. Use the structure of the passage to help eliminate answers. Remove choices that are

- **Too specific:** Watch out for choices that contain specific facts or details. Make sure you don't include examples! Remember, examples only support the main point; they don't state it.
- **Not mentioned:** Make sure the information in the choice is actually found in the passage. Some answer choices are cleverly worded to distract you.

These questions can be very difficult, but if you've been practicing the active reading strategies in this book, they should be much easier. Still, save these questions for last.

Summary: Reading

Congratulations! You've just cracked the first section of the TOEFL. Before we give you a drill to practice your new skills, let's review some of the key ideas from this chapter.

Basic Ideas

- **It's in there:** No matter how difficult the question may seem, remember that the answer is somewhere in the passage.

- **Two-pass system:** Not all questions are created equal. Do all the questions that you find easier first, and save the killer questions for last.

- **POE:** Sometimes it's easier to find the wrong answer than the right answer. Make sure you know the POE guidelines for the test.

The Approach

1. **Actively read the passage,** looking for the purpose, structure, and main idea.

2. **Attack the questions** based on question type.

3. **Find the answer** to the question in the passage.

4. **Use POE** to eliminate bad answers.

Chapter 7
Reading Practice Drills

Here are some practice reading passages. Remember to use the two-pass approach you just learned in the previous chapter. At this point, don't worry about time—just focus on getting the right answers and understanding the process. After you've completed these drills, be sure to read through the explanations of the right and wrong answers in the next chapter.

READING DRILL #1

The First Environmentalist: Rachel Carson

Rachel Louise Carson received her degrees in marine biology from the Pennsylvania College for Women and in zoology from the Johns Hopkins University. Her true calling turned out to be much broader in range than the academic study of wildlife, however. As Carson's career as a scientific writer progressed, she became interested in the effects of artificial chemicals on the natural environment. Through her published research, she was the first to direct public attention to the environmental damage caused by the indiscriminate use of pesticides in agriculture. She is thus regarded as the public figure who launched the environmentalist movement.

Upon enrolling in college, Carson had initially intended to major in English and become a journalist or novelist. Her attentiveness to presentation allowed her to convey even rather dry facts in an evocative prose style that held the attention of the general reader. **Wedded to her extensive academic training in biology, Carson's talent for expressive writing positioned her ideally to bring scientific findings about ecology to a mass audience.** She published a famous trilogy about the delicate and complex ecology of the sea, beginning with *Under the Sea-Wind*. That first volume took a large-scale approach, describing the living systems of the ocean in everyday, easily understood terms. *Under the Sea-Wind* was only a moderate commercial success, but it, along with Carson's writings for the United States Fish and Wildlife Service, set the stage for her second volume, published ten years after the first. *The Sea Around Us* made Rachel Carson a household name. It became not only a bestseller but also a National Book Award winner. In it, Carson examined more explicitly than before the effects of human action on the creatures of the ocean. The last book in the trilogy was *The Edge of the Sea,* in which Carson trained her writerly and scientific gaze on the shoreline of the East Coast to examine the endangered organisms that populated it.

➤These books established Carson as a public figure who advocated respect for the environment, but the work that would be her most lasting legacy was yet to come. She began to examine data on the effects of agricultural pesticides, spurred in part by a letter from two friends who owned a farm in Massachusetts and expressed concern that sprayed pesticides were causing harm to local wildlife. Carson's research convinced her that high exposure to pesticides such as DDT threatened not only beneficial insects and birds but also people. She put her conclusions in a landmark fourth scientific volume, *Silent Spring*. In the famous image that gave the book its title, Carson hypothesized about an ecosystem in which the calling of birds had been silenced by poison in soil and groundwater.

Carson alleged that the regulations governing use of these chemicals were inadequate, though her positions were not as extreme as they are sometimes now characterized. She did not support the outright banning of pesticides. Rather, she objected to "indiscriminate" use, which is to say, use without any thought for caution and moderation. Eventually, Carson's views were taken seriously at the highest levels of government. President John F. Kennedy's Science Advisory Committee solicited her advice on how to improve rules about pesticide use. She also testified before Congress. Through her influence, she assisted in bringing about far stricter controls on toxic chemicals such as DDT, which deteriorates slowly and thus remains in soil and groundwater for very long periods of time.

Although Carson's fame meant that she was in demand as a public speaker, she much preferred the solitude of research and writing. She employed assistants but frequently did even tedious archival research herself to avoid wasting time reviewing material with which she was already familiar. The same concern with clarity and elimination of waste characterized her writing itself. Though Carson died in 1964, two years after the publication of *Silent Spring,* that book is still frequently cited in environmental policy recommendations by analysts and regulators. Her best-selling work, it also remains a staple of high school and college science classes. Indeed, more than one major publication has deemed Carson one of the most influential figures of the twentieth century.

1. The word launched in the passage is closest in meaning to

   (A) wrote about
   (B) reorganized
   (C) began
   (D) researched

2. The author uses the word dry in the passage to indicate that the facts discussed are

   (A) not interesting
   (B) not related to marine life
   (C) not difficult to explain
   (D) available in the works of other scientists

3. Which of the sentences below best expresses the essential information in the boldfaced sentence in the passage? *Incorrect* answer choices change the meaning in important ways or leave out essential information.

   (A) Carson felt it necessary to choose between becoming a scientist and becoming a popular writer.
   (B) People were surprised at the large-scale damage Carson's writings brought to their attention.
   (C) Carson initially found it difficult to write about ecology for a mass audience.
   (D) Carson was able to popularize her views by combining her writing talent and knowledge of biology.

4. The author uses the phrase a household name to indicate that Carson

   (A) became famous
   (B) wrote very slowly
   (C) did not socialize much
   (D) was already planning her third book

5. The word trained in the passage is closest in meaning to

   (A) questioned
   (B) studied
   (C) reviewed
   (D) aimed

6. According to paragraph 3 of the passage, Carson was influenced to write *Silent Spring* by

   (A) observing the use of pesticides at her farm
   (B) a letter from friends
   (C) the public reaction to her first three books
   (D) her illnesses caused by DDT

   Paragraph 3 is marked with an arrow [➤]

7. It can be inferred from the passage that DDT is especially dangerous because

   (A) it is the most commonly used pesticide
   (B) its taste attracts birds
   (C) it does not disappear quickly
   (D) it takes a long time to kill insects

8. The "silent spring" in the title of Carson's fourth major book refers to

   (A) the long gap between her two books
   (B) people's unwillingness to speak out against pollution
   (C) the death of wildlife from agricultural chemicals
   (D) the hidden dangers of pesticides

9. The word alleged in the passage is closest in meaning to

   (A) ruled
   (B) argued
   (C) disproved
   (D) limited

10. The word indiscriminate in the passage is closest in meaning to

   (A) ineffective
   (B) uncontrolled
   (C) illegal
   (D) funded

11. Which of the following is NOT mentioned in the passage as evidence of Carson's influence on the regulation of pesticides?

   (A) She spoke before Congress.
   (B) She served on a presidential committee.
   (C) Her work is still cited by regulators.
   (D) She wrote the first set of pesticide regulations.

12. **Directions:** An introductory sentence for a brief summary of the passage is provided below. Complete the summary by selecting the THREE answer choices that express the most important ideas in the passage. Some sentences do not belong in the summary because they express ideas that are not presented in the passage or are minor ideas in the passage. *This question is worth 2 points.*

Rachel Carson was a pioneering environmentalist who helped draw public attention to the effects of human activity on wildlife.

-
-
-

Answer Choices	
Carson at first considered majoring in English and becoming a nonscientific writer.	Carson's three books about ocean ecology increasingly focused on the dangers humans posed to marine life.
The government considered Carson a valued expert and invited her input on ecological policy.	Many scientists doubted Carson's conclusions, causing her to write more books to support them.
The book *Silent Spring* has had both immediate and long-term influence on environmentalism.	Carson did much of her research by talking to people with everyday experience using pesticides.

READING DRILL #2

National Flags

➤ The flag, the most common symbol of national identity in the modern world, is also one of the most ancient. The traditional flag of fabric is still used to mark buildings, ships, and diplomatic caravans by national affiliation, but its visual design makes it adaptable for other roles as well. Most flags have a compact, rectangular shape and distinct visual symbolism. Their strong colors and geometric patterns are usually instantly recognizable even if miniaturized to less than a square centimeter. Images of flags can thus serve as identifying icons on airliners, television broadcasts, and computer displays.

Despite its simplicity, the national flag as we know it today is in no way a primitive artifact. It is, rather, the product of millennia of development in many corners of the globe. Historians believe it had two major ancestors, of which the earlier served to indicate wind direction. ■ Early human societies used very fragile shelters and boats. ■ Their food sources were similarly vulnerable to disruption. ■ Even after various grains had been domesticated, people needed cooperation from the elements to assure good harvests. For all these reasons, they feared and depended on the power of the wind, which could bring warmth from one direction and cold from another.

Ascertaining the direction of the wind using a simple strip of cloth tied to the top of a post was more reliable than earlier methods, such as watching the rising of smoke from a fire or the swaying of field grasses. The association of these prototypes of the flag with divine power was therefore a natural one. ■ Tribes began to fix long cloth flutters to the tops of totems before carrying them into battle, believing that the magical assistance of the wind would be added to the blessings of the gods and ancestors represented by the totem itself.

➤ These flutters may seem like close kin of our present-day flags, but the path through history from one to the other wanders through thousands of years and over several continents. The first known flag of a nation or ruler was unmarked: The king who established the Chou Dynasty in China (around 1000 B.C.) was reputed to have a white flag carried ahead of him. This practice may have been adopted from Egyptians even further in the past, but it was from China that it spread over trade routes through India, then across Arab lands, and finally to medieval Europe.

In Europe, the Chinese-derived flag met up with the modern flag's second ancestor, the heraldic crest. The flags used in Asia may have been differentiated by color, but they rarely featured emblems or pictures. European nobles of the medieval period had, however, developed a system of crests (symbols or insignias specific to particular families) that were commonly mounted on hard surfaces; shields to be used in battle often displayed them especially prominently.

➤ The production of these crests on flags permitted them to be used as heralds, meaning that they functioned as visual announcements that a member of an important household was present. While crests began to appear on flags as well as shields, the number of prominent families was also increasing. They required an ever greater number of combinations of stripes, crosses, flowers, and mythical animals to distinguish themselves. These survived as the basic components of flag design when small regional kingdoms were later combined into larger nation-states. They remain such for many European countries today.

Some nations, particularly those whose colors and emblems date back several hundred years, have different flags for different official uses. For example, the flag of Poland is a simple rectangle with a white upper half and red lower half. The colors themselves have been associated with Polish nationalism since the 1700s. They originated as the colors of the Piast family, which during its rule displayed a crest bearing a white eagle on a red field. Homage is paid to the Piast Dynasty in the

Polish ensign, the flag officially used at sea. Unlike the familiar plain flag flown on land, the ensign has a red shield with a white eagle centered on its upper white stripe.

1. Paragraph 1 of the passage describes the design of the typical flag as

   (A) unfamiliar to people from other countries
   (B) likely to change as technology improves
   (C) suited to many different uses
   (D) older than the country it represents

   Paragraph 1 is marked with an arrow [➤]

2. The word miniaturized in the passage is closest in meaning to

   (A) publicized
   (B) colored
   (C) made brighter
   (D) made smaller

3. The word primitive in the passage is closest in meaning to

   (A) ancient
   (B) unsophisticated
   (C) identifiable
   (D) replaceable

4. The word they in the passage refers to

   (A) grains
   (B) people
   (C) elements
   (D) harvests

5. The earliest ancestors of the flag were associated with divine power because

   (A) they were flown as high in the sky as people could reach
   (B) they were woven from valuable field grasses
   (C) they moved with the wind
   (D) tribes that flew them always won battles

6. The word fix in the passage is closest in
   meaning to

   (A)   create
   (B)   respect
   (C)   attach
   (D)   blow

7. Which of the sentences below best expresses the essential
   information in the boldfaced sentence in the passage? *Incorrect*
   answer choices change the meaning in important ways or leave
   out essential information.

   (A)   Despite the obvious similarities between the two, ancient flutters
         developed very slowly and indirectly into modern flags.
   (B)   Despite the widespread use of modern flags, flutters in the ancient style
         are still used in some parts of the world.
   (C)   Historians are slowly discovering evidence of how the flutters used on
         ancient totems developed into modern flags.
   (D)   Ancient flutters are still sometimes used instead of modern flags to
         represent a country over official journeys.

8. According to paragraph 4 of the passage, the first known national
   flag in history

   (A)   was not carried into battle
   (B)   is still used in China today
   (C)   was copied by the Egyptians
   (D)   was not colored or patterned

   Paragraph 4 is marked with an arrow [➤]

9. As discussed in the passage, a crest is

   (A)   the most important member of a household
   (B)   the color of a particular flag
   (C)   the symbol of a particular family
   (D)   a European noble

10. According to paragraph 6 of the passage, the number of flag
    designs increased because

    (A)   fewer shields were being made for battle
    (B)   nation-states were becoming larger
    (C)   artists had greater freedom in creating flags
    (D)   more families wanted their own symbols

    Paragraph 6 is marked with an arrow [➤]

11. The word them in the passage refers to

    (A) crests
    (B) families
    (C) hard surfaces
    (D) shields

12. The word components in the passage is closest in meaning to

    (A) styles
    (B) makers
    (C) countries
    (D) parts

13. The two flags of Poland mentioned in the passage differ in that

    (A) they do not use the same colors
    (B) they originally represented different families
    (C) only one is used officially
    (D) one does not have a crest

14. Look at the four squares [■] that indicate
    where the following sentence could be added to the passage.

    **Therefore, strong winds could easily tear
    roofs from houses or cause high waves that imperiled travelers.**

    Where would the sentence best fit?

    Click on a square [■] to add the sentence to
    the passage.

15. **Directions:** An introductory sentence for a brief summary of the passage is provided below. Complete the summary by selecting the THREE answer choices that express the most important ideas in the passage. Some sentences do not belong in the summary because they express ideas that are not presented in the passage or are minor ideas in the passage. *This question is worth 2 points.*

There were many historical steps in the evolution of the national flag as it's known today.

-
-
-

Answer Choices	
A Chinese king's practice of having a flag carried ahead of him spread across Asia to Europe.	Ancient tribes respected the power of the wind and began to carry totem poles with flutters for good luck in battle.
Many countries have followed Poland's example and used an eagle on their flags to symbolize strength and power.	Heraldic crests and colors combined with a standard rectangular shape to make a symbol with many uses.
Early humans lived lives that were vulnerable to disruption by natural forces.	Some flags used in Asian countries may have been colored in distinct ways.

READING DRILL #3

Salamanders and Species Names

➤When reviewing the current journals of taxonomy, the science of organizing animals into neat classifications, it is important to remember that names are a human convenience. Nature is not concerned with putting her creations into simple and objective categories. The classifications that we now have are the result of scientists' need to put some sort of order into what is a very chaotic situation. And although taxonomists have the best intentions when naming and classifying new or existing species, there are many occasions when naming a species causes quite a bit of confusion.

An excellent example of the problem with naming species is the case of *Ensatina,* a genus of salamander found in the Central Valley area of California. Central Valley is about 40 miles wide, and although salamanders do not live in the valley itself, they are found in the forests and mountains that ring the valley. At the southern tip of the valley live two distinct types of salamander—one salamander is characterized by its yellow and black spots, whereas the other is light brown in color and has no spots.

■ In biology, a species is typically defined as a group of animals that breed only with one another. ■ Thus, any two animals that can breed belong to the same species, whereas animals that are unable to breed with each other are of a different species. ■ The two Central Valley salamanders do not interbreed, which would seem to make it pretty clear that the salamanders should be classified as different species. ■

➤But there is one interesting problem with these salamanders. A number of other salamanders inhabit the ring surrounding Central Valley. Moving north along the eastern side of the valley, the salamanders have fewer and fewer blotches. At the northern end of the valley, the salamanders appear to be a mixture of the two species; these salamanders are mostly brown, but they still have visible blotches.

Now, moving south along the western end of the valley, the salamanders have blotches that are more and more pronounced. Finally, by the time the southern tip of the valley is reached, the salamanders fully resemble the yellow and black spotted species. The salamanders in effect form an almost continuous ring around the outside of the Central Valley, and although the two distinct species at the "ends" of the ring do not interbreed, the salamanders can and do breed with "the intermediates" along the ring. So although it is fairly clear that the salamanders at the ends of the ring are distinct species, what of the other salamanders found around the valley?

This situation presents quite a problem in classification. Most taxonomists have decided that the best solution is to put each of the intermediary salamanders into its own subspecies. However, this messy solution results in ten different species names for a salamander that is found only in the Central Valley. One can imagine how such a solution, applied to other species, could result in hundreds of thousands of subspecies for each species.

➤Further complicating the situation is the new evidence from genetic studies. It appears that the salamanders in Central Valley are all rather closely related, meaning that they all probably evolved from a common ancestor. A likely scenario is that the ancestral salamander species arrived at either the northern or southern tip of the valley and dispersed from there, with the offspring moving farther and farther down the eastern and western sides of the valley. In any case, the genetic evidence indicates a continuous gene flow along the Central Valley.

The case of the Central Valley salamander, sometimes called a "ring species," is not unique. The salamander shows the difficulty of attempting to place animals into neat compartments; although classification may be helpful to scientists and researchers, it is not a primary concern of the animals themselves—the salamander certainly doesn't care what species it belongs to! Still, despite the problems with the current taxonomic system, it is admittedly useful. There is simply no other consistent way to label or classify the gradations found in nature, so the use of distinct species names will continue.

1. The word convenience in the passage is closest in meaning to

    (A) comfort
    (B) support
    (C) aid
    (D) luxury

2. The word genus as used in the passage is closest in meaning to

    (A) kind
    (B) color
    (C) location
    (D) quality

3. Based on the information in paragraph 1, which of the following can be properly inferred?

    (A) Nature's creations cannot be put into simple categories.
    (B) Some scientists are concerned with sorting and arranging natural phenomena.
    (C) Scientists do not agree on the value of taxonomy.
    (D) The confusion caused by naming species is not worth the value gained from such a practice.

    Paragraph 1 is marked with an arrow [➤]

4. According to the passage, which of the following is true in the biological definition of a species?

    (A) A member of one species is unable to breed with a member of a different species.
    (B) A member of one species often lives more than 40 miles away from a member of another species.
    (C) Species classification is based on coloration and markings, such as black and yellow spots.
    (D) There is no clear definition of what a species is.

5. In paragraph 4, the author states that

    (A)   many different species of salamanders live along the Central Valley
    (B)   salamanders along the western end of the valley have fewer spots
    (C)   salamanders found at the northern end of the valley cannot interbreed
          with salamanders found at the
          southern end
    (D)   the range of salamanders found along the valley presents a difficulty

    Paragraph 4 is marked with an arrow [➤]

6. The phrase the intermediates refers to

    (A)   salamanders found outside the Central Valley ring
    (B)   distinct species of salamanders found only in the
          Central Valley
    (C)   a range of salamanders that do not fit neatly into a species classification
    (D)   salamanders found at the ends of the "ring" around the Central Valley

7. Which of the sentences below best expresses the meaning
   of the highlighted sentence in the passage? *Incorrect* answer
   choices change the meaning in important ways or leave out
   essential information.

    (A)   It is possible that all the salamanders found along the valley are
          descended from one early species.
    (B)   Salamander species are typically descended from a common ancestor.
    (C)   The ancestor of all salamander species found in the valley initially lived at
          the southern tip of the valley.
    (D)   Some theories on the emergence of salamander species focus on the
          existence of an ancestral species.

8. In paragraph 7, the author provides information about genetic
   studies to

    (A)   suggest that researchers have ignored a crucial piece
          of evidence
    (B)   support an earlier assertion about the problem
          with classification
    (C)   argue that new studies will eventually prove that the salamanders are
          part of the same species
    (D)   assert that the presence of a common ancestor is the most likely
          explanation for the different types of salamanders found in the valley

    Paragraph 7 is marked with an arrow [➤]

9. The phrase neat compartments most nearly means

   (A) clear areas
   (B) distinct groups
   (C) different times
   (D) main division

10. The word admittedly as used in the passage is closest to

    (A) precisely
    (B) literally
    (C) certainly
    (D) rarely

11. The author's opinion about species classification would best be described as

    (A) uncertain of the need for a system of species classification
    (B) dismissive toward species classification because of the many problems it creates
    (C) assured of the need for species classification despite its difficulties
    (D) optimistic that the problems with species classification will soon be overcome

12. There are four black squares [■] in the passage, indicating where the following sentence could be added.

    This definition is widely accepted by biologists and zoologists, but its application isn't always simple.

    Where would the sentence fit best?

    Click on a square [■] to add the sentence to the passage.

13. **Directions:** An introductory sentence for a brief summary of the passage is provided below. Complete the summary by selecting the THREE answer choices that express the most important ideas in the passage. Some sentences do not belong in the summary because they express ideas that are not presented in the passage or are minor ideas in the passage. *This question is worth 2 points.*

Using species classifications is a human convenience.

-
-
-

Answer Choices	
It is likely that the Central Valley salamanders were all descended from a common ancestor.	Despite the difficulties found in species classification, there is a need for it in science.
Although scientists may have a need to place animals into classes, nature is not always so easily categorized.	The Central Valley salamander and other "ring species" illustrate the difficulties in classifying animals.
Any two animals that can breed with each other are considered members of the same species.	One solution to the problem involves placing animals into subspecies, but this approach results in problems of its own.

READING DRILL #4

Solutions to Spam

▶Although it seems like the proliferation of spam—junk E-mails sent unsolicited to millions of people each day—is a recent problem, spam has been around as long as the Internet has. In fact, the first documented case of spam occurred in 1978, when a computer company sent out 400 E-mails via the Arpanet, the precursor to the modern Internet. Now, spam E-mails account for more than two-thirds of all the E-mail sent over the Internet, and for some unlucky users, spam makes up 80 percent of the messages they receive. And, despite technological innovations such as spam filters and even new legislation designed to combat spam, the problem will not go away easily.

The reason spammers (the people who and businesses that spread spam) are difficult to stop is that spam is so cost effective. It costs a spammer roughly one-hundredth of a cent to send spam, which means that a spammer can still make a profit even with an abysmally low response rate, as low as one sale per 100,000 E-mails sent. This low rate gives spammers a tremendous incentive to continue sending out millions and millions of E-mails, even if the average person never purchases anything from them. With so much at stake, spammers have gone to great lengths to avoid or defeat spam blockers and filters.

Most spam filters rely on a fairly primitive "fingerprinting" system. In this system, a program analyzes several typical spam messages and identifies common features in them. Any arriving E-mails that match these features are deleted. But the fingerprinting defense proves quite easy for spammers to defeat. To confuse the program, a spammer simply has to include a series of random characters or numbers. These additions to the spam message change its "fingerprint" and thus allow the spam to escape detection. And when programmers modify the fingerprint software to look for random strings of letters, spammers respond by including nonrandom content, such as sports scores or stock prices, which again defeats the system.

▶A second possible solution takes advantage of a computer's limited learning abilities. So-called "smart filters" use complex algorithms, which allow them to recognize new versions of spam messages. These filters may be initially fooled by random characters or bogus content, but they soon learn to identify these features. Unfortunately, spammers have learned how to avoid these smart filters as well. **The smart filter functions by looking for words and phrases that are normally used in a spam message, but spammers have learned to hide words and phrases by using numbers or other characters to stand in for letters.** For example, the word "money" might appear with a zero replacing the letter "o." Alternatively, spammers send their messages in the form of a picture or graphic, which cannot be scanned in the same way a message can.

Another spam stopper uses a proof system. With this system, a user must first verify that he or she is a person before the E-mail is sent by solving a simple puzzle or answering a question. This system prevents automated spam systems from sending out mass E-mails since computers are often unable to pass the verification tests. With a proof system in place, spam no longer becomes cost effective because each E-mail would have to be individually verified by a person before it could be sent. So far, spammers have been unable to defeat proof systems, but most E-mail users are reluctant to adopt these systems because they make sending E-mails inconvenient. ■A similar problem prevents another effective spam blocker from widespread use. ■This system involves charging a minimal fee for each E-mail sent. ■The fee, set at one penny, would appear as an electronic check included with the E-mail. ■Users can choose to waive the fee if the E-mail is from a legitimate source; however, users can collect the fee from a spammer. A fee system would most likely eliminate a great deal of spam, but unfortunately many users find such a system too intrusive and inconvenient.

➤In some ways, the battles being fought over intrusive E-mails are very much an arms race. Computer engineers will continue to devise new and more sophisticated ways of blocking spam, while spammers will respond with innovations of their own. It is unfortunate that the casualties in this technological war will be average E-mail users.

1. The word proliferation most nearly means

    (A)   addition
    (B)   spread
    (C)   diminishment
    (D)   enlargement

2. In paragraph 1, the author describes spam as

    (A)   a recent problem that affects millions of users
    (B)   totaling more than 80 percent of E-mails sent via the Internet
    (C)   a technological innovation
    (D)   unwanted messages sent to a mass audience

    Paragraph 1 is marked with an arrow [➤]

3. In the passage, the word abysmally is closest in meaning to

    (A)   unknowingly
    (B)   disastrously
    (C)   disappointingly
    (D)   extremely

4. The phrase the program refers to

    (A)   spam messages
    (B)   random characters and numbers
    (C)   a type of spam filter
    (D)   common features

5. According to paragraph 4, smart filters are superior to fingerprinting systems because smart filters

    (A)   are eventually able to recognize new versions of spam messages
    (B)   are able to learn from their mistakes
    (C)   do not need to find common features to detect spam
    (D)   are not fooled by random characters or content

    Paragraph 4 is marked with an arrow [➤]

6. Which of the choices below best expresses the meaning of the highlighted sentence in the passage? *Incorrect* answer choices change the meaning in important ways or leave out essential information.

   (A) Once spammers figured out how smart filters functioned, they were able to defeat them by changing words in the message.
   (B) Spammers can avoid smart filters by replacing certain letters in words or phrases with other characters.
   (C) Smart filters function by looking for words that have certain letters replaced by numbers.
   (D) A smart filter is easily defeated by spammers who are able to disguise words and phrases with numbers and characters.

7. The word automated as used in the passage most nearly means

   (A) computerized
   (B) automatic
   (C) costly
   (D) illegal

8. The passage mentions all of the following as hindrances to adopting verification systems EXCEPT

   (A) user reluctance
   (B) inconvenience
   (C) ineffectiveness
   (D) violation of privacy

9. The author describes the fight over spam as an arms race because

   (A) computer engineers and spammers are constantly reacting to each other's strategies
   (B) some of the techniques used by spammers may cause harm to E-mail users
   (C) there is no peaceful solution to the problem of spam
   (D) computer engineers will never be able to completely protect against spam E-mails

10. In paragraph 6, the author implies that

    (A)   most spam E-mails will eventually be blocked
    (B)   E-mail users suffer the greatest costs from the fight over spam
    (C)   there is no way to stop new and more sophisticated spam E-mails
    (D)   the battle over spam E-mails will never end

Paragraph 6 is marked with an arrow [➤]

11. There are four black squares [■] in the passage, indicating where the following sentence could be added.

Although a fee to send an E-mail seems an extreme solution, the fee is more of a verification device than an actual payment.

Click on a square [■] to add the sentence to the passage.

12. **Directions:** Select the appropriate phrases from the answer choices and match them to the type of strategy to which they relate. TWO of the answer choices will NOT be used. *This question is worth 4 points.*

Answer Choices		Spammers
Take advantage of computer learning abilities	•	
Require a verification test to send E-mails	•	
Insert random characters and numbers into messages	•	
Develop a "fingerprint" of E-mail messages	•	
Benefit from the low cost of sending E-mail messages		**Spam Blockers**
Require users to include a small payment with each E-mail	•	
Rely on the convenience of E-mail	•	
Use automated systems	•	
Do not want to be inconvenienced when sending E-mails	•	

Chapter 8
Reading Practice
Answers and Explanations

READING DRILL #1

1.   **C**   This is a *vocabulary in context* question. Go back to the passage and read a few lines before the shaded word to try to come up with your own word to replace the one in the question. The passage tells us that

> Through her published research, she was the first to direct public attention to the environmental damage caused by the indiscriminate use of pesticides in agriculture. She is thus regarded as the public figure who _____ the environmentalist movement.

The clue is that she was the "first to direct public attention to the environmentalist movement." Thus, a good word for the blank would be *started* or *began*. Here's why the other answer choices are incorrect.
   - There is no evidence for choice (B), "reorganized," so eliminate it.
   - Although it is true that she was a science writer, the passage doesn't say she "wrote about" the environmentalist movement, so (A) is incorrect.
   - Similarly, although she researched scientific issues, she didn't research the movement itself, so choice (D) is wrong as well.

2.   **A**   Question 2 is another *vocabulary in context* question. Return to the passage and read a few lines before and after the word in question.

> Upon enrolling in college, Carson had initially intended to major in English and become a journalist or novelist. Her attentiveness to presentation allowed her to convey even rather ____ facts in an evocative prose style that held the attention of the general reader.

In this case, the clues are that Carson could write in a way that "held the attention of the general reader." The words *even rather* mean that the facts do not usually hold the attention of people. So our word for the blank may be *boring* or *uninteresting*. Here's why the other answer choices are incorrect.
   - There is no support for answer choice (B): The sentences do not talk about marine life.
   - Additionally, the lines talk about Carson's ability to write, not explain, so choice (C) should be eliminated.
   - Finally, no mention is made of other scientists, so eliminate answer choice (D).

3.   **D**   This is a *paraphrase* question. Remember to trim the fat on these questions. Here's the sentence we have to work with.

> Wedded to her extensive academic training in biology, Carson's talent for expressive writing positioned her ideally to bring scientific findings about ecology to a mass audience.

Let's get rid of some of the modifiers.

> ~~Wedded to her extensive academic training in biology,~~ Carson's talent ~~for expressive writing~~ positioned her ~~ideally~~ to bring scientific findings ~~about ecology~~ to a mass audience.

So the sentence is stating basically that Carson had the talent to bring science to a large audience. Here's why the other answer choices are incorrect.

- Answer choice (A) says Carson had to choose between being a writer and a scientist, but that is not stated at all in this sentence.
- Choice (B) is about how people *reacted* to her findings, not Carson's ability to bring science to the people so eliminate this choice.
- Finally, choice (C) states that Carson found it hard to write for a mass audience, but this sentence states the *opposite*.

Remember to answer questions of this type during your second pass, especially if you're having trouble understanding the sentence.

4. **A** Here we have another *vocabulary in context* question. This one asks about a phrase instead of a single word, but our approach is still the same. Let's look at a few lines from the passage.

> *The Sea Around Us* made Rachel Carson _____.
> It became not only a best-seller but also a National Book Award winner.

The sentence tells us that the book was a best-seller and an award winner. What sort of word would make sense in the blank? Even if you are unable to come up with a good word for the blank, you can often figure out if the word should be positive or negative. In this case, we need a positive word. Here's why the other answer choices are incorrect.
- We can eliminate answers (B) and (C) because these choices are not very positive.
- That leaves us with either (A) or (D). Because there is no information about Carson planning her next book, (D) should be eliminated.

5. **D** Here's another *vocabulary in context* question, and this one is kind of tough. However, we can still use Process of Elimination (POE) to help us out. Let's look at the following lines from the passage.

> The last book in the trilogy was *The Edge of the Sea,* in which Carson _____ her writerly and scientific gaze on the shoreline of the East Coast to examine the endangered organisms that populated it.

It seems as if the blank is referring to Carson's "gaze." According to the sentence, what did she do with her gaze? She focused it on the shoreline. So we want a word that means something like *focused*. Of the choices, only "aimed" is close. Here's why the other answer choices are incorrect.
- Even if you were unable to come up with a word for the sentence, you should still be able to eliminate choice (A). Nothing in the sentence says she "questioned" anything.
- Choice (C) can be eliminated for the same reason. There is nothing in the sentence to suggest that she "reviewed" something.
- That leaves you with choices (B) and (D). Answer (B) is a good trap answer because *studied* is very close to the word *examine*, which does appear in the sentence. However, if you are going to guess on the TOEFL, it's a good strategy to avoid answers that seem too easy or obvious.

6. **B** This question is a *detail* question. Make sure you rephrase the question first so you know what you're looking for in the passage. A good paraphrase of this question would be

> What influenced Carson to write *Silent Spring*?

The question helpfully told us that the answer is somewhere in paragraph 3, so let's go back and look for it.

She began to examine data on the effects of agricultural pesticides, spurred in part by a letter from two friends who owned a farm in Massachusetts and expressed concern that sprayed pesticides were causing harm to local wildlife. Carson's research convinced her that high exposure to pesticides such as DDT threatened not only beneficial insects and birds but also people. She put her conclusions in a landmark fourth scientific volume, *Silent Spring*.

Try to answer in your own words before returning to the choices. According to these lines, what influenced Carson? It appears that the letter from two friends impacted her. This information should lead us to answer choice (B). Here's why the other answer choices are incorrect.

- Choice (A) is wrong because it states that Carson observed pesticides at "her" farm, but the passage states that the farm belongs to her friends.
- Eliminate choice (C) because it talks about public reaction, but that topic doesn't appear in this paragraph.
- Choice (D) is incorrect because the passage does not state that Carson was sick.

7. **C** Question 7 asks us to make an inference about DDT. Use DDT as your lead word and return to the passage. There are two places in the passage that refer to DDT. Here's the first.

Carson's research convinced her that high exposure to pesticides such as DDT threatened not only beneficial insects and birds but also people. She put her conclusions in a landmark fourth scientific volume, *Silent Spring*.

However, this part of the passage doesn't answer the question of why DDT is especially dangerous. If you are unable to answer the question in your own words after reading a portion of the passage, look for another part of the passage that also contains the lead word. DDT is mentioned again in the following paragraph:

Through her influence, she assisted in bringing about far stricter controls on toxic chemicals such as DDT, which deteriorates slowly and thus remains in soil and groundwater for very long periods of time.

This part of the passage seems to be more helpful. It states that DDT deteriorates "slowly and thus remains in soil...for very long periods of time," which matches answer choice (C). Here's why the other answer choices are incorrect.

- Watch out for answer choice (A), which states that DDT is the "most" used pesticide. That is an extreme answer and should be eliminated on an inference question.
- There is no mention of the information in choices (B) or (D).

8. **C** Here we have a *reference* question. If we rephrase this one, it asks the following:

To what does the phrase *silent spring* refer?

Once again, we'll use a lead word to help us find our answer. Go back to the passage and look for the phrase *silent spring*. Look at this part of the passage.

She put her conclusions in a landmark fourth scientific volume, *Silent Spring*. In the famous image that gave the book its title, Carson hypothesized about an ecosystem in which the calling of birds had been silenced by poison in soil and groundwater.

Thus, based on these lines, (C) is the best answer. Here's why the other answer choices are incorrect.

- The information mentioned in choice (A) appears earlier in the passage, but it is not related to this question.
- Choice (B) may seem to be common sense, but there is no support for it in the passage.
- Choice (D) is wrong as well; there is no mention of "hidden" dangers in reference to the title of Carson's book.

9. **B** Here's another *vocabulary in context* question. Let's go back to the passage and find some clues. Take a look at the following lines:

> Carson _____ that the regulations governing use of these chemicals were inadequate, though her positions were not as extreme as they are sometimes now characterized. She did not support the outright banning of pesticides.

These lines talk about Carson's "positions" and state that she did "not support" banning pesticides. Therefore, we need a word for the blank that is related to these words. You may have come up with a word such as *believed* or *thought*. Looking at the answer choices, only choice (B) is close to these words. Here's why the other answer choices are incorrect.
- Based on the sentence and the rest of the passage at which we've looked, it's clear that Carson is in no position to make a ruling, so (A) is out as well.
- There is no evidence that Carson disproved anything, so eliminate choice (C).
- She did not limit something, so (D) must be wrong.

10. **B** On some *vocabulary in context* questions, you'll see that the author does you a favor by actually defining a word for you. Usually, when this occurs, the definition will be set off by commas and come directly after the word in question. The lines below are an example.

> She did not support the outright banning of pesticides. Rather, she objected to "indiscriminate" use, which is to say, use without any thought for caution and moderation.

Notice how the definition follows right after the highlighted word. In this context, *indiscriminate* means "without any thought for caution and moderation." Of course, if you're still unsure, POE is very helpful. Here's how POE can help you identify why the other answer choices are incorrect.
- There are no words about the effectiveness of the pesticides, so choice (A) can't be right.
- You may be tempted to pick (C), but remember to always find proof for your answer. Nowhere does it say that using pesticides are against the law.
- Likewise, nowhere does the passage mention spending money for pesticides, so eliminate (D).

11. **D** Remember for an *EXCEPT/NOT/LEAST* question to go through the answer choices one by one and see if you find evidence for them in the passage. If you can find evidence, then mark the answer as "true."
(A)   True: "She also testified before Congress."
(B)   True: "President John F. Kennedy's Science Advisory Committee solicited her advice on how to improve rules about pesticide use."
(C)   True: "...that book is still frequently cited in environmental policy recommendations by analysts and regulators."
(D)   False: There is no evidence of this in the passage.

12.   This final *summary* question requires you to work with the main idea of the passage. As we've learned, the main idea appears throughout the passage; use the active reading strategies discussed earlier to find it. For this type of question, avoid picking answers that refer to specific details. Here are the correct answers.

> **Rachel Carson was a pioneering environmentalist who helped draw public attention to the effects of human activity on wildlife.**
>
> - Carson's three books about ocean ecology increasingly focused on the dangers humans posed to marine life.
> - The book *Silent Spring* has had both immediate and long-term influence on environmentalism.
> - The government considered Carson a valued expert and invited her input on ecological policy.

Each of the correct answers is somehow related to the initial boldfaced statement. The first correct response refers to the effects of "human activity on wildlife," and the second and third refer to Carson's environmental influence.

For this question, it is helpful to look at the wrong answers. Here's the first one that we eliminated.

> Carson at first considered majoring in English and becoming a nonscientific writer.

This is a detail mentioned in the paragraph, but it is not related to the summary, which focuses on Carson as a "pioneering environmentalist who helped draw public attention to the effects of human activity on wildlife."

Let's look at another incorrect answer choice.

> Many scientists doubted Carson's conclusions, causing her to write more books to support them.

This choice mentions scientists doubting Carson's conclusions, which doesn't match the summary. Look to eliminate answers that are opposite of the tone of the summary.

Here's the last incorrect answer choice.

> Carson did much of her research by talking to people with everyday experience using pesticides.

Once again, we have a specific detail. Eliminate this choice because it doesn't touch on the main themes of environmentalism or drawing people's attention to the problem. Instead, it focuses on research methods.

READING DRILL #2

1.   **C**   Our first question is a *detail* question. Return to the first paragraph and look for the information about the "design of the typical flag."

> The traditional flag of fabric is still used to mark buildings, ships, and diplomatic caravans by national affiliation, but its visual design makes it adaptable for other roles as well.

This matches nicely with answer choice (C). Here's why the other answer choices are incorrect.

- Choice (A) is wrong; if anything, the passage states that flags are "instantly recognizable."
- There is no mention of flags changing with technology, so eliminate choice (B).
- Choice (D) states that the flag is older than the country it represents, but this is beyond the information in the passage. The passage only states that flags are an "ancient" symbol.

2. **D** For this *vocabulary in context* question, let's look at the following lines:

> Their strong colors and geometric patterns are usually instantly recognizable even if _____ to less than a square centimeter. Images of flags can thus serve as identifying icons on airliners, television broadcasts, and computer displays.

A good word for the blank may be something like *reduced* because the flag is "less than a square centimeter" and can fit on "television broadcasts" and "computer displays." Only answer choice (D) fits this meaning. Here's why the other answer choices are incorrect.

- Answer choice (A) is a trap answer. Be careful not to add your own interpretation to the passage.
- Although you may think that putting the flag on an airliner or a computer is a form of publicity, the passage doesn't state that. There is no support for either answer (B) or (C).

3. **B** Here's another *vocabulary in context* question. Look at the following sentences from the passage:

> Despite its simplicity, the national flag as we know it today is in no way a _____ artifact. It is, rather, the product of millennia of development in many corners of the globe.

This sentence has some good context clues. The first sentence says *despite its simplicity*, which means the shaded word should have a meaning close to *simplicity*. Also, the next line states that the flag is "the product of...development..." which means a good word for the blank could be *simple* or *undeveloped*. Often on vocabulary questions, the right answer is found in the text. Here's why the other answer choices are incorrect.

- Choice (A) is the trap answer. One way of avoiding it is to notice that *ancient* shows up earlier in the passage, in the first line. Remember that for vocabulary questions, you should be looking at only the two or three lines closest to the word you're being questioned about. Therefore, if you see a word that appears outside of that range, it is probably a trap answer.
- Choice (C) is similar to choice (A) in that the first paragraph mentions how easy it is to identify a flag, but that information is not relevant to this sentence.
- There is no support for answer choice (D).

4. **B** This *reference* question asks us to find the word to which a pronoun refers. Here are the sentences in question.

> Even after various grains had been domesticated, people needed cooperation from the elements to assure good harvests. For all these reasons, they feared and depended on the power of the wind, which could bring warmth from one direction and cold from another.

For a pronoun reference, it is sometimes helpful to "trim the fat." Let's get rid of some of the extra information.

~~Even after various grains had been domesticated,~~ people needed cooperation from the elements to assure good harvests. ~~For all these reasons,~~ they feared and depended on the power of the wind~~, which could bring warmth from one direction and cold from another.~~

Based on this, who "feared and depended on the power of wind"? It must be the "people" from the first sentence. It wouldn't make sense for any of the other answers to fear and depend on wind.

5. **C** Make sure you rephrase the question first. This is a *detail* question that asks.

Why were flags associated with divine power?

Look in the passage for the phrase *divine power*. Here are the lines we need.

> Ascertaining the direction of the wind using a simple strip of cloth tied to the top of a post was more reliable than earlier methods, such as watching the rising of smoke from a fire or the swaying of field grasses. The association of these prototypes of the flag with divine power was therefore a natural one. ■ Tribes began to fix long cloth flutters to the tops of totems before carrying them into battle, believing that the magical assistance of the wind would be added to the blessings of the gods and ancestors represented by the totem itself.

From these lines, it seems that there is a connection between the wind and divine power, hence choice (C). Here's why the other answer choices are incorrect.

- Look for extreme wording in answers, such as in choices (A) and (D). The first choice says flags were flown "as high as people could reach" whereas (D) says that tribes with flags "always won" battles. These concepts are not supported in the passage.
- There is no mention of "valuable" field grasses, as in choice (B).

6. **C** The same lines will help us with this *lead word* question. The first line tells us that tribes used a "simple strip of cloth tied to the top of a post." This matches with the sentence "Tribes began to ____ long cloth flutters to the tops of totems." Thus, a good word for the blank may be *tie*. That makes (C) the best choice. The other answers are tempting, but they do not relate to the shaded word.

7. **A** Question 7 is a *paraphrase* question. Here's the boldfaced sentence.

> These flutters may seem like close kin of our present-day flags, but the path through history from one to the other wanders through thousands of years and over several continents.

This sentence doesn't have a lot of fat to trim, so POE may be a good strategy here.

- Start with the first part of the sentence and find the subject—it's referring to flags. Therefore, we can eliminate choice (C), which is about historians, not flags.
- Now look at the second part of the sentence. It says the path "through history…wanders through thousands of years and…several continents." Eliminate answers that bring in new information not related to these terms. Choice (D) mentions *official journeys*, which is not part of the sentence. Eliminate it.
- Choice (B) states that ancient flags are "still used in some parts of the world." Nothing about that appears in the sentence, so the answer must be (A).

8.   **D**   First rephrase the question, which asks about a *detail* from the passage. It asks us

What do we know about the first known flag in history?

Return to paragraph 4 and read these lines.

> The first known flag of a nation or ruler was unmarked: The king who established the Chou Dynasty in China (around 1000 B.C.) was reputed to have a white flag carried ahead of him.

Thus, the flag was unmarked, which makes choice (D) the best. You may have noticed that the answer to reading questions on the TOEFL are often very close to the lead word or line reference provided in the question. Remembering this will help you avoid many trap answers. Notice how the other answers are not mentioned at all in the relevant line, making them all easy to eliminate.

9.   **C**   This *vocabulary in context* question asks "What is a crest?" Let's look for the word "crest" in the passage. We find it in the following lines:

> In Europe, the Chinese-derived flag met up with the modern flag's second ancestor, the heraldic crest. The flags used in Asia may have been differentiated by color, but they rarely featured emblems or pictures. European nobles of the medieval period had, however, developed a system of crests (symbols or insignias specific to particular families) that were commonly mounted on hard surfaces; shields to be used in battle often displayed them especially prominently.

The first line tells us that the crest was the flag's "second ancestor." However, that is not mentioned in the answer choices, so keep reading. The next mention of crests states that nobles had "developed a system of crests (symbols or insignias specific to particular families)...." This information is what we need. Here's why the other answer choices are incorrect.
   - Answers (A) and (D) don't make sense because they state that the crest is a person instead of an object.
   - Answer (B) is wrong because it refers to flags, not crests.

10.   **D**   We know the answer to this *detail* question is somewhere in paragraph 6, so let's find it. The question asks

Why did the number of flag designs increase?

Take a look at the following lines, which mention the word "increasing":

> While crests began to appear on flags as well as shields, the number of prominent families was also increasing. They required an ever greater number of combinations of stripes, crosses, flowers, and mythical animals to distinguish themselves. These survived as the basic components of flag design when small regional kingdoms were later combined into larger nation-states. They remain such for many European countries today.

These lines state that there were more families, and they needed an "ever greater number of combinations of stripes, crosses, flowers, and mythical animals to distinguish themselves." Therefore, choice (D) must be correct. Here's why the other answer choices are incorrect.
   - Answer choice (A) states the opposite of what the passage says.
   - Although it is true that kingdoms were combined into "larger" nation-states, this doesn't answer the question of why flag designs increased, which eliminates choice (B).

- Finally, eliminate choice (C) because there is no mention of artists having greater freedom.

11. **A** This is another *pronoun reference* question. Let's look at the passage excerpt again.

> European nobles of the medieval period had, however, developed a system of crests (symbols or insignias specific to particular families) that were commonly mounted on hard surfaces; shields to be used in battle often displayed _____ especially prominently.

Try to put your own word in the blank. According to the sentence, what is being "displayed"? It must be the crests. It wouldn't make sense for the other choices to be displayed.

12. **D** Question 12 is a more typical *vocabulary in context* question. Again, let's look at the passage excerpt.

> They required an ever greater number of combinations of stripes, crosses, flowers, and mythical animals to distinguish themselves. These survived as the basic _____ of flag design when small regional kingdoms were later combined into larger nation-states.

What word would fit in the blank? We need a word that would mean *stripes, crosses, flowers, and mythical animals* because these are the items that are referred to by the sentence. A good choice for the shaded portion may be *things* or *items*, and choice (D) comes closest to that. Here's why the other answer choices are incorrect.

- Answers (B) and (C) don't make sense; the sentence says "these survived...," which must refer to the things in the previous sentence.
- Choice (A) may be tempting, but the sentence refers to individual parts of the flags, not the overall style.

13. **D** Start by taking a moment to understand what this *detail* question is asking you to find.

How do the two flags of Poland differ?

Go back to the final passage and read about the two flags of Poland, looking for something different between them.

> For example, the flag of Poland is a simple rectangle with a white upper half and red lower half. The colors themselves have been associated with Polish nationalism since the 1700s. They originated as the colors of the Piast family, which during its rule displayed a crest bearing a white eagle on a red field. Homage is paid to the Piast Dynasty in the Polish ensign, the flag officially used at sea. Unlike the familiar plain flag flown on land, the ensign has a red shield with a white eagle centered on its upper white stripe.

One difference mentioned in the passage is that one flag is flown at sea and one on land; however, that difference is not one of our choices. If you're not sure what the answer is based on your reading, don't forget the importance of POE. Here's how to use POE to determine why the other answer choices are incorrect.

- Answer (A) says the two flags don't use the same colors, but that is incorrect—they both use red and white, according to the passage.

- The next choice says that the flags represented different families. Be careful on this one. The passage states the flag used at sea represents the Piast Dynasty, but there is no mention of any other family. So eliminate choice (B).
- Choice (C) must be wrong as well because the passage doesn't state that the flag used on land isn't the official flag.

Therefore, we're left with choice (D). The sea flag, according to the passage, has "a red shield with a white eagle," which is "unlike the plain flag flown on land."

14. This is a *sentence insertion* question. Recall that for this question type, you have to look at the sentences before and after the black squares (■) to try to match the information in those sentences with the new sentence. Here's the sentence we are going to add.

> **Therefore, strong winds could easily tear roofs from houses or cause high waves that imperiled travelers.**

Now we'll check each of the potential insertion places.

> Historians believe it had two major ancestors, of which the earlier served to indicate wind direction. **Therefore, strong winds could easily tear roofs from houses or cause high waves that imperiled travelers.** Early human societies used very fragile shelters and boats.

How well do these sentences match? Not very well, as you can see. The boldface sentence talks about strong winds tearing off roofs, but the first sentence doesn't talk about houses at all. The second sentence does, but it doesn't make sense to provide a detail about the houses before introducing the idea. So, let's look at the next black square.

> Early human societies used very fragile shelters and boats. **Therefore, strong winds could easily tear roofs from houses or cause high waves that imperiled travelers.** Their food sources were similarly vulnerable to disruption.

Now look at how well these sentences match. The first sentence introduces "fragile shelters and boats," which matches with the boldfaced sentence's mention of "houses" and "high waves." And the second sentence says that the "food sources were similarly vulnerable," which links the ideas of dangers encountered by the early human ancestors. Thus, the second square is our choice.

15. The final question of the group is a *summary* question. From the previous questions and our initial reading of the passage, you should have a pretty good sense of the main idea. Use this to help you eliminate answers. Here's the completed table.

> There were many historical steps in the evolution of the national flag as it's known today.
>
> - Ancient tribes respected the power of the wind and began to carry totem poles with flutters for good luck in battle.
> - A Chinese king's practice of having a flag carried ahead of him spread across Asia to Europe.
> - Heraldic crests and colors combined with a standard rectangular shape to make a symbol with many uses.

The first sentence refers to the "steps" in the development of the flag, and each of these three choices gives one of the steps.

Looking at the wrong answers is helpful as well.
- "Early humans lived lives that were vulnerable to disruption by natural forces" doesn't mention flags at all, so you should eliminate it.
- "Many countries have followed Poland's example and used an eagle on their flags to symbolize strength and power" is mentioned as an example, not a main part of the passage. Remember to eliminate choices that refer to specific details.
- "Some flags used in Asian countries may have been colored in distinct ways" is just a minor detail. Eliminate it.

READING DRILL #3

1.   **C**   This *vocabulary in context* question requires us to look at the following lines:

> When reviewing the current journals of taxonomy, the science of organizing animals into neat classifications, it is important to remember that names are a human _____ _____. Nature is not concerned with putting her creations into simple and objective categories.

Based on these lines, it appears that although nature doesn't put animals into "simple and objective categories," humans do. So our word for the blank should be something that has to do with this idea of making things simple. We may use the word *help* or *assistance*. Choice (C) is the closest match to this word. Here's why the other answer choices are incorrect.
- Choices (A) and (D) are similar in meaning to the word *convenience*, but they don't make sense in this context. Nothing in the sentence indicates that the names comfort anything or are luxurious.
- Similarly, there is no evidence that the names support anything, so eliminate choice (B).

2.   **A**   On this *vocabulary in context* question, you may have to read a few more lines than you are accustomed to. Let's look at the passage.

> An excellent example of the problem with naming species is the case of *Ensatina,* a _____ of salamander found in the Central Valley area of California. Central Valley is about 40 miles wide, and although salamanders do not live in the valley itself, they are found in the forests and mountains that ring the valley. At the southern tip of the valley live two distinct types of salamander....

For this question, you may be able to figure out the answer right away if you know the word *species*. If not, don't give up! Read a few more lines, and you'll see that the passage refers to "two distinct types of salamander." This is to what the blank refers. Another way of approaching this question is with POE. Here's how to use POE to determine why the other answer choices are incorrect.
- There is no mention of the color of the salamanders or the quality, so eliminate (B) and (D).
- Answer choice (C) doesn't make sense either because you wouldn't say a "location" of salamander.

3. **B**   This is an *inference* question. What makes this question a little more difficult is that there is no lead word or line reference to help us find the answer. In such a situation, you have two options. The first is to read the entire passage to try to answer the question based on your reading. A second approach involves using the answer choices to guide your reading. Here's the first paragraph of the passage.

> When reviewing the current journals of taxonomy, the science of organizing animals into neat classifications, it is important to remember that names are a human convenience. Nature is not concerned with putting her creations into simple and objective categories. The classifications that we now have are the result of scientists' need to put some sort of order into what is a very chaotic situation. And although taxonomists have the best intentions when naming and classifying new or existing species, there are many occasions when naming a species causes quite a bit of confusion.

Using the second approach to answering this question, let's look at each answer choice.
- Start with answer choice (A) and look for evidence that nature's creations "cannot" be put into simple categories. The passage does mention something that is fairly similar to this idea, but on inference questions, you have to read very carefully. The passage only says that nature is "not concerned" with putting animals into categories, not that they "cannot" be put into categories. Eliminate this choice.
- For answer choice (C), we should try to find evidence of what scientists believe. The only thing the first paragraph says about scientists is that they have a "need to put some sort of order into…a very chaotic situation." That's not the same as answer (C), so eliminate it.
- With answer choice (D), look for the part of the paragraph that talks about the "confusion caused" by taxonomy. This phrase appears near the end of the paragraph, but nowhere does it say that the difficulties outweigh the value of classification.
- Answer (B) is correct because the passage says that taxonomy is the "science of organizing animals" and that there is a "scientists' need to put some sort of order" into the system.

4. **A**   This is a *lead word* question. If you find the part of the passage that talks about the "biological definition of a species," you'll find the answer to this question. Recall that the questions are arranged in order, roughly based on the passage. Therefore, because this is an early question, focus your efforts toward the beginning of the passage. Here are the lines we need.

> ■ In biology, a species is typically defined as a group of animals that breed only with one another. ■ Thus, any two animals that can breed belong to the same species, whereas animals that are unable to breed with each other are of a different species. ■

As we can see from these lines, a species is a group of animals that "breed only with one another." Therefore, (A) is the best choice. Here's why the other answer choices are incorrect.
- Answer choices (B) and (C) both refer to information that is contained in the previous paragraph. Because the lead word is in the third paragraph, we should only be reading that paragraph.
- Answer choice (D) is contradicted by the third paragraph.

5. **D**   This is a *reference* question. We need to return to paragraph 4 and see what point the author makes in it. Here's the paragraph.

➤But there is one interesting problem with these salamanders. A number of other salamanders inhabit the ring surrounding Central Valley. Moving north along the eastern side of the valley, the salamanders have fewer and fewer blotches. At the northern end of the valley, the salamanders appear to be a mixture of the two species; these salamanders are mostly brown but still have visible blotches.

Let's use POE to eliminate some of the answer choices.

- Answer choice (A) is wrong because although the lines say there are "a number of other salamanders," they do not say there is a number of different "species."
- Choice (B) is a good trap for test takers who don't return to the passage to verify their answers. According to these lines, it is the salamanders along the *eastern* side of the valley, not the western, that have fewer spots.
- There is no mention of the breeding habits of salamanders in this paragraph, so eliminate (C).
- That leaves (D) as our answer, based on the first line of the paragraph.

6. **C** This *reference* question is similar to questions that ask to what a pronoun refers. You should know the drill by now. Here are the lines to focus on.

The salamanders in effect form an almost continuous ring around the outside of the Central Valley, and although the two distinct species at the "ends" of the ring do not interbreed, the salamanders can and do breed with _____ along the ring.

With what must the salamanders breed? Other salamanders, hopefully! And based on these lines, which salamanders are they? Because the two species at the "ends" of the ring "do not interbreed," the ones not at the ends must do so. Here's why the other answer choices are incorrect.

- Eliminate choice (A) because the passage doesn't mention any salamanders "outside" of the Central Valley.
- You can also eliminate answer choice (B) because the passage never states that the salamanders live only in the Central Valley.
- Answer choice (D) is the opposite of what we need; the salamanders at the ends of the ring do not interbreed.

7. **A** This is a *paraphrase* question. Let's look at the highlighted sentence to try to find the important parts.

A likely scenario is that the ancestral salamander species arrived at either the northern or southern tip of the valley and dispersed from there, with the offspring moving farther and farther down the eastern and western sides of the valley.

The first part of the sentence says that "the ancestral salamander species arrived at the...valley." The second part states the "offspring" moved down the "eastern and western sides of the valley." Answer choice (A) mentions both of these important points. Here's why the other answer choices are incorrect.

- Answer choice (B) is wrong because it doesn't mention anything about the valley; it just talks about salamanders in general.
- Answer choice (C) is wrong because the sentence doesn't say that the ancestors definitely lived in the southern part. It could have been the northern or southern tip, according to the sentence.
- Answer choice (D) is wrong because it is about "theories," not salamanders.

8. **B** Make sure you rephrase this *lead word* question before returning to the passage. This question is asking the following:

Why does the author provide information about genetic studies?

Using the phrase *genetic studies* as your lead word, you should find your answer in the following lines:

> ➤ Further complicating the situation is the new evidence from genetic studies. It appears that the salamanders in Central Valley are all rather closely related, meaning that they all probably evolved from a common ancestor.

Based on these lines, it appears that the author mentions the genetic studies because they "further complicate" the situation. Therefore, answer choice (B) makes most sense. Here's why the other answer choices are incorrect.

- Eliminate choice (A) because there is no suggestion that evidence was "ignored."
- The passage never proves that the salamanders are part of the same species, so choice (C) must be wrong.
- Choice (D) is wrong because the lines do not state that a common ancestor is the "most likely" explanation for the situation.

9. **B** This *vocabulary in context* question asks you to find the meaning of two words instead of one. Don't worry, however, because our technique is still the same. Look at these lines from the passage.

> The salamander shows the difficulty of attempting to place animals into _____; although classification may be helpful to scientists and researchers, it is not a primary concern of the animals themselves—the salamander certainly doesn't care what species it belongs to!

Based on what we've read, what do the scientists try to place animals into? Our word may be *species* or *classes*. These words match best with choice (B). Here's why the other answer choices are incorrect.

- Choice (A) doesn't work with these sentences. There are no "clear areas" in these sentences.
- Similarly, choice (D) doesn't work with these sentences: The scientists aren't trying to divide up the animals.
- Choice (C) refers to time periods, which are also not mentioned in these lines. Eliminate it.

10. **C** Take a look at the following lines to answer this *vocabulary in context* question:

> Still, despite the problems with the current taxonomic system, it is _____ useful. There is simply no other consistent way to label or classify the gradations found in nature, so the use of distinct species names will continue.

The sentence says that "despite the problems," the system is the only "consistent way to label or classify." Our word for the blank should support the idea that the system works. You may not be able to come up with a good word for the blank, but you can use POE.

- First eliminate choice (D) because it is a negative word.
- For answer choice (A), can you find any words in these lines that correspond to the word *precisely*? No. So, eliminate choice (A).
- Similarly, there is no support that the shaded word means *literally*, which is choice (B).
- Only answer choice (C) works.

11. **C** This *inference* question asks for the author's general opinion about species classification. Use your understanding of the main idea to try to answer in your own words. Based on the passage, the author states that there are problems with species classification, but it is still useful. This makes (C) the best answer. Here's why the other answer choices are incorrect.
- Choice (A) is wrong because in the last paragraph, the author states that a classification system is "useful."
- Answer choice (B) is too negative; the author talks about some positive aspects of species classification.
- Answer (D) is incorrect because the author never states that the problems will soon be solved.

12. Once again, you are asked to add a sentence to the passage (this is a *sentence insertion* question). Here is the sentence we need to add.

> **This definition is widely accepted by biologists and zoologists, but its application isn't always simple.**

Let's check the sentences before and after the black squares (■) for a match.

Look at the first option.

> At the southern tip of the valley live two distinct types of salamander—one salamander is characterized by its yellow and black spots, whereas the other is light brown in color and has no spots. **This definition is widely accepted by biologists and zoologists, but its application isn't always simple.** In biology, a species is typically defined as a group of animals that breed only with one another.

This isn't a very good match. The first sentence talks about color and spots, but the boldfaced sentence mentions a definition. The second sentence doesn't have any "application" of the definition.

Let's move on to the next choice.

> In biology, a species is typically defined as a group of animals that breed only with one another. **This definition is widely accepted by biologists and zoologists, but its application isn't always simple.** Thus, any two animals that can breed belong to the same species, while animals that are unable to breed with one another are of a different species.

In this case, the first sentence does match well with the "definition" mentioned in the highlighted sentence. However, the problem is with the second sentence. The sentence we are trying to add talks about some "application" of the definition, but there is nothing in the second sentence that corresponds to this.

Here's the third choice.

> Thus, any two animals that can breed belong to the same species, whereas animals that are unable to breed with one another are of a different species. **This definition is widely accepted by biologists and zoologists, but its application isn't always simple.** The two Central Valley salamanders do not interbreed, which would seem to make it pretty clear that the salamanders should be classified as different species.

Here, the first sentence gives a definition of a species, which matches with the beginning of the highlighted sentence. And the second sentence introduces the salamanders, which present a problem with using the species definition. This is the place where the highlighted sentence belongs, but let's look at the last choice to be sure.

> The two Central Valley salamanders do not interbreed, which would seem to make it pretty clear that the salamanders should be classified as different species. **This definition is widely accepted by biologists and zoologists, but its application isn't always simple.** But there is one interesting problem with these salamanders.

Here, the highlighted sentence comes too late in the paragraph. It refers to the definition that was introduced prior to the discussion, and therefore, its placement here does not make sense.

13.　　Now we have to do our final *summary*. This is the correctly completed summary.

> **Using species classifications is a human convenience.**
>
> - Although scientists may have a need to place animals into classes, nature is not always so easily categorized.
> - The Central Valley salamander and other "ring species" illustrate the difficulties in classifying animals.
> - Despite the difficulties found in species classification, there is a need for it in science.

Each of the correct answers refers to some part of the main idea of the passage. You'll notice that the first correct response roughly matches with the first paragraph, the second response corresponds to the body paragraphs, and the last correct answer is supported by the final paragraph.

Let's look at why the other answer choices are wrong.

The first one says

> It is likely that the Central Valley salamanders were all descended from a common ancestor.

This choice gives information about the salamanders, but the salamanders are used only to support the author's point; they are not part of the main idea.

The second incorrect choice reads

> Any two animals that can breed with each other are considered members of the same species.

This answer gives the definition of a species, but the summary is related more to the difficulties with species classifications, so this detail is not part of the main idea.

The final wrong answer says

> One solution to the problem involves placing animals into subspecies, but this approach results in problems of its own.

Our final answer presents a solution to a problem mentioned in the passage, but that problem was presented to support the author's larger point about the difficulties with species classification. So once again, this answer simply refers to a specific *detail,* not a main idea.

READING DRILL #4

1.   **B**   The first question is a *vocabulary in context* question. Let's look at the following lines:

> Although it seems like the _____ of spam—junk E-mails sent unsolicited to millions of people each day—is a recent problem, spam has been around as long as the Internet has.

The clue is that junk E-mails are "sent" to "millions of people." We need a word that matches this idea. Let's look at which answers are incorrect.
- Eliminate choice (A), because although "addition" is one part of the definition of *proliferation*, in this context there is no evidence that the spam is being added to anything. Instead, it's spreading to "millions of people."
- Eliminate choice (C); it is the opposite of the word we need!
- Eliminate choice (D); it is not close to the word we need.
- Thus, choice (B) is best.

2.   **D**   This question wants to know how the author describes spam. Using "spam" as the *lead word*, go back and read these lines.

> Although it seems like the proliferation of spam—junk E-mails sent unsolicited to millions of people each day—is a recent problem, spam has been around as long as the Internet has. In fact, the first documented case of spam occurred in 1978, when a computer company sent out 400 E-mails via the Arpanet, the precursor to the modern Internet.

According to the author, spam is "junk E-mails sent unsolicited to millions of people." The answer that best matches this is (D). Here's why the other choices are incorrect.
- Answer choice (A) is contradicted by the passage, which says that spam has been around for a while, not that it is a "recent" problem.
- Answer choice (B) is a trap. If you read carefully, the lines say that spam makes up 80 percent of the E-mails received by "some unlucky users," not 80 percent of *all* messages, as the answer choice states.
- Answer choice (C) is not mentioned.

3.   **D**   Here we have another *vocabulary in context* question. The lines we need are as follows:

> It costs a spammer roughly one-hundredth of a cent to send spam, which means that a spammer can still make a profit even with an _____ low response rate, as low as one sale per 100,000 E-mails sent.

We are looking for a word that relates to the clue of "one sale per 100,000 E-mails sent." Use POE to eliminate wrong answers.
- Answer choice (A) is out because nothing in the sentence has to do with *unknowingly*.
- Choice (B) is wrong because the lines state that the spammer still makes a profit, so it isn't a "disaster."
- Similarly, choice (C) doesn't work because there is no indication that the spammer is "disappointed" with the results.

4. **C** For this question, we need to figure out to what the phrase is referring. It is very similar to a *vocabulary in context* question. Look at the following lines:

> But the fingerprinting defense proves quite easy for spammers to defeat. To confuse _____, a spammer simply has to include a series of random characters or numbers.

Ask yourself "What is it that the spammer wants to confuse?" It must be the fingerprinting defense mentioned in the previous line. So, eliminate the wrong answers.

- Answers (A) and (B) are related to spam messages, not the fingerprinting defense.
- Answer choice (D) is not mentioned.
- Thus, choice (C) is best: The fingerprinting defense is "a type of spam filter."

5. **A** Make sure you know what the question is asking before you return to the text. This question asks why smart filters are better than fingerprinting systems, so use *smart filters* as your *lead word*. Here are the lines at which to look.

> A second possible solution takes advantage of a computer's limited learning abilities. So-called "smart filters" use complex algorithms, which allow them to recognize new versions of spam messages. These filters may be initially fooled by random characters or bogus content, but they soon learn to identify these features.

These lines state that the smart filter may "initially be fooled" by certain messages, but "they soon learn to identify" them. This is closest to choice (A). Here's why the other choices are incorrect.

- Answer choice (B) goes too far beyond the information given. It is not stated that the filters learn from their "mistakes."
- Also, the passage doesn't state how smart filters work, so choice (C) is not necessarily true.
- Choice (D) is wrong because the filters can be fooled by spam, even if they later are able to recognize it.

6. **B** This question asks us to *paraphrase* a sentence from the passage. Let's look at the sentence and see what we can trim out of it.

> The smart filter functions by looking for words and phrases ~~that are normally used in a spam message~~, but spammers have learned to hide words and phrases by using numbers or other characters to stand in for letters.

Basically, the sentence is saying that the filters work in one sort of way, but spammers have figured out a way to confuse the filters. Let's use POE.

- Eliminate choice (C) because it talks only about *filters,* whereas our sentence should refer to *spammers* as well.
- Answer choice (D) adds in new information: It states that the filters are "easily" defeated, but the original sentence didn't state that.
- Now we're left with answers (A) and (B). Although they are fairly similar, answer choice (B) is, in fact, correct. The sentence states that the spammers hide words by using "other characters to stand in for letters." This is what (B) says.
- (A) states that the spammers "change words" in the message, which isn't the same as "standing in."

7. **A** For this *vocabulary in context* question, we should look at these lines.

> This system prevents _____ spam systems from sending out mass E-mails since computers are often unable to pass the verification tests.

Ask yourself what type of word would go in the blank. What type of spam systems are we discussing? The sentence states that "computers" are unable to pass the test, so that is the clue. Here's why the other choices are incorrect.

- Watch out for choice (B): This is a trap answer because *automatic* means "to operate independently," but this is not stated in the sentence.
- There is no evidence that the systems are "costly" or "illegal," so eliminate (C) and (D).

8. **C** For an *EXCEPT* question, remember to go back to the passage and look for each answer choice. Then check off each one for which you find support.

(A) "but most E-mail users are reluctant to adopt these systems"
(B) "they make sending E-mails inconvenient"
(C) not stated in the passage
(D) "unfortunately many users find such a system too intrusive"

Because there is no evidence for (C), it is our answer.

9. **A** Once again, take a moment to understand the question. It asks, "Why does the author call the fight over spam an arms race?" The *lead word* here is *arms race*, which is discussed in the following lines:

> In some ways, the battles being fought over intrusive E-mails are very much an arms race. Computer engineers will continue to devise new and more sophisticated ways of blocking spam, while spammers respond with innovations of their own.

Thus, the author indicates that while engineers will "continue" to make new spam blockers, spammers will "respond" with new devices of their own. This makes choice (A) the best answer. Here's why the other choices are incorrect.

- Answer choice (B) is not stated in the passage—nowhere does it say that users will be "harmed."
- Answers (C) and (D) are both too extreme. They say that there is "no solution" to spam and that engineers will "never" be able to defeat spam.

10. **B** This is an *inference* question. The answer is in the final paragraph, which states

> In some ways, the battles being fought over intrusive E-mails are very much an arms race. Computer engineers will continue to devise new and more sophisticated ways of blocking spam, while spammers respond with innovations of their own. It is unfortunate that the casualties in this technological war will be average E-mail users.

Here are the incorrect answers.

- Answer choice (A) is not mentioned by the author. In fact, the author implies that the spam battle will continue, not "eventually be blocked."
- Choice (C) is too extreme; there are *some* ways to stop spam.
- Choice (D) is extreme as well. It is not known if the battle will end.
- Thus, choice (B) is best. The author states that it is "unfortunate that the casualties in this technological war will be average E-mail users."

11.　For a *sentence insertion* question, remember to make sure the ideas in the new sentence match up with the sentences surrounding it. Let's look at the first square.

> So far, spammers have been unable to defeat proof systems, but most E-mail users are reluctant to adopt these systems because they make sending E-mails inconvenient. **Although a fee to send an E-mail seems an extreme solution, the fee is more of a verification device than an actual payment.** A similar problem prevents another effective spam blocker from widespread use.

This doesn't seem to match very well. The first sentence doesn't mention a "fee," which is part of the inserted sentence. And the second sentence seems to be introducing a new system, which doesn't match up with the idea of a "verification device" found in the boldfaced sentence. Let's try the next square.

> A similar problem prevents another effective spam blocker from widespread use. **Although a fee to send an E-mail seems an extreme solution, the fee is more of a verification device than an actual payment.** This system involves charging a minimal fee for each E-mail sent.

Again, this doesn't seem to be a good match. The first sentence doesn't mention a fee at all. The second sentence does, but it is introducing the system. Now let's try the third square.

> This system involves charging a minimal fee for each E-mail sent. **Although a fee to send an E-mail seems an extreme solution, the fee is more of a verification device than an actual payment.** The fee, set at one penny, would appear as an electronic check included with the E-mail.

This almost works. The first sentence does talk about a fee, and it matches with the beginning of the added sentence. But the second part of the new sentence—about the verification device—doesn't connect to the next sentence, which still talks about the fee. Thus, the final square must be the answer. Let's look at it.

> The fee, set at one penny, would appear as an electronic check included with the E-mail. **Although a fee to send an E-mail seems an extreme solution, the fee is more of a verification device than an actual payment.** Users can choose to waive the fee if the E-mail is from a legitimate source; however, users can collect the fee from a spammer.

This is the best fit. The first sentence does indeed refer to a fee, as does the beginning of the inserted sentence. The second sentence describes how users can waive the fee for some people or charge the fee for spammers. This matches up with the "verification" system mentioned in the inserted sentence.

12.　This question requires you to summarize the tactics mentioned in the passage. Although your understanding of the main idea may help, it is still a good idea to refer back to the passage to double-check your response. Here is the completed table.

Answer Choices	Spammers
Require users to include a small payment with each E-mail	• Use automated systems
Do not want to be inconvenienced when sending E-mails	• Insert random characters and numbers into messages
	• Rely on the convenience of E-mail
	• Benefit from the low cost of sending E-mail messages

Spam Blockers

- Take advantage of computer learning abilities
- Require a verification test to send E-mails
- Develop a "fingerprint" of E-mail messages

The remaining answer choices, which are not used, refer to E-mail users, not spammers or spam blockers.

Chapter 9
Cracking the
Listening Section

The Listening section of the TOEFL consists of the following tasks:

- Four to six **academic lectures**, at least two of which contain classroom dialogue
  - Each lecture is three to five minutes long.
  - A lecture may involve one speaker or multiple speakers.
  - Each lecture is followed by six questions.
- Two to three **conversations** involving two or more speakers
  - Each conversation is three to four minutes long.
  - A conversation has 12–25 exchanges.
  - Each conversation is followed by five questions.
- You will have 60–90 minutes to complete the entire section.

The Listening section measures your ability to follow and understand lectures and conversations that are typical of an American educational setting. You will hear each lecture or conversation only once, but you are allowed to take notes while you are listening.

At the beginning of the Listening section, you'll be instructed to put on your headset. An example of the screen is shown below.

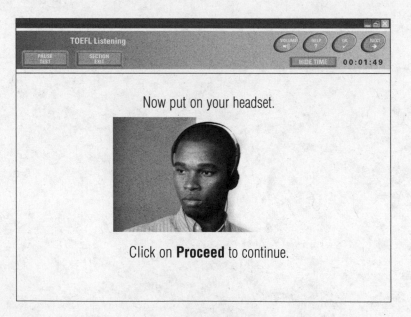

You'll also receive instructions on how to adjust the volume of the headset. Make sure the volume is at a comfortable level before the section begins.

LISTENING DIRECTIONS

You should be aware of a few special aspects of the Listening section before you take the TOEFL. First, unlike the Reading section, you are not allowed to skip questions and return to them later. *You must answer each question before you can proceed to the next one.* Second, some of the questions on the Listening section are heard, not read. These questions are indicated by a special headset icon, similar to what you've seen in this book.

It is important to be prepared for these audio questions. In this book, we use the headset icon to indicate when you should listen to the accompanying CD. On the actual test, you will only hear this material; it will *not* appear on your screen.

CRACKING THE LISTENING SECTION: BASIC PRINCIPLES

One of the most common mistakes students make in the Listening section is to try to do too much. Some students try to take notes on every detail offered, and they end up not hearing important information. Other students try to understand every single word in the lecture, and they panic when they miss a word or phrase. Neither of these approaches is very helpful on the test.

Instead, you must do your best to think of the lectures and conversations as being similar to the reading passages on which we've worked. Each lecture or conversation will have a purpose, a main idea, and supporting details. Your goal on the Listening section will be to find these items in each selection. Because there are only five or six questions per listening task, there is no need to memorize or comprehend every single detail.

The Listening section requires you to do the following:

- **Find the main idea or purpose.** Each lecture or conversation will have a main idea or purpose. Find and note this theme, which is usually stated at the beginning of the discussion or talk.
- **Focus on the structure.** Pay attention to how the main idea develops. Look for examples, comparisons, and cause-and-effect relationships.
- **Listen for tone and attitude.** Try to figure out if the speakers are positive, negative, or neutral toward the topic.

- **Pay attention to transitions.** Make sure you are listening for transition words and phrases. These help you follow the logic of the lecture or conversation.

We'll look at all of these points in more detail in a moment, but there are two other important things to keep in mind when you approach the Listening section.

- **Don't memorize.** As we said earlier, there is far too much information to try to memorize or retain. So, don't even bother trying. Keep in mind that the TOEFL is testing you on your ability to follow a logical flow of ideas, not on your ability to memorize information. Just relax and try to focus on the big issues, not the minor ones.

- **Don't take too many notes.** One easy way to get sidetracked on the Listening section is to write down too many notes. Writing requires your concentration, and if you're concentrating on writing, you're probably not concentrating on listening. Focus on listening; in fact, if you are not comfortable taking notes, don't take any at all.

Basic Principle #1: Find the Main Idea or Purpose

We've spent a lot of time practicing this step with reading passages. Now we will apply our understanding of the main idea or purpose to a listening task. Fortunately, the patterns in the Listening section are very similar to the patterns in the Reading section. Lectures are designed around a main idea, whereas conversations are centered on a purpose.

In **lectures,** the speaker will typically introduce the main idea at the very beginning of the talk. Listen for phrases similar to the following:

- "Okay, today I want to talk about...."
- "What we're going to talk about today is...."
- "Today, we're going to look at...."
- "Tonight, I wanted to look at...."

The professor will then follow with the topic of discussion. If you're taking notes, you should write the topic down. Once you have the main topic, you can expect the lecturer to provide a purpose, explanation, or more information.

In a **conversation,** the beginning sentences will reveal the speaker's purpose. Listen for the purpose to appear after an initial greeting, as in the following examples:

- "Hi, what can I do for you?"
- "Hello, how can I help you?"
- "What can I do for you today?"
- "Is there something I can do for you?"

After this initial question, the other speaker will state his or her purpose. Usually this involves asking for some sort of help or assistance. If you are taking notes, you should write down what the purpose of the conversation is.

Basic Principle #2: Focus on the Structure

After finding the main idea or purpose, focus on the structure of the talk. Lectures and conversations each have standard structures. Listen for them as you take the TOEFL.

Types of Lecture Structures

Most lectures will have one of the following basic structures:

Lecture Structure #1: Compare/Contrast

This type of lecture involves finding similarities and differences between two or more things. Listen for the speaker to introduce this framework by using one of the following phrases:

- "several theories"
- "possible explanations"
- "many different views"

After the framework is introduced, the speaker will list each item to be discussed and mention its characteristics. Listen for words that indicate compare/contrast, such as

- "in contrast"
- "on the other hand"
- "similarly"
- "however"
- "additionally"
- "also"

Lecture Structure #2: Cause-and-Effect Relationships

Some lectures attempt to explain why a certain situation occurs. Listen for the speaker to introduce this type of framework with the following phrases:

- "Why would this happen?"
- "What is the reason for this?"
- "How could this happen?"
- "What leads to this?"

If it seems that the speaker is describing a cause-and-effect situation, listen for the cause. A speaker will often use the following phrases to introduce the cause:

- "x causes y"
- "x results in y"
- "x produces y"

- "*x* leads to *y*"
- "*x* brings about *y*"
- "*x* is responsible for *y*"

After identifying the cause, look for the speaker to detail the effects with a phrase similar to the following:

- "*y* is caused by *x*"
- "*y* results from *x*"
- "*y* is due to *x*"
- "*y* can be blamed on *x*"
- "*y* is attributable to *x*"
- "*y* happens because of *x*"

Lecture Structure #3: Abstract Category/Specific Examples   Another common lecture structure involves moving from an abstract category to a specific example. A lecture may also sometimes begin with specific examples and end with a more general interpretation of the examples. A speaker may introduce an abstract concept with one of the following phrases:

- "one approach..."
- "one theory..."
- "the idea is..."
- "the concept..."
- "the basic premise is..."

Next, the speaker will move to the examples, typically using the following phrases:

- "for example..."
- "one instance of this is..."
- "consider..."
- "we see this in/with..."
- "this is illustrated by/with..."

Even if you have difficulty understanding the abstract idea, you can usually figure it out by paying close attention to the examples used.

Lecture Structure #4: Sequences   A lecture may present a series of steps or stages. Listen for the lecturer to mention the following clues:

- "process"
- "development"
- "stages"
- "transition"

The steps or parts will typically be introduced with clear transitions, such as

- "first...second...third..."
- "next..."
- "then..."
- "initially..."
- "finally..."

Types of Conversation Structures

Conversations on the TOEFL also fall into some predictable patterns. Try to identify the pattern when listening to the people speak.

Conversation Structure #1: Problem/Solution This is a typical conversation type on the TOEFL. One student has a problem, and another student offers advice or a possible solution. Listen for the first student to introduce the problem by mentioning one of the following:

- "problem"
- "issue"
- "difficulty"
- "trouble"

After describing the problem, the other person will offer some sort of advice or solution. Listen for the following phrases:

- "why don't you..."
- "if I were you, I'd..."
- "maybe you should..."
- "have you tried/thought of..."

For this structure, it is important to listen for what the problem is and what steps or solutions the speaker may take to solve it.

Conversation Structure #2: Service Encounter Another common conversation on the TOEFL is the service encounter. In this encounter, a student will discuss a problem with a professional—usually a professor, a librarian, or an office worker. The problem will be introduced in the same way as in the previous conversation type, but the response may differ. The service professional will usually explain *exactly* what the student needs to do to solve the problem. The solution may involve several parts. If so, listen for the following words to indicate the steps the student must take:

- "requirement"
- "application"
- "form"
- "recommendation"
- "prohibited"

Conversation Structure #3: Significant Event   Some conversations on the TOEFL revolve around a significant event. This could be a meeting, an announcement, or a social event. Usually, the first speaker will introduce the event with one of the following phrases:

- "have you heard about..."
- "did you see..."
- "let you know about..."
- "program/event/opportunity/chance"

After noting the event, listen to any details about it. Also note what the speaker's plans are concerning the event. Listen for the following key words:

- "participate"
- "plans"
- "open to"
- "free" or "busy"

Basic Principle #3: Listen for Tone and Attitude

Although you are unlikely to be asked a tone question in the Listening section, an understanding of the speaker's tone or attitude is helpful on many types of questions. Speakers on the TOEFL often use phrases or words that can have more than one interpretation. However, if you are aware of the speaker's tone, you are less likely to misinterpret the phrase.

For example, lecturers on the TOEFL often say something like the following:

> "...and after the war, the country experienced a prolonged period of economic growth, right?"

Even though the speaker *appears* to be asking a question, he is actually just *emphasizing his point*. Being aware of the tone will help you interpret statements such as this one.

The tone of most lectures is fairly straightforward. Because the speaker is teaching a class, the tone will usually be similar to one of the following types:

- **Objective:** The speaker is simply listing facts or providing information. The speaker is an authority on his or her subject and so will not be unsure or uncertain about the topic. This type of tone can appear in any of the four common lecture types.
- **Subjective:** In some cases, the speaker will be presenting a position or making an argument. The speaker will try to convince the listeners about a certain view. This type of tone is more likely to appear in *compare/contrast* and *cause-and-effect* lectures.

- **Inquisitive:** There are also classroom discussions on the TOEFL. During a discussion, the professor leads the class through a number of questions, so the tone is inquisitive. The professor considers and responds to the students' questions as the lecture progresses. *Abstract category/specific example* lectures typically involve discussion, although other lecture types may as well.

Conversations tend to have slightly more personal tones. You can expect the tone to be similar to one of the following types:

- **Excited:** This tone is typical of the *significant event* conversation. The speaker is interested in the event and may be trying to influence others about it.
- **Disappointed/upset:** In this case, the speaker is not happy about the situation. He or she may express dissatisfaction with things or events. This usually occurs during the *problem/solution* encounter, although it can appear in other conversations too.
- **Uncertain or confused:** Sometimes the speaker is uncertain or confused, especially in *service encounters*. The speaker will be unsure of what action to take or how to proceed.

Of course, you don't have to spend valuable time during your test trying to figure out the exact tone. However, having a basic idea of the tone—as well as of the purpose of the lecture or conversation—will aid you when you are eliminating answers.

Basic Principle #4: Pay Attention to Transitions

From your work on the Reading section of the TOEFL, you should have a pretty good understanding of the common transitions used in writing. These transitions show up in lectures and conversations as well, and it is good to note them. However, two other types of transitions to be especially alert for are *reversals* and *negations*.

Reversal Transitions

Often, speakers on the TOEFL will reverse the direction or logic of the conversation or lecture. If you're not listening carefully, you may misunderstand the speaker. For example, look at the following lines:

"First, I want to look at the mechanism by which single-celled organisms reproduce...um, actually, let's come back to that in a moment. We need to talk about..."

In this situation, the speaker abruptly changes the topic. These reversals happen occasionally during lectures and somewhat more frequently during conversations. Here are some phrases for which to listen.

- "you know what?"
- "we'll come back to that in a moment"
- "actually, let's"
- "instead"
- "better yet"
- "I don't want to get into that now"

Negation Transitions

Also, speakers will sometimes use a positive word to indicate a negation. Look for phrases like the following, where the negation words are italicized:

- "I don't have to explain that, *right*?"
- "You guys are okay with this, *correct*?"
- "We don't need to go into that now, *okay*?"

In each case, the speaker uses a positive word to express a negative statement. When used in this way, the positive words indicate that the speaker assumes the listener knows what the speaker is talking about and no further discussion or explanation is needed.

Reversals and negations can by tricky, but if you're on the lookout for them, they'll be easier to handle.

CRACKING THE LISTENING SECTION: BASIC APPROACH

Now we're ready to crack the Listening section. Here are the steps.

1. **Actively listen to the selection,** noting the main idea or purpose, structure, and tone.
2. **Attack the question.** There's no skipping in the Listening section, so you'll have to do each question as it appears.
3. **Use POE aggressively,** using your understanding of the main idea, previous questions, and any notes you've taken to help you.

Let's try the steps on a practice passage. Use your CD to follow along.

Step 1: Actively Listen to the Selection

If you intend to take notes, take a moment to organize your scrap paper. Remember, you don't want to try to write down everything. Instead, as we've discussed, focus on the main topic, structure, and tone. Listen carefully for these parts and be sure to write them down.

Keep in mind the basic principles you have learned throughout this book. You should expect to hear the main idea or purpose at the very beginning of the speech and the majority of the details and supporting examples throughout the rest. A lecture or conversation usually will have a conclusion as well. Screens similar to the ones that follow will introduce each passage.

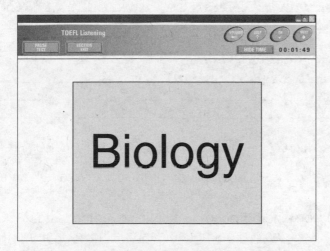

When you are ready, play Track 3 on the accompanying CD. After you are finished listening to the lecture and questions that follow, try to answer the questions below. If you are having difficulty answering the questions, replay the selection. A transcript of the lecture is also included on the next two pages for your reference. (But don't cheat and read along as you listen to the track!)

What is the *main idea* of the lecture?

_____
_____
_____

What is the *structure* of the lecture?

_____
_____
_____

What is the lecturer's *tone*?

_____
_____
_____

Let's look at a transcript of the lecture and find the important points.

Narrator: Listen to a biology professor give a talk on an environmental issue.

Professor: There's been a lot of talk over the last few decades about greenhouse gases—those gases in the atmosphere that trap radiation from the sun so that after it passes into the atmosphere it doesn't pass out. People are increasingly conscious of the environmental effects of their daily activities, which is a good thing. But all the publicity can be confusing too. I think writing for the general public about science is a real service, but...well, it's not nice to say, but...I wish some of these people would verify things with real scientists more often. They'd save themselves some embarrassment.

With that in mind, I'd like to clear up some things about that hot topic: carbon dioxide. Carbon dioxide is a greenhouse gas; it absorbs energy from the sun. In that respect, it's like water vapor and methane, two other naturally occurring greenhouse gases. You all know that carbon dioxide is produced when we burn fossil fuels—coal, petroleum products, natural gas—and that those fuels run a lot of the machines and manufacturing processes that drive modern life.

Those are the sources that get all the public attention, but, of course, we produce carbon dioxide as a waste product too. It's one of the by-products of respiration. We breathe in air, use up some of the oxygen, and breathe out air that contains carbon dioxide. So do other animals. Because carbon dioxide is part of the natural life cycle, nature has a way of dealing with it. How does nature control the amount of carbon dioxide floating around in the atmosphere?

Male Student: I thought the ocean soaked it up.

Professor: Yes, that's one way. Carbon dioxide is very soluble in water. Soluble...uh, I don't have to explain that one to you because the root's related to the word *dissolve*, right? So carbon dioxide is pulled readily out of the air and into the water. Now, the oceans also release some of their carbon dioxide, but on balance, they absorb more; so that means that, if we produce artificially more than would naturally be emitted through life processes, the ocean could, as Jason put it, soak it up.

Unfortunately, if we're looking for a solution to carbon dioxide pollution, the ocean isn't it, and that's because the ocean absorbs gases from the atmosphere very, very slowly. If we suddenly increased the amount of carbon dioxide we produced, current models suggest that it would take 1,000 years for it to mix into seawater. And even then, there would still be a small amount left. So over the short and medium term, we can't rely on the ocean to take up the slack for us.

Okay, so that's one way nature deals with carbon dioxide. What's the other?

Female Student: Plants, isn't it? I mean, plants breathe carbon dioxide the way we breathe air.

Professor: Sure—I was actually kind of surprised that wasn't the one mentioned first. Yes, plants require carbon dioxide for photosynthesis. The more dense the growth of large plants, the more carbon dioxide is absorbed. Such an area—including forests of large, old-growth trees, and also the ocean—where carbon dioxide is absorbed in large quantities, is called a carbon sink. The carbon dioxide gas is sucked in kind of the way water is sucked down the drain in your sink after you wash the dishes. In fact, in the ocean, there are algae, seaweed...um, other kinds of marine plants too that rely on carbon dioxide to perform photosynthesis, just like the green plants on land. It's just that algae are far, far smaller.

Now, here's something interesting: Like the ocean, green plants release carbon dioxide into the atmosphere as well as absorb it—uh, when a plant dies...you know, if it burns in a forest fire or just dies of old age and decays, then its carbon dioxide is back in the air. So it only holds it in over its lifetime. However—this is the interesting part—unlike the ocean, green plants soak up carbon dioxide to use it—to make the energy they need to live and grow. So what they've found in some regions...populated, industrialized regions...is that increased levels of carbon dioxide can stimulate plant growth. There's more of the fuel the plants need for energy, so they grow more green and dense and lush and use more of it—in other words, the amount of carbon dioxide used up by plants can increase quickly in response to the environment. Some people have suggested that we can use that natural phenomenon to help deal with increased levels of greenhouse gases in the atmosphere.

Narrator: What is the discussion mainly about?

What is the problem with relying on the oceans to solve the problem of excess amounts of carbon dioxide? Why does the professor mention that carbon dioxide is a by-product of respiration? What did the professor call areas where carbon dioxide is absorbed in large quantities? What did the professor mean by this?

As stated earlier, expect the main idea to show up early in the lecture. The very first line of the lecture gives us the topic.

"There's been a lot of talk over the last few decades about **greenhouse gases**—those gases in the atmosphere that trap radiation from the sun so that after it passes into the atmosphere it doesn't pass out."

Of the 37 words in this sentence, you really only needed to note the two boldfaced ones. A little later on, the professor specifies exactly what aspect of greenhouse gases the lecture will discuss.

"With that in mind, I'd like to **clear up some things about** that hot topic **carbon dioxide**."

From these lines, we now have the *basic purpose* of the lecture. Hopefully, you were now on the lookout for the things the professor wanted to clear up. The professor continues to talk about two major areas. The first is in the following lines:

> *Professor:* How does **nature control the amount** of carbon dioxide floating around in the atmosphere?
>
> *Male Student:* I thought the **ocean soaked it up.**
>
> *Professor:* Yes, that's one way.

This is the first important *detail* in the lecture. You may have noticed that the professor also mentioned the following:

> "**Unfortunately,** if we're looking for a solution to carbon dioxide pollution, the ocean isn't it, **and that's because** the ocean absorbs gases from the atmosphere very, very slowly."

These lines have a good *tone* indicator ("unfortunately") and a good *transition* ("and that's because"). You should also note that the professor repeats the fact about the ocean not being suitable for absorbing carbon dioxide in the next four lines as well, so you have a few opportunities to pick up this important point.

The next major detail occurs here.

> *Professor:* Okay, so that's one way nature deals with carbon dioxide. **What's the other?**
>
> *Female Student:* **Plants,** isn't it? I mean, plants breathe carbon dioxide the way we breathe air.

The professor continues with the following, which you may have noted:

> **However**—this is the **interesting part**—unlike the ocean, **green plants soak up carbon dioxide to use it**—to make the energy they need to live and grow.

Once again, the lecturer uses strong *transitions,* such as "however," and *tone* words, such as "interesting part," to alert you to important details. If you were able to pick up on these parts of the lecture, chances are you'll be in pretty good shape for the Listening section. As we've mentioned before, you're *not* expected to memorize or comprehend every detail of the lecture.

Here are some possible responses to the earlier questions.

- What is the *main idea* of the lecture? <u>Oceans and plants are nature's way of controlling carbon dioxide.</u>
- What is the *structure* of the lecture? <u>It's mostly compare and contrast. Two methods are looked at.</u>
- What is the lecturer's *tone*? <u>Mostly neutral, with occasional positive ("here's the interesting part") and negative ("unfortunately") digressions</u>

You'll find that a basic understanding of these major points will help you to answer most of the questions following the lecture or conversation. The important thing is not to become stressed or worried that you didn't understand every single part of the talk.

Step 2: Attack the Questions

The questions in the Listening section are very similar to the questions in the Reading section. Of course, the major differences are that you will hear the lecture or conversation only *once* and that you will *not* be able to skip questions and come back to them later.

The following types of questions appear most often on the Listening section:

1. **Main idea questions:** The first question of the set will typically be a main idea question. Considering the work you've done up to this point, the main idea question shouldn't be too difficult for you to answer. However, we'll go over some POE strategies just in case.

2. **Detail questions:** The majority of the questions following the lectures or conversations will ask about facts from the selections. The details will not be about minor points, but rather about major points.

3. **Purpose questions:** Some questions will ask you *why* the speaker mentioned a particular detail or fact. For these questions, it is helpful to think about the overall structure of the selection.

4. **Definition questions:** Often, during a lecture (definitions rarely, if ever, show up in conversations), the lecturer will define a particular term for his or her students. Pay attention if you hear the speaker signal a definition with one of the following expressions:
    *   "A *caucus* **is** a secret party meeting."
    *   "A *caucus* **is defined as** a secret party meeting."
    *   "A *caucus* **is the word used for** a secret party meeting."
    Sometimes the speaker will reverse the order of the term and the definition.
    *   "A secret party meeting **is known as** a *caucus.*"
    *   "A secret party meeting **is called** a *caucus.*"
    *   "A secret party meeting **is referred to as** a *caucus.*"
    Finally the definition may be placed in the middle of a larger phrase.
    *   "A *caucus*—a secret party meeting—is usually held in emergencies."
    *   "A *caucus*, **that is,** a secret party meeting, is usually held in emergencies."
    *   "A *caucus*, **or** a secret party meeting, is usually held in emergencies."

5. **Inference or suggestion questions:** The TOEFL will often test your ability to "read between the lines" (or more precisely, "listen between the lines"). There will often be questions asking what the speaker is suggesting or what he or she really means by a particular phrase. A person will often suggest something by using one of the following phrases:

- "**Why not** come back later?"
- "**How about** coming back later?"
- "**What about** coming back later?"
- "**Why don't you** come back later?"
- "**If I were you, I'd** come back later."
- "**You should** come back later."
- "**You could always** come back later."
- "**Maybe you could** come back later."
- "**It may not be a bad idea** to come back later."

Each of these constructions is a way of expressing the same basic idea that someone may return later.

6. **Multiple-multiple-choice questions:** Some questions in the Listening section require you to select more than one example. Many times, these questions ask you to list the main details or points made in the lecture.

Step 3: Use POE Aggressively

Because you are unable to listen to the lecture or conversation more than once, you'll have to focus on using good POE strategies when answering the questions. If you've missed a key point of the lecture or conversation, you can still increase your chances of getting a question correct by eliminating answers that aren't likely to be correct.

Before we go through the question types and the POE strategies, you may want to listen to Track 3 on the accompanying CD again. We'll identify the question types and apply test-taking techniques to work through the questions that follow.

Main Idea Questions
Question 1 is a typical main idea question on the TOEFL.

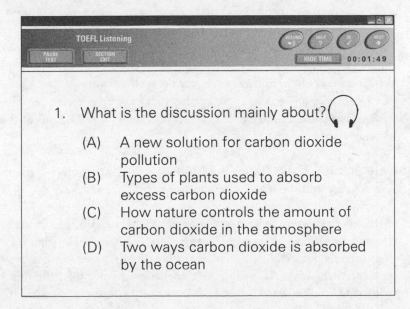

1. What is the discussion mainly about?

    (A) A new solution for carbon dioxide pollution

    (B) Types of plants used to absorb excess carbon dioxide

    (C) How nature controls the amount of carbon dioxide in the atmosphere

    (D) Two ways carbon dioxide is absorbed by the ocean

As we saw earlier in our active listening section, the speaker began by talking about carbon dioxide and mentioned two major ways that carbon dioxide is absorbed by nature—by oceans and by plants. Thus, choice (C) is the best answer.

Here's why the other answer choices are incorrect.

- For main idea questions, wrong answer choices may be *too specific*. For example, answer choice (B) talks only about plants. Even if you weren't sure exactly what the lecture was about, you may have noticed that plants did not appear until the end of the lecture. Any details that you hear mentioned only toward the *end* of the lecture will *never* be the main idea.

- Of course, some answers will contain information that is *not mentioned* at all. Answer choice (A) states that the lecture was about a "solution" for pollution. But no solution was offered. Even if you feel that you missed something important during the lecture, be aggressive. The lecture mentioned two key points: the ocean and plants. Answer choice (A) states there is "one solution." The great thing about a multiple-choice test is that there are usually a few ways to look at wrong answers.

- Questions on the TOEFL will also typically contain a *trap* answer, which uses words or phrases from the lecture or conversation in a deceptive manner. Answer choice (D) is a good example of a trap answer. The first part of the choice talks about "two ways." This matches up with the two key examples used in the lecture. Next, the choice talks about "carbon dioxide," which obviously is part of the lecture also. Finally, the choice contains "the ocean," a match with one of the examples in the lecture. Unfortunately, the lecture is about two ways *nature* absorbs carbon dioxide, not two ways the ocean absorbs it. The lesson here is that if you are uncertain of the right answer, and if one of the choices seems too good to be true, it's a trap. Still, be careful to use this advice only when you're stuck; otherwise, you'll drive yourself crazy over-analyzing the answer choices.

- One other wrong answer type that may appear on a main idea question is a choice that is *too broad*. This is the opposite of an overly specific answer choice. For example, suppose there had been the following answer choice:
(E) The effect of environmental issues on everyday life
This answer is too general. The lecture does have an environmental theme, but the correct answer has to reflect more of the details of the talk, not just the basic idea.

POE Strategies for Main Idea Questions   When answering a main idea question, make sure you avoid the following answer types:

- **Answers that are *too specific*:** Remember that the main idea should be something that ties into the entire lecture. If the answer choice focuses on a detail that you remember hearing only once, it is too specific. Similarly, an answer choice that focuses on something that is mentioned only toward the end of the lecture will not be correct.

- **Answers that are *too broad***: If the answer choice deals with a topic or theme mentioned early in the lecture but doesn't address the *details* of the talk, it is too broad and therefore incorrect.
- **Answers that are *not mentioned***: The TOEFL is not a memorization test. If you don't recall hearing anything about the focus of a particular answer choice, then that choice is most likely incorrect. The selections on the TOEFL are centered on a topic and continually refer back to it; thus, it is unlikely that you somehow missed the main idea.
- **Answers that are *traps***: Use this only as a last resort. If you are really stuck on a question, avoid answers that seem too good to be true.

Once you've answered the main idea question, keep the answer you've selected in mind. It can help you on some of the other questions.

Detail Questions

As you know from the Reading section, detail questions ask you about specific facts from the discussion. Fortunately, the wrong answers to detail questions in the Listening section tend to be a little more obviously wrong. Question 2 is a typical detail question.

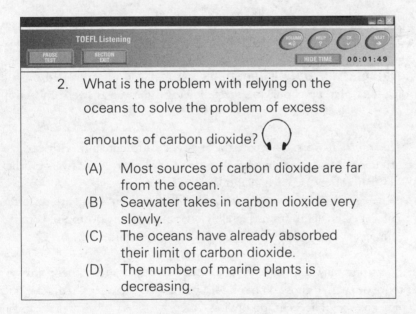

The answer to this question was one of the key points in the lecture. Recall that the professor alerted us to an important point by saying the following:

"Unfortunately, if we're looking for a solution to carbon dioxide pollution, the ocean isn't it, and that's because the ocean absorbs gases from the atmosphere very, very slowly."

We noted this because of the speaker's use of the important tone indicator word *unfortunately*. Thus, the correct answer is choice (B).

If you are having trouble identifying the incorrect answer, you may still be able to eliminate some answers. *Extreme* answers, for example, are usually incorrect. You've seen these answers in the Reading section, and they appear in the Listening section as well. Answer choice (C) is a good example of an extreme choice. It makes a pretty absolute statement: that oceans have "absorbed their limit" of carbon dioxide. Many extreme answers use words such as the following:

always	*never*	*all*
none	*every*	*everything*
nothing	*only*	*impossible*

Another way of eliminating answers on detail questions is to cross off choices that are *contrary to the main idea*. For example, in this lecture, if you were able to figure out that the speaker gave oceans and plants as the two main examples, you should eliminate answer choice (D) because that focuses on marine plants, which was a separate example in the lecture.

If you keep your eyes out for these two common types of wrong answers, you will have a 50 percent chance of getting the question right; those odds aren't so bad!

POE Strategies for Detail Questions   When you are stumped on a detail question, don't give up. Look for the following types of answers and eliminate them:

- *Extreme* answers: Compare the answers. Eliminate any with extreme wording, and go with the safe answer. Correct answers on the TOEFL often use fairly bland language.
- Answers that are *contrary to the main idea*: Even if you are uncertain of a specific detail from the selection, you may be able to use your understanding of the main idea to eliminate choices.

Detail questions may also have *trap answers*. Unfortunately, these answers are harder to identify than those on main idea questions. But again, if all else fails, try not to pick answers that seem too obvious or easy.

Purpose Questions

It is important to try to pay attention to the structure of the selection as you listen. If you grasp the structure, it will make purpose questions, like the one on the next page, easier.

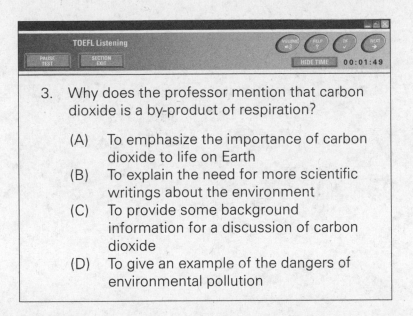

3. Why does the professor mention that carbon dioxide is a by-product of respiration?

(A) To emphasize the importance of carbon dioxide to life on Earth
(B) To explain the need for more scientific writings about the environment
(C) To provide some background information for a discussion of carbon dioxide
(D) To give an example of the dangers of environmental pollution

Before trying to answer this question, think about the structure of the lecture. We saw earlier that the professor looks at two key examples (oceans and plants) and compares and contrasts them. Although the lectures on the TOEFL may have some minor digressions, most of the information should in some way relate to the big picture. That means you can safely eliminate answers that seem to introduce *new ideas*. For example, answer choice (B) should be eliminated. The lecture is not about scientific writings (although they are mentioned once, they never appear again). Similarly, answer choice (D) can be eliminated as well: The lecture doesn't focus on environmental pollution or its dangers.

That leaves choices (A) and (C). Once again, think about the big picture and look for the answer containing information that is *contrary to the main idea*. Answer choice (A) talks about "life on Earth." But half of the lecture is about the ocean, which is not alive, so eliminate choice (A). That leaves us with answer choice (C) as the correct answer.

POE Strategies for Purpose Questions   Keep the main idea in mind as you attack purpose questions. Get rid of answers that contain the following:

- **New ideas:** The purpose of examples and details are to support the main idea. Answer choices that contain new information not related to the main idea are wrong.
- **Information contrary to the main idea:** You should also eliminate any answers that seem to go against the main idea of the lecture.

Definition Questions

Definition questions require you to recall a very specific part of the lecture. Thus, they can be very difficult. Question 4 is an example of one.

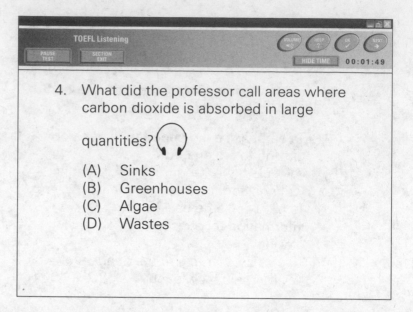

4. What did the professor call areas where carbon dioxide is absorbed in large quantities?

(A) Sinks
(B) Greenhouses
(C) Algae
(D) Wastes

Unfortunately, if you didn't catch this part of the lecture, POE won't help you much. You can use your knowledge of the words and common sense to eliminate choices, but if you're unsure of the words, you'll have to take a blind guess.

The professor defined the word at this point in the lecture:

"Such an area—including forests of large, old-growth trees, and also the ocean—where carbon dioxide is absorbed in large quantities, is called a carbon sink. The carbon dioxide gas is sucked in kind of the way water is sucked down the drain in your sink after you wash the dishes."

Therefore, the correct answer is (A).

POE Strategies for Definition Questions
Your best option when trying to use POE on definition questions is to

- **Use your vocabulary:** If you happen to know one or more of the words in the answer choices, see if any of the words will work. It is unlikely that the correct definition for a question on the TOEFL will be radically different from the standard definition of the word.

Inference/Suggestion Questions

For inference and suggestion questions, you will often hear a portion of the speech replayed before you answer the questions. When a portion of the lecture is going to be repeated, you will always see a screen similar to the one below.

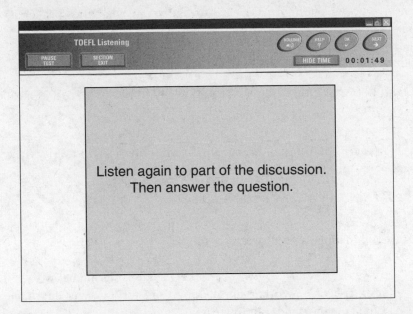

On the actual test, the excerpt from the selection will not appear on the screen; you will only hear it.

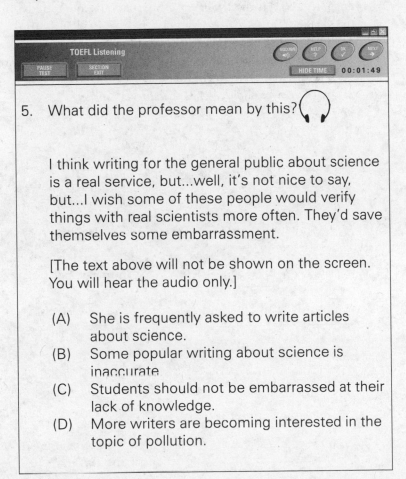

5. What did the professor mean by this?

I think writing for the general public about science is a real service, but...well, it's not nice to say, but...I wish some of these people would verify things with real scientists more often. They'd save themselves some embarrassment.

[The text above will not be shown on the screen. You will hear the audio only.]

(A) She is frequently asked to write articles about science.

(B) Some popular writing about science is inaccurate.

(C) Students should not be embarrassed at their lack of knowledge.

(D) More writers are becoming interested in the topic of pollution.

For these types of questions, we have to figure out what the speaker is *really* saying.

The phrase in question contains a suggestion.

> "I wish some of these people would verify things with real scientists more often."

Thus, the speaker is indicating that she thinks the writers need to verify their work. The next part of the selection clarifies this suggestion further.

> "They'd save themselves some embarrassment."

Let's start eliminating some answers.

- Answer (A) is on the *wrong topic*. The speaker is stating her wish for other people's writing, not making a suggestion to herself; that wouldn't make sense. Eliminate it.
- Answer choice (C) has the same problem. The professor is talking about *writers,* not students.
- Answer choice (D) has the *wrong tone*. Even if you're not exactly sure what the speaker is trying to say, you may be able to identify the selection as positive or negative. In this case, the selection is somewhat negative ("They'd save themselves some embarrassment"), but answer choice (D) is fairly *positive*. So eliminate it.
- We're left with answer choice (B) as the correct answer.

Let's try it again, this time with an inference question.

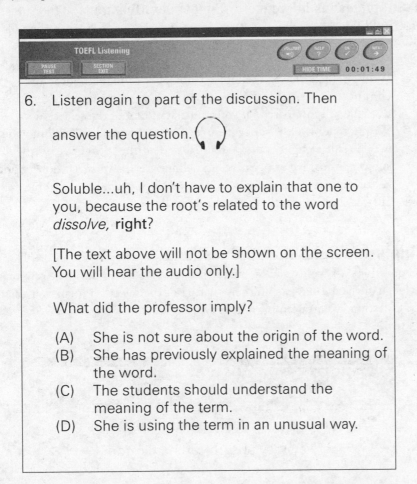

This selection contains a good example of the negations we mentioned earlier when discussing transitions. As used in this context, the word *right* means that the speaker assumes the students understand the topic without needing any further explanation. We also have some POE options on this question.

- Answer choice (A) is on the *wrong topic*. The professor is addressing the students, not herself. Eliminate this choice.
- Answer choice (D) has the *wrong tone*. The professor is indicating that she doesn't "have to explain" the term, so it doesn't make sense for her to use the term in an unusual way and not explain it.
- That leaves answers (B) and (C). Answer choice (B) is tempting, but we have no way of knowing whether it's true; remember that on the TOEFL, we should be able to support our inferences.
- Therefore, answer choice (C) is the best answer.

POE Strategies for Inference or Suggestion Questions The three most important POE strategies for these questions are to pay attention to the following types of answers:

- **Wrong topic:** Stick to the topic. Think about the main idea, and eliminate answers that don't relate to it. Also, eliminate answers that don't make sense based on your understanding of the selection.
- **Wrong tone:** Even if you're unsure of what the speaker is saying, you may be able to figure out the tone. Decide if the speaker views the subject as positive or negative, and eliminate answers that don't work.
- **Extreme:** Inference and suggestion questions often have extreme answer choices as well. If you see one, eliminate it.

Multiple-Multiple-Choice Questions

These questions ask you to select more than one answer. You must rely on your knowledge of the main idea and the structure of the selection to answer them correctly. Question 7 is an example of this type.

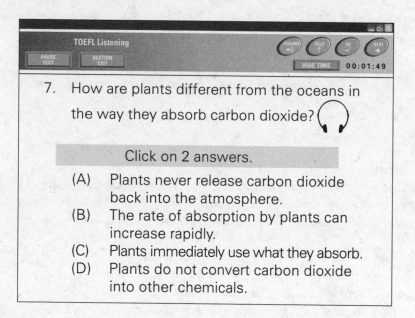

As you can see, it's important while you're listening to try to understand the structure of the lecture. This lecture involved a *comparison and contrast* between two ways in which carbon dioxide is absorbed by nature. You may remember that the professor hinted that some important information was about to come when he said

"However—this is the interesting part—unlike the ocean, green plants soak up carbon dioxide to use it—to make the energy they need to live and grow."

Thus, we know that plants use the carbon dioxide they absorb. Now, let's use POE. You may have noticed that both answer choice (A) and answer choice (C) contain *extreme* language: the words "never" and "immediately." Thus, as with other questions on the TOEFL, they're wrong. So, even if you didn't remember the exact differences mentioned in the talk, you can still get the question right.

POE Strategies for Multiple-Multiple-Choice Questions Multiple-multiple-choice questions are typically either *detail* questions or *main idea* questions, so use the same POE strategies provided earlier in this chapter.

Listening Summary

Good job! You are halfway through your TOEFL preparation. Here are some important points to remember that will help you crack the Listening section.

- o **Don't memorize; understand!** The most common mistake on the Listening section is to try to do too much. Look for the big picture: main idea, structure, and tone. Don't get lost in the details.

- o **Taking notes is optional:** If taking notes interferes with your ability to comprehend what you're listening to, then don't do it. Take notes only if you are able to write and maintain your focus on the selection.

- o **Know what bad answers look like:** Make sure you're familiar with the kinds of bad answers that appear most frequently on the TOEFL.

- o **Stay aggressive!** If you don't catch an important detail, don't panic. Stay aggressive and eliminate answers based on your knowledge of the main idea, structure, tone, and previous questions.

Now that we've worked with the passages and lectures on the TOEFL, it's time to create some passages and speeches of our own. Let's practice the Listening section with some drills, and then move on to the Speaking and Writing sections.

Chapter 10
Listening Practice Drills

You're now ready to crack the Listening section. Remember to use the strategies and guidelines you learned in the previous chapter. Pay special attention to POE (Process of Elimination). If you're stuck, get rid of as many bad answers as you can. After you've finished, check your answers and look over the explanations provided in the next chapter. Good luck!

DRILL #1: A CONVERSATION

On the TOEFL you will see screens similar to the ones shown below and on the pages that follow. Listen to Track 4 on the CD. Then answer the following questions.

1. What is the man's problem?

   (A) He was unable to concentrate during the biology test.
   (B) He has a hard time understanding biology.
   (C) He is distracted by noise while studying.
   (D) His television is broken.

2. What has the man been using to create white noise?

   (A) A radio
   (B) The noise from the radiator
   (C) A television
   (D) A fan

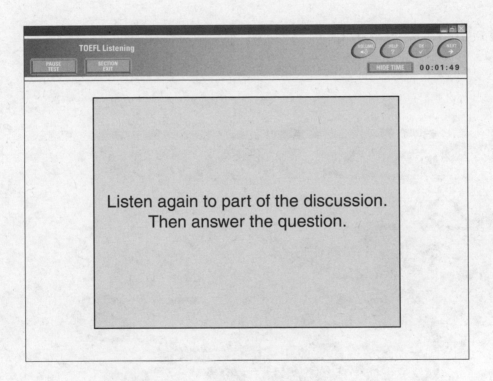

Male Student: I just bought my fan new this year; it's the quiet kind.

Female Student: Well, sure...I was, you know, just giving an example....

3. What did the woman mean by this?

   (A) She misunderstood the nature of the man's problem.
   (B) She was not specifically recommending the use of a fan.
   (C) She thought the man had a different kind of fan.
   (D) She has a fan the man can use.

4. Why does the woman suggest the man keep his window open?

    (A)   He can be comfortable in less clothing.
    (B)   The air from the fan may be too warm.
    (C)   The noise from outside will help him concentrate.
    (D)   People study better in cool rooms.

5. What do the speakers imply is the major problem with the heating system?

    (A)   Its controls are confusing.
    (B)   It is very old.
    (C)   The noise it makes is too loud to drown out.
    (D)   It doesn't heat the rooms effectively.

DRILL #2: A CONVERSATION

Listen to Track 5 on the CD. Then answer the following questions.

1. Why is the woman speaking to the man?

   (A) She wants the results of her allergy test.
   (B) She is supposed to receive an injection.
   (C) She needs to set up an appointment.
   (D) She cannot decide which test to use.

2. Why must the man wait to give the woman instructions?

   (A) He cannot get in contact with her doctor.
   (B) She hasn't been on her special diet long enough.
   (C) He hasn't received her file yet.
   (D) He hasn't observed her symptoms.

3. Why is the elimination test more difficult?

   (A) It must be performed at the student health center.
   (B) There is more danger of a serious reaction.
   (C) It takes more time and effort.
   (D) It requires injections.

4. When can the spot test described by the man be used?

   (A) When the elimination test did not produce results
   (B) When the symptoms are becoming worse over time
   (C) When the patient has too little time for the elimination test
   (D) When the doctor has some idea of the cause of the allergy

5. What will the woman do next?

   (A) Get her file from the student health center
   (B) Tell the man when she can meet next
   (C) Tell the man what she has eaten lately
   (D) Start the diet for the elimination test

DRILL #3: A LECTURE

Listen to Track 6 on the CD. Then answer the following questions.

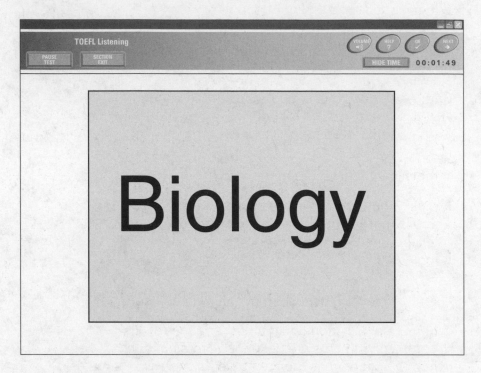

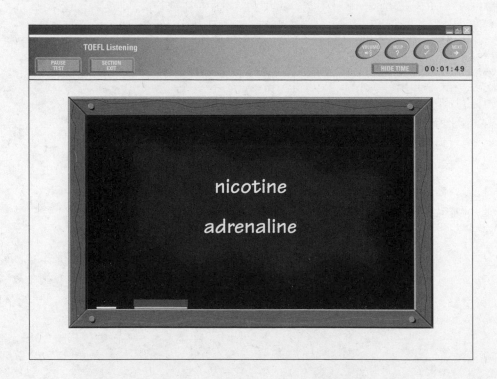

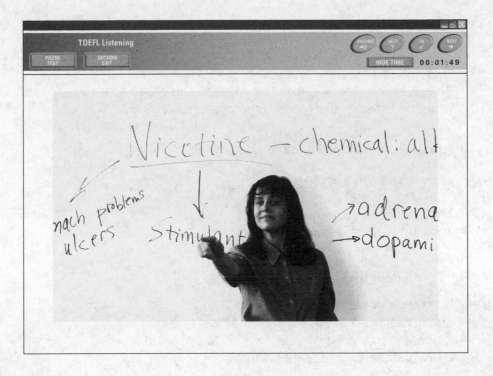

1. Listen again to part of the lecture. Then answer the question.

   Okay, I know from having taught this class before that the topic I'm about to cover has the potential to get people's blood boiling, so I'd like to start off by making something clear: I'm going to discuss the physical effects of tobacco on the body. This is not the place for a debate over social issues.

   What can be inferred about the professor?

   (A) She is not used to teaching students about the effects of tobacco.
   (B) She thinks the topic may be confusing.
   (C) She wants to avoid a controversial discussion.
   (D) She thinks the debate over tobacco is interesting.

2. Why is only a small amount of nicotine ingested in smoking?

   Click on 2 answers.

   (A) The processing of tobacco removes a lot of nicotine.
   (B) The body does not absorb nicotine easily.
   (C) Most of the nicotine is destroyed by burning.
   (D) The tobacco plant contains little nicotine.

3. Why does nicotine affect the nervous system powerfully?

   (A) The brain has a large surface area.
   (B) Nicotine is similar in structure to some hormones.
   (C) Blood travels directly from the lungs to the brain.
   (D) Nicotine crosses the blood-brain barrier quickly.

4. What effect does adrenaline have on people's moods?

   (A) They feel more alert.
   (B) They feel calmer.
   (C) They become more nervous.
   (D) They think more slowly and carefully.

5. How does dopamine contribute to cigarette addiction?

   (A) It makes people more energetic.
   (B) It sends signals associated with pleasure.
   (C) It decreases the amount of oxygen to the brain.
   (D) It lowers heart and breathing rates.

6. What kinds of illnesses used to be treated with tobacco?

   Click on 2 answers.

   (A) Heart disease
   (B) Anxiety
   (C) Poor digestion
   (D) Breathing problems

DRILL #4: A LECTURE

Listen to Track 7 on the CD. Then answer the following questions.

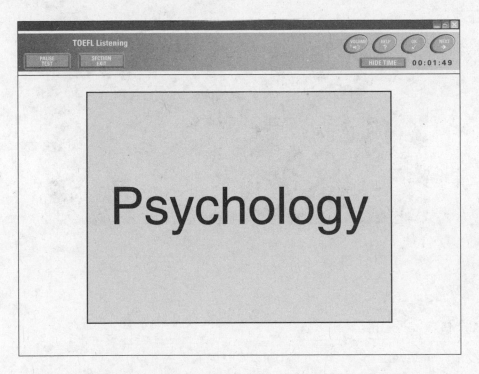

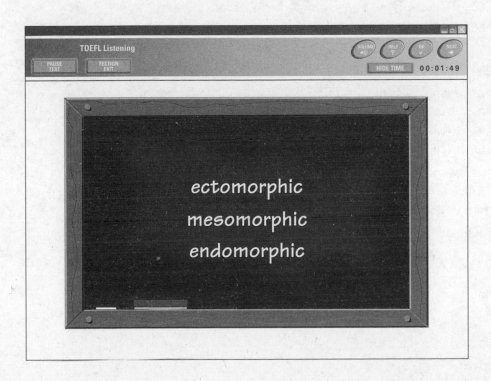

1. What is the lecture mainly about?

   (A) The layers of the human body
   (B) A way of categorizing people's personalities
   (C) The best kind of exercise for different body types
   (D) How students can identify their own body types

2. What do biologists use to divide the body into layers?

   (A) The amount of fat in each type of tissue
   (B) The origins of the different cells
   (C) The type of personality in which each area is dominant
   (D) The kind of activity with which the tissues are associated

3. Listen again to part of the lecture. Then answer the question.

So when biologists talk about the layers of the body, that's what they mean: The outermost is the skin and nervous system, the middle is the muscles, and the innermost is the stomach, basically. It's important to get that straight right from the beginning because most people—well, isn't it natural to think of the bones as the innermost layer?

What did the professor mean by this?

...well, isn't it natural to think of the bones as the innermost layer?

(A)   The layers of the body do not include the bones.
(B)   Most people are familiar with the categories.
(C)   Scientists have recently changed their thinking.
(D)   The mistake is understandable.

4. Which of the following are characteristics of an ectomorphic body?

Click on 2 answers.

(A)   Lack of fat
(B)   Strong bones
(C)   Low muscle development
(D)   Enlarged stomach

5. What will the professor discuss next?

(A)   Problems with Sheldon's theory
(B)   The questions Sheldon used in his interviews
(C)   A newer theory of personality types
(D)   Studies that have tested Sheldon's theory

6. Based on the information in the lecture, indicate whether the following are characteristics of the mesomorphic or endomorphic personality type.

	Mesomorphic	Endomorphic
Seeks ways to fulfill appetites		
Friendly and outgoing		
Reacts to situations physically		
Physically inactive		
Attacks problems without planning		

DRILL #5: A LECTURE

Listen to Track 8 on the CD. Then answer the following questions.

1. According to the professor, why was trade with nonessential goods difficult?

(A) Poor societies cannot devote resources to making nonessential goods.
(B) Nonessential goods are often large and heavy to carry.
(C) Different societies have different systems of value.
(D) The decorations used by early societies were too simple to be valuable.

2. Why did people begin relying on gold and gold specialists?

Click on 3 answers.

(A) Gold had to be imported over long distances.
(B) Travelers were in danger from thieves.
(C) Only specialists could determine its value.
(D) Gold doesn't spoil.
(E) Gold was difficult to transport.

3. How did gold specialists indicate the value of the gold they received?

(A) They recorded where it had been mined.
(B) They recorded its purity and density.
(C) They only lent out the highest-quality gold.
(D) They issued receipts in different colors.

4. Listen again to part of the lecture. Then answer the question.

MS: So if you were storing 500 ounces of gold of whatever percent purity, you'd give the receipt back, and get your 500 ounces of gold back? They kept it for you in your own little drawer or something?

MP: Whoops! I guess I did make it sound that way—thanks for catching that!

What did the professor mean by this?

Whoops! I guess I did make it sound that way—thanks for catching that!

(A) He was not sure what the student said.
(B) His statement was misleading.
(C) He wanted to emphasize a different point.
(D) The man's interpretation is correct.

5. Why did the professor say the receipts issued by gold shops were the first ancestors of money?

(A) All gold shops used the same standard format.
(B) They were written on small slips of paper.
(C) They represented the value of something else.
(D) They were used in societies where bartering was still practiced.

6. What is an ingot?

(A) A piece of gold
(B) A gold specialist's shop
(C) A receipt
(D) A cultural object

Chapter 11
Listening Practice
Answers and Explanations

DRILL #1: A CONVERSATION

Here is the transcript for Drill #1. Read through it and pay attention to the structure and purpose of the talk.

Male Student: I can't believe it! Professor Blake gave me a C on my biology test.

Female Student: Of course he did. You only answered 80 percent of the questions right. Next time, maybe you should consider studying without the television on.

MS: But I wasn't watching it! I really was paying attention to my notes and the book and stuff; I'm just the sort of person who needs white noise in the background in order to concentrate—I mean, I'm usually *good* at biology.

FS: Oh? My sister says she's like that.

MS: Okay, so you know what I mean? If I'm in the middle of a quiet room, every little noise is distracting. It's like it's magnified...I mean, amplified...whatever. If the radiator starts making little noises—

FS: Boy, how old is the heating system in these old dorm rooms, anyway, huh?

MS: Yeah, really? Or someone's having a conversation in the hall and it comes in through the door. I just start fixating on it.

FS: I get that, but is it a good idea to use the television for white noise? Don't you get distracted if something funny comes on...you know, or interesting?

MS: Sometimes, I guess. But most of the time, I can focus just fine. I think.

FS: Uh, all right. But, you know, though, um, you can use other things to drown out noises. Like, my sister—I'm not making this up—she had an old fan, and it made kind of a hum when she ran it.

MS: Those old fans do.

FS: Right? A steady sound, rhythmic...not loud...and it turned out that if she put it on, it was soft enough that she could think, and loud enough that the little distracting stuff in the background, like, she couldn't hear *that*.

MS: I just bought my fan new this year; it's the quiet kind.

FS: Well, sure...I was, you know, just giving an example. In our psychology course last year, didn't they say that tuning the radio in to static is okay too? For people who need white noise, I mean?

MS: Static on the radio? You know the hissing sound that makes! I'll never get any work done!

FS: That's if you have it at normal volume. With trial and error, you might be able to make it softer so it doesn't annoy you but loud enough to drown out other stuff—

MS: Uh-huh.

FS: —like my sister's fan.

MS: I guess.

FS: It has to be better than the television. Just look at that biology score again.

MS: Don't make me, please. Yeah, I mean, you may be right. I'll see how it works studying without the television.

FS: Ooh, something else I just thought of.

MS: What?

FS: Well, you were talking about the radiator, and I think...I don't remember which class it was, but we were told that people find it harder to concentrate when they're in a warm room. It helps if the temperature's a little on the cool side. Sharpens your concentration.

MS: I do get drowsy when the radiator's on full blast, but the radiators in our rooms aren't very easy to, uh, control. It's not surprising after they've been used so many years, but—

FS: I'm with you there. You could always try cracking the window, though. Or maybe wearing fewer layers of clothing. It might be a little uncomfortable, but it's your grades we're talking about, after all.

This conversation falls into the *students discussing a problem* category, a very typical pattern on the TOEFL. Our first goal with a conversation is to identify the purpose of the interaction. Like the main idea, the purpose appears early in the conversation. In this case, the following lines reveal the purpose:

MS: I can't believe it! Professor Blake gave me a C on my biology test.

FS: Of course he did. You only answered 80 percent of the questions right. Next time, maybe you should consider studying without the television on.

Once you identify a problem, your next goal is to try to listen for the solutions offered. In many cases, one listener will offer a solution, only to have the other speaker reject it. The listener will then advise another possible solution. In this case, the listener offers the following advice:

"Next time, maybe you should consider studying without the television on."

After the speaker claims he needs the television on, the listener proposes two other solutions.

"But, you know, though, um, you can use other things to drown out noises. Like, my sister— I'm not making this up—she had an old fan, and it made kind of a hum when she ran it."

"In our psychology course last year, didn't they say that tuning the radio in to static is okay too?"

After discussing these options, the woman offers one final solution.

"I don't remember which class it was, but we were told that people find it harder to concentrate when they're in a warm room. It helps if the temperature's a little on the cool side. Sharpens your concentration."

It is also very important to pay attention to tone when listening to conversations. Does the speaker accept the solutions or reject them? Was the problem solved by the end of the conversation or will it still be an issue? Paying attention to the tone will help you with POE.

Look at some of the man's responses. What is his tone?

"Static on the radio? You know the hissing sound that makes! I'll never get any work done!"

"Yeah, I mean, you may be right. I'll see how it works studying without the television."

"I do get drowsy when the radiator's on full blast, but the radiators in our rooms aren't very easy to, uh, control."

It appears that the man is initially against listening to the radio to solve his problem, but he then offers to try the suggestion. As for the radiator solution, he feels it might work, but he's not sure he will be able to adjust the temperature. Based on these lines, the man's tone is not extremely positive or extremely negative, but it doesn't seem as if his problems are completely solved.

Now let's see how this understanding of the purpose and the tone helps us attack the questions.

1. **C**   This question asks about the purpose of the selection. As we've seen, the conversation involves solutions to the man's studying problems. Eliminate answer choice (A) because it focuses on the test, not the man's studying habits. Answer choice (B) is a trap answer; the student actually says he's good at biology. He received a low score on the test because of his studying problems. Answer choice (D) is obviously incorrect. The issue is the student's academic performance.

2. **C**   This is a detail question. Recall that in the beginning of the talk, the man and woman had the following exchange:

    > FS: …Next time, maybe you should consider studying without the television on.
    > MS: But I wasn't watching it! I really was paying attention to my notes and the book and stuff; I'm just the sort of person who needs white noise in the background in order to concentrate…

    However, if you missed that, you may have noticed that answers (A) and (D) are the solutions offered by the woman, so you can eliminate them. The man says that the noises made by the radiator are distracting, but he doesn't use them for white noise so answer choice (B) is wrong.

3. **B**   For this question, we have to figure out what the woman is suggesting. The following is stated:

    > MS: I just bought my fan new this year; it's the quiet kind.
    > FS: Well, sure…I was, you know, just giving an example.

    Eliminate (A). The main purpose of the conversation is to solve a problem and the woman offered a few different solutions, so she did not misunderstand the problem. Also, eliminate (D). The woman offers another solution. Therefore, the fan doesn't solve the problem. This is a good example of how knowing the purpose and the structure can help you eliminate answers. After the man says he has a quiet fan, the woman suggests using a radio instead, which makes answer choice (B) the best option.

4. **D**   This is another suggestion/inference question. Once again, use the purpose to help you. The answer should have something to do with studying and the problems the man is having. Thus, eliminate answers (A) and (B) right away. They have nothing to do with studying. Answer choice (C) is the trap answer. Although the woman suggests a number of solutions to help the man, she doesn't suggest using noise from the outside. However, in her discussion of the radiator, she does mention that it's easier to study in a cool room, making choice (D) the answer.

5. **B** This final question asks for a detail from the passage. There are two hints about the heating system, one in the beginning of the talk and one toward the end. The first hint is when the woman says:

"Boy, how old is the heating system in these old dorm rooms, anyway, huh?"

Later, the man states the following:

"It's not surprising after they've been used so many years, but—"

Thus, choice (B) is best. If you missed those details, you can still eliminate answer choice (C)—the purpose of the conversation is to offer solutions to a problem. If there was no solution, the woman wouldn't offer any advice. Answers (A) and (D) are not mentioned during the conversation.

DRILL #2: A CONVERSATION

Here is a transcript of the conversation heard for these questions.

Make sure to read through the transcript below to familiarize yourself with the types of structures you will see on the TOEFL.

Narrator: Listen to a conversation at a university guidance office.

Woman: Uh, excuse me—are you Dr. Martin?

Man: I'm Greg Martin, and I don't think there are any other Martins in the office, but I'm a nutritionist, not a doctor.

W: Oh, sorry. I guess I was confused. The doctor at the student health center told me I should see you because I need an allergy test. I was hoping I'd be able to make an appointment.

M: Sure.

W: I would have called, but I was right here, so I figured I'd stop in and—

M: No problem at all. Since your file hasn't come to me from student health—

W: Oh, right, I mean, I just left there, so you wouldn't have it yet. I'll come back.

M: Well, no, actually, if you have a minute, I'll just give you a general explanation of what we're going to ask you to do. I can't actually give you instructions specific to your case without looking at your file, but here's the basic idea.

W: Okay, can I—

M: Oh, sure, sure, I'm sorry, please have a seat here.

W: Thanks. I thought they tested for allergies by injecting you with things?

M: Sometimes. In the case of food allergies, where your symptoms aren't life-threatening, it's more helpful to check by adjusting your diet.

W: Uh-huh, so what do I have to do?

M: As I said, it's going to depend on what your doctor's written in your file for me, but there are two major kinds of dietary tests for food allergies. One is an elimination diet. We'll use that if your doctor is pretty stumped about what's causing your problem. For a few weeks, you'll have to eat a bland diet—just foods that we know are safe—that's pretty certain to eliminate the offending food.

W: A few weeks?

M: Well, it can take a while for the food you eat to clear out of your system. We want a totally blank canvas because then what we do is, one by one, you add in foods that a lot of people have allergies to.

W: Oh, I get it, and then if my symptoms come back, we know what food must be doing it.

M: It's not always that exact, but that's the idea.

W: Well, okay, but what's the other test? You said there were two.

M: The other test is more of a spot test. If your doctor knows from your symptoms that there are only a few foods that are likely culprits, you'll stop eating just those foods for a week or so. Then, you'll eat one of them on an empty stomach, and we'll wait to see whether your symptoms come back.

W: Okay.

M: But as I said, that test is really only useful if your doctor's already got a pretty good sense of what your problem might be.

W: Well, it sounds like it's a lot easier to go through, so, you know, I'm hoping…

M: Of course. Let me look at my schedule and see whether I have a slot open on...uh, Friday, maybe? Your doctor should have gotten your information to me by then.

Once again, our first challenge during a conversation on the TOEFL is to identify the purpose. The purpose should appear within the first two to four exchanges between the speakers.

In this conversation, the purpose is stated in the following lines:

W: Uh, excuse me—are you Dr. Martin?

M: I'm Greg Martin, and I don't think there are any other Martins in the office, but I'm a nutritionist, not a doctor.

W: Oh, sorry. I guess I was confused. The doctor at the student health center told me I should see you because I need an allergy test. I was hoping I'd be able to make an appointment.

This conversation is about what we'd call a "service encounter." The woman needs to make an appointment with the nutritionist. After identifying a conversation as a service encounter, listen for any problems the student may have encountered and any actions the professional recommends to the student. The first problem occurs at the following point in the conversation:

M: …I'll just give you a general explanation of what we're going to ask you to do. I can't actually give you instructions specific to your case without looking at your file, but here's the basic idea.

The first point to note is that the nutritionist is unable to give the student specific instructions until he looks at the file. Next, the nutritionist says the following:

M: As I said, it's going to depend on what your doctor's written in your file for me, but there are two major kinds of dietary tests for food allergies. One is an elimination diet.

After hearing the nutritionist introduce this possible solution, listen for the details. The man continues by saying

M: Well, it can take a while for the food you eat to clear out of your system. We want a totally blank canvas because then what we do is, one by one, you add in foods that a lot of people have allergies to.

The second solution is described as follows:

W: Well, okay, but what's the other test? You said there were two.

M: The other test is more of a spot test. If your doctor knows from your symptoms that there are only a few foods that are likely culprits, you'll stop eating just those foods for a week or so. Then, you'll eat one of them on an empty stomach, and we'll wait to see whether your symptoms come back.

That's the important information from the conversation. Notice once again that all of the information is not absolutely essential. As long as you have a basic understanding of the purpose and the structure you should be able to answer the questions effectively.

Let's go through the questions and see what answers can be eliminated.

1. **C** The first question typically asks about the purpose. Eliminate answer choice (A) because the nutritionist doesn't have any results. Watch out for answer choice (B)—be suspicious of an answer choice that focuses on a specific detail from the passage. We want an answer that covers the whole selection, not just one part of it. Answer choice (D) is incorrect as well; the nutritionist recommends two tests, but the purpose of the visit is not for the woman to decide between them.

2. **C** This is a good example of the type of specific information of which you'll need to be aware on the TOEFL. However, if you recognized the conversation as a service encounter, you may have been listening for a problem or complication. You may be able to eliminate (B) based on the structure. The problem was mentioned at the beginning of the conversation, while the "special diet" doesn't show up until the end of the talk. Also, if you're torn between (A) and (C), go with (C) because it's less extreme; while answer (C) says he hasn't received the file *yet,* answer (A) says he *cannot* reach the doctor.

3. **C** Here is another detail question. Fortunately, it asks about a problem with the first method of testing. Remember to listen for complications and problems during conversations because the TOEFL asks about them often. In any case, you can eliminate answer choice (A) because it's extreme. Also, you may have eliminated answer choice (D) if you noticed that the nutritionist never mentions injections; only the student does.

4. **D** This is yet another specific question. The nutritionist mentioned the answer to this question when he introduced the second solution.

> *M:* The other test is more of a spot test. If your doctor knows from your symptoms that there are only a few foods that are likely culprits, you'll stop eating just those foods for a week or so.

If you missed that information, use your knowledge of the structure to help you. The nutritionist describes two solutions to the problem but never indicated that the student had to do both or that the two tests were related. Thus, eliminate answers (A) and (C).

5. **B** This question is an inference question. Based on the conversation, what will the woman do next? Stick to the purpose of the conversation. She's there to make an appointment, so answer (B) is the most logical answer. Get rid of answer choice (A). The nutritionist said earlier that he would get the file. And the woman must meet with the nutritionist before she can begin the tests, so answers (C) and (D) cannot be correct.

DRILL #3: A LECTURE

Read the following transcript of the first lecture. Ask yourself how the lecture compares with reading selections with which you've worked.

Female Professor: Okay, I know from having taught this class before that the topic I'm about to cover has the potential to get people's blood boiling, so I'd like to start off by making something clear: I'm going to discuss the physical effects of tobacco on the body. This is not the place for a debate over social issues. If you all want to get into it over lunch after class is over, you're welcome to. Just don't expect me to join in.

Anyway, what we want to talk about is what happens to your body when you smoke or chew tobacco. The primary active ingredient in tobacco is one you're probably all familiar with: nicotine. Nicotine is a class of chemical called an alkaloid, meaning that it's a close relative of the caffeine in coffee and the natural drugs found in some plants. It generally has a stimulant effect—it gets your body systems going, makes them more active. It actually makes up a very small percent of the tobacco plant—about 5 percent by mass—not much, right? Also, when you smoke tobacco, most of the nicotine burns away before you can even inhale it. That means that most of the nicotine in your cigarettes never gets to your lungs. It's not ingested. So between those two things—the low proportion of nicotine in the tobacco plant, and the high proportion of the nicotine that's destroyed before you ingest it—you're not really getting a whole lot with each puff.

Even so, the nicotine in cigarettes has a powerful effect on the body for a few reasons. For one thing, while some drugs pass through the body largely without being absorbed, nicotine inhaled into the lungs is absorbed almost completely. This is because the lungs have a lot of surface area that's usually used to exchange oxygen and carbon dioxide when you breathe. All that surface area provides lots and lots of places for nicotine to pass into the bloodstream. Then there's the fact that nicotine crosses the blood-brain barrier quickly. The blood-brain barrier is a sort of gate-keeping system in the bloodstream. It severely limits the ability of substances and organisms to pass from the blood into the brain. This helps keep the chemical environment of the brain stable, which it needs to function properly, and it also keeps the brain clean...you know, nasty infections can't get in, even if the rest of the body is sick fighting them off.

Because nicotine is one of those chemicals that crosses the blood-brain barrier quickly, it affects the nervous system right from its command center. And it has two big effects. One is that it stimulates the production of the hormone adrenaline. More adrenaline means an increase in your heartbeat, your breathing, and possibly even cognition—that is, the thinking and perceiving nerves in your brain. That would help...right?...to explain why people report feeling energized and sharper, more aware, after smoking a cigarette. Their breathing and heart rates are jazzed up, and their thinking nerves are, too.

You might be thinking at this point, *Well, that's how people get addicted to smoking—it makes them feel more energetic and stuff,* and you're partially right, but there's another physiological reason. Scientists have evidence that nicotine stimulates the production of not only adrenaline but also another chemical: dopamine. Levels of dopamine rise when you're doing something enjoyable, like eating your favorite food. So what happens is...some researchers refer to it as a reinforcement or reward mechanism. Dopamine signals well-being, so when nicotine stimulates dopamine production, it's kind of like exciting your pleasure center. That's probably the source of the rush people associate with smoking, and why they keep reaching for more cigarettes to get that same feeling again after it passes.

Now, those are the most obvious direct effects, but nicotine alters body functions in other ways that are also significant. For instance, it decreases the amount of oxygen that gets to the brain, which can make you feel more relaxed. It also, at least in the short term, relaxes the stomach. In fact—some of you may know this, but—nicotine used to be prescribed as medicine for these reasons. Doctors would tell people to use tobacco if they were nervous or anxious because the nicotine calmed them down. Likewise, people with upset stomachs would be told to use nicotine because the relaxing effect on the stomach helped digestion. Now, the problem—the biggest problem—is that these are short-term effects, but as you continue to use nicotine a lot over a period of time, it has bad effects that aren't immediately obvious. Nicotine can cause stomach ulcers and make heart problems worse. You may get short-term relief, but you'll eventually be worse off.

Just as with a reading passage, a lecture will state its main purpose first. However, since the lectures are spoken, you will probably hear a brief introduction or greeting before the main idea is introduced. Here's an example.

P: Okay, I know from having taught this class before that the topic I'm about to cover has the potential to get people's blood boiling, so I'd like to start off by making something clear: I'm going to discuss the physical effects of tobacco on the body. This is not the place for a debate over social issues.

The first part of the excerpt is a brief introduction ("Okay, I know...clear"), after which the professor states the main purpose—"I'm going to discuss the physical effects of tobacco on the body."

Based on this statement, the lecture is most likely going to fit into the cause-and-effect category of lectures. That means we have to look for the effects of nicotine mentioned in the lecture. Here's the first.

> P: Nicotine is a class of chemical called an alkaloid, meaning that it's a close relative of the caffeine in coffee and the natural drugs found in some plants. It generally has a stimulant effect—it gets your body systems going, makes them more active.

This is the first important point to note, that nicotine is a stimulant. The professor uses good transitions to introduce the following important points:

> P: Even so, the nicotine in cigarettes has a powerful effect on the body for a few reasons. For one thing, while some drugs pass through the body largely without being absorbed, nicotine inhaled into the lungs is absorbed almost completely.

> P: Then there's the fact that nicotine crosses the blood-brain barrier quickly.

Although there is a lot of information contained in this lecture, try not to become overwhelmed. Listen for the transition words and direction markers and focus on the important details. Note the following emphasis used by the professor at the point in the lecture below.

> P: Because nicotine is one of those chemicals that crosses the blood-brain barrier quickly, it affects the nervous system right from its command center. And it has two big effects.

After hearing that, listen for the two big effects, which are as follows:

> P: One is that it stimulates the production of the hormone adrenaline. More adrenaline means an increase in your heartbeat, your breathing, and possibly even cognition—that is, the thinking and perceiving nerves in your brain.

> P: Scientists have evidence that nicotine stimulates the production of not only adrenaline but also another chemical: dopamine. Levels of dopamine rise when you're doing something enjoyable, like eating your favorite food.

While it may seem like there is a lot of detail here, remember that as you listen you are trying to get the general idea of the talk. You are not trying to write down or recall every detail. The last thing to listen for is how the lecture ends.

> P: For instance, it decreases the amount of oxygen that gets to the brain, which can make you feel more relaxed. It also, at least in the short term, relaxes the stomach.

Those were the key parts of the lecture. Let's go to the questions and see how you did.

1. **C** The first question is an inference question. Fortunately, it's rather easy if you managed to grasp the main idea of the lecture. Here are the relevant lines.

> P: Okay, I know from having taught this class before that the topic I'm about to cover has the potential to get people's blood boiling, so I'd like to start off by making something clear: I'm going to discuss the physical effects of tobacco on the body. This is not the place for a debate over social issues.

You can eliminate answer choice (A) immediately; a professor would not be lecturing on a subject he or she is unfamiliar with. You can also eliminate (D). The tone of the lecture is mostly objective—there is nothing that indicates the professor is especially interested in the topic. Answer choice (B) doesn't work either; at no point in the lecture did the professor say anything about the topic being confusing or hard to follow. All the professor said was that "this is not the place for a debate over social issues."

2. **C & D** This information is revealed at the beginning of the lecture, when the professor begins talking about nicotine. However, some smart use of POE can also lead you to the right answers. For example, the professor later talks about nicotine's ability to cross the "blood-brain barrier" and the strong effects nicotine has on the body. Thus, choice (B) is unlikely. And choice (A) mentions the processing of tobacco, a topic that is never addressed in the lecture.

3. **D** The answer to this question is in one of the key areas of the lecture, which the professor indicated with the use of transitions.

> P: Even so, the nicotine in cigarettes has a powerful effect on the body for a few reasons. For one thing, while some drugs pass through the body largely without being absorbed, nicotine inhaled into the lungs is absorbed almost completely.
>
> P: Then there's the fact that nicotine crosses the blood-brain barrier quickly.

In any case, eliminate choice (C), which says the blood travels "directly" to the brain. Answer choice (A) is a clever trap because the lecture states that the lungs, not the brain, have a large surface area. And (B) is wrong because while hormones are discussed in the lecture, it is never stated that they are similar to nicotine.

4. **A** The answer to this question is one of the two "big effects" the professor mentioned. If you missed it, you may have been able to eliminate answer choice (C). The professor later mentions that nicotine was sometimes used as a medicine, so it's unlikely to have a negative effect. Also, answer choice (D) contradicts the beginning of the lecture in which the speaker describes nicotine as a "stimulant."

5. **B** This question deals with the other "big" effect stated by the professor. You can see why it is so important to pay attention to transitions and to direction markers. Sometimes you can also use previous questions to help you answer a question, provided that you are confident you got the question right. But if you found the right answer to question 4, then you can eliminate answer choices (A) and (D) because we've already learned that adrenaline increases heart rates and makes people more energetic. Answer choice (C) is mentioned as an effect of nicotine, but not dopamine.

6. **B & C** The final question is easier if you keep the main idea in mind. We've learned that nicotine can stimulate a person and also cause pleasurable sensations. Which of the conditions are likely to be affected by nicotine? It seems unlikely that heart disease would be affected, so eliminate choice (A), but pleasurable sensations could perhaps reduce anxiety. You can also get rid of (D) because it is obviously wrong; smoking would not help breathing problems. That leaves (B) as the second right answer.

DRILL #4: A LECTURE

Here is a transcript of the second lecture. Try to use the active reading strategies you learned to identify the key parts.

Narrator: Listen to part of a lecture in a psychology class.

Professor: People have been trying to figure out the ways and extent to which our personalities are determined by our bodies since ancient times, but the personality typology—the categorization—that you see used most frequently now was developed by a psychologist in the 1940s. His name was William Sheldon and what he did was study photographs of college-aged men, then interview them. He was trying to figure out whether body shape somehow indicated something about personality, so he started looking at the layers of the body.

I know from experience that when I say "layers of the body," only a few of you will really know what I'm talking about, so let me just explain quickly: The way a biologist divides the body into layers is according to how cells in each tissue are first formed when you're an embryo. There's one type of cell that turns into the skin and nervous system—including the brain and spinal cord and the rest of the nerves. Then you have another type of cell that turns into the muscles and bones. And there's a third kind that becomes the lining of the digestive system. So when biologists talk about the layers of the body, that's what they mean: The outermost is the skin and nervous system, the middle is the muscles, and the innermost is the stomach, basically. It's important to get that straight right from the beginning because most people—well, isn't it natural to think of the bones as the innermost layer?

So here's what Sheldon did. He categorized his subjects' body types according to which biological layer was dominant—you know, which was most highly developed. That gave him three separate categories, with one for each layer: I'll write them down for you because they're kind of a mouthful.

An ectomorphic body type is dominated by the skin and nerves of the outer layer. The muscles and the stomach are less emphasized, so you end up with a body that has relatively little muscle and fat. In other words, an ectomorphic body tends to be skinny. If you're ectomorphic, you may not be all that tall, but your body is narrow for your height. You can kind of get a sense of the connection Sheldon was trying to make to personality here, can't you? If you have little fat, and muscles that don't develop easily—but on the other hand, your nerves are very active, very easily stimulated—well, it's kind of like, you have little insulation against the world around you. That could make you feel sort of vulnerable; you might be more likely to like reading and writing, exercise for the mind rather than the body. And that's what Sheldon concluded: The ectomorphic body type is associated with people who do a lot of thinking but aren't physically very aggressive.

The mesomorphic body type is the next one, and its focus is the next layer down. That was the muscles. A mesomorphic body has powerful, well-developed bones and muscles that are easy to strengthen through training and exercise. What kind of personality does that suggest to you—a body type in which the muscles take on strength easily, but the sensitive nervous system and the stomach are less dominant? It's the type of person who's physically active and takes a positive...a kind of can-do approach to things. A mesomorphic person likes physical exercise and will tend to try to solve problems by getting into gear right away, rather than sitting back and thinking for a while about the best plan.

The endomorphic body type is dominated by the very innermost layer of the body. That layer is, of course, the digestive tract, including the stomach. Endomorphs do tend to have rounder bodies and to go for...uh, not just food but sensuality and enjoyment in general. They look for ways to fulfill their appetites, which is why I said a few minutes back that you could think of them as being oriented toward the stomach. Endomorphs tend to be jolly and outgoing and sociable, and they also tend to be less physically active. They like to sit back and enjoy life. They're laid-back. Unlike mesomorphs, who are always ready for action—go, go, go!—endomorphs have a tendency to sit still and see what happens. But they don't overthink things the way ectomorphs do.

So Sheldon built this model and interviewed his subjects to see whether their personalities and bodies corresponded, and his conclusion was that they did. But the next obvious question is whether anyone else has been able to prove any of this, right? So we'll talk about a few other studies scientists have done recently.

Lectures on the TOEFL are laid out in a way that is very similar to the layout of reading passages. This lecture gets right to the point. The speaker states

P: People have been trying to figure out the ways and extent to which our personalities are determined by our bodies since ancient times, but the personality typology—the categorization—that you see used most frequently now was developed by a psychologist in the 1940s.

Those lines provide us with the basic topic—personalities and body types. It appears that this lecture will fit into the abstract model/specific examples type of lectures as indicated by the professor's use of the term *categorization*.

The lecture moves on to describe the three basic body layers.

P: There's one type of cell that turns into the skin and nervous system—including the brain and spinal cord and the rest of the nerves. Then you have another type of cell that turns into the muscles and bones. And there's a third kind that becomes the lining of the digestive system.

Now we need to listen for the characteristics of each category. The important characteristics of the first category are given as follows:

> *P:* In other words, an ectomorphic body tends to be skinny.
>
> *P:* …the ectomorphic body type is associated with people who do a lot of thinking but aren't physically very aggressive.

Of course, the professor mentions some other details, but these are the important ones on which to focus. The lecture continues on to the next category.

> *P:* A mesomorphic body has powerful, well-developed bones and muscles that are easy to strengthen through training and exercise.
>
> *P:* A mesomorphic person likes physical exercise and will tend to try to solve problems by getting into gear right away…

And the final category is described as follows:

> *P:* Endomorphs do tend to have rounder bodies and to go for...uh, not just food but sensuality and enjoyment in general.
>
> *P:* Endomorphs tend to be jolly and outgoing and sociable, and they also tend to be less physically active.

Notice how the speaker also summarizes the previous points in the lecture, saying

> *P:* Unlike mesomorphs, who are always ready for action—go, go, go!—endomorphs have a tendency to sit still and see what happens. But they don't overthink things the way ectomorphs do.

Also, don't forget to listen for how the lecture ends. In this case, the speaker indicates a new topic for study.

> *P:* But the next obvious question is whether anyone else has been able to prove any of this, right? So we'll talk about a few other studies scientists have done recently.

Thus, we have a pretty clear introduction, body paragraphs, and conclusion, just as we've seen in the Reading section. Now let's look at the questions.

1. **B** This first question asks for the main idea. The speaker refers throughout the lecture to body types and personality types, so answer choice (B) is best. Eliminate (A) because the layers of the body is only half the story; remember the main idea should cover all parts of the talk. If you're unsure, definitely don't pick answer (C), which talks about the "best" forms of exercise—that's an extreme answer. And (D) is no good either. The speaker doesn't address the students at all in the lecture.

2. **B** The second question is a tougher detail question. Using the main idea of the selection may help you eliminate answers. Get rid of answer choice (C) because biologists don't focus on personality, psychologists do (which is why "psychology" is the heading for the lecture). Answer choice (D) doesn't make

sense; the tissues aren't associated with activities. That leaves (A) and (B). If you're really stuck, you should pick choice (B), only because the other answer mentions the word *fat*, which makes it more tempting. Remember that some answers are traps! If you are stuck and one answer seems to look attractive, you may want to pick the other answer instead.

3. **D** Here is an inference question, which requires you to listen to the portion of the lecture reproduced below.

> P: So when biologists talk about the layers of the body, that's what they mean: The outermost is the skin and nervous system, the middle is the muscles, and the innermost is the stomach, basically. It's important to get that straight right from the beginning because most people—well, isn't it natural to think of the bones as the innermost layer?

Eliminate answer choice (B) right away because it's too strong. We don't know anything about what "most" people think. And (C) is wrong as well. The comment isn't about what scientists think—the lecturer is making sure the class understands the subject. Answer choice (A) is the trap. While it may be true that the bones are not one of the layers, that is not what the speaker means with the line "isn't it natural to think of the bones as the innermost layer?"

4. **A & C** If you took notes on the key characteristics of the category you may have found this question fairly straightforward. If not, you should eliminate answer (B). Bones are not part of the categories; we just heard that very fact repeated in the previous question. And it wouldn't make sense to choose both (A) and (D), so you know that one of them is wrong.

5. **D** The answer to this question is found at the end of the lecture, when the professor states

> P: But the next obvious question is whether anyone else has been able to prove any of this, right? So we'll talk about a few other studies scientists have done recently.

Of the answer choices, answer choice (B) is the best candidate for POE if you're unsure of the answer. The questions used by the interviewer are a minor detail. You may also eliminate answer choice (C) because it seems likely that the professor should continue discussing Sheldon.

6. Here's the correctly completed chart.

	Mesomorphic	Endomorphic
Seeks ways to fulfill appetites		x
Friendly and outgoing		x
Reacts to situations physically	x	
Physically inactive		x
Attacks problems without planning	x	

Although you can't really use POE on this type of question, you can note that choices one, two, and four are related, as are choices three and five. Thus, if you know which personality type is which, you'll be able to correctly place all the choices.

DRILL #5: A LECTURE

Read the transcript of the lecture, noting the main idea, structure, and tone. How do the students' questions relate to the main idea?

Male Professor: Since yesterday's brief introduction on the origin of banking confused some of you, today I would like to review it a little bit. Banking the way we know it today is a convenience. The money used in banking represents a certain amount of value, but the money itself isn't valuable; it's just paper. To see how we got here...suppose we think about a society far, far back in history—what would it have used before the paper money we have today?

Female Student: Didn't they trade with the goods themselves?

MP: Sure. The system of exchanging one good for another of equal value is called *bartering*. Bartering was common in early societies, first with essential goods, then with nonessential goods. By nonessential, I mean, for example, art or cultural objects. You might trade a curtain that had been dyed in a decorative pattern for some wheat. The curtain's decorative value isn't essential to survival the way the food value of the grain is. That's the first step toward a money economy: recognizing trade-worthy value in something that isn't essential to survival.

Of course, you may see a hitch. Different cultures don't value the same decorations, so something could be worth a lot to one tribe and nothing to another. With food, that's not a problem—everyone has to eat—but with nonessential items, you're going to use something with cross-cultural value. Can anyone think of anything that would work?

Male Student: How about gold? It's durable...easy to shape...and it's beautiful. Is that why cultures started using it as money?

MP: Well, you can't refer to the earliest trade with gold as a money economy, but yes. Gold is a perfect example. As societies grew more stable and trade flourished, gold, usually molded into small ingots, gradually replaced the system of bartering. There were problems with gold, though.

FS: Yeah, I was going to say, gold is heavy, isn't it? How did people carry enough of it around to buy things? And wasn't it dangerous—like, you'd get robbed if people knew you had money with you?

MP: Definitely. Hauling all your gold around was a real risk in early societies, when there were bandits roaming around and no police to help you. And as you say, gold is heavy and unwieldy. One advantage it has, though, is that, unlike livestock or food, it doesn't go bad, so you don't have to use it up immediately.

That combination of characteristics gave people an idea. They started leaving their gold ingots with gold specialists for safekeeping. The specialists stored the gold for a small fee, and they gave their customers receipts, the way you'd get today. So you'd get something that said that, you know, you were the owner of such-and-such an amount of gold stored at this particular shop. The quality of gold from different mines varies, so the purity and density of your gold ingots—you know, how heavy they were for their size—determined their value and would also be recorded.

Then, when you wanted to use it, you just went back, gave the shopkeeper the receipt, and he gave you your gold.

MS: So if you were storing 500 ounces of gold of whatever percent purity, you'd give the receipt back, and get your 500 ounces of gold back? They kept it for you in your own little drawer or something?

MP: Whoops! I guess I did make it sound that way—thanks for catching that! No, you'd get 500 ounces of gold of the same purity back. They would have equal value, but would not necessarily be the exact same pile of ingots that you originally gave to the shopkeeper.

FS: The shopkeeper would use the gold or lend it out while you were storing it?

MP: Sure, and you can see how that's another of the beginnings of banking as we know it. You wouldn't get back your very own pile of gold; you'd get back a pile of equal value. It was the value itself that was important.

MS: So how did it become like money? I mean, we're still talking about big, heavy stacks of things, and—

MP: Well, that's the last point. Eventually, people figured out that they could use their receipts from storing gold to trade with one another. If they wanted to buy something, instead of running to the gold shop, withdrawing gold, and bringing it to another shop to pay for food or clay pots or whatever, they just gave the food merchant a receipt for the appropriate amount of gold. The merchant could then cash it in for gold, and the trade would be complete. And that's the last major step: The receipts became the first real ancestor of the money we use today because they stood for value actually attached to goods somewhere else.

Some of the academic lectures will include questions from the students and other forms of discussion. While this may appear to make the lectures more confusing, the student questions actually help you to follow the lecture and figure out the main idea.

First let's figure out what the main topic is. As always, the professor mentions it at the very beginning of the lecture.

> MP: Banking the way we know it today is a convenience. The money used in banking represents a certain amount of value, but the money itself isn't valuable; it's just paper. To see how we got here...suppose we think about a society far, far back in history—what would it have used before the paper money we have today?

Now that we know the lecture will be about the beginnings of banking, we should look for a sequence of ideas. The first student question introduces a key point.

> FS: Didn't they trade with the goods themselves?

As we said earlier, the students' comments and questions provide an easy way to follow the development of the lecture. Now the professor will explain the important idea below.

> MP: Sure. The system of exchanging one good for another of equal value is called *bartering*. Bartering was common in early societies, first with essential goods, then with nonessential goods...Of course, you may see a hitch. Different cultures don't value the same decorations, so something could be worth a lot to one tribe and nothing to another.

A student now asks a question, which again helps us understand the progression of ideas in the lecture.

> MS: How about gold? It's durable...easy to shape...and it's beautiful. Is that why cultures started using it as money?

> MP: Well, you can't refer to the earliest trade with gold as a money economy, but yes. Gold is a perfect example. As societies grew more stable and trade flourished, gold, usually molded into small ingots, gradually replaced the system of bartering. There were problems with gold, though.

This exchange brings us to another key part of the lecture. The professor details the problems.

> MP: Definitely. Hauling all your gold around was a real risk in early societies, when there were bandits roaming around and no police to help you. And as you say, gold is heavy and unwieldy. One advantage it has, though, is that, unlike livestock or food, it doesn't go bad, so you don't have to use it up immediately.

The lecture then continues with a longer explanation of how the problems with gold lead to a new idea. But even if you missed some of that discussion, notice how the next student comment helps you figure out the key point.

> MS: So if you were storing 500 ounces of gold of whatever percent purity, you'd give the receipt back, and get your 500 ounces of gold back? They kept it for you in your own little drawer or something?

This comment gives us some clue as to what the professor was talking about before—the ability to store gold. Now the professor continues with the sequence.

> MP: Sure, and you can see how that's another of the beginnings of banking as we know it.
>
> MS: So how did it become like money? I mean, we're still talking about big, heavy stacks of things, and—
>
> MP: Well, that's the last point. Eventually, people figured out that they could use their receipts from storing gold to trade with one another.

As you can see, in each case the discussion between student and professor helped to clarify the major points of the lecture. So, make sure to be aware of this when dealing with an academic discussion on the TOEFL.

Now let's take care of the questions.

1. **C** This question was answered when the professor talked about bartering and the point was introduced with the use of a direction marker: "of course...." The answer choices in this question are very good candidates for POE. The first choice is extreme. It says that societies "cannot" devote resources. This is an absolute statement and should be eliminated. Answer choice (D) is another type of extreme answer, one that shows up every once in a while. The problem with this answer is that it can be seen as somewhat offensive. It judges the decorations as "too simple." The TOEFL will never have a correct answer that makes a negative value judgment. The characteristics in answer choice (B) refer to gold.

2. **B, D, & E** Get rid of answer choice (C), which is extreme because it states that "only" specialists could determine the value of gold. The discussion never mentions shipping as a problem, so choice (A) is wrong.

3. **B** Once again, answer choice (C) is extreme, so eliminate it. Answer choice (D) never appears in the lecture, so eliminate it as well. Answer choice (A) is certainly tempting, but the lecture said that "the quality of gold from different mines varies, so the purity and density of your gold ingots—you know, how heavy they were for their size—determined their value and would also be recorded." Thus, choice (B) is best.

4. **B** Here's a transcription of the excerpt to which you're asked to listen for this question.

> MS: So if you were storing 500 ounces of gold of whatever percent purity, you'd give the receipt back, and get your 500 ounces of gold back? They kept it for you in your own little drawer or something?
>
> MP: Whoops! I guess I did make it sound that way—thanks for catching that!

The professor's use of the word *whoops* indicates a mistake of some sort. Eliminate choice (A) and choice (D) because the line in question is about the professor ("I guess I did make it sound that way..."), not the student. And no point is introduced in this line, so choice (C) is incorrect.

5. **C** The professor mentions the answer to this question at the end of the lecture. Alternatively, use POE. Choice (A) is extreme; it says "all" gold shops used the same format. Choice (D) refers to bartering, which was mentioned in the beginning of the sequence as something that came before money. Eliminate it. Answer choice (B) is not mentioned.

6. **A** This is a definition question. These can be tough because if you miss the definition during the lecture it's hard to use POE. If you recalled that the word *ingot* appeared during the discussion of gold, you may be able to eliminate choices (C) and (D) because they don't refer to gold. The professor defines the term here.

> *MP:* The quality of gold from different mines varies, so the purity and density of your gold ingots—you know, how heavy they were for their size—determined their value and would also be recorded.

Chapter 12
Cracking the
Speaking Section

Of all the sections on the TOEFL, the Speaking section often causes the most anxiety in test takers. Of course, we're going to talk about some ways to help you crack this section, but first let's look at what you can expect in the Speaking section.

> - **Two Independent Tasks,** with one question asking about a personal preference and another asking you to choose an option. Here's the time breakdown to complete these tasks.
>   - 15 seconds preparation time
>   - 45 seconds speaking time
> - **Two Integrated Tasks** that require you to read a passage, listen to a conversation or lecture, and respond. Here's the time breakdown to complete these two tasks.
>   - 45 seconds reading time
>   - 60- to 90-second conversation/lecture
>   - 30 seconds preparation time
>   - 60 seconds speaking time
> - **Two Integrated Tasks** that require you to listen to a conversation or lecture and respond. Here's the time breakdown for these tasks.
>   - 1- to 2-minute conversation/lecture
>   - 20 seconds preparation time
>   - 60 seconds speaking time
> - You will have 20 minutes to complete the entire section.

As you can see, one of the challenges of the Speaking section is the way in which the questions require you to apply a variety of different skills—reading, listening, and, of course, speaking.

HOW THE SPEAKING SECTION IS SCORED

Each of your spoken responses will be graded on a scale of 0 to 4. The graders consider three major areas when judging the quality of your response—let's look at each in detail.

1. **Delivery:** On the TOEFL, delivery refers to both the flow and clarity of your speech. A higher-scoring response will be well paced and free of long pauses and unnecessary interjections. Although the speech may contain minor pronunciation errors or problems with intonation, these errors do not detract from understanding the speech.

2. **Language use:** The scorers are looking for effective use of grammar and vocabulary. Complexity of sentence structure will also be considered. A higher-scoring response generally contains a variety of sentence structures, a range of vocabulary, and few grammatical errors. Once again, a top response doesn't have to be perfect, but the errors shouldn't affect the listener's ability to understand the speech.

3.   **Topic development:** This includes how well your response addresses the task as well as the development of your ideas. Thus, the graders are judging you not only on *how* you speak, but also on *what* you say. This is an important point because test takers who are comfortable speaking in English may not achieve a top score if they do not structure their responses appropriately.

SPEAKING SECTION DIRECTIONS

The Speaking section has a fairly unique format, so it is helpful to familiarize yourself with the directions before you take the test. That way, you'll feel prepared and more comfortable when you actually take the TOEFL.

The Speaking section begins with a microphone test. At the beginning of the section, you'll be asked to answer a sample question. This question does not affect your TOEFL score, so don't worry about it. Your response is used simply to adjust the microphone volume, which will be done automatically at the conclusion of your response. The microphone test screen will look similar to the one shown below.

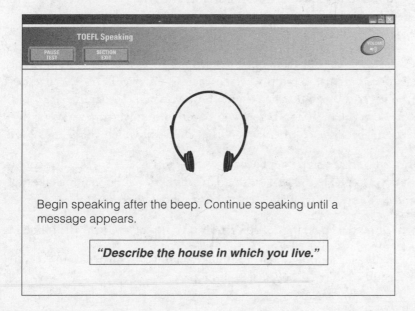

As you speak, the computer will adjust the volume of the microphone. When a message appears on the screen that tells you to stop speaking, the adjustment has finished.

After the adjustment is finished, the directions appear. The first two questions will ask you to respond to familiar topics—these are the tasks (discussed in the shaded box on the previous page) that ask you to state your personal preference and to choose between two options.

The next two questions require you to read a short text. You will have 45 seconds to read the selection, after which the text is removed from the screen. Next you will listen to a talk on the same topic as the reading. Your response will have to combine information from both the talk and the reading.

The final two questions ask you to listen to a conversation or lecture and respond to it. You will be allowed to take notes during all readings, conversations, and lectures. However, the directions for each question will not appear on the screen; you'll only be able to listen to them once.

CRACKING THE SPEAKING SECTION: BASIC PRINCIPLES

The Speaking section of the TOEFL can be very intimidating, but it doesn't have to be. The first important point about the Speaking section is that although there are six different questions, the *types* of responses you will give are all fairly similar. Basically, your goal when speaking is to use the structures you've seen throughout the Reading and Listening sections. If you are comfortable with the work we've done in those sections, you'll be comfortable with the types of responses that are rewarded on the TOEFL.

Another important point to consider is the *score range* of the programs to which you're applying. The top score on the Speaking section is 30 (although there are only six questions and the top score on each is a 4, the TOEFL converts your 0 to 24 points to a 0 to 30 scaled score); however, many programs are looking for scores far lower than 30. So before you devote too much time to worrying about this section, check the requirements of the schools in which you're interested.

Finally, realize that you *do not* have to sound like a native speaker to score well. It is perfectly acceptable to speak with an accent and make some mistakes in grammar and word use. What ultimately matters is how *understandable* your speech is.

Thus, cracking the Speaking section requires you to be aware of the following:

- **How you sound.** When speaking, you must try to avoid unnecessary pauses and try to speak at an even pace.
- **What you say.** Good responses have a clear flow of ideas and use appropriate transitions to link topics.
- **Your command of English grammar and vocabulary.** A top-scoring response uses a variety of words and contains some complex sentence structures.

Let's examine each of these requirements in more detail.

Basic Principle #1: How You Sound

As mentioned earlier, this doesn't mean you have to sound like a native speaker. It means that you should speak confidently and clearly. The two biggest problems are

- pausing often and breaking up the flow of your speech with unnecessary words such as *um* and *uh*
- delivering your speech in a mechanical "robot" voice, as if you were reading the response from a page

The best way to avoid the first problem is to use our speaking templates. These are basic patterns that you can use to organize your speech. We'll talk about the templates a little later in this chapter, and if you master these templates, you'll know exactly what you need to say for each task. That should help you avoid too many pauses in your speech.

As for the second issue, the best way to avoid a mechanical delivery is to practice. Once you familiarize yourself with the templates, practice using them with a variety of different topics. The more you practice using the templates, the more natural your speech will sound.

Basic Principle #2: What You Say

One key to scoring well on the Speaking section is to make sure the ideas about which you are talking are clearly connected to one another. You should use transitions to relate the parts of your speech together.

Here are some of the common transition words you will need to use on the TOEFL.

Words that indicate a *sequence* or progression					
First	Second	Third	Next	After	Lastly
Then	Previously	Before	Following	Finally	

Words that indicate a *connection* between ideas			
Because	Therefore	Thus	And
Also	Furthermore	Additionally	So

> **Words that indicate a *contradiction* between ideas**
>
> However   Despite   Yet   Although
>
> But   In contrast to   On the other hand

Now practice using these transitions in the exercise that follows.

Practice: Using Transitions

Read the following sentences aloud, connecting them with the appropriate transition word or words.

1. Jane would like to go home during the holiday break, _____ she doesn't have enough money.

2. Sasha intends to major in mathematics _____ it is her favorite subject.

3. First, you must mix the two chemicals together. _____, wait for the reaction to occur.

4. One of the main reasons Jose took the job was the salary; _____, the location was a factor.

5. _____ Ming had never met Anna before, they acted like old friends.

6. The professor is known for his harsh grading scale; _____, students say that he is one of the best teachers at the school.

7. The class requires students to write a 20-page research paper. _____, the students have to complete a group project.

8. Marco had _____ believed that he wanted to go to business school, but now he plans to attend law school.

9. It is very difficult to do well in this class without doing the required reading. _____, I recommend keeping up with the assignments.

10. Neela was sure that she had failed the exam _____ she received a passing grade.

Answers and Explanations for Practice: Using Transitions

Here are the appropriate transitions.

1. Jane would like to go home during the holiday break, **but** she doesn't have enough money.

This sentence *contrasts* two ideas. You also could have used *although*.

2. Sasha intends to major in mathematics **because** it is her favorite subject.

Here, we need to *connect* the two ideas. The first part is explained by the second part of the sentence.

3. First, you must mix the two chemicals together. **Then** wait for the reaction to occur.

There is a *progression* of ideas in this sentence. You also may have used *next* or *second*.

4. One of the main reasons Jose took the job was the salary; **additionally,** the location was a factor.

We need to *connect* both of the reasons together. Other possible responses include *furthermore* and *also*.

5. **Although** Ming had never met Anna before, they acted like old friends.

There is a *contrast* between the first idea and the second one.

6. The professor is known for his harsh grading scale; **however,** students say that he is one of the best teachers at the school.

Another *contrasting* set of ideas. The first part says something negative, whereas the second part expresses something positive.

7. The class requires students to write a 20-page research paper. **Furthermore**, the students have to complete a group project.

Both of the requirements need to be *connected*. You could have used *also* or *additionally* as well.

8. Marco had **previously** believed that he wanted to go to business school, but now he plans to attend law school.

This sentence shows a *progression* of ideas.

9. It is very difficult to do well in this class without doing the required reading. **Therefore**, I recommend keeping up with the assignments.

The first part and the second part are *connected* to each other. You could have also used *thus*.

10. Neela was sure that she had failed the exam **yet** she received a passing grade.

These two ideas *contrast* with one another. You also could have used *but*.

You can practice this drill on your own. Try making statements that require using each of the transitions presented on the previous page.

Basic Principle #3: Your Command of English Grammar and Vocabulary

This book is not intended to be a comprehensive grammar handbook; however, we will give you some basic grammatical structures to follow, and you should make sure to memorize the Grammar Review at the end of Chapter 5. (Check out The Princeton Review's *Grammar Smart* if you need more work with grammar.) Similarly, although working on your vocabulary is a worthwhile goal, we're only going to focus on some of the words that will be useful to you on the TOEFL. The Princeton Review also publishes *Word Smart for the TOEFL* for additional vocabulary practice.

Improving and Varying Sentence Structure

Let's start with some common sentence structures. Here is the most basic type of sentence.

Ichiro hit the ball.

This sentence has a simple pattern: *subject* (Ichiro), *verb* (hit), *object* (the ball). Although many of your constructions will follow this simple pattern, you'll have to vary your sentence structure somewhat to achieve a higher score on the TOEFL. For example, here's another way we can express the same idea.

The ball was hit by Ichiro.

This sentence moves the words around and creates a different emphasis. By using "the ball" as the *subject,* we give it more emphasis. Furthermore, by moving "Ichiro" to the *object* of the sentence, we de-emphasize him. If we add some more information to the sentence, we can use the following construction:

After hitting the ball, Ichiro ran to first base.

This sentence structure allows us to express two different actions, "hitting the ball" and "ran." And as you've seen, we can use *transitions* to make our sentences even more complex.

> Although Ichiro hit the ball, he was unable to reach first base safely.
> Ichiro hit the ball, but he was unable to reach first base safely.
> Ichiro hit the ball and reached first base safely.

All of these are types of sentences that you can use to increase your TOEFL Speaking score. Let's practice some of them.

Practice Using Complex Sentence Structures   Rewrite each of the following sentences by first switching the subject and the object. Next, add in the new information by using one of the complex structures discussed earlier. Don't forget to use transitions.

For example

> Maria bought a picture frame.
> Rewrite: <u>A picture frame was bought by Maria.</u>

Now add in this new information: "She needed it for her house."

Combine and rewrite: <u>Needing a picture frame for her house, Maria bought one. Also: A picture frame was bought by Maria because she needed it for her house.</u>

Now try it.

1. Steve attended class.
   Rewrite: _____
   Add new information: "Steve did not do his homework."
   Combine and rewrite: _____

2. Ellen chose the black shirt.
   Rewrite: _____
   Add new information: "Ellen prefers the color black."
   Combine and rewrite: _____

3. The professor gave two reasons for the behavior.
   Rewrite: _____
   Add new information: "The professor described the behavior first."
   Combine and rewrite: _____

4. The class required both a midterm and final exam.
   Rewrite: _____
   Add new information: "A student cannot pass the class without passing the midterm and final exam."
   Combine and rewrite: _____

5. The firm hired Ivan.
   Rewrite: _____
   Add new information: "Ivan was the most qualified candidate."
   Combine and rewrite: _____

6. Soccer is Andrew's favorite sport.
   Rewrite: _____
   Add new information: "Andrew started playing soccer when he was very young."
   Combine and rewrite: _____

7. Jaime asked a question.
   Rewrite: _____
   Add new information: "Jaime needed directions to the student center."
   Combine and rewrite: _____

8. Guillermo read the book.
   Rewrite: _____
   Add new information: "Guillermo wrote a paper on the book."
   Combine and rewrite: _____

9. Heather forgot her book.
   Rewrite: _____
   Add new information: "She needed it for class."
   Combine and rewrite: _____

10. Dennis plays the guitar.
    Rewrite: _____
    Add new information: "Dennis is learning to play the piano."
    Combine and rewrite: _____

Answers to Practice Using Complex Sentence Structures   Here are the rewritten versions of the sentence and some suggested ways of combining the sentences with the new information provided.

1. Steve attended class.
   Rewrite: The class was attended by Steve.
   Add new information: "Steve did not do his homework."
   Possible responses: Steve attended the class, although he did not do his homework. Despite not doing his homework, Steve attended the class. Steve attended the class even though he did not do his homework.

2. Ellen chose the black shirt.
   Rewrite: The black shirt was chosen by Ellen.
   Add new information: "Ellen prefers black."

Possible responses:	<u>Preferring black, Ellen chose that shirt. Because she preferred black, Ellen chose that shirt. Ellen chose that shirt because she prefers black.</u>

3. The professor gave two reasons for the behavior.

Rewrite:	<u>Two reasons for the behavior were given by the professor.</u>
Add new information:	"The professor described the behavior first."
Possible responses:	<u>After describing the behavior first, the professor gave two reasons for it. The professor first described the behavior and gave two reasons for it. The professor gave two reasons for the behavior after first describing it.</u>

4. The class required both a midterm and final exam.

Rewrite:	<u>A midterm and final exam were both required by the class.</u>
Add new information:	"A student cannot pass the class without passing the midterm and final exam."
Possible responses:	<u>Because the class requires both a midterm and final exam, a student cannot pass the class without passing both exams. Requiring a midterm and final exam, the class cannot be passed unless a student passes the exams. The class requires a midterm and final exam, and a student cannot pass the class unless he or she passes both exams.</u>

5. The firm hired Ivan.

Rewrite:	<u>Ivan was hired by the firm.</u>
Add new information:	"Ivan was the most qualified candidate."
Possible responses:	<u>Being the most qualified candidate, Ivan was hired by the firm. Because he was the most qualified candidate, Ivan was hired by the firm. The firm hired Ivan because he was the most qualified candidate.</u>

6. Soccer is Andrew's favorite sport.

Rewrite:	<u>Andrew's favorite sport is soccer.</u>
Add new information:	"Andrew started playing soccer when he was very young."

Possible responses: <u>Andrew's favorite sport is soccer because he started playing it when he was very young. Because he started playing it when he was very young, Andrew's favorite sport is soccer. Having played since he was very young, Andrew's favorite sport is soccer.</u>

7. Jaime asked a question.
    Rewrite: <u>A question was asked by Jaime.</u>
    Add new information: "Jaime needed directions to the student center."

    Possible responses: <u>Needing directions to the student center, Jaime asked a question. Jaime asked a question because she needed directions to the student center. Because she needed directions to the student center, Jaime asked a question.</u>

8. Guillermo read the book.
    Rewrite: <u>The book was read by Guillermo.</u>
    Add new information: "Guillermo wrote a paper on the book."
    Possible responses: <u>Guillermo read the book and also wrote a paper on it. Guillermo read the book because he had to write a paper on it. The book was read by Guillermo so that he could write a paper on it.</u>

9. Heather forgot her book.
    Rewrite: <u>The book was forgotten by Heather.</u>
    Add new information: "She needed it for class."
    Possible responses: <u>Although she needed it for class, Heather forgot her book. Heather forgot her book although she needed it for class. Heather forgot her book even though she needed it for class.</u>

10. Dennis plays the guitar.
    Rewrite: <u>The guitar was played by Dennis.</u>
    Add new information: "Dennis is learning to play the piano."
    Possible responses: <u>Dennis plays the guitar and is also learning to play the piano. Dennis is learning to play the piano, although he can play the guitar already. Although he plays the guitar, Dennis is learning to play the piano.</u>

The important point from this exercise is to see that there are many ways of expressing the same idea. You'll need to use a variety of sentence structures to score well on the TOEFL. You can practice this exercise on your own also. Take sentences from a book, magazine, or newspaper article and practice rewriting them in a variety of different ways.

Improving and Building Your Vocabulary

As for the vocabulary aspect, certain words are more suitable for certain tasks. Basically, the Speaking section asks to you do the following tasks:

- Describe
- Summarize
- Contrast

Let's look at each task and the types of phrases that are appropriate.

Descriptions   Some tasks ask you to describe a problem, an opinion, or a personal preference. If you are describing details, try using the following phrases:

- one aspect of...
- one characteristic of...
- one quality of...
- one issue (for describing a problem)...
- one feature...
- one attribute...
- one element...
- one thing...

For example, you may be asked to do the following on the TOEFL:

Describe a friend of yours, and explain why you consider this person a friend. Use details and examples to support your view.

For this task, we are asked to describe our friend. Our response may look like the sample below (note the descriptions are in boldface type).

One of my best friends is Joel. He is my friend for many reasons. One **characteristic** of Joel's that I really admire is his honesty. He always tells the truth to me. Another **quality** of Joel's that I like is his optimistic attitude. Joel always has a positive word for everyone. Joel's sense of humor is a final **aspect of** his personality that I admire. He is always able to make me laugh. For these reasons, I consider Joel a great friend.

As you can see, each of the words listed above can be used when describing a specific detail. Now it's your turn to try answering the above question, using as many of the above phrases as possible.

_____

_____

_____

_____

_____

_____

Summaries Another common task on the TOEFL Speaking section involves summarizing a reading or lecture. When summarizing, try using some of the following phrases:

- **according to** the reading/lecture/speaker...
- the reading/lecture/speaker **states that**...
- the reading/lecture/speaker **argues that**...
- the reading/lecture/speaker **holds that**...
- the reading/lecture/speaker **asserts that**...
- one reason/explanation **presented by** the reading/lecture/speaker...
- the reading/lecture/speaker **claims that**...
- the reading/lecture/speaker **expresses** the point/reason/opinion...

Here's an example of a summary.

Read the following passage and then summarize the points made by the author.

New research in the field of neuroscience is leading some researchers to change their beliefs about how the brain forms. An early view of the brain held that intelligence was primarily determined by genes. Now, however, a new study casts doubt on that view. Researchers have discovered that the neurons in the brain develop in the early stages of infancy. The more stimulation these neurons receive, the more connections the neurons make with other neurons. Cognitive scientists believe that intelligence is partly based on the number of connections between neurons in the brain.

Now we have to summarize the important parts of the passage. Our response might look like the following (again, with the summarizing terms shown in boldface):

According to the reading, some scientists have to change their views about the brain. The reading **states that** the early view of the brain is wrong. One reason given, **according to** the reading, is that there is a new study. The reading **claims that** the new study shows that brain development occurs during childhood. It also **argues that** the amount of stimulation a child receives leads to a higher intelligence.

Now try your own summary. Practice by using the passage on page 348 or parts of some of the other reading passages in this book.

_____

_____

_____

_____

_____

Contrasts　The final type of speaking task asks you to contrast ideas. Here are some helpful phrases to use when contrasting ideas.

- in contrast to...
- one difference between...
- unlike...
- one distinction between...
- dissimilarly...
- one disagreement between...
- one inconsistency between...
- one point at issue is...

Let's look at a task that requires us to contrast two things.

Read the following passage:

For more than three hundred years, the world understood physics as a predictable system. Isaac Newton's three laws of motion allowed physicists to predict the motion of not just falling apples and thrown balls, but comets, planets, and stars as well. The amazing degree of accuracy these predictions had convinced scientists that the universe obeyed precise laws, a belief that in many ways was reassuring because it was comforting to think of the universe as an orderly, predictable place.

Now read the following lecture on the same topic:

What would you guys think if I told you I could walk right through that wall over there? You probably wouldn't believe me. As you all know from, uh, basic physics, two solid objects cannot occupy the same space. But the truth is that...is that neither I nor the wall is really solid. That's right...I am mostly made up of empty space. I know it's weird, but think about it. I'm made of atoms, and atoms are mostly empty space. And it was in the early um, early twentieth century when the discovery was made that atoms can pass through other objects. If you shoot a number of atoms...I think it was Neils Bohr who did this experiment...at a sheet of metal, some of them will pass right through it. And although the probability is extremely unlikely...because I have so many atoms in my body... if I walked into that wall an infinite number of times, at some point I would pass right through it. So our world isn't as nice and predictable as we may believe.

Explain how the lecture casts doubt on or otherwise relates to the reading.

This asks us to contrast the information presented in both selections. Here's a sample response, with the contrasting terms shown in boldface.

One **difference between** the two is the predictable nature of physics. The reading states that the universe is predictable. In **contrast to** this idea, the professor says the world isn't always predictable. **Unlike** the reading, the lecture gives some information on how atoms can be unpredictable. This is **inconsistent with** the reading, which talks about larger objects, such as planets. However, the biggest **point at issue between** the two is whether or not we can predict events in the universe.

See if you can find other things to contrast in the lecture. Try to use the contrasting phrases listed above in your response. You can also practice on your own. A good place to look for contrasting ideas is in the editorial pages of your local newspaper. Find two articles or opinions on the same topic and try to contrast them.

CRACKING THE SPEAKING SECTION: BASIC APPROACH

Now that we've gone over the basic principles, we're ready to crack the Speaking section. To do so, do the following:

> 1. **Learn the appropriate template for each task,** and use it for your response.
> 2. **Learn the appropriate vocabulary for each task.** These words were covered in the previous section.
> 3. **Listen to spoken English as often as possible.** There's no better way to improve your speaking ability.

Let's spend some more time on the first step because it is one of the keys to doing well on this section.

Step 1: Learn the Appropriate Templates
The following templates are effective ways of organizing your speech. Learn them and you will be less likely to freeze up during the Speaking section. Let's go through the templates one by one.

Template #1: Personal Preference Question

The first speaking task on the TOEFL typically asks you to describe something that you would prefer to do, see, or experience. These tasks may also ask you to talk about something important to you. Regardless of the exact question, these tasks require you to pick the thing, person, or event you are going to discuss.

Here's a typical example.

> Describe a place you would like to visit, and explain why you chose this location. Use details and examples to support your position.

For this type of question, we'll use the following template:

State personal preference	I would like to visit Italy.
Reason #1	I would choose to visit Italy **because** it has a lot of history.
Specific detail for reason #1	**For example**, Italy has many interesting Roman ruins. It would be interesting to see these historic sites.
Reason #2	**Another reason** I would like to visit Italy is for the culture.
Specific detail for reason #2	Italy has been home to many great artists and the museums there contain some of the most famous works of art.
Reason #3	**Finally,** I would like to visit Italy to sample the food.
Specific detail for reason #3	I love Italian food and would really like the chance to try some authentic Italian cooking.

The boldfaced words are examples of transitions and other phrases you can use in your speech.

Depending on how fast you speak, you may only be able to provide two reasons in the time given. That's acceptable. And although this response may appear simple, it is much harder when you are under pressure. Now, try to use the template for the following prompt. Time yourself. Give yourself 15 seconds to prepare and 45 seconds to respond.

> Describe your favorite hobby, and explain why you enjoy it. Use details and examples to support your point.

State personal preference	
Reason #1	
Specific detail for reason #1	
Reason #2	
Specific detail for reason #2	
Reason #3	
Specific detail for reason #3	

Practice using this template on your own. Think of your favorite food, color, article of clothing, activity, and so on, and try to provide reasons and details as to why they are your favorites. Don't forget to use transitions.

Template #2: Choose an Option Question

The second type of task on the TOEFL presents you with two options. You'll have to decide which one is best and support your decision. Here's an example.

> Some universities give financial aid in the form of grants, which don't have to be paid back, whereas others provide financial assistance in the form of loans, which must be paid back. Which option do you think is better and why? Support your decision with reasons and examples.

Here's the template we'll use.

State option	I think it is **better** to offer students' loans.
Reason #1	I **prefer** loans **because** they make the student responsible.
Specific detail for reason #1	A student who has to pay back a loan becomes personally responsible for his or her education.
Reason #2	**Furthermore,** loans are safer for the school.
Specific detail for reason #2	Grants require the school to give away large amounts of money, and there is no guarantee that the school will get the money back.
Reason #3	**Lastly,** a student with a loan is probably more likely to stay in school.
Specific detail for reason #3	If the student doesn't complete the degree, it will be harder to pay back the money.

Try out this template. As before, keep track of your time. Give yourself 15 seconds to prepare and 45 seconds to respond.

> Some people believe that universities should require students to take classes on ethics, whereas others believe a school should focus only on academic issues. Which do you think is better? Support your decision with reasons and examples.

State option	
Reason #1	
Specific detail for reason #1	
Reason #2	
Specific detail for reason #2	
Reason #3	
Specific detail for reason #3	

You can try out this template on your own as well. Newspaper editorial pages often present two sides of an issue. Also, political issues are good practice.

Template #3: Summarize an Opinion Question

The third type of task requires you to read a brief passage and listen to a conversation about it. You'll then have to summarize the opinion or position given in the conversation. This task is different from the first two in that it has both reading and listening elements.

While *reading* the passage, you most likely won't need to take notes. The passage will usually discuss some sort of campus life issue. While *listening* to the conversation, pay attention to the speaker's opinion or attitude about the reading. You should pay particular attention to the reasons the speaker gives for his or her position. Write them down if you can.

Here's an example.

> Read the following announcement from the university president:
>
> Due to recent budget constraints, the university has decided to close the computer labs during weekends and reduce their operating hours during the week from 8:00 A.M. to 10:00 P.M. to 9:00 A.M. to 8:00 P.M. These changes are necessary in order to compensate for an unexpected budget shortfall. Without these cutbacks, the school would be forced to reduce service in other important areas, such as the library and the cafeteria.

Play Track 9 on the accompanying CD. (Transcripts of all the audio tracks in this chapter can be found beginning on page 330.)

The woman offers her opinion of the announcement. State what her opinion is and what reasons she gives for having that view.

Here's the template for our response.

State opinion	The woman **believes** that the decision to reduce the hours of the computer lab is a **bad** idea.
Reason #1	Her first **reason for claiming this** is that she needs a computer for her class work.
Details for reason #1	The woman **states that** she doesn't have a computer and that some of her classes require her to use one.
Reason #2	**Also,** the woman **claims** it will be harder to complete all of her work.
Detail for reason #2	**According** to the woman, the best time to do work is on the weekends. Now she fears that the labs will be too full during the week.

As you can see, all you have to do is basically repeat the reasons given by the speaker. You won't be required to do anything else. Now, it's your turn to try the template with the following example. Give yourself 30 seconds to prepare and 60 seconds to respond.

Read the following announcement from the president of a university:

Effective immediately, the university is instituting a new policy on off-campus visitors. Any guests are now required to register with campus security and obtain a guest pass which must be worn at all times. This new policy is necessary in order to keep all the students safe and to increase campus safety's knowledge of who is on campus.

Play Track 10 on the accompanying CD.

The man gives his opinion on the announcement. State the man's opinion and provide the reasons he gives for holding it.

State opinion	
Reason #1	
Details for reason #1	
Reason #2	
Detail for reason #2	

Template #4: Summarize/Contrast Question

The fourth template involves your response to a reading and an academic lecture. The goal of this task is to show how the lecture relates to or contrasts with the reading. Both the lecture and the reading will present some characteristics of a given topic. While *reading* the passage, write down the characteristics mentioned—typically there will be three to five of them. While *listening* to the lecture, listen for the characteristics and jot them down if you can. Think about how the characteristics in the lecture agree or disagree with the information in the reading.

Here's a sample.

> Read the following passage about captive breeding:
>
> Both environmentalists and animal rights activists consider captive breeding a solution to the threat of extinction of certain endangered species. In captive breeding, endangered animals are caught and bred, and the offspring is then released back into the wild. Unfortunately, the results of this program have been mixed. In many cases, the animals that are released back into the wild are unable to survive. The time spent in human captivity makes it more difficult for them to acquire food and to fit in with other members of their species.

Play Track 11 on the accompanying CD.

> The professor describes the results of a captive breeding experiment. Explain how the results of the experiment relate to the reading on the topic.

For this response, we need to combine information from the lecture and the reading, so our template will be a little different. Here's how we'll do it.

Main response	The experiment with the lynx shows that captive breeding can be successful.
Characteristic #1 from reading	**One problem** with captive breeding, **according to** the reading, is that animals do not always survive when reintroduced into the wild.
Detail #1 from lecture	**But** the scientists were able to successfully reintroduce the lynx into the wild.
Characteristic #2 from reading	The reading **states that** a major problem is that the animals don't know how to hunt.
Detail #2 from lecture	**However,** for the experiment, biologists first taught the animals how to hunt before releasing them.
Characteristic #3 from reading	**Another** problem in the reading is that the animals don't know how to interact with other members of the species.
Detail #3 from lecture	Scientists were able to get around this, **however,** by keeping the lynx together in a group.

For this type of question, it's acceptable if you run out of time before you list all of the characteristics. Your goal while speaking is to be as clear as possible, so don't rush through the details because it may make you harder to understand.

Try this template with the following example. You have 30 seconds to prepare and 60 seconds to respond.

Read the following passage about methane:

Methane is a colorless, odorless gas that occurs naturally as a result of the decomposition of plant and animal matters. Methane is a hydrocarbon like coal and oil, and it's all that remains of long-dead plants, dinosaurs, and other prehistoric animals. Although methane can be produced by volcanic activity, scientists usually connect the presence of methane with the presence of biological life. Many microorganisms excrete methane as a waste product, and scientists often infer the presence of these creatures by measuring the amount of methane in the air.

Play Track 12 on the accompanying CD.

The professor presents some facts about Mars. Explain how these facts may indicate life.

Main response	
Characteristic #1 from reading	
Detail #1 from lecture	
Characteristic #2 from reading	
Detail #2 from lecture	
Characteristic #3 from reading	
Detail #3 from lecture	

Template #5: Summarize/Preference Question

The fifth type of task asks you to listen to a conversation, usually about a problem. After listening, you'll have to summarize the problem and any solutions offered and state your preference. As you're *listening,* pay attention to the problem and the solutions offered. Here's an example.

Play Track 13 on the accompanying CD.

> The students discuss two possible solutions to the problem. Describe the problem and state which of the two solutions you prefer and why.

The important thing for this task is that you are able to list the solutions to the problem. There is no "right" or "wrong" answer, so when it comes time to state your preference, just pick whichever solution is easier for you to talk about. Here's the template, with the summarizing and preference terms shown in boldface.

State the problem	The man's problem is that he has two projects due at the same time.
State the solutions	His friend **offers** two possible solutions. He can ask for an extension, or he can drop the class.
State your preference	I think asking for an extension is a **better** solution.

Reason #1	An extension is better **because** dropping the class is too drastic.
Detail for reason #1	It seems silly to drop the entire class just because of one conflict.
Reason #2	I **also** think an extension is better because the professor will probably give the student one.
Detail for reason #2	The woman told of a similar situation, and she was able to get an extension.

Now try the template on the following example; you have 20 seconds to prepare and 60 seconds to respond.

Play Track 14 on the accompanying CD.

> The students discuss two possible solutions to the problem. Describe the problem and state which of the two solutions you prefer and why.

State the problem	
State the solutions	
State your preference	
Reason #1	
Detail for reason #1	
Reason #2	
Detail for reason #2	

Template #6: Summarize Question

The final task on the TOEFL also asks you to summarize a lecture. The template is somewhat different, however, because you have to link the points of a lecture to the main idea of the talk. Also, it may be a little more difficult than tasks three or four because you have only one chance to figure out the main idea. Thus, while *listening*, try to identify the main idea. Don't try to catch all of the details provided; you need only enough details so that you can talk for a minute.

Here's an example.

Play Track 15 on the accompanying CD.

> Using points and examples from the talk, explain how the Internet has contributed to censorship.

For this task, make sure you state the main idea right away. If you focus too much on the details, you'll lose points. Use the following template, with the key terms shown in boldface.

State main idea	The professor **argues that** the Internet actually promotes censorship, rather than fights it.
Reason #1	The **first** reason given by the professor is that the Internet has so much information on it.
Detail for reason #1	The Internet contains information from a wide variety of sources, including the government and companies.
Link between reason #1 and main idea	This censors information **because** the huge amount of information means that some views will never be heard.
Reason #2	**Furthermore,** the Internet makes it harder to find information.
Detail for reason #2	**For example,** the professor **states that** search engines only show the most popular websites.
Link between reason #2 and main idea	This contributes to censorship by leading users to a very small number of websites and hiding the other sites from them.

Now it's your turn. Listen to the following excerpt, and respond to it using the template; give yourself 20 seconds to prepare and 60 seconds to respond.

Play Track 16 on the accompanying CD.

Using points and examples from the talk, explain how the participants and items in a ritual represent other things.

State main idea	
Reason #1	
Detail for reason #1	
Link between reason #1 and main idea	
Reason #2	
Detail for reason #2	
Link between reason #2 and main idea	

Step 2: Learn the Appropriate Vocabulary

Throughout this lesson, certain words and phrases have appeared in **bold**. These words and phrases are particularly important on the Speaking section of the TOEFL. Go through this chapter and any other passages in the book and study the types of vocabulary words used.

For the Speaking section, you'll need to use three major categories of words. They are as follows:

- **Words that indicate preference.** This category includes words such as **favorite, best, most, better, superior,** and **favorable.** These are types of words that are helpful when explaining your opinion or preference. You'll also use these words on one of your Writing tasks. This category would also include the opposites of the above words, such as **worse, less, inferior, worst,** and **least.** Try to find other examples of preference words in this book.
- **Words that describe.** This category of words is useful when describing someone else's speech or conversation. These are the words that were discussed in the "Basic Principles" section. Make sure to review them frequently.
- **Transition words.** Be certain to familiarize yourself with the words in this category. See pages 307–308 for a refresher.

Step 3: Listen to Spoken English

This book has shown you how to construct responses, but you'll have to continue practicing by speaking aloud. One of the best ways of increasing your speaking ability is to listen to spoken English as often as possible. If you don't live in an English-speaking country, you can still hear English spoken in movies or on the Internet.

APPENDIX: TRANSCRIPTS TO AUDIO TRACKS

Track 9

Now listen to two students discuss the announcement.

Woman: Did you hear the announcement? They're cutting back the computer lab hours!

Man: Yeah, but it's better that they cut down there than at the library or the cafeteria.

W: Maybe for you, but I don't have a computer. I use the computer lab a lot. Plus, I need to have access to a computer for my economics class.

M: Well, they'll still be open during the week.

W: I know. But I get most of my work done during the weekend. The labs are usually empty then. They'll probably be filled with students now. It's going to make it really hard for me to get all my class work done.

M: Hmm. I didn't really think of that.

Track 10

Now listen to the following conversation about the announcement:

Man: I think the university's new policy is great.

Woman: Really? I think it's going to be annoying. I have some friends visiting, and they're going to have to spend all this time registering. And what if they lose their passes?

M: True. But that's a minor inconvenience. It's worth it if the campus is safer. Remember that vandalism that took place at the library was done by someone from off-campus.

W: I still think the school is overreacting. One bad thing happens, and they go and change the policy.

M: No, there have been other incidents. A couple months ago, there were some things stolen from one of the dorms. And the students reported seeing a suspicious figure.

W: I guess you're right.

Track 11

Now listen to a professor lecture about the same topic.

Okay, so we've been talking about some problems faced by biologists when they try to reintroduce species into the wild. As we've um...ah, talked about, sometimes the animals aren't ready or able to go...to fit into their native habitats. But there have been some new strategies used which seem to be, uh, working out. For example, biologists recently reintroduced four lynx—you guys know what a lynx is, right?—into the wild. The first time they tried it, the cats died of starvation—they didn't know how or where to hunt. This time, they kept the animals longer and let them mature. They also forced the animals to hunt for food instead of giving them the food directly. And finally, they kept the lynx together in a big pen so they know how to get along with other members of their species.

Track 12

Now listen to a professor give a talk about the same topic.

So, there's been some interesting news for those of you who dream of life on other planets. It turns out that Mars has a pretty high concentration of methane in its atmosphere. Now, usually when we think of life, we associate it with oxygen, right? But that's because we're kind of prejudiced. A whole host of creatures need no oxygen whatsoever.

The reason that this is important is that it looks like Mars has very little geologic activity. Methane can be produced without life, but as far as we know, there are no active volcanoes on Mars. Plus, here's another interesting point—methane only lasts about 300 years in the atmosphere. So that means the methane we're seeing now is fairly new...and it's being replenished somehow.

Listen to a conversation between two students.

Man: It looks like I've got a big problem on my hands.

Woman: Yeah? What's wrong?

M: I think I overbooked myself this semester. I took five classes, and two of them are really demanding. I have two really big projects due, and I don't think I can do both of them.

W: Oh no. It really sounds like you've got a lot of stuff on your plate. Have you talked to your professors yet?

M: No. I don't see how that would help.

W: Well, you could ask for an extension. Last semester, I asked Professor Miller for an extension on my psychology project. She was really nice about it and gave me two more weeks to finish it.

M: Hmm...I could do that. But I can't take extensions forever. The fact is that I still have a lot of work to do for these classes.

W: I guess. But it could help you open up your schedule for now so you're not so stressed out, you know?

M: Right.

W: Of course, there is one other option—but it's kind of drastic. You could drop one of the classes and take it next semester. It's still early enough to do it.

M: That could work, but I really didn't want to think about it. But I may have to.

Track 14

Listen to a conversation between two students.

Woman: Did you hear about the school's new parking policy? It's going to be a problem.

Man: No. I don't drive. So what's the deal with it?

W: Well, they changed the rules so that freshmen have to park all the way down near the athletic center. That's so far away!

M: Why did they do that?

W: I don't know. I think because the seniors have complained that there's not enough parking on the main campus. All I know is that it's going to be a big inconvenience for me.

M: Is there anywhere else you can park? I mean, the athletic center is pretty far. Maybe you can park off campus.

W: I don't know. I think I'd be afraid that something would happen to my car. I don't use it all the time, so it would be unattended for a lot of time.

M: I guess I didn't think of that. I have an idea.... Maybe you could find a garage for the car. It probably wouldn't cost any more than you pay now for a parking tag.

W: Maybe. But I'd have to find a garage close enough to campus that I could walk to.

Track 15

Listen to a lecture given in a sociology class.

Now oftentimes, when we think of the Internet, we think of it as the ultimate expression of free speech. There is no regulation of content on the Internet. People and organizations can put anything they want on the Web. Also, the Internet allows access to a huge amount of information. You can find almost anything you want there, but social scientists have argued that the Internet is actually responsible for a new type of censorship. In most cases, censorship involves a suppression of ideas. But the Internet censors material in a different way.

According to these sociologists, the censorship found on the Internet is subtle, but just as bad as any form of censorship. Basically, the Internet censors viewpoints by having too much information. That's right. Because the Internet contains information from companies, organizations, individuals, and even the government, any one viewpoint or idea can easily be buried under the tide, meaning that no one is exposed to it. Another way the Internet increases censorship is that because it is so vast, information becomes harder to find. Popular search engines direct users to the most popular websites and very seldom do people take the time to look at any more than the first two or three sites listed. Thus, these search engines are practicing an electronic form of censorship—unpopular ideas are hidden and inaccessible to the average user.

Track 16

Listen to a talk in an anthropology class.

All cultures partake in certain rituals and ceremonies. Although these rituals and ceremonies may sometimes seem hard to decipher, the essence of these actions is representation—the motions and the items used in the ceremony or ritual stand in for, or symbolize, something else. Usually, the members of the ritual are trying to control or affect something that lies outside their power, such as the weather or the gods, so they must use symbols to stand in for it.

For example, the Dieri people of central Australia use a very symbolic rainmaking ceremony. First, the rainmakers are bled. Their blood drips into a hole in the ground, which represents rain dropping from the sky. Next, the rainmakers take two rounded stones, which stand for clouds, and carry them some distance away. They then place the stones high up in a tree, which symbolizes the height of the clouds in the sky. Or, for another example, there is the fairly common ceremony in which a victim is chosen to symbolize all the sins and wrongdoings of a culture. The victim is then cleansed, either through a ritual bath or through death, in order to wash away the sins of the people. In fact, this is where the term "scapegoat" comes from, because one culture used a goat as its ceremonial symbol.

Speaking Summary

All right, only one more section to crack before you're ready to take the TOEFL! Let's review what you should do on the Speaking tasks.

o   **Know what the graders want:** Remember that graders are looking for the following: *delivery, language use,* and *topic development.* All three are important to your score. Even if you speak perfect English, if you don't answer the question correctly, your score will suffer.

o   **Don't try to be perfect:** You don't need to speak English as if you were a native speaker. The graders are concerned only with how easy it is to understand what you say. It's acceptable to have errors in your speech.

o   **Speak smoothly and confidently**, even if you make mistakes.

o   **Connect your ideas** with transitions.

o   **Use the templates:** It is very easy to lose track of what you are saying, and 60 seconds is not much time, so it's hard to recover if you get sidetracked. Practice the templates so you know exactly how your responses will be structured.

Let's go over those templates again:
*   **Personal preference**: state your preference and list 3 reasons with details.
*   **Choose an option**: choose whichever option you have more to say about, state it, and present your reasons and details.
*   **Summarize an opinion**: repeat the speaker's opinions and reasons but restate them in your own words.
*   **Summarize/contrast**: compare the points in the reading and the lecture and say why they are similar or different.
*   **Summarize/preference**: state the problem and the possible solutions, say which you prefer, and then give reasons and details why you think that one is better.

- **Summarize a passage or lecture:** listen carefully and state the main idea of the lecture. Restate the points of the lecture in your own words and explain the reasons and details given in the lecture.

○ **Practice, practice, practice:** There is no substitute for practice. Keep working on your speaking ability. Have an English-speaking friend listen to you as you speak, if possible.

Practice your speaking skills with the drills in the next chapter, and then we'll tackle cracking the Writing section. Almost done!

Chapter 13
Speaking Practice Drills

Now we're ready to practice the Speaking section. If possible, record or ask a friend to record your responses so you can review them later. Remember to use the templates we covered in the previous chapter.

Throughout the Speaking section on the actual test, you will be instructed to listen carefully with a screen that looks like the one below.

Questions will be introduced by a screen that looks like the one shown here.

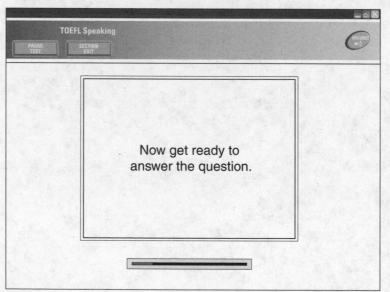

You will also see photographs of relevant scenes with each question. Some examples are included here with the question templates.

1. PERSONAL PREFERENCE QUESTION (TEMPLATE #1)

Listen to Track 17 on the accompanying CD. After the narrator reads the question, the track is finished, so you should pause the CD. Here's the question.

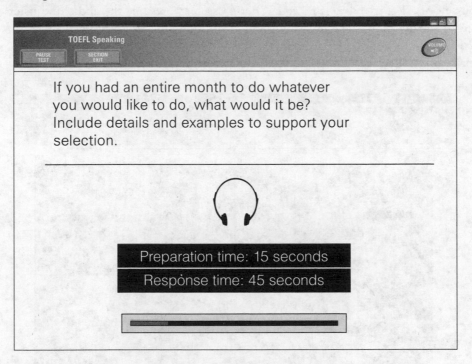

TOEFL Speaking

If you had an entire month to do whatever you would like to do, what would it be? Include details and examples to support your selection.

Preparation time: 15 seconds
Response time: 45 seconds

2. CHOOSE AN OPTION QUESTION (TEMPLATE #2)

Listen to Track 18 on the accompanying CD. After the narrator reads the question, the track is finished, so you should pause the CD. Here's the question.

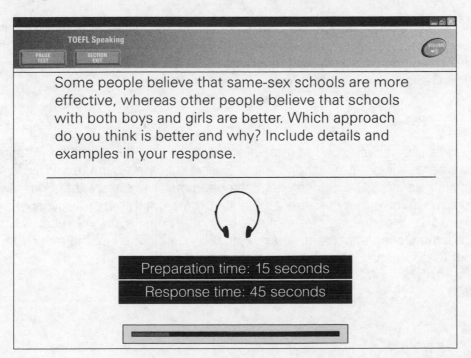

TOEFL Speaking

Some people believe that same-sex schools are more effective, whereas other people believe that schools with both boys and girls are better. Which approach do you think is better and why? Include details and examples in your response.

Preparation time: 15 seconds
Response time: 45 seconds

3. SUMMARIZE AN OPINION QUESTION (TEMPLATE #3)

For summarize an opinion questions on the actual test, you will see a series of screens similar to the ones that follow and hear a prompt to read a passage in 45 seconds. For our purposes here, you will need to stop the audio to read the passage and either time yourself or ask a friend to time you. After 45 seconds, resume the audio and listen to the conversation. After the narrator reads the question, the track is finished, so you should pause the CD.

Now listen to Track 19 on the accompanying CD (a transcript is also provided below).

Narrator: The University of Hartsdale has responded to budget constraints by eliminating some academic departments from its College of Liberal Arts. The campus newspaper printed the following report about the announcement of the department cuts. You have 45 seconds to read the report. Begin reading now.

[Stop the CD for 45 seconds.]

The university has announced that, effective at the beginning of the fall semester, three departments will be eliminated from the College of Liberal Arts: ecology, folklore studies, and textile sciences. Arrangements have been made to ensure that currently enrolled majors will receive their degrees as planned, but no new major applications have been approved for the affected departments during this past academic year. A statement by the dean of the College of Liberal Arts expressed confidence that the money thus saved would be put to good use elsewhere in the university.

[Restart the audio CD.]

Narrator: Now listen to two students as they discuss the announcement.

Woman: Did you see about those three departments being cut next year? It's a shame.

Man: Maybe. But you know, there were only two or three professors in each of those programs, and none of them is being let go. They're just being moved to bigger departments—you know, like, the folklore professors are going to be in anthropology. They'll still do the same research and teach the same classes.

W: They haven't let any professors go? I thought this was supposed to save money.

M: Well, it will. Each department has to have an administrative office, with a secretary and a budget manager. Those things add up. Moving the professors to bigger departments means a big savings on operations.

W: But it still means students have fewer options for majors.

M: You could say that, I guess. On the other hand, each of those departments only had, like, one major per year to begin with. They just weren't very popular. I really don't think we're going to be losing any important scholarship just because those things aren't full departments anymore.

Narrator: The man explains his opinion of the announcement made by the College of Liberal Arts. State his opinion, and explain the reasons he gives for holding that opinion.

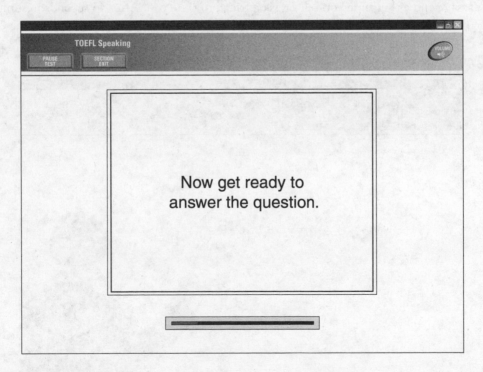

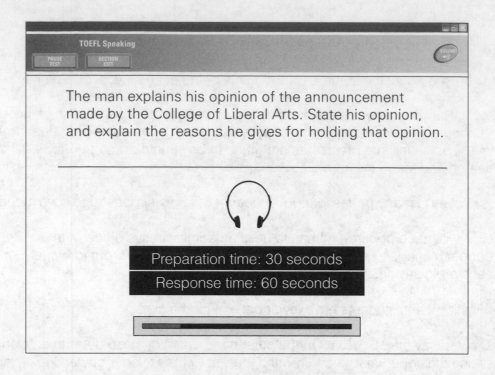

The man explains his opinion of the announcement made by the College of Liberal Arts. State his opinion, and explain the reasons he gives for holding that opinion.

Preparation time: 30 seconds

Response time: 60 seconds

4. SUMMARIZE/CONTRAST QUESTION (TEMPLATE #4)

Now, let's look at a contrast question. On the actual test, you will see a series of screens similar to the ones that follow and hear a prompt that will ask you to read a passage in 45 seconds. For our purposes here, you will need to stop the audio to read the passage and either time yourself or ask a friend to time you. After 45 seconds, resume the audio for the listening passage. After the narrator reads the question, the track is finished, so you should pause the CD.

Listen to Track 20 on the accompanying CD (a transcript is also provided below).

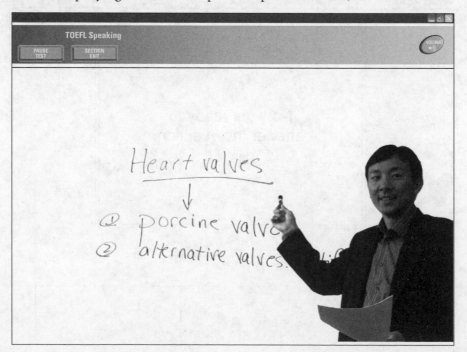

Narrator: Now read the passage about surgery to replace heart valves. You have 45 seconds to read the passage. Begin reading now.

[Stop the CD for 45 seconds.]

Heart Valve Replacement

Valves in the heart regulate the flow of blood, like gates or the locks of a canal. When a valve malfunctions and needs to be replaced, several factors need to be considered. The biggest is the age of the patient. Younger patients require valves that will last for many years; they also tend to be healthy enough to withstand courses of supplementary treatment that are hard on the body. Older patients, on the other hand, are often too weak for such supplementary treatments and can make do with replacement valves that are less durable.

[Restart the CD.]

Narrator: Now listen to part of a lecture on this topic given in a biology class.

Professor: People with defective heart valves need them replaced, and what's often used is the heart valve from a pig. It's called a "porcine valve" because of that. A pig's valve is very similar to a person's, and because pig valves are natural and tend to be accepted by the body, patients who receive them require little treatment after surgery...relatively, for transplant patients, I mean. Now, there *are* problems. For example, pig valves tend to last around ten years—not very long.

Actually, now that I'm on that topic, I might mention that porcine valves are not the only option. Alternative valves have been developed that are entirely artificial. They're made of plastic and metal. These valves can last for decades, certainly a lot longer than pig valves. But the human body recognizes that plastic and metal are artificial. So what happens is that blood sticks to them, and blood clots form around them. These clots are dangerous because they can block the flow of blood. For that reason, patients who receive artificial valves spend the rest of their lives taking drugs that prevent blood from clotting. The drugs can be tough for the body to handle, but they're worth it for the sake of having a functioning heart valve.

Narrator: The professor discussed the characteristics of two kinds of heart valves. Explain how their characteristics are related to their suitability for younger and older transplant patients.

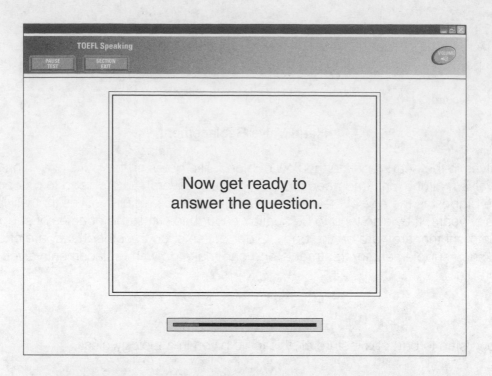

Now get ready to
answer the question.

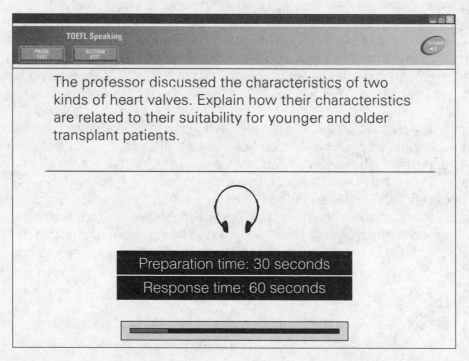

The professor discussed the characteristics of two kinds of heart valves. Explain how their characteristics are related to their suitability for younger and older transplant patients.

Preparation time: 30 seconds
Response time: 60 seconds

5. SUMMARIZE/PREFERENCE QUESTION (TEMPLATE #5)

For summarize/preference questions on the actual test, you will see a series of screens similar to the ones that follow and hear a prompt to listen to a conversation. For our purposes, after the narrator reads the question, the track is finished, so you should pause the CD.

Now listen to Track 21 on the accompanying CD (a transcript is also provided below).

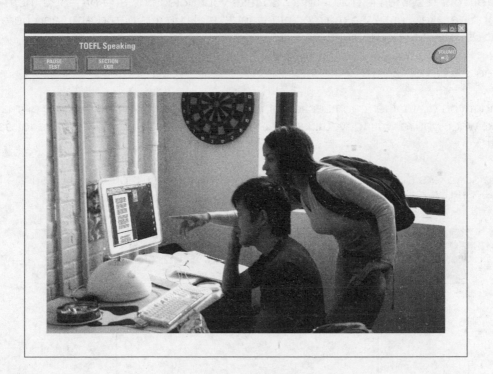

Narrator: Now listen to a conversation between two students.

Woman: How's that paper coming along, Chris?

Man: Coming along? You're joking, right?

W: Stuck, huh?

M: Yeah. The problem is, I can't get started. I mean, I have all the information I want to use—that's the frustrating thing. For once, I started my research early rather than leaving it to the last minute.

W: Uhhhh.... Have you considered just sitting at the computer and making yourself type? Sometimes that helps if you have writer's block.

M: Just typing whatever comes to mind?

W: Uh-huh. You can't force inspiration, but if you just let yourself relax and let your thoughts flow and type them out, you'll eventually get into the rhythm, and you'll start writing good stuff for your paper.

M: I don't know.

W: Okay, well, the other thing is, what about making an outline?

M: An outline?

W: Sure. Your research is done, right? So take your notecards and organize them on paper first. See, like, here's the main point I want to make in this paragraph, and here are the three details I want to use to support it.

M: I see.

W: And if you do that for each section of your paper, you have the structure all mapped out, and when you're writing, you just need to connect the pieces. It can be a lot easier to deal with.

Narrator: The speakers discuss two possible solutions for the man's problem. Describe the problem. Then state which of the two solutions you prefer and explain why.

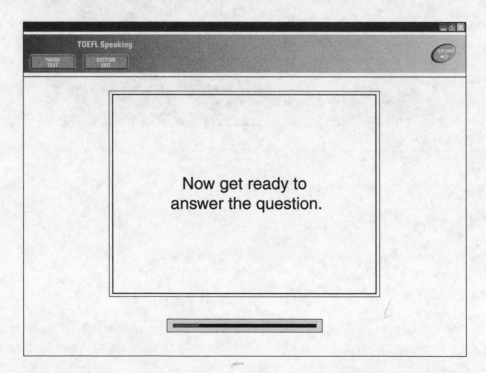

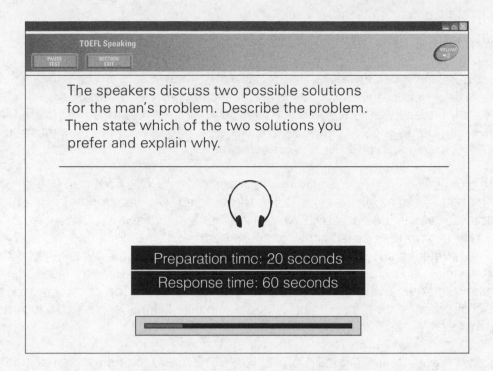

The speakers discuss two possible solutions for the man's problem. Describe the problem. Then state which of the two solutions you prefer and explain why.

Preparation time: 20 seconds

Response time: 60 seconds

6. SUMMARIZE QUESTION (TEMPLATE #6)

Now lets look at a summarize question. On the actual test, you will see a series of screens similar to the ones that follow and hear a prompt that will ask you to listen to a lecture. For our purposes, after the narrator reads the question, the track is finished, so you should pause the CD.

Now listen to Track 22 on the accompanying CD (a transcript is also provided below).

Narrator: Now listen to part of a talk in an archaeology class.

Professor: Most gems weren't formed by life processes, so they're very durable. If you're one of the lucky few archaeologists who discover an ancient crown inlaid with, say, rubies, you'll probably have to worry more about damage to the metal than to the stones themselves. But, some gemstones *are* organic. They're more fragile and can present special problems if you've dug them up and need to preserve them.

One example is amber, which formed millions of years ago from tree sap. The tree sap breaks down on exposure to air, but if the tree died and was buried in an airtight space before decaying, the sap could harden into amber. That's where amber gets its liquid clarity and smoothness. Uh, now, once it's hardened, you don't need to worry about oxygen breaking it down. What you do need to worry about is...well, think of it as being like hardened wax. If it comes too near to heat, it might melt or deform. Also, contact with oils or strong acids can injure the surface and make it cloudy. The basic thing to remember is, avoid sudden temperature changes and any contact with cleaning solutions and other such chemicals.

Another organic gem is coral. Coral is sort of the skeleton of creatures from the ocean floor, made of calcium carbonate, often with carotene mixed in. That's what makes it pinkish and orangish. You don't have to worry about melting coral, but you do have to worry about scratching it. Calcium carbonate is naturally rather powdery, so it chips easily. Also, it's very porous, so it absorbs liquids quickly. You need to make sure that you never soak coral in water or pour chemicals over it.

Narrator: Using points and examples from the talk, explain how archaeologists must take the origins of amber and coral into consideration when caring for them.

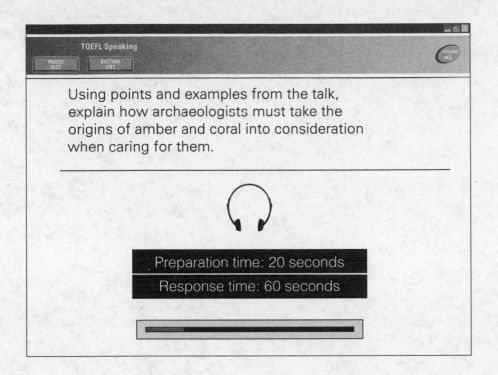

Using points and examples from the talk, explain how archaeologists must take the origins of amber and coral into consideration when caring for them.

Preparation time: 20 seconds

Response time: 60 seconds

Chapter 14
Speaking Practice
Answers and Explanations

In this chapter, you'll find transcripts of the questions in the previous chapter and sample responses. Use these to help you pinpoint areas for improvement in your speaking. Your answers will vary from the samples, but make sure you stick to the templates and fulfill the tasks.

1. PERSONAL PREFERENCE QUESTION (TEMPLATE #1)

Narrator: If you had an entire month to do whatever you would like to do, what would it be? Include details and examples to support your selection.

Preparation time: 15 seconds

Response time: 45 seconds

Sample Response

State personal preference	If I had that much time, I would like to travel around the world.
Reason #1	I would choose this **because** I am curious about other places in the world.
Specific detail for reason #1	**So far,** I have visited four different countries, **but** there are many more I would like to visit.
Reason #2	**Another reason** I would like to travel around the world is so I can meet many interesting people.
Specific detail for reason #2	I enjoy meeting new people and I am **especially** interested in meeting people from different cultures.
Reason #3	A **final** reason I would like to travel is because I plan to study international business.
Specific detail for reason #3	I think that traveling around the world would help me in the field of international business.

2. CHOOSE AN OPTION QUESTION (TEMPLATE #2)

Narrator: Some people believe that same-sex schools are more effective, whereas other people believe that schools with both boys and girls are better. Which approach do you think is better and why? Include details and examples in your response.

Preparation time: 15 seconds

Response time: 45 seconds

State option	I **believe that** schools should have both male and female students in order to be effective.
Reason #1	**The first reason** I believe this is that a mixed school is a better example of the real world.
Specific detail for reason #1	Any job that a student gets will involve both men and women, so a mixed school will prepare the student for that.
Reason #2	**Secondly,** going to a same-sex school may cause some difficulties for students.
Specific detail for reason #2	**For example,** students at a same-sex school may not know how to get along well with the opposite sex.
Reason #3	**Finally,** I think that being exposed to a variety of opinions is important to education.
Specific detail for reason #3	A mixed school exposes students to more opinions, which is very important.

3. SUMMARIZE AN OPINION QUESTION (TEMPLATE #3)

Narrator: The University of Hartsdale has responded to budget constraints by eliminating some academic departments from its College of Liberal Arts. The campus newspaper printed the following report about the announcement of the department cuts. You have 45 seconds to read the report. Begin reading now.

The university has announced that, effective at the beginning of the fall semester, three departments will be eliminated from the College of Liberal Arts: ecology, folklore studies, and textile sciences. Arrangements have been made to ensure that currently enrolled majors will receive their degrees as planned, but no new major applications have been approved for the affected departments during this past academic year. A statement by the dean of the College of Liberal Arts expressed confidence that the money thus saved would be put to good use elsewhere in the university.

Narrator: Now listen to two students as they discuss the announcement.

Woman: Did you see about those three departments being cut next year? It's a shame.

Man: Maybe. But you know, there were only two or three professors in each of those programs, and none of them is being let go. They're just being moved to bigger departments—you know, like, the folklore professors are going to be in anthropology. They'll still do the same research and teach the same classes.

W: They haven't let any professors go? I thought this was supposed to save money.

M: Well, it will. Each department has to have an administrative office, with a secretary and a budget manager. Those things add up. Moving the professors to bigger departments means a big savings on operations.

W: But it still means students have fewer options for majors.

M: You could say that, I guess. On the other hand, each of those departments only had, like, one major per year to begin with. They just weren't very popular. I really don't think we're going to be losing any important scholarship just because those things aren't full departments anymore.

Narrator: The man explains his opinion of the announcement made by the College of Liberal Arts. State his opinion, and explain the reasons he gives for holding that opinion.

Preparation time: 30 seconds

Response time: 60 seconds

Sample Response

State opinion	The man **believes that** the decision to cut the departments is a good one.
Reason #1	The man **contends that** no professors will lose their jobs when the departments are eliminated.
Details for reason #1	**According to** the student, the professors will simply join other departments.
Reason #2	**Furthermore,** the student states that there were not many majors in those departments.
Detail for reason #2	There was only one major per year in the eliminated departments.

4. SUMMARIZE/CONTRAST QUESTION (TEMPLATE #4)

Narrator: Now read the passage about surgery to replace heart valves. You have 45 seconds to read the passage. Begin reading now.

Heart Valve Replacement

Valves in the heart regulate the flow of blood, like gates or the locks of a canal. When a valve malfunctions and needs to be replaced, several factors need to be considered. The biggest is the age of the patient. Younger patients require valves that will last for many years; they also tend to be healthy enough to withstand courses of supplementary treatment that are hard on the body. Older patients, on the other hand, are often too weak for such supplementary treatments and can make do with replacement valves that are less durable.

Narrator: Now listen to part of a lecture on this topic given in a biology class.

Professor: People with defective heart valves need them replaced, and what's often used is the heart valve from a pig. It's called a "porcine valve" because of that: A pig's valve is very similar to a person's, and because pig valves are natural and tend to be accepted by the body, patients who receive them require little treatment after surgery...relatively, for transplant patients, I mean. Now, there *are* problems. For example, pig valves tend to last around ten years—not very long.

Actually, now that I'm on that topic, I might mention that porcine valves are not the only option. Alternative valves have been developed that are entirely artificial. They're made of plastic and metal. These valves can last for decades—certainly a lot longer than pig valves. But the human body recognizes that plastic and metal are artificial. So what happens is that blood sticks to them, and blood clots form around them. These clots are dangerous because they can block the flow of blood. For that reason, patients who receive artificial valves spend the rest of their lives taking drugs that prevent blood from clotting. The drugs can be tough for the body to handle, but they're worth it for the sake of having a functioning heart valve.

Narrator: The professor discussed the characteristics of two kinds of heart valves. Explain how their characteristics are related to their suitability for younger and older transplant patients.

Preparation time: 30 seconds

Response time: 60 seconds

Main response	The professor **discussed** two types of valves. One is from a pig, the other is made of plastic and metal.
Characteristic #1 from reading	**One aspect** of heart valves that is very important is how long they last.
Detail #1 from lecture	Pig valves can be used, **but** they last for only ten years. This makes them unsuitable for younger patients.
Characteristic #2 from reading	**Another characteristic** that is important is the need for additional treatments.
Detail #2 from lecture	Plastic and metal valves require special drugs that stop the blood from clotting.
Characteristic #3 from reading	**According to** the reading, old patients and young patients have different needs. Old patients should avoid extra treatments, **whereas** young patients need a valve that lasts for a long time.
Detail #3 from lecture	**Thus,** pig valves may be suited to older patients, **and** plastic or metal valves for younger patients.

5. SUMMARIZE/PREFERENCE QUESTION (TEMPLATE #5)

Narrator: Now listen to a conversation between two students.

Woman: How's that paper coming along, Chris?

Man: Coming along? You're joking, right?

W: Stuck, huh?

M: Yeah. The problem is, I can't get started. I mean, I have all the information I want to use—that's the frustrating thing. For once, I started my research early rather than leaving it to the last minute.

W: Uhhhh....Have you considered just sitting at the computer and making yourself type? Sometimes that helps if you have writer's block.

M: Just typing whatever comes to mind?

W: Uh-huh. You can't force inspiration, but if you just let yourself relax and let your thoughts flow and type them out, you'll eventually get into the rhythm, and you'll start writing good stuff for your paper.

M: I don't know.

W: Okay, well, the other thing is, what about making an outline?

M: An outline?

W: Sure. Your research is done, right? So take your notecards and organize them on paper first. See, like, here's the main point I want to make in this paragraph, and here are the three details I want to use to support it.

M: I see.

W: And if you do that for each section of your paper, you have the structure all mapped out, and when you're writing, you just need to connect the pieces. It can be a lot easier to deal with.

Narrator: The speakers discuss two possible solutions for the man's problem. Describe the problem. Then state which of the two solutions you prefer and explain why.

Preparation time: 20 seconds

Response time: 60 seconds

Sample Response

State the problem	The problem is that the man is unable to write his paper.
State the solutions	His friend **proposes** two different solutions. The **first** is just to try to write whatever comes into his head. The **second** is to make an outline.
State your preference	I think that writing an outline is a **better** solution.
Reason #1	An outline is the **best** way of organizing your thoughts.
Detail for reason #1	**Because** the student already has done the research, all he needs to do is figure out how to put all the information together.
Reason #2	**Additionally,** making an outline is more productive than just writing whatever you think of.
Detail for reason #2	The student could waste a lot of time writing stuff that isn't good, **but** working on an outline will directly contribute to the paper.

6. SUMMARIZE QUESTION (TEMPLATE #6)

Narrator: Now listen to part of a talk in an archaeology class.

Professor: Most gems weren't formed by life processes, so they're very durable. If you're one of the lucky few archaeologists who discover an ancient crown inlaid with, say, rubies, you'll probably have to worry more about damage to the metal than to the stones themselves. But, some gemstones *are* organic. They're more fragile and can present special problems if you've dug them up and need to preserve them.

One example is amber, which formed millions of years ago from tree sap. The tree sap breaks down on exposure to air, but if the tree died and was buried in an airtight space before decaying, the sap could harden into amber. That's where amber gets its liquid clarity and smoothness. Now, once it's hardened, you don't need to worry about oxygen breaking it down. What you do need to worry about is...well, think of it as being like hardened wax. If it comes too near to heat, it might melt or deform. Also, contact with oils or strong acids can injure the surface and make it cloudy. The basic thing to remember is, avoid sudden temperature changes and any contact with cleaning solutions and other such chemicals.

Another organic gem is coral. Coral is sort of the skeleton of creatures from the ocean floor, made of calcium carbonate, often with carotene mixed in—that's what makes it pinkish and orangish. You don't have to worry about melting coral, but you do have to worry about scratching it. Calcium carbonate is naturally rather powdery, so it chips easily. Also, it's very porous, so it absorbs liquids quickly. You need to make sure that you never soak coral in water or pour chemicals over it.

Narrator: Using points and examples from the talk, explain how archaeologists must take the origins of amber and coral into consideration when caring for them.

Preparation time: 20 seconds

Response time: 60 seconds

Sample Response

State main idea	**According to** the professor, both amber and coral can be harmed by certain processes.
Reason #1	Amber is made from hardened tree sap.
Detail for reason #1	**Because of** this fact, amber can be damaged by heat, oils, and acids.
Link between reason #1 and main idea	**Thus,** archaeologists have to be careful not to expose amber to high temperatures, which can affect the shape of the amber. **Also,** some liquids will make the amber cloudy.
Reason #2	Coral is made up of the skeletons of ocean creatures.
Detail for reason #2	**Because** it is brittle, it can be scratched or chipped. **Additionally,** it can absorb liquid.
Link between reason #2 and main idea	Archaeologists **therefore** must be careful not to soak coral or handle it roughly.

Chapter 15
Cracking the
Writing Section

The final section of the TOEFL measures your ability to communicate in an academic environment. This is supposed to check to see if you can write a college-level paper when you get to college. There are only two writing tasks, and they combine many of the qualities present in the Reading, Listening, and Speaking sections. On the Writing section, you'll be asked to do the following:

- **Read** a passage on an academic subject, **listen** to a lecture on the same topic, and **write** an essay that discusses the relationship between the two. You'll have three minutes to read and 20 minutes to respond.
- **Write** an essay that states, explains, and supports your position on an issue. You'll have 30 minutes to write this essay.

You will have 50 minutes to complete both tasks.

HOW THE WRITING SECTION IS SCORED

Your TOEFL essays are graded on a 0 to 5 scale. A top-scoring essay on the TOEFL accomplishes the following:

- addresses the topic and the task
- is well organized and uses appropriate examples
- displays unity, progress, and coherence
- displays consistent facility in the use of language

It is worth noting that of the four criteria, only one focuses on your use of language. The rest are concerned with how well you complete the task and how organized your writing is.

Your goal in the Writing section is to make the grader's job as easy as possible. Essays that are disorganized or lack focus are difficult to read. An essay that is difficult to read is going to receive a low score. Instead of making the grader's life difficult, you want to show the grader that your writing conforms to the above standards. By writing a focused, organized essay, you'll make it easy for the grader to give you a score of 4 or 5.

WRITING SECTION DIRECTIONS

It is important to note that your first writing task will require both a reading and listening part, so you'll need to leave your headset on. Your essay must be typed, so you should have some familiarity with the keyboard before you take the TOEFL. The word processor used for the TOEFL is very simple; it only has *cut*, *copy*, and *paste* functions.

For the first task, you will have three minutes to read a passage. After that time is finished, the passage is removed from the screen, and you will listen to a lecture on the same topic. You may take notes during the reading and the lecture. When the lecture is finished, you'll have 20 minutes to write an essay on the relationship between the reading and the lecture. Your response must *not* include personal opinions. The reading passage will reappear on the screen for your reference.

The second task is much simpler. You will have 30 minutes to write a response to a prompt. There is no reading or lecture; you *are* asked to provide your personal views on a subject.

CRACKING THE WRITING SECTION: BASIC PRINCIPLES

There are a few things to keep in mind when writing your essays for the TOEFL. As with the Speaking section, the graders are not expecting perfection. They realize that you are essentially writing the first draft of an essay. Given the limited amount of time provided, they expect you to make a few grammatical mistakes and misspell a few words. Furthermore, in many ways the graders are looking more at *how* you write, not *what* you write. The structure and organization of your essay is just as important as the content of your essay.

When writing your essay, be aware of the following important points:

- Make sure you answer the question appropriately.
- Make sure your essay is long enough.
- Make sure your essay is clearly organized.

Paying attention to these three basic points will put you on the right track. Let's look at them in further detail.

Basic Principle #1: Make Sure You Answer the Question Appropriately

One of the first things the graders will look at when reading your essay is if you answered the question in the prompt. Well-written essays that don't address the task will lose points. Therefore, it is important that you know about the two different tasks you will be asked to do.

The first task asks you to **summarize** and **relate** the points in a lecture to those in a reading. Thus, your essay should contain *only* facts from the material. All you are expected to do is report the main points mentioned and show how they are related to each other. You should *not* give your opinion on any of the topics. The first task should be written entirely in the third person—that is, using words such as *he, she, the professor, the student,* and so on. You should never use *I* or *me* in the first essay.

The second task requires you to state your **opinion.** This task requires you to argue what option or choice you believe to be better. Thus, the essay should be written in the first person—it's acceptable to use *I* and *my* for the second essay.

It is important that you understand the tasks. Knowing exactly what your purpose is makes the essays easier to write.

Basic Principle #2: Make Sure Your Essay Is Long Enough

On the TOEFL, quantity makes a difference. To a grader, a longer essay is a better essay. Why? Because a longer essay shows the grader that you are comfortable writing and are able to produce a sustained, focused piece. When writing, you must make sure your essay falls within the TOEFL's suggested guidelines for length.

- For the first task, the TOEFL states that an "effective" response is between 150 to 225 words.
- A minimum of 300 words is required for the second task.

Although these word counts may seem intimidating, they're not as bad as you may think. For example, the section that you are now reading is more than 100 words. In fact, a 200-word essay basically consists of an introduction, one or two body paragraphs, and a conclusion—about the same length as half of this page. That's it.

A 300-word essay is approximately two-thirds of this page. You'll find that when you use the essay templates in this chapter, you shouldn't have any problem writing 300 words, but you should nonetheless count the words of your practice essays to make sure they are long enough.

Basic Principle #3: Make Sure Your Essay Is Clearly Organized

Organized essays are easy to read. Essays that are easy to read are easy to understand. TOEFL graders like both of those qualities. Your written responses on the TOEFL should contain the following:

- **an introduction,** containing your thesis statement
- **body paragraphs,** containing examples and details that support your thesis
- **a conclusion,** containing a final restatement of your thesis
- **appropriate transitions,** linking your paragraphs and ideas together

Now would be a good time to return to Core Concept: Writing, especially if you haven't read through it yet. That section provides all the necessary information on how to organize your essay and use transitions.

CRACKING THE WRITING SECTION: BASIC APPROACH

You will achieve a good score on the TOEFL Writing section if you do the following:

1. **Know what you're going to write *before* you write.** Master the writing templates in this chapter so you are confident on test day.
2. **Organize your essay first.** Don't just start writing; spend a few minutes outlining your essay. It will make writing it much easier.
3. **Consider your audience.** TOEFL graders are trained to look for certain things in an essay. Make sure your essay contains these key elements.
4. **Use your time wisely.** You have only 20 or 30 minutes to write. Make efficient use of your time.

Let's look at each of these steps.

Step 1: Know What You're Going to Write

The biggest danger in trying to write under timed conditions is writer's block—that is, you have absolutely no idea what to write. While you struggle with how to put your thoughts on paper, valuable time slips away. Fortunately, there is an easy solution to this problem: Know exactly what you need to write *before* you sit down at the testing center.

We're going to look at templates for each of the writing tasks. Use these templates and familiarize yourself with their basic structures. That way, all you'll have to do is adjust the template to the specific topic.

Template #1: Casting Doubt on a Lecture

For the first essay, you will usually be asked to perform the following task:

> Summarize the points made in the lecture, explaining how they cast doubt on the reading.

The template for this task is as follows:

> **Paragraph #1: Introduction**
> I. Topic sentence
>   **In the lecture, the** (professor/teacher/instructor) **made several points about** (topic).

II. State main idea of lecture
   The (professor/teacher/instructor) **argues that** (the main idea of the lecture).
III. Transition/main idea of reading
   However, the reading contends that (the main idea of the reading).
IV. Thesis statement
   The professor's lecture casts doubt on the reading by using a number of points that are contrary to (the main idea of the reading).

Paragraph #2: Body Paragraph
I. Transition/point #1 from lecture
   The first point that the (professor/teacher/instructor) **uses to cast doubt on the reading is** (point #1 from lecture).
II. Detail for point #1
   According to the (professor/teacher/instructor), (detail for point #1 from the lecture).
III. Opposing point from reading
   (Point #1) **differs from the reading in that the reading states** (point #1 of the reading).
IV. Explanation of relationship between reading and lecture
   The point made by the (professor/lecturer/instructor) **casts doubt on the reading because** (how lecture is different from reading).

Paragraph #3: Body Paragraph
I. Transition/point #2 from lecture
   Another point that the (professor/teacher/instructor) **uses to cast doubt on the reading is** (point #2 from lecture).
II. Detail for point #2
   The (professor/teacher/instructor) **claims that** (detail for point #2 from the lecture).
III. Opposing point from reading
   However, the reading states (point #2 from reading).
IV. Explanation of relationship between reading and lecture
   This point is contradicted by (point #2 from lecture).

Paragraph #4: Conclusion
I. Topic sentence
   In conclusion, the points made in the lecture contrast with the reading.
II. Summary
   (Points #1 and #2 from the lecture) **demonstrate that** (main idea of the reading) **is in doubt.**

The words in bold are suggestions; you don't have to use them exactly. You may also find that you have time to write a third body paragraph. If so, repeat the formula from the first two body paragraphs. However, your writing should still follow the general pattern established in the outline. In the next chapter, you'll have the opportunity to see the template in action on a sample question.

Template #2: Showing Support for a Reading Passage

You may also see a prompt like the following:

Summarize the points made in the lecture, explaining how they support the reading.

This task is simply the opposite of the first. The template is fairly similar.

Paragraph #1: Introduction
I. Topic sentence
In the lecture, the (professor/teacher/instructor) **made several points about** (the topic).
II. State main idea of lecture
The (professor/teacher/instructor) **argues that** (main idea of the lecture).
III. Transition/main idea of reading
The points made by the (professor/teacher/instructor) **agree with** (main idea of the reading passage).
IV. Thesis statement
In fact, the examples used by the (professor/teacher/instructor) **support** (main idea of the reading passage).

Paragraph #2: Body Paragraph
I. Transition/point #1 from lecture
The first point that the (professor/teacher/instructor) **uses to support the reading is** (point #1 from the lecture).
II. Detail for point #1
According to the (professor/teacher/instructor), (detail for point #1 from the lecture).
III. Opposing point from reading
(Point #1) **supports the reading, which holds that** (point #1 from the reading passage).
IV. Explanation of relationship between reading and lecture
The point made by the (professor/lecturer/instructor) **supports the reading because** (why lecture agrees with the reading).

Paragraph #3: Body Paragraph
I. Transition/point #2 from lecture
Furthermore, the (professor/teacher/instructor) **bolsters the reading by stating that** (point #2 from the lecture).
II. Detail for point #2
The (professor/teacher/instructor) **claims that** (detail for point #2 from the lecture).
III. Opposing point from reading
This point agrees with the reading, which contends that (point #2 from the reading).
IV. Explanation of relationship between reading and lecture
The (point #2 from lecture) **shows the truth of the reading because** (how point #2 agrees with the reading).

Paragraph #4: Conclusion

I. Topic sentence
In conclusion, the points made in the lecture support the reading.

II. Summary
(Points #1 and #2 from the lecture) **demonstrate that** (main idea of the reading) **is valid.**

Template #3: Using Specific Details and Examples to Support Your Opinion

The second task on the TOEFL simply asks for your opinion on a matter. The prompt will look something like the example shown below.

Do you agree or disagree with the following statement?

(statement)

Use specific details and examples to support your answer.

For the second task, we'll use the following template:

Paragraph #1: Introduction

I. Topic sentence/paraphrase prompt
The issue at hand is (choice offered by the prompt).

II. Interpret the prompt
This issue is (important/difficult/troubling) **because** (what is important/difficult/troubling about the prompt).

III. State your thesis
I believe that (state your choice) **is the better option because** (reasons why you believe your option is preferable).

Paragraph #2: Body Paragraph

I. Transition/first reason
(Your choice of options) **is preferable because** (reason #1).

II. Detail for reason #1
(Details about reason #1)

III. Tie reason #1 back to thesis
Because (details about reason #1), **I think that** (your choice) **is superior to** (the other option).

Paragraph #3: Body Paragraph

I. Transition/second reason
Additionally, (your choice) **is better because** (reason #2).

II. Detail for reason #2
(Details about reason #2)

III. Tie reason #2 back to thesis
Based on (details about reason #2), (your choice) **is a better option than** (the other option).

Paragraph #4: Body Paragraph
   I. Transition/third reason
   Finally, I think (your choice) **is the right choice because** (reason #3).
  II. Detail for reason #3
   (Details about reason #3).
 III. Tie reason #3 back to thesis
   I like (your choice) **over** (the other option) **due to** (details about reason #3).

Paragraph #5: Conclusion
   I. Transition/restate thesis
   Ultimately, I feel that (your choice) **is the correct one.**
  II. Final statement
   I believe this because (why you believe your choice is best).

In summary, familiarize yourself with these templates. If you know exactly what your essay is supposed to look like, you'll have an easier time writing.

Step 2: Organize Your Essay

In the first step, we looked at how your essay should *be structured*. Now we need to talk about what your essay will *contain*. Before you start writing, spend about five minutes brainstorming examples and points for your essay. Failing to do so may lead you to write an essay that lacks focus and coherence.

For the first task, you'll be presented with a short reading passage. While reading, take notes on the main idea and some of the major facts presented. Your notes do not have to be very detailed—you'll be able to refer back to the passage while you are writing. However, it is important to know the general idea of the reading so that you can relate it back to the lecture.

During the lecture, try to note the major points presented by the professor. There will usually be three to five points, but you won't need all of them: Two or three points will be sufficient for the task. You will not be able to hear the lecture again, so it is important to remember some of the points.

Try to organize your notes in the following way:

Reading:
  Main idea: _____
 Example/reason: _____
 Example/reason: _____
 Example/reason: _____

Remember, if it's too difficult to read and take notes, then do not attempt to do so. The reading passage will be available for reference while you write. For the lecture, the main idea is generally opposite that of the reading, so don't worry about noting that. The examples offered in the lecture are the parts you have to concentrate on. During the lecture, try to organize your notes as follows:

Lecture:
Point #1: _____
Detail #1: _____
Point #2: _____
Detail #2: _____
Point #3: _____
Detail #3: _____

Even if you are unable to write down the details for the example, you'll need to try to remember them so you can refer to them in your essay. If you don't mention specific points from the lecture, you will receive a lower score.

For the second task, it is very important that you come up with good reasons for your viewpoint. You need to tell the reader why you believe your opinion is better. Here's a good way to organize your thoughts.

Issue:
Your opinion: _____
Why? _____
Reason #1: _____
Detail #1: _____
Reason #2: _____
Detail #2: _____
Reason #3: _____
Detail #3: _____

A Sample Response: A Well-Organized Essay

Let's look at a sample response for the second writing task. Here's the prompt.

Do you agree or disagree with the following statement?

The purpose of education should be to teach skills, not values.

Support your position with details and examples.

Before you start writing, take time to organize. First, write down what the issue is.

Issue: _Should schools teach only skills and not values?_

Putting the statement into your own words or rephrasing it as a question is a helpful way to approach the prompt. Now, figure out which side of the issue you are on.

Your opinion: <u>Disagree—I believe schools should teach values as well as skills.</u>

After figuring out your opinion, ask yourself why you have that opinion. This information will be useful for your introduction.

Why? <u>Because students need to know how to act in the world.</u>

Once you ask yourself why you have your opinion, you then need to list some specific examples.

Reason #1: <u>Students may not get educated about values at home.</u>

Detail #1: <u>Some parents don't teach values to their children. Thus, schools should teach them.</u>

Reason #2: <u>Education is more than just skills.</u>

Detail #2: <u>Students are going to use their education in the outside world. They need to know what's right and wrong.</u>

Reason #3: <u>It is easier to teach values when students are younger.</u>

Detail #3: <u>Education plays an important role in a young person's life, so schools are a good place to teach values.</u>

Your Turn: Practice Writing a Well-Organized Essay

Now it's your turn to organize your thoughts on the prompt that follows.

Do you agree or disagree with the following statement?

Students should be required to take regular standardized tests to prove that they are learning.

Support your position with details and examples.

Issue:

     Your opinion: _____

     Why? _____

     Reason #1: _____

     Detail #1: _____

     Reason #2: _____

     Detail #2: _____

     Reason #3: _____

     Detail #3: _____

Now try it again, and time yourself. See if you can brainstorm some examples within five or six minutes.

Do you agree or disagree with the following statement?

The best way to teach is by example.

Support your position with details and examples.

Issue:

Your opinion: _____
Why? _____
Reason #1: _____
Detail #1: _____
Reason #2: _____
Detail #2: _____
Reason #3: _____
Detail #3: _____

Step 3: Consider Your Audience

TOEFL graders are trained to look for certain features in your writing. By ensuring that your essay contains these features, you'll improve your score. Similarly, there are some elements to avoid in your writing. Make sure your essay contains the following:

1. **An introduction, body paragraphs, and a conclusion.** More details on these can be found in Core Concept: Writing.
2. **Specific examples.** Your essay must use specific examples. The more detail you use, the better your essay will be.
3. **Transitions.** One of the things TOEFL graders look for in an essay is "unity and coherence." That means that all the ideas are linked together with appropriate transitions.

In addition, you'll want to avoid the following:

1. **Repeating phrases from the reading or prompt word for word.** Always put the examples and reasons into your own words. Although repeating a word or two is acceptable, you should *never* copy long phrases directly from the text on screen. TOEFL graders will penalize you for this.
2. **Writing your essay as one long paragraph.** Make sure you divide your essay into separate paragraphs. *Do not* just write a single block of text.
3. **Including material not relevant to the task.** Your essay must remain on topic. *Do not* include any reasons or examples that do not connect or relate to the task.

By keeping these points in mind, you'll ensure that your essay is well received by the TOEFL graders.

Step 4: Use Your Time Wisely

If you had unlimited time, you would surely be able to achieve a top score on the Writing section. Unfortunately, your time on the TOEFL is extremely limited. Thus, you must make sure to use your time wisely. The following tables provide a good guide for how to spend your time:

Task #1: 20 minutes

Time	Task
5 minutes	Organize your essay.
2 minutes	Write your introduction.
10 minutes	Write your body paragraphs.
2 minutes	Write your conclusion.
1 minute	Proofread your essay to correct any mistakes.

Task #2: 30 minutes

Time	Task
7 minutes	Organize your essay.
2 minutes	Write your introduction.
16 minutes	Write your body paragraphs.
2 minutes	Write your conclusion.
3 minutes	Proofread your essay to correct any mistakes.

To stick to these guidelines, you'll have to know exactly what your essay is going to look like. Use the templates from Step 1 to focus as you read.

Now you're ready to try some practice writing drills.

Writing Summary

Congratulations! You now know how to crack all parts of the TOEFL. But before you move on, keep the following points in mind for cracking the Writing section:

- **Answer the question!** Even if you write well, you won't receive a top score unless you address the task. Make sure you know what each task requires.

- **Focus on form.** The structure and organization of your essay is crucial. Make sure you know how to put your essay together.

- **Make the graders' jobs easy.** You know what the TOEFL graders are looking for, so make them happy by giving them a structured essay that uses detailed examples and good transitions.

Let's practice some writing with the drills in the next chapter. Then, if you feel ready, go on to Part IV and take the full-length practice TOEFL exam. If not, review the lessons in the previous chapters until you are confident you know how to crack the test.

Chapter 16
Writing Practice Drills

You're now ready to crack the Writing section. We've provided lined pages on which to write your responses, but it would be better to practice typing your answers on a computer because that's how you'll be doing it on the actual TOEFL. Try the following practice prompts. After you've finished, read through the sample essays in the next chapter to get an idea of what TOEFL graders are looking for in the essay responses.

WRITING PRACTICE DRILL #1

The first type of writing question will provide you with the following directions:

> You will have 3 minutes to read the following passage. You may take notes during your reading. After the 3 minutes are up, you will hear a lecture on the topic. You may take notes during the lecture as well.
>
> After the lecture ends, you will have 20 minutes to write your response. An effective response is generally 150 to 225 words long. You may use your notes to help you answer, and you may refer to the reading passage. Your essay will be graded on the quality of your writing and on the completeness of the content.

Now let's look at a writing question. On the actual test, you will hear a prompt that will ask you to read a passage in 3 minutes. For our purposes here, you will need to stop the audio to read the passage and either time yourself or ask a friend to time you. After 3 minutes, resume the audio for the listening passage.

Begin playing Track 23 on the CD.

Narrator: Now read the passage about the first grain-based food. You have 3 minutes to read the passage. Begin reading now.

[Stop the CD for 3 minutes while you read the passage on page 377.]

Scant physical evidence remains of the first human domestication of grain. Still, there is enough to conclude that ancient peoples, motivated by the nutritional value of bread or cakes made of wild wheat, looked for controlled ways to grow it to provide a consistent food supply. Three related discoveries are likely to have led to the introduction of bread as the first grain-based food.

The first discovery was that wheat could be prepared for use by grinding. People probably began consuming wheat by chewing it raw. Because wheat is very hard, they gradually discovered that it was less trouble to eat if crushed to paste between two stones. The result would have been the ancestor of the drier, more powdery wheat flour we use today.

From there, it was a short step to the next breakthrough—baking the simplest bread, which requires no technology but fire. Loaves of wheat paste, when baked into bread, could be stored for long periods, certainly longer than raw seeds. This kept the food value of wheat available for an extended period after it had been harvested.

Finally, ancient peoples found that, if the paste was allowed to sit in the open, yeast spores from the air settled on it and began fermenting the wheat. This natural process of fermentation caused bubbles to form in the wheat paste, suggesting that it would be lighter in texture and even easier to eat when baked.

Resume playing Track 23 on the CD.

N: Now listen to part of a lecture on the topic you just read about.

N: Summarize the points made in the lecture you just heard, explaining how they cast doubt on the contents of the reading. You may refer to the passage as you write.

Directions: You have 20 minutes to plan and write your response. Your response will be graded on the quality of your writing and on how well your response presents the points in the lecture and their relationship to the reading passage. Typically, an effective response will be 150 to 225 words.

Question: Summarize the points made in the lecture you just heard, explaining how they cast doubt on the contents of reading. You may refer to the passage as you write.

Copy Cut Paste

Word Count: 0

Scant physical evidence remains of the first human domestication of grain. Still, there is enough to conclude that ancient peoples, motivated by the nutritional value of bread or cakes made of wild wheat, looked for controlled ways to grow it to provide a consistent food supply. Three related discoveries are likely to have led to the introduction of bread as the first grain-based food.

The first discovery was that wheat could be prepared for use by grinding. People probably began consuming wheat by chewing it raw. Because wheat is very hard, they gradually discovered that it was less trouble to eat if crushed to paste between two stones—the result would have been the ancestor of the drier, more powdery wheat flour we use today.

From there, it was a short step to the next breakthrough: baking the simplest bread, which requires no technology but fire. Loaves of wheat paste, when baked into bread, could be stored for long periods, certainly longer than raw seeds. This kept the food value of wheat available for an extended period after it had been harvested.

Finally, ancient peoples found that, if the paste was allowed to sit in the open, yeast spores from the air settled on it and began fermenting the wheat. This natural process of fermentation caused bubbles to form in the wheat paste, suggesting that it would be lighter in texture and even easier to eat when baked.

WRITING PRACTICE DRILL #2

The second type of writing question asks you to write a response to a question in 30 minutes. It will look something like the following:

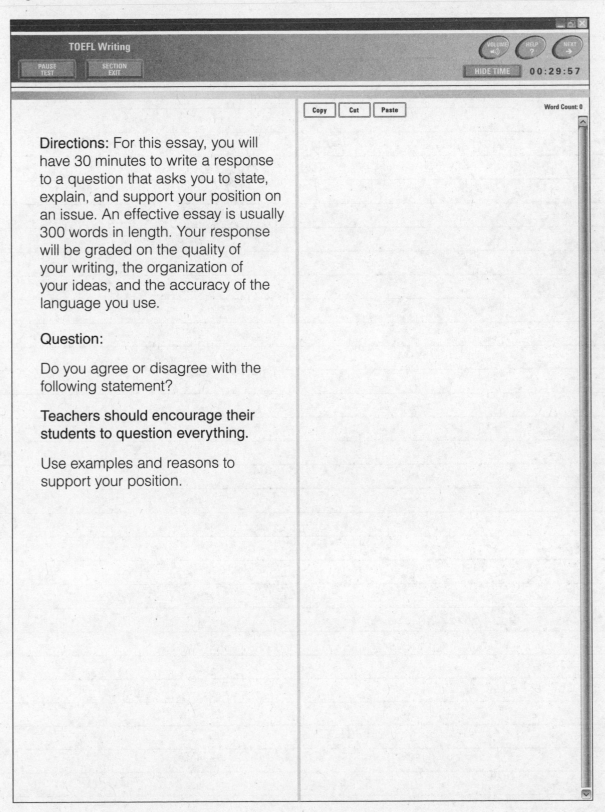

Directions: For this essay, you will have 30 minutes to write a response to a question that asks you to state, explain, and support your position on an issue. An effective essay is usually 300 words in length. Your response will be graded on the quality of your writing, the organization of your ideas, and the accuracy of the language you use.

Question:

Do you agree or disagree with the following statement?

Teachers should encourage their students to question everything.

Use examples and reasons to support your position.

WRITING PRACTICE DRILL #3

This drill again asks you to write a response to a question in 30 minutes.

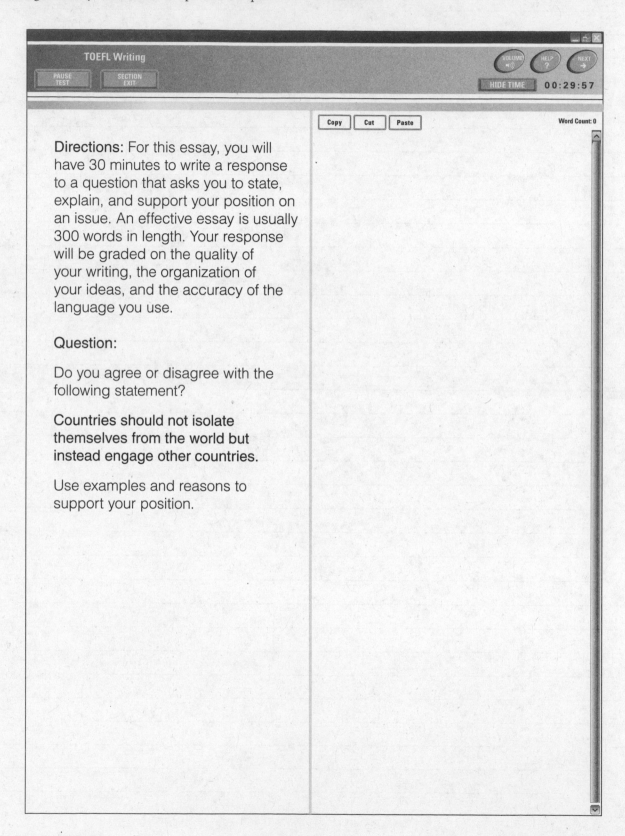

TOEFL Writing

PAUSE TEST   SECTION EXIT

VOLUME   HELP ?   NEXT →

HIDE TIME   00:29:57

Copy   Cut   Paste

Word Count: 0

Directions: For this essay, you will have 30 minutes to write a response to a question that asks you to state, explain, and support your position on an issue. An effective essay is usually 300 words in length. Your response will be graded on the quality of your writing, the organization of your ideas, and the accuracy of the language you use.

Question:

Do you agree or disagree with the following statement?

Countries should not isolate themselves from the world but instead engage other countries.

Use examples and reasons to support your position.

WRITING PRACTICE DRILL #4

This is another opportunity for you to write a response to a question in 30 minutes.

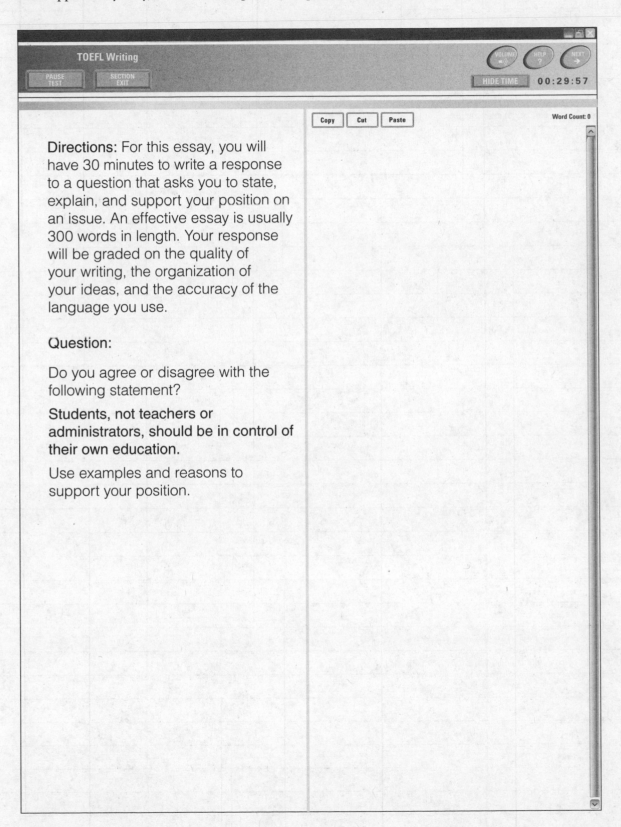

TOEFL Writing

PAUSE TEST   SECTION EXIT

VOLUME   HELP ?   NEXT →

HIDE TIME   00:29:57

Copy   Cut   Paste

Word Count: 0

Directions: For this essay, you will have 30 minutes to write a response to a question that asks you to state, explain, and support your position on an issue. An effective essay is usually 300 words in length. Your response will be graded on the quality of your writing, the organization of your ideas, and the accuracy of the language you use.

Question:

Do you agree or disagree with the following statement?

Students, not teachers or administrators, should be in control of their own education.

Use examples and reasons to support your position.

WRITING PRACTICE DRILL #5

Here's another chance to write a response to a question in 30 minutes.

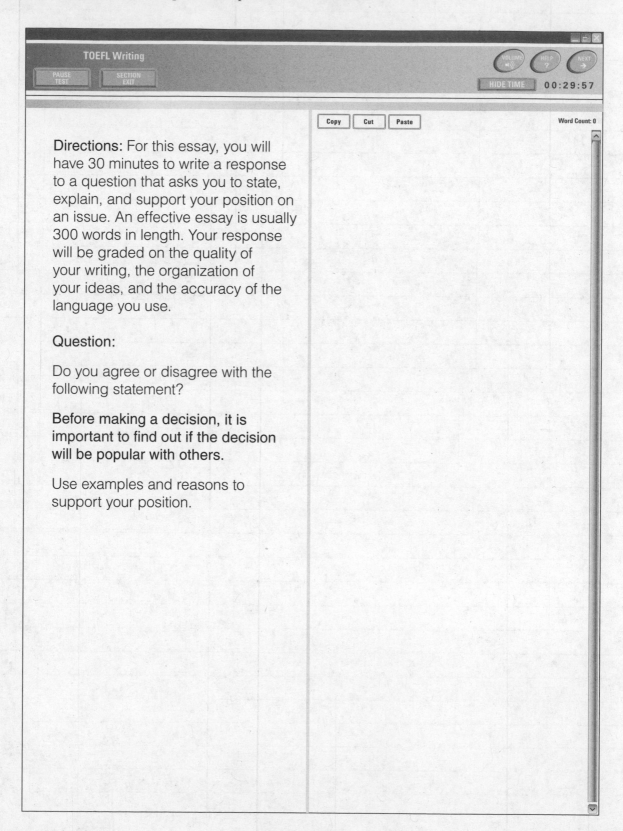

PAUSE TEST

SECTION EXIT

VOLUME

HELP ?

NEXT →

HIDE TIME   00:29:57

Copy   Cut   Paste

Word Count: 0

Directions: For this essay, you will have 30 minutes to write a response to a question that asks you to state, explain, and support your position on an issue. An effective essay is usually 300 words in length. Your response will be graded on the quality of your writing, the organization of your ideas, and the accuracy of the language you use.

Question:

Do you agree or disagree with the following statement?

Before making a decision, it is important to find out if the decision will be popular with others.

Use examples and reasons to support your position.

Chapter 17
Writing Practice
Answers and
Explanations

Read through the following sample responses to the drill you completed in the previous chapter, and compare your essays with them. If possible, have a friend who is proficient in English look over your essays.

WRITING PRACTICE DRILL #1

Take a look at the first task.

> *Narrator:* Now read the passage about the first grain-based food. You have 3 minutes to read the passage. Begin reading now.

Scant physical evidence remains of the first human domestication of grain. Still, there is enough to conclude that ancient peoples, motivated by the nutritional value of bread or cakes made of wild wheat, looked for controlled ways to grow it to provide a consistent food supply. Three related discoveries are likely to have led to the introduction of bread as the first grain-based food.

The first discovery was that wheat could be prepared for use by grinding. People probably began consuming wheat by chewing it raw. Because wheat is very hard, they gradually discovered that it was less trouble to eat if crushed to paste between two stones—the result would have been the ancestor of the drier, more powdery wheat flour we use today.

From there, it was a short step to the next breakthrough: baking the simplest bread, which requires no technology but fire. Loaves of wheat paste, when baked into bread, could be stored for long periods, certainly longer than raw seeds. This kept the food value of wheat available for an extended period after it had been harvested.

Finally, ancient peoples found that, if the paste was allowed to sit in the open, yeast spores from the air settled on it and began fermenting the wheat. This natural process of fermentation caused bubbles to form in the wheat paste that suggested it would be lighter in texture and even easier to eat when baked.

> *Narrator:* Now listen to part of a lecture on the topic you just read about.

> *Professor:* Conventional wisdom says that a very primitive kind of bread was the first grain food that human societies ate. But, you know, for the last few decades, there's been an alternative hypothesis that quite a few anthropologists are starting to give a closer look. That hypothesis says that it was, in fact, beer—not bread—that was the first grain food. Sound strange? Consider a couple of things.
>
> For one thing, you don't have to grind wheat to make it easier to eat. If you keep it in a moist environment, it naturally starts sprouting, with a new baby plant splitting the hard seed case in half. Sprouted wheat is sweeter, softer, and actually more nutritious than whole wheat seeds—and it would have developed without human effort. In order to discover the usefulness of ground wheat, someone had to get the bright idea of crushing it. To discover the usefulness of sprouted wheat, people just had to do nothing and let it sit. Which do you think happened first?

Another thing: What turns grain into beer is fermentation, and wheat begins to ferment almost as soon as it's stored—from water and yeasts in the air. After the wheat sprouted, it would have started to ferment. The process would have been obvious because of the bubbles and foam that formed. People could have experimented by tasting it and discovering the first beer.

And even if you assume that people were already grinding wheat to paste, think about it. The paste ferments and bubbles. Is it likely that early peoples would have thought to fire it before eating? We're used to cooking our food, but in prehistoric times, the idea that you would take fire to food to improve it for eating was not obvious.

N: Summarize the points made in the lecture you just heard, explaining how they cast doubt on the contents of the reading. You may refer to the passage as you write.

Let's look at some notes you may have jotted down.

Reading:
       Main Idea: Bread was the first grain-based food
       Example/reason: Wheat is hard to eat, and people probably ground it into a paste.
       Example/reason: The wheat paste could be baked with fire.
       Example/reason: Wheat ferments naturally, which makes it easier to eat when baked.
Lecture:
       Point #1: Wheat doesn't need to be ground.
       Detail #1: Sprouted wheat is easy to eat and tastes better than normal wheat.
       Point #2: Fermenting happens very quickly.
       Detail #2: People tasting the foam from fermenting may have created the first beer.
       Point #3: It's unlikely that people would think to bake wheat.
       Detail #3: Early people did not cook things.

With that information, let's construct our essay. The following sections offer a variety of responses, scored from high to low. All spelling and grammatical errors are intentional—to demonstrate the factors behind an assigned score. As you read the response, think of what numerical value the grader might have assigned, and check to see how your assessment matches up to the actual score. As you know, the scale is from 0 to 5.

A High-Scoring Response

The following is an example of a high-scoring response:

In the lecture, the profesor makes several points about the first wheat product. The profesor argues that beer was the first wheat product. This is different from the reading, which states that bread came first. However, the teacher cast doubt on the reading with several points.

First of all, the teacher says that wheat doesn't have to be ground. It is easy to people to eat wheat when it sprouts. This is not what the reading states, it says that early people ground wheat into a paste because it hard to eat. The lecture casts doubt on this by showing another way to eat wheat.

Also, the talk says that fermenting happens very fast. This fermenting leads to a foam, which people probably tasted as the first beer. In the reading, it is argued that fermenting made people think to bake the bread. The professor doubts this point by stating it is unlikely.

Finally, the profesor argues that people woud not think to bake the wheat. The point is made that early people do not cook things. These points made by the teacher cast doubt on the reading. It seems like beer not bread was the first wheat food.

Score and Analysis of This Response

Score: 5   This essay received the highest possible score of 5 because it does many things well.

- First, it is extremely well organized. It has a clear introduction, body paragraphs, and a conclusion. It is also easy to follow because the essay uses appropriate transitions to link ideas.
- Also, the essay has a good length—199 words.
- More important, the author mentions several specific examples from the talk and shows how they are different from the points in the reading. That level of detail is necessary for a top score on the TOEFL.

This essay is by no means perfect. The writer misspelled "professor" throughout the essay and makes a number of errors with subject-verb agreement (for example, "the teacher cast doubt" instead of "casts doubt"). However, the errors do not detract from the overall message of the essay.

A Lower-Scoring Response

Following is an example of a lower-scoring response to the first practice drill.

In early cultures there were different ways of using wheat. Some cultures use wheat for making bread and some ohers used it to make beer. It is said by the instructor though that it is the beer that was made first.

Another thing is that fermenting of the wheat created beer, not bread. The professor said that the people would not bake the foam but instead they would drink it like beer.

the lecture shows that early peoples rarely used fire to make things. They didn't think to make the bread form the wheat that they had ground. That is to say that it seems like beer was more likely to be make by people than was bread.

Score and Analysis of This Response

Score: 2   This weaker response scored much lower because the essay has numerous problems.

- The first problem is that the ideas in the essay are not clearly expressed. The writing style makes it difficult to understand exactly what the author is trying to demonstrate.
- Also, the ideas are not linked together, making the essay difficult to follow.

- The first two sentences indicate that the writer did not grasp the main point of the reading and the lecture. Plus, the first sentence of the third paragraph is not mentioned in either the reading or the lecture.
- The response is also rather short, only 118 words long.

On the positive side, the response does include some points from the lecture, even if they are slightly unclear.

WRITING PRACTICE DRILL #2

Now let's look at the second task from the previous chapter.

Question:

Do you agree or disagree with the following statement?

Teachers should encourage their students to question everything.

Use examples and reasons to support your position.

Here are some sample notes for this topic.

Issue: *Should teachers encourage their students to question what they learn?*

Your opinion:	Agree—teachers should encourage students to question things.
Why?	Because education requires curiosity.
Reason #1:	Many things that are thought to be true turn out to be false.
Detail #1:	People thought Earth was flat, but it's round.
Reason #2:	Students shouldn't accept everything a teacher says.
Detail #2:	It could be dangerous for students to blindly accept statements from their teacher.
Reason #3:	Teachers should prepare students for when they are out of school.
Detail #3:	There won't always be a teacher around to guide students.

Now let's put it together in our essay.

A High-Scoring Response

The following is a higher-scoring essay.

The question being asked is if teachers should advise their students to question things in their lives. This is a very important issue because it has to do with what kind of persons are schools are creating. In my opinion, I believe that a teacher must teacher their students to question everything. Because the most important thing about eductation is curiousity.

The reason I prefer that teachers make their students question them is that it often the case that in education and science, many things people think are true are not. An example—for many years it was thouht that the earth was flat. But of course it turn out that the earth is round. If scientists did not question what everyone thought was true this discovry may not have happened when it did. Since things can be wrong, teachers should help the students to question thier education.

Second, it can be very dangerous for students to not question what the teacher says. If you believe everything that people tells you, you might end up doing things you wouldn't do on your onw. This could lead to many problems, such as the rise of a dictatorship. Thus, it is clear that a teacher should show the student how to question what is being taught in class.

And lastly, I believe that it is best for teachers to make their students question everything. When the students leave the school, they will not have the teacher around to guide them. A student needs to know how to judge the things they find. So it is necessary for them to question things. I think questioning is always beter than just believing things.

In conclusion, I have shown that it better for teachers to encourage their students to question things. Without curiousity there is no education.

Score and Analysis of This Response

Score: 5   This response received the highest possible score for the following reasons:

- The writer keeps the essay focused on the topic. Everything relates to the thesis.
- The writer goes into a good amount of detail for each of the reasons.
- The essay is just the right length.
- There are clear transitions, and the essay is easy to follow.
- The writer does a nice job of tying the conclusion back to the introduction by repeating the line about curiosity and education.

Again, the essay is not perfect, but it's good enough to get a top score on the TOEFL.

A Lower-Scoring Response

Now take a look at a lower-scoring response.

It really depens on the case for this question. I'm not sure if it is better or worst for a teacher to tell the students to question. I think there are times and places for it, definitly. For example, if a student is very young, then it is bad for that student to question the teacher. This doesn't show the respekt to the teacher that belongs in a student. There fore there shouldn't be any questioning done in this class.

And yet sometimes it is good to the student to question. There are students who interested in becoming a scientist and they must be taught to question. If a sceintist does not question, then he cannot do his job. or at least he cannot do his job right. So for this example I would say that questioning is important.

Now we have two situations and they are both very different. So which is the correct choice. This is why I said first that it all depends on the case at hand. In the first case, with the young child it is not right to question. Yet in the second case with the scientist is right to question. I think that in the end the teacher must decide. The teacher must decide whether or not to encourage the students to question everything. And that is the final opinion on this subject.

Score and Analysis of This Response
Score: 2 This essay received a much lower score than the previous response for the following reasons:

- One of the most glaring problems with this essay is that it does not satisfy the task. The assignment asks you to state whether you agree or disagree, so make sure you pick a side. Don't try to defend both sides of the issue.
- Furthermore, this essay is not very well planned out. It is clear that the author didn't think before writing.
- There are not enough examples.
- The author begins to repeat information in the final paragraph.

Although this is not the worst possible essay, it is not going to receive a good score.

WRITING PRACTICE DRILL #3
Here are sample responses to Drill #3 from the previous chapter.

Question:

Do you agree or disagree with the following statement?

Countries should not isolate themselves from the world, but instead engage other countries.

Use examples and reasons to support your position.

Here are some sample notes for the topic.

Issue: *Should countries isolate themselves or engage other countries?*

Your opinion:	Agree—countries need to work with other countries in the world.
Why?	Because countries can't succeed without cooperating with others.
Reason #1:	New technologies make countries more interconnected.
Detail #1:	Outsourcing allows people in one country to work for companies in other countries.
Reason #2:	Countries need to trade with others to prosper.
Detail #2:	There is now a global marketplace for goods and countries can take advantage of it.
Reason #3:	Countries should exchange information in order to take advantage of progress.
Detail #3:	New discoveries and technologies can be shared with other countries.

Let's see how we can put this information into an essay.

A High-Scoring Response

Here's an example of a higher-scoring response.

I believe that countries should be engaged with other, not isolate. This is true to me because there are many avantages to a country working with others. For example, new technology, trade, and information is shared.

First, there are many new technologys that make the countries more connected. The most important one is the outsourcing. Because of it people can get jobs even if the company is an another country. This is very good because it brings jobs to countries and helps the people.

Also, trade is very useful to a country. Without trade, a countries economic will be hurt. There are now many planes, ships, and trains that can sent goods around the world countries should use these in order to help there economy. With lots of trade, a country will be made more prosperuos.

Lastly, there is much information now available in the world. Without working with other countries it might not be possible to use this. I know that in my situation, I learned about many things going on in the world. I was helped by this in my studies.

In conclusion, I think it obvious that countries must engage, not isolate. For the reasons above, such as trade, tecnology, and information it is obvious that countries should work with other countries and not be isolated.

Score and Analysis of This Response

Score: 4   This response scored a solid grade of 4. There are several good things in this essay.

- The essay stays on topic, with only a minor digression or two.
- The essay is well organized, with a clear introduction, body paragraphs, and conclusion. The writer uses obvious transitions.
- There are three good examples provided for the topic, and the writer gives some details for each of them.

However, there are a few issues that prevented the writer from achieving the top score.

- The essay is too short, only using about 220 words.
- In the fourth paragraph, the author digresses from the topic and provides an inappropriate personal example.
- The conclusion basically repeats the same information in both sentences ("I think it obvious that countries must engage, not isolate" and "...it is obvious that countries should work with other countries and not be isolated.")

Overall, however, this is a good response for the TOEFL.

A Lower-Scoring Response

Now look at a lower-scoring essay. What are some of its problems?

Yes, a country must engage other countries. This is very true. Because of the reasons like technology, trade, and information. For the first example, you see that technology is importance. Without the technology a country is not productive. Also there is trade to think of. No trade mean a country does not make money. This is why a country should not be isolated. Last there is the information. Information is now one of the worlds top commodity. It is so important now that without infomation a country cannot succeed. There fore countries should not isolate but they should engage the world they live in.

Score and Analysis of This Response

Score: 1   This essay received only a 1, the lowest score possible (remember, a score of 0 is for a blank essay or one written in a foreign language). Here are some reasons why.

- Although the essay does address the task, there is no organization. The essay contains only one paragraph.
- The examples are not explained in sufficient detail.
- The essay is too short.

The writer needs to better organize this essay and develop the examples more to gain a higher score.

WRITING PRACTICE DRILL #4

The following are sample responses to Drill #4 from the previous chapter.

> Question:
>
> Do you agree or disagree with the following statement?
>
> Students, not teachers or administrators, should be in control of their own education.
>
> Use examples and reasons to support your position.

Here are some sample notes for the topic.

Issue: *Should students be in control of the educational process?*

Your opinion:	Disagree. Students should not be in control.
Why?	Teachers and administrators are better at the job than the students are.
Reason #1:	Students may be too immature or inexperienced to make the right choices.
Detail #1:	Elementary school students are unable to make the right decisions. High school students may not be as interested in education.
Reason #2:	Students might not study areas outside of their interests.

Detail #2:	If students are in control, they may pick a limited program of study and not be exposed to other areas.
Reason #3:	Teachers and administrators have more experience in the area.
Detail #3:	Teachers and administrators go to school to learn theories of education and know best how to educate students.

Let's see how we can put this information into an essay.

A Higher-Scoring Response
Here's an example of a higher-scoring response.

Should students be in control of their education? This is a good question. Many people think that everyone has the right to control their own destiny. Especially since education is so important, they think that maybe it best for people to be in charge of what they learned. But I don't agree with this. It is better if teachers and admistrators are in charge because they are professionals and know best.

Obviously, in many times, a student cannot make the best decision for their education. Think about a young child in elementery school—they are too inexperienced to be in charge of what is learned. Or what about high school students. It is known that most high school students are not caring about education. They are usually caring more about meeting boyfriends and girlfriends and maybe getting jobs. This means that they would not be best at making decisions.

Another reason I'm against students being in control is that it means students won't study as much. By this I mean that if a student get to pick the program, they will pick only the areas that they like. Maybe one student will only study history, another chemsitry. This can be good, but a student should study all subjects. Teachers can make sure the students study everything and get a better education.

Finally, the teacher and administrator have the most experience. They go to school and college to learn the best ways of teaching. With their knowlege they can help students learn the most. They are professional in the field and must be in charge of education, not the students.

And so, it is shown that students should not be in control of their educations. It is to important to the student and to the society. A teacher is more experienced and more able to pick best for what a student should learn.

Score and Analysis of This Response
Score: 5   This is a top-scoring essay. Here's why.

- The essay is focused and clearly addresses the question task.
- The essay is well organized, with a clear introduction, body paragraphs, conclusion, and good transitions.
- Each example is supported by significant details.
- The essay is of an appropriate length, more than 300 words long.

This is an excellent response for the TOEFL.

A Lower-Scoring Response

Here is a lower-scoring essay. As you read it, think about how the essay could be improved.

Whose better at the decision for education? The student or the teacher? It is the teacher. Only teachers have knowlegde, and experience to do this job. A student is too unknown to do this job right.

Because the student is young, they can't make the right decide. That is why they are in school. To learn enough. But teachers can do this job. When I put a child into school, I expect the teacher to educate. That is the job they are suposed to do. It is like any other job, such as doctor. They go to school to learn how to do the job the best way and we expect them to do that.

Plus a children doesn't know what's best for them. There is a student who doesn't like math, then what does he learn? Same things for history, science, and langauge. If the student is in control, then maybe he doesn't pick the studies he needs. Now whose fallt is it for the education? A bad education is not good for anyone. This means that it must be the teacher in charge. Students can't be trusted to do right in this decision.

In conclusion, we must lest the teachers make this decision. That is there job so they should do it. The students cannot make this decision on their own.

Score and Analysis of This Response

Score: 3   Although this essay is organized and manages to address the topic, it has several problems.

- The paragraphs don't remain focused on the topic; they have too many digressions.
- The essay is very repetitive.
- The language is distracting or confusing, enough so that the writer's meaning is sometimes unclear.
- The response is too short.

Despite these problems, the graders will give credit for the organization of the essay and the fact that it more or less supports its thesis.

WRITING PRACTICE DRILL #5

The following are sample responses to Drill #5 from the previous chapter.

Question:

Do you agree or disagree with the following statement?

Before making a decision, it is important to find out if the decision will be popular with others.

Use examples and reasons to support your position.

Here are some sample notes for the topic.

Issue: *Should you make a decision based on how popular it will be with others?*

Your opinion:	Disagree. Popularity should not be a factor in decisions.
Why?	Sometimes unpopular decisions are the best decisions.
Reason #1:	Just because a decision is popular doesn't make it right.
Detail #1:	In some cases, like discrimination, a majority might agree with it but it's still wrong.
Reason #2:	There are other factors that are more important than popularity.
Detail #2:	A person should look at the consequences of the decision, not just its popularity.
Reason #3:	The person who made the decision feels responsible for it.
Detail #3:	Making a decision based on other people's morals might make you feel guilty.

Let's see how we can put this information into an essay.

A Higher-Scoring Response

Here's an example of a higher-scoring response.

Many times, people worry about that their decisions will be popular with others. They do this because it is nice to think that everyone suports you. However, this is not necessary the best way of making a decision. I say this because sometimes there are things that are more important than popular decisions. A person needs to be aware of these when he decides.

First of all, not all popular decisions are the right decisions. In many places, alot of people think something is okay, but that doesn't mean it is. For example, some countries discriminate against people. These peolple are not allowed to vote or have other rights. Even if other people think this is okay, it is not. So a popular decision is not always a right decision.

Another reason I don't think popular is a good way to make decisions is because there are many things to think about with a decision. For example, who does the decision help? Who does it hurt? How much will the decision cost? I think these things are more important than making decision popular to people. So a person should think of these ideas first.

Finally, every person lives with the decisions they make. By this I mean that a person who decides something will feel good or bad for it. If the decision is bad, then the person who made it feels bad. And the same for a good decision. As already stated, a popular decision is not always good. So a person might have to feel bad to make a decsion that is popular with others.

To conclude, a popular decision is not the best decision. As shown in this essay, there are many other things to think about when deciding. A person should know that a popular decision isn't always the right and he can still feel bad making a decision that other people want.

Score and Analysis of This Response

Score: 5 This is a top-scoring essay. Here's why.

- The essay stays on topic; everything in it is relevant to the topic and the thesis.
- The essay's organization is very good. Each body paragraph flows well by introducing a reason, providing details, and providing a summary.
- The essay is detailed and of a good length.
- There are very few grammatical and spelling mistakes.

This qualifies as a great essay on the TOEFL.

A Lower-Scoring Response

Here is a lower-scoring essay. As you read it, think about how the essay could be improved.

A popular decision is not best decision. Why, because many reasons. Number one is popular decisions are not always the best. Two, is there other things that are more important that popular. Three, there are moral feelings with decision that can be bad.

Popular decisions are not always the best. In one country they do not women vote. Is this right, no. Every body should be able to vote. I think it very important to vote. Without vote, there is no way to have power. Therefore each person has to vote. Next, besides popular, is other things more important. I think cost of decision is more popular. I think whether decision is hurtful or helpful is more important. Last, there is an important thing. This is how you feel about the decision. If you feel bad then decision not good, even if it popular. The way you feel about the decision is important.

Finally, we see that that popular decision isn't best way. Popular decisions are not always the best. There are other things that are more important than popular.

Score and Analysis of This Response

Score: 1 This essay is very weak and has the following problems:

- The writing is very repetitive, using the same or similar sentences throughout.
- The essay strays from the topic to talk about voting.
- The writer's use of the language is troublesome and the grammatical problems distract the reader from the essay.
- The response is too short, and the examples are not explained in sufficient detail.

This writer will have to spend more time practicing writing in English and mastering grammar to get a better score.

Part IV
Taking a
Practice Test

Now that you've completed your TOEFL preparation, it's time to try a full-length TOEFL practice exam. Use the test in the next chapter to practice the techniques and approaches you've worked on throughout the book and to familiarize yourself with the types of questions you'll see on test day. Make sure to time yourself as accurately as possible while taking the test.

EVALUATING YOUR PERFORMANCE

Because of the nature of the TOEFL iBT exam, it is difficult to obtain a scaled score that precisely matches the one you'll receive after taking your actual exam. However, it is still possible to evaluate your performance and get an idea of how you'll do on the real thing.

Reading and Listening Sections

For these two sections, go through each question and analyze your performance. Keep track of questions that you got correct and see if you can categorize them as follows (jot down the abbreviations in parentheses next to the question numbers):

- **Correct (C):** These are questions that you fully understood. You had no problem answering them and spent very little time on them.
- **Correct, guessed (CG):** These are questions you got right, but you guessed the correct answer. For these questions, make sure you try to figure out *why* the answer is correct. Also, look at the other choices. What made you eliminate them?
- **Incorrect, mistake (I):** This means that you got the question wrong, but you see your mistake. This type of situation is very common. Often, it results from not using the techniques described in this book or from going too quickly on the test and not reading carefully enough. Minimize the number of questions that fall into this category, and you'll do well on the TOEFL.
- **Incorrect, don't understand (I?):** This is for the questions that you got wrong and you're not sure why. It could be a comprehension problem. Or maybe you misunderstood what the question was asking. For these questions, look back at the choices. Were there any obviously wrong answers? Did you fall for a *trap* answer? What could you have done differently?

Speaking and Writing Sections

If at all possible, try to record your spoken responses. Listen to them, and see how closely they match the templates we've provided. If possible, play the responses for an English speaker and ask that person to evaluate your response.

Do the same for your written responses. Compare what you've written with the samples provided in this book. Do you have a clear introduction? Does your response include transition words? Do you use examples appropriately?

WHAT NOW?

After you've finished our practice test and your self-evaluation, you should take the full-length practice test available from ETS (**www.ets.org**). This will give you an opportunity to get a scored result.

Don't forget to refer back to the section on "The Week Before the Test" in the Introduction of this book for more tips on your final preparation.

Chapter 18
The Princeton Review
TOEFL iBT Practice Test

THE READING SECTION

For this section, you will read three passages and answer questions about their content. You will have 60 minutes to answer all the questions. You may begin.

More Available

The Veneration of Trees

In *The Golden Bough,* his classic catalog of mythologies, Sir James George Frazer extensively documents the significance of trees in world religion. His chapters on tree spirits roam from Northern Europe to the Eastern Seaboard of what is now the United States to the islands of the Pacific. Despite the lack of contact among these regions, the veneration of trees united them. The woods that covered large areas of Europe and North America, in particular, were difficult to penetrate and dangerous to cross. It was not a great mental leap for people to see the trees that populated them as embodiments of the natural forces that governed their lives.

On the basis of Frazer's classification, one can derive three loose stages of tree worship. In the first, a society sees the tree as the physical body of the spirit that inhabits it, much as the human body can be seen as housing the mind. It is known that both the Celtic and the Germanic tribes that inhabited ancient Northern Europe regarded certain trees as sacred, setting them apart by species (as the Druids worshipped oaks) or by location (the way certain natural groves were regarded as natural temples or sacred spaces in what is now Germany). Early on, each of these trees was regarded as an animate being with both spirit and body. It had a distinct identity, like an individual person. This suggests that it was believed to have the same impulses and reactions as the people who venerated it.

Accordingly, ancient peoples had elaborate taboos designed to avoid causing offense to trees. These taboos were taken very seriously.

More Available

In some places, one could be punished severely for injuring the bark of a tree or stealing its fruit. Before a tree was felled for human use, woodcutters in many world cultures would offer it both apologies and thanks for the resources it was about to provide them. This was necessary to avoid insulting the tree and inviting bad fortune. It was also the case, however, that injuries were said to cause suffering to trees as they did to people. In some societies, it was claimed that trees cry out in pain when struck or cut into. A tree's spirit and body are considered inseparable in this first stage.

A society makes a leap in sophistication and reaches Frazer's second stage when it begins to regard them as separate. That is, the spirit exists independently of the physical tree, even if it chooses to dwell there most of the time. The same spirit may thus take up residence in any tree of a forest; it is not killed when an individual tree is cut down. It is not bound to a single tree but rather stands for a group. The distinction may seem small, but it is a significant first step toward symbolic thinking. A forest, after all, is more than the sum of its parts. It encompasses not only its trees but also the animals and brush that flourish among them. The dangers of the forest are hidden; a traveler may or may not encounter them on a given journey. To think about a tree spirit identified with the forest as a whole, therefore, people had to think about phenomena that were removed from them in time and space—ideas rather than things. Such a tree spirit represented the potential and abstract rather than the concrete and immediate.

That transition is completed in the third stage. Liberated from each other, trees and their spirits can begin to be seen as symbols and embodiments of other natural processes of significance to primitive life: the power

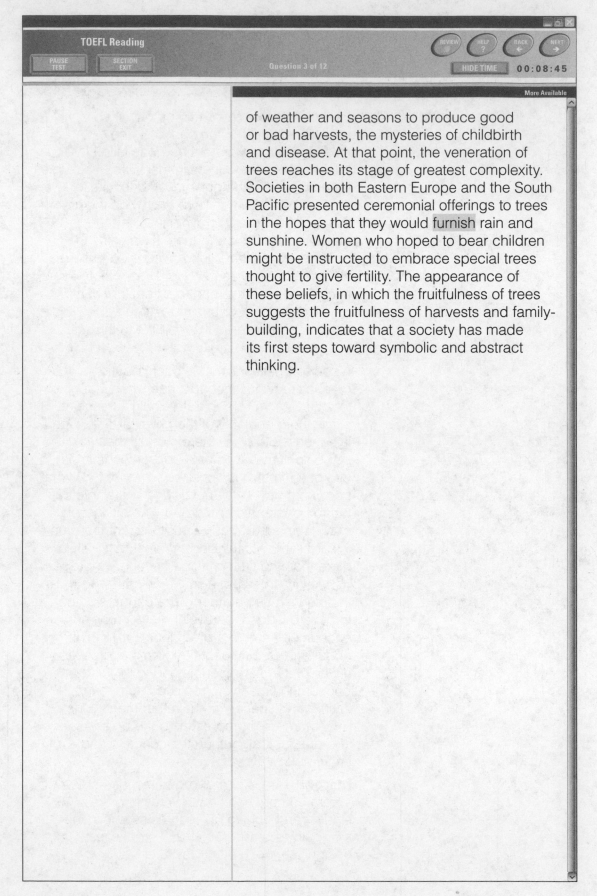

More Available

of weather and seasons to produce good or bad harvests, the mysteries of childbirth and disease. At that point, the veneration of trees reaches its stage of greatest complexity. Societies in both Eastern Europe and the South Pacific presented ceremonial offerings to trees in the hopes that they would furnish rain and sunshine. Women who hoped to bear children might be instructed to embrace special trees thought to give fertility. The appearance of these beliefs, in which the fruitfulness of trees suggests the fruitfulness of harvests and family-building, indicates that a society has made its first steps toward symbolic and abstract thinking.

More Available

1. It can be inferred from paragraph 1 of the passage that the peoples of Europe and North America associated trees with

(A) travel to distant places
(B) the religions of older tribes
(C) dangerous forces of nature
(D) the common culture of humanity

Paragraph 1 is marked with an arrow [➤]

The Veneration of Trees

➤In *The Golden Bough*, his classic catalog of mythologies, Sir James George Frazer extensively documents the significance of trees in world religion. His chapters on tree spirits roam from Northern Europe to the Eastern Seaboard of what is now the United States to the islands of the Pacific. Despite the lack of contact among these regions, the veneration of trees united them. The woods that covered large areas of Europe and North America, in particular, were difficult to penetrate and dangerous to cross. It was not a great mental leap for people to see the trees that populated them as embodiments of the natural forces that governed their lives.

On the basis of Frazer's classification, one can derive three loose stages of tree worship. In the first, a society sees the tree as the physical body of the spirit that inhabits it, much as the human body can be seen as housing the mind. It is known that both the Celtic and the Germanic tribes that inhabited ancient Northern Europe regarded certain trees as sacred, setting them apart by species (as the Druids worshipped oaks) or by location (the way certain natural groves were regarded as natural temples or sacred spaces in what is now Germany). Early on, each of these trees was regarded as an animate being with both spirit and body. It had a distinct identity, like an individual person. This suggests that it was believed to have the same impulses and reactions as the people who venerated it.

Accordingly, ancient peoples had elaborate taboos designed to avoid causing offense to trees. These taboos were taken very seriously. In some places, one could be punished severely for injuring the bark of a tree or stealing its fruit. Before a tree was felled for human use, woodcutters in many world cultures would offer it both apologies and thanks for the resources it was about to provide them. This was necessary to avoid insulting the tree and inviting bad fortune. It was also the case, however, that injuries were said to cause suffering to trees as they did to people. In some societies, it was claimed that trees cry out in pain when struck or cut into. A tree's spirit and body are considered inseparable in this first stage.

A society makes a leap in sophistication and reaches Frazer's second stage when it begins to regard them as separate. That is, the spirit exists independently of the physical tree, even if it chooses to dwell there most of the time. The same spirit may thus take up residence in any tree of a forest; it is not killed when an individual tree is cut down. It is not bound to a single tree but rather stands for a group. The distinction may seem small, but it is a significant first step toward symbolic thinking. A forest, after all, is more than the sum of its parts. It encompasses not only its trees but also the animals and brush that flourish among them. The dangers of the forest are hidden; a traveler may or may not encounter them on a given journey. To think about a tree spirit identified with the forest as a whole, therefore, people had to think about phenomena that were removed from them in time and space—ideas rather than things. Such a tree spirit represented the potential and abstract rather than the concrete and immediate.

That transition is completed in the third stage. Liberated from each other, trees and their spirits can begin to be seen as symbols and embodiments of other natural processes of significance to primitive life: the power of weather and seasons to produce good or bad harvests, the mysteries of childbirth and disease. At that point, the veneration of trees reaches its stage of greatest complexity. Societies in both Eastern Europe and the South Pacific presented ceremonial offerings to trees in the hopes that they would furnish rain and sunshine. Women who hoped to bear children might be instructed to embrace special trees thought to give fertility. The appearance of these beliefs, in which the fruitfulness of trees suggests the fruitfulness of harvests and family-building, indicates that a society has made its first steps toward symbolic and abstract thinking.

More Available

2. The word penetrate in the passage is closest in meaning to

(A) enter
(B) locate
(C) survive
(D) consider

The Veneration of Trees

In *The Golden Bough*, his classic catalog of mythologies, Sir James George Frazer extensively documents the significance of trees in world religion. His chapters on tree spirits roam from Northern Europe to the Eastern Seaboard of what is now the United States to the islands of the Pacific. Despite the lack of contact among these regions, the veneration of trees united them. The woods that covered large areas of Europe and North America, in particular, were difficult to penetrate and dangerous to cross. It was not a great mental leap for people to see the trees that populated them as embodiments of the natural forces that governed their lives.

On the basis of Frazer's classification, one can derive three loose stages of tree worship. In the first, a society sees the tree as the physical body of the spirit that inhabits it, much as the human body can be seen as housing the mind. It is known that both the Celtic and the Germanic tribes that inhabited ancient Northern Europe regarded certain trees as sacred, setting them apart by species (as the Druids worshipped oaks) or by location (the way certain natural groves were regarded as natural temples or sacred spaces in what is now Germany). Early on, each of these trees was regarded as an animate being with both spirit and body. It had a distinct identity, like an individual person. This suggests that it was believed to have the same impulses and reactions as the people who venerated it.

Accordingly, ancient peoples had elaborate taboos designed to avoid causing offense to trees. These taboos were taken very seriously. In some places, one could be punished severely for injuring the bark of a tree or stealing its fruit. Before a tree was felled for human use, woodcutters in many world cultures would offer it both apologies and thanks for the resources it was about to provide them. This was necessary to avoid insulting the tree and inviting bad fortune. It was also the case, however, that injuries were said to cause suffering to trees as they did to people. In some societies, it was claimed that trees cry out in pain when struck or cut into. A tree's spirit and body are considered inseparable in this first stage.

A society makes a leap in sophistication and reaches Frazer's second stage when it begins to regard them as separate. That is, the spirit exists independently of the physical tree, even if it chooses to dwell there most of the time. The same spirit may thus take up residence in any tree of a forest; it is not killed when an individual tree is cut down. It is not bound to a single tree but rather stands for a group. The distinction may seem small, but it is a significant first step toward symbolic thinking. A forest, after all, is more than the sum of its parts. It encompasses not only its trees but also the animals and brush that flourish among them. The dangers of the forest are hidden; a traveler may or may not encounter them on a given journey. To think about a tree spirit identified with the forest as a whole, therefore, people had to think about phenomena that were removed from them in time and space—ideas rather than things. Such a tree spirit represented the potential and abstract rather than the concrete and immediate.

That transition is completed in the third stage. Liberated from each other, trees and their spirits can begin to be seen as symbols and embodiments of other natural processes of significance to primitive life: the power of weather and seasons to produce good or bad harvests, the mysteries of childbirth and disease. At that point, the veneration of trees reaches its stage of greatest complexity. Societies in both Eastern Europe and the South Pacific presented ceremonial offerings to trees in the hopes that they would furnish rain and sunshine. Women who hoped to bear children might be instructed to embrace special trees thought to give fertility. The appearance of these beliefs, in which the fruitfulness of trees suggests the fruitfulness of harvests and family-building, indicates that a society has made its first steps toward symbolic and abstract thinking.

More Available

3. The author mentions the Druids in paragraph 2 as an example of a people that

(A) exhibited all three stages of tree worship

(B) punished people for stealing fruit

(C) worshipped a particular species of tree

(D) cut down many trees as its civilization expanded

Paragraph 2 is marked with an arrow [➤]

The Veneration of Trees

In *The Golden Bough,* his classic catalog of mythologies, Sir James George Frazer extensively documents the significance of trees in world religion. His chapters on tree spirits roam from Northern Europe to the Eastern Seaboard of what is now the United States to the islands of the Pacific. Despite the lack of contact among these regions, the veneration of trees united them. The woods that covered large areas of Europe and North America, in particular, were difficult to penetrate and dangerous to cross. It was not a great mental leap for people to see the trees that populated them as embodiments of the natural forces that governed their lives.

➤On the basis of Frazer's classification, one can derive three loose stages of tree worship. In the first, a society sees the tree as the physical body of the spirit that inhabits it, much as the human body can be seen as housing the mind. It is known that both the Celtic and the Germanic tribes that inhabited ancient Northern Europe regarded certain trees as sacred, setting them apart by species (as the Druids worshipped oaks) or by location (the way certain natural groves were regarded as natural temples or sacred spaces in what is now Germany). Early on, each of these trees was regarded as an animate being with both spirit and body. It had a distinct identity, like an individual person. This suggests that it was believed to have the same impulses and reactions as the people who venerated it.

Accordingly, ancient peoples had elaborate taboos designed to avoid causing offense to trees. These taboos were taken very seriously. In some places, one could be punished severely for injuring the bark of a tree or stealing its fruit. Before a tree was felled for human use, woodcutters in many world cultures would offer it both apologies and thanks for the resources it was about to provide them. This was necessary to avoid insulting the tree and inviting bad fortune. It was also the case, however, that injuries were said to cause suffering to trees as they did to people. In some societies, it was claimed that trees cry out in pain when struck or cut into. A tree's spirit and body are considered inseparable in this first stage.

A society makes a leap in sophistication and reaches Frazer's second stage when it begins to regard them as separate. That is, the spirit exists independently of the physical tree, even if it chooses to dwell there most of the time. The same spirit may thus take up residence in any tree of a forest; it is not killed when an individual tree is cut down. It is not bound to a single tree but rather stands for a group. The distinction may seem small, but it is a significant first step toward symbolic thinking. A forest, after all, is more than the sum of its parts. It encompasses not only its trees but also the animals and brush that flourish among them. The dangers of the forest are hidden; a traveler may or may not encounter them on a given journey. To think about a tree spirit identified with the forest as a whole, therefore, people had to think about phenomena that were removed from them in time and space—ideas rather than things. Such a tree spirit represented the potential and abstract rather than the concrete and immediate.

That transition is completed in the third stage. Liberated from each other, trees and their spirits can begin to be seen as symbols and embodiments of other natural processes of significance to primitive life: the power of weather and seasons to produce good or bad harvests, the mysteries of childbirth and disease. At that point, the veneration of trees reaches its stage of greatest complexity. Societies in both Eastern Europe and the South Pacific presented ceremonial offerings to trees in the hopes that they would furnish rain and sunshine. Women who hoped to bear children might be instructed to embrace special trees thought to give fertility. The appearance of these beliefs, in which the fruitfulness of trees suggests the fruitfulness of harvests and family-building, indicates that a society has made its first steps toward symbolic and abstract thinking.

More Available

4. The word severely in the passage is closest in meaning to

(A)   occasionally
(B)   harshly
(C)   repeatedly
(D)   secretly

The Veneration of Trees

In *The Golden Bough*, his classic catalog of mythologies, Sir James George Frazer extensively documents the significance of trees in world religion. His chapters on tree spirits roam from Northern Europe to the Eastern Seaboard of what is now the United States to the islands of the Pacific. Despite the lack of contact among these regions, the veneration of trees united them. The woods that covered large areas of Europe and North America, in particular, were difficult to penetrate and dangerous to cross. It was not a great mental leap for people to see the trees that populated them as embodiments of the natural forces that governed their lives.

On the basis of Frazer's classification, one can derive three loose stages of tree worship. In the first, a society sees the tree as the physical body of the spirit that inhabits it, much as the human body can be seen as housing the mind. It is known that both the Celtic and the Germanic tribes that inhabited ancient Northern Europe regarded certain trees as sacred, setting them apart by species (as the Druids worshipped oaks) or by location (the way certain natural groves were regarded as natural temples or sacred spaces in what is now Germany). Early on, each of these trees was regarded as an animate being with both spirit and body. It had a distinct identity, like an individual person. This suggests that it was believed to have the same impulses and reactions as the people who venerated it.

Accordingly, ancient peoples had elaborate taboos designed to avoid causing offense to trees. These taboos were taken very seriously. In some places, one could be punished severely for injuring the bark of a tree or stealing its fruit. Before a tree was felled for human use, woodcutters in many world cultures would offer it both apologies and thanks for the resources it was about to provide them. This was necessary to avoid insulting the tree and inviting bad fortune. It was also the case, however, that injuries were said to cause suffering to trees as they did to people. In some societies, it was claimed that trees cry out in pain when struck or cut into. A tree's spirit and body are considered inseparable in this first stage.

A society makes a leap in sophistication and reaches Frazer's second stage when it begins to regard them as separate. That is, the spirit exists independently of the physical tree, even if it chooses to dwell there most of the time. The same spirit may thus take up residence in any tree of a forest; it is not killed when an individual tree is cut down. It is not bound to a single tree but rather stands for a group. The distinction may seem small, but it is a significant first step toward symbolic thinking. A forest, after all, is more than the sum of its parts. It encompasses not only its trees but also the animals and brush that flourish among them. The dangers of the forest are hidden; a traveler may or may not encounter them on a given journey. To think about a tree spirit identified with the forest as a whole, therefore, people had to think about phenomena that were removed from them in time and space—ideas rather than things. Such a tree spirit represented the potential and abstract rather than the concrete and immediate.

That transition is completed in the third stage. Liberated from each other, trees and their spirits can begin to be seen as symbols and embodiments of other natural processes of significance to primitive life: the power of weather and seasons to produce good or bad harvests, the mysteries of childbirth and disease. At that point, the veneration of trees reaches its stage of greatest complexity. Societies in both Eastern Europe and the South Pacific presented ceremonial offerings to trees in the hopes that they would furnish rain and sunshine. Women who hoped to bear children might be instructed to embrace special trees thought to give fertility. The appearance of these beliefs, in which the fruitfulness of trees suggests the fruitfulness of harvests and family-building, indicates that a society has made its first steps toward symbolic and abstract thinking.

More Available

5. Which of the following is NOT mentioned as evidence that ancient peoples believed trees had individual spirits?

(A) They apologized to a tree before cutting it down.

(B) They had rules against injuring tree bark.

(C) They thought trees could express pain.

(D) They gave each tree a personal name.

The Veneration of Trees

In *The Golden Bough*, his classic catalog of mythologies, Sir James George Frazer extensively documents the significance of trees in world religion. His chapters on tree spirits roam from Northern Europe to the Eastern Seaboard of what is now the United States to the islands of the Pacific. Despite the lack of contact among these regions, the veneration of trees united them. The woods that covered large areas of Europe and North America, in particular, were difficult to penetrate and dangerous to cross. It was not a great mental leap for people to see the trees that populated them as embodiments of the natural forces that governed their lives.

On the basis of Frazer's classification, one can derive three loose stages of tree worship. In the first, a society sees the tree as the physical body of the spirit that inhabits it, much as the human body can be seen as housing the mind. It is known that both the Celtic and the Germanic tribes that inhabited ancient Northern Europe regarded certain trees as sacred, setting them apart by species (as the Druids worshipped oaks) or by location (the way certain natural groves were regarded as natural temples or sacred spaces in what is now Germany). Early on, each of these trees was regarded as an animate being with both spirit and body. It had a distinct identity, like an individual person. This suggests that it was believed to have the same impulses and reactions as the people who venerated it.

Accordingly, ancient peoples had elaborate taboos designed to avoid causing offense to trees. These taboos were taken very seriously. In some places, one could be punished severely for injuring the bark of a tree or stealing its fruit. Before a tree was felled for human use, woodcutters in many world cultures would offer it both apologies and thanks for the resources it was about to provide them. This was necessary to avoid insulting the tree and inviting bad fortune. It was also the case, however, that injuries were said to cause suffering to trees as they did to people. In some societies, it was claimed that trees cry out in pain when struck or cut into. A tree's spirit and body are considered inseparable in this first stage.

A society makes a leap in sophistication and reaches Frazer's second stage when it begins to regard them as separate. That is, the spirit exists independently of the physical tree, even if it chooses to dwell there most of the time. The same spirit may thus take up residence in any tree of a forest; it is not killed when an individual tree is cut down. It is not bound to a single tree but rather stands for a group. The distinction may seem small, but it is a significant first step toward symbolic thinking. A forest, after all, is more than the sum of its parts. It encompasses not only its trees but also the animals and brush that flourish among them. The dangers of the forest are hidden; a traveler may or may not encounter them on a given journey. To think about a tree spirit identified with the forest as a whole, therefore, people had to think about phenomena that were removed from them in time and space—ideas rather than things. Such a tree spirit represented the potential and abstract rather than the concrete and immediate.

That transition is completed in the third stage. Liberated from each other, trees and their spirits can begin to be seen as symbols and embodiments of other natural processes of significance to primitive life: the power of weather and seasons to produce good or bad harvests, the mysteries of childbirth and disease. At that point, the veneration of trees reaches its stage of greatest complexity. Societies in both Eastern Europe and the South Pacific presented ceremonial offerings to trees in the hopes that they would furnish rain and sunshine. Women who hoped to bear children might be instructed to embrace special trees thought to give fertility. The appearance of these beliefs, in which the fruitfulness of trees suggests the fruitfulness of harvests and family-building, indicates that a society has made its first steps toward symbolic and abstract thinking.

More Available

6. The second stage of tree worship discussed in the passage involves a distinction between

(A)   sacred trees and ordinary trees

(B)   the spirit and the body of a tree

(C)   trees with and without spirits

(D)   single trees and trees in forests

The Veneration of Trees

In *The Golden Bough*, his classic catalog of mythologies, Sir James George Frazer extensively documents the significance of trees in world religion. His chapters on tree spirits roam from Northern Europe to the Eastern Seaboard of what is now the United States to the islands of the Pacific. Despite the lack of contact among these regions, the veneration of trees united them. The woods that covered large areas of Europe and North America, in particular, were difficult to penetrate and dangerous to cross. It was not a great mental leap for people to see the trees that populated them as embodiments of the natural forces that governed their lives.

On the basis of Frazer's classification, one can derive three loose stages of tree worship. In the first, a society sees the tree as the physical body of the spirit that inhabits it, much as the human body can be seen as housing the mind. It is known that both the Celtic and the Germanic tribes that inhabited ancient Northern Europe regarded certain trees as sacred, setting them apart by species (as the Druids worshipped oaks) or by location (the way certain natural groves were regarded as natural temples or sacred spaces in what is now Germany). Early on, each of these trees was regarded as an animate being with both spirit and body. It had a distinct identity, like an individual person. This suggests that it was believed to have the same impulses and reactions as the people who venerated it.

Accordingly, ancient peoples had elaborate taboos designed to avoid causing offense to trees. These taboos were taken very seriously. In some places, one could be punished severely for injuring the bark of a tree or stealing its fruit. Before a tree was felled for human use, woodcutters in many world cultures would offer it both apologies and thanks for the resources it was about to provide them. This was necessary to avoid insulting the tree and inviting bad fortune. It was also the case, however, that injuries were said to cause suffering to trees as they did to people. In some societies, it was claimed that trees cry out in pain when struck or cut into. A tree's spirit and body are considered inseparable in this first stage.

A society makes a leap in sophistication and reaches Frazer's second stage when it begins to regard them as separate. That is, the spirit exists independently of the physical tree, even if it chooses to dwell there most of the time. The same spirit may thus take up residence in any tree of a forest; it is not killed when an individual tree is cut down. It is not bound to a single tree but rather stands for a group. The distinction may seem small, but it is a significant first step toward symbolic thinking. A forest, after all, is more than the sum of its parts. It encompasses not only its trees but also the animals and brush that flourish among them. The dangers of the forest are hidden; a traveler may or may not encounter them on a given journey. To think about a tree spirit identified with the forest as a whole, therefore, people had to think about phenomena that were removed from them in time and space—ideas rather than things. Such a tree spirit represented the potential and abstract rather than the concrete and immediate.

That transition is completed in the third stage. Liberated from each other, trees and their spirits can begin to be seen as symbols and embodiments of other natural processes of significance to primitive life: the power of weather and seasons to produce good or bad harvests, the mysteries of childbirth and disease. At that point, the veneration of trees reaches its stage of greatest complexity. Societies in both Eastern Europe and the South Pacific presented ceremonial offerings to trees in the hopes that they would furnish rain and sunshine. Women who hoped to bear children might be instructed to embrace special trees thought to give fertility. The appearance of these beliefs, in which the fruitfulness of trees suggests the fruitfulness of harvests and family-building, indicates that a society has made its first steps toward symbolic and abstract thinking.

More Available

7. The phrase bound to in the passage is closest in meaning to

(A) limited to
(B) hidden within
(C) regarded as
(D) venerated as

The Veneration of Trees

In *The Golden Bough,* his classic catalog of mythologies, Sir James George Frazer extensively documents the significance of trees in world religion. His chapters on tree spirits roam from Northern Europe to the Eastern Seaboard of what is now the United States to the islands of the Pacific. Despite the lack of contact among these regions, the veneration of trees united them. The woods that covered large areas of Europe and North America, in particular, were difficult to penetrate and dangerous to cross. It was not a great mental leap for people to see the trees that populated them as embodiments of the natural forces that governed their lives.

On the basis of Frazer's classification, one can derive three loose stages of tree worship. In the first, a society sees the tree as the physical body of the spirit that inhabits it, much as the human body can be seen as housing the mind. It is known that both the Celtic and the Germanic tribes that inhabited ancient Northern Europe regarded certain trees as sacred, setting them apart by species (as the Druids worshipped oaks) or by location (the way certain natural groves were regarded as natural temples or sacred spaces in what is now Germany). Early on, each of these trees was regarded as an animate being with both spirit and body. It had a distinct identity, like an individual person. This suggests that it was believed to have the same impulses and reactions as the people who venerated it.

Accordingly, ancient peoples had elaborate taboos designed to avoid causing offense to trees. These taboos were taken very seriously. In some places, one could be punished severely for injuring the bark of a tree or stealing its fruit. Before a tree was felled for human use, woodcutters in many world cultures would offer it both apologies and thanks for the resources it was about to provide them. This was necessary to avoid insulting the tree and inviting bad fortune. It was also the case, however, that injuries were said to cause suffering to trees as they did to people. In some societies, it was claimed that trees cry out in pain when struck or cut into. A tree's spirit and body are considered inseparable in this first stage.

A society makes a leap in sophistication and reaches Frazer's second stage when it begins to regard them as separate. That is, the spirit exists independently of the physical tree, even if it chooses to dwell there most of the time. The same spirit may thus take up residence in any tree of a forest; it is not killed when an individual tree is cut down. It is not bound to a single tree but rather stands for a group. The distinction may seem small, but it is a significant first step toward symbolic thinking. A forest, after all, is more than the sum of its parts. It encompasses not only its trees but also the animals and brush that flourish among them. The dangers of the forest are hidden; a traveler may or may not encounter them on a given journey. To think about a tree spirit identified with the forest as a whole, therefore, people had to think about phenomena that were removed from them in time and space—ideas rather than things. Such a tree spirit represented the potential and abstract rather than the concrete and immediate.

That transition is completed in the third stage. Liberated from each other, trees and their spirits can begin to be seen as symbols and embodiments of other natural processes of significance to primitive life: the power of weather and seasons to produce good or bad harvests, the mysteries of childbirth and disease. At that point, the veneration of trees reaches its stage of greatest complexity. Societies in both Eastern Europe and the South Pacific presented ceremonial offerings to trees in the hopes that they would furnish rain and sunshine. Women who hoped to bear children might be instructed to embrace special trees thought to give fertility. The appearance of these beliefs, in which the fruitfulness of trees suggests the fruitfulness of harvests and family-building, indicates that a society has made its first steps toward symbolic and abstract thinking.

TOEFL Reading

PAUSE TEST   SECTION EXIT

8 of 39

REVIEW   HELP ?   BACK   NEXT →

HIDE TIME   00:08:45

More Available

8. The author of the passage uses the phrase ideas rather than things to indicate that

(A) the forest was actually much less dangerous than people thought it to be

(B) people stopped fearing the forest at the second stage of tree worship

(C) some aspects of the forest can be imagined but not seen

(D) many travelers were seriously hurt in the forest

The Veneration of Trees

In *The Golden Bough*, his classic catalog of mythologies, Sir James George Frazer extensively documents the significance of trees in world religion. His chapters on tree spirits roam from Northern Europe to the Eastern Seaboard of what is now the United States to the islands of the Pacific. Despite the lack of contact among these regions, the veneration of trees united them. The woods that covered large areas of Europe and North America, in particular, were difficult to penetrate and dangerous to cross. It was not a great mental leap for people to see the trees that populated them as embodiments of the natural forces that governed their lives.

On the basis of Frazer's classification, one can derive three loose stages of tree worship. In the first, a society sees the tree as the physical body of the spirit that inhabits it, much as the human body can be seen as housing the mind. It is known that both the Celtic and the Germanic tribes that inhabited ancient Northern Europe regarded certain trees as sacred, setting them apart by species (as the Druids worshipped oaks) or by location (the way certain natural groves were regarded as natural temples or sacred spaces in what is now Germany). Early on, each of these trees was regarded as an animate being with both spirit and body. It had a distinct identity, like an individual person. This suggests that it was believed to have the same impulses and reactions as the people who venerated it.

Accordingly, ancient peoples had elaborate taboos designed to avoid causing offense to trees. These taboos were taken very seriously. In some places, one could be punished severely for injuring the bark of a tree or stealing its fruit. Before a tree was felled for human use, woodcutters in many world cultures would offer it both apologies and thanks for the resources it was about to provide them. This was necessary to avoid insulting the tree and inviting bad fortune. It was also the case, however, that injuries were said to cause suffering to trees as they did to people. In some societies, it was claimed that trees cry out in pain when struck or cut into. A tree's spirit and body are considered inseparable in this first stage.

A society makes a leap in sophistication and reaches Frazer's second stage when it begins to regard them as separate. That is, the spirit exists independently of the physical tree, even if it chooses to dwell there most of the time. The same spirit may thus take up residence in any tree of a forest; it is not killed when an individual tree is cut down. It is not bound to a single tree but rather stands for a group. The distinction may seem small, but it is a significant first step toward symbolic thinking. A forest, after all, is more than the sum of its parts. It encompasses not only its trees but also the animals and brush that flourish among them. The dangers of the forest are hidden; a traveler may or may not encounter them on a given journey. To think about a tree spirit identified with the forest as a whole, therefore, people had to think about phenomena that were removed from them in time and space—ideas rather than things. Such a tree spirit represented the potential and abstract rather than the concrete and immediate.

That transition is completed in the third stage. Liberated from each other, trees and their spirits can begin to be seen as symbols and embodiments of other natural processes of significance to primitive life: the power of weather and seasons to produce good or bad harvests, the mysteries of childbirth and disease. At that point, the veneration of trees reaches its stage of greatest complexity. Societies in both Eastern Europe and the South Pacific presented ceremonial offerings to trees in the hopes that they would furnish rain and sunshine. Women who hoped to bear children might be instructed to embrace special trees thought to give fertility. The appearance of these beliefs, in which the fruitfulness of trees suggests the fruitfulness of harvests and family-building, indicates that a society has made its first steps toward symbolic and abstract thinking.

More Available

9. The author implies that the most complex phase of tree worship involves

(A) the belief that all trees are sacred

(B) distinguishing between male and female tree spirits

(C) different ceremonies for different seasons

(D) the use of trees as symbols

The Veneration of Trees

In *The Golden Bough,* his classic catalog of mythologies, Sir James George Frazer extensively documents the significance of trees in world religion. His chapters on tree spirits roam from Northern Europe to the Eastern Seaboard of what is now the United States to the islands of the Pacific. Despite the lack of contact among these regions, the veneration of trees united them. The woods that covered large areas of Europe and North America, in particular, were difficult to penetrate and dangerous to cross. It was not a great mental leap for people to see the trees that populated them as embodiments of the natural forces that governed their lives.

On the basis of Frazer's classification, one can derive three loose stages of tree worship. In the first, a society sees the tree as the physical body of the spirit that inhabits it, much as the human body can be seen as housing the mind. It is known that both the Celtic and the Germanic tribes that inhabited ancient Northern Europe regarded certain trees as sacred, setting them apart by species (as the Druids worshipped oaks) or by location (the way certain natural groves were regarded as natural temples or sacred spaces in what is now Germany). Early on, each of these trees was regarded as an animate being with both spirit and body. It had a distinct identity, like an individual person. This suggests that it was believed to have the same impulses and reactions as the people who venerated it.

Accordingly, ancient peoples had elaborate taboos designed to avoid causing offense to trees. These taboos were taken very seriously. In some places, one could be punished severely for injuring the bark of a tree or stealing its fruit. Before a tree was felled for human use, woodcutters in many world cultures would offer it both apologies and thanks for the resources it was about to provide them. This was necessary to avoid insulting the tree and inviting bad fortune. It was also the case, however, that injuries were said to cause suffering to trees as they did to people. In some societies, it was claimed that trees cry out in pain when struck or cut into. A tree's spirit and body are considered inseparable in this first stage.

A society makes a leap in sophistication and reaches Frazer's second stage when it begins to regard them as separate. That is, the spirit exists independently of the physical tree, even if it chooses to dwell there most of the time. The same spirit may thus take up residence in any tree of a forest; it is not killed when an individual tree is cut down. It is not bound to a single tree but rather stands for a group. The distinction may seem small, but it is a significant first step toward symbolic thinking. A forest, after all, is more than the sum of its parts. It encompasses not only its trees but also the animals and brush that flourish among them. The dangers of the forest are hidden; a traveler may or may not encounter them on a given journey. To think about a tree spirit identified with the forest as a whole, therefore, people had to think about phenomena that were removed from them in time and space—ideas rather than things. Such a tree spirit represented the potential and abstract rather than the concrete and immediate.

That transition is completed in the third stage. Liberated from each other, trees and their spirits can begin to be seen as symbols and embodiments of other natural processes of significance to primitive life: the power of weather and seasons to produce good or bad harvests, the mysteries of childbirth and disease. At that point, the veneration of trees reaches its stage of greatest complexity. Societies in both Eastern Europe and the South Pacific presented ceremonial offerings to trees in the hopes that they would furnish rain and sunshine. Women who hoped to bear children might be instructed to embrace special trees thought to give fertility. The appearance of these beliefs, in which the fruitfulness of trees suggests the fruitfulness of harvests and family building, indicates that a society has made its first steps toward symbolic and abstract thinking.

More Available

10. The word furnish in the passage is closest in meaning to

(A) explain

(B) provide

(C) avoid

(D) refuse

The Veneration of Trees

In *The Golden Bough*, his classic catalog of mythologies, Sir James George Frazer extensively documents the significance of trees in world religion. His chapters on tree spirits roam from Northern Europe to the Eastern Seaboard of what is now the United States to the islands of the Pacific. Despite the lack of contact among these regions, the veneration of trees united them. The woods that covered large areas of Europe and North America, in particular, were difficult to penetrate and dangerous to cross. It was not a great mental leap for people to see the trees that populated them as embodiments of the natural forces that governed their lives.

On the basis of Frazer's classification, one can derive three loose stages of tree worship. In the first, a society sees the tree as the physical body of the spirit that inhabits it, much as the human body can be seen as housing the mind. It is known that both the Celtic and the Germanic tribes that inhabited ancient Northern Europe regarded certain trees as sacred, setting them apart by species (as the Druids worshipped oaks) or by location (the way certain natural groves were regarded as natural temples or sacred spaces in what is now Germany). Early on, each of these trees was regarded as an animate being with both spirit and body. It had a distinct identity, like an individual person. This suggests that it was believed to have the same impulses and reactions as the people who venerated it.

Accordingly, ancient peoples had elaborate taboos designed to avoid causing offense to trees. These taboos were taken very seriously. In some places, one could be punished severely for injuring the bark of a tree or stealing its fruit. Before a tree was felled for human use, woodcutters in many world cultures would offer it both apologies and thanks for the resources it was about to provide them. This was necessary to avoid insulting the tree and inviting bad fortune. It was also the case, however, that injuries were said to cause suffering to trees as they did to people. In some societies, it was claimed that trees cry out in pain when struck or cut into. A tree's spirit and body are considered inseparable in this first stage.

A society makes a leap in sophistication and reaches Frazer's second stage when it begins to regard them as separate. That is, the spirit exists independently of the physical tree, even if it chooses to dwell there most of the time. The same spirit may thus take up residence in any tree of a forest; it is not killed when an individual tree is cut down. It is not bound to a single tree but rather stands for a group. The distinction may seem small, but it is a significant first step toward symbolic thinking. A forest, after all, is more than the sum of its parts. It encompasses not only its trees but also the animals and brush that flourish among them. The dangers of the forest are hidden; a traveler may or may not encounter them on a given journey. To think about a tree spirit identified with the forest as a whole, therefore, people had to think about phenomena that were removed from them in time and space—ideas rather than things. Such a tree spirit represented the potential and abstract rather than the concrete and immediate.

That transition is completed in the third stage. Liberated from each other, trees and their spirits can begin to be seen as symbols and embodiments of other natural processes of significance to primitive life: the power of weather and seasons to produce good or bad harvests, the mysteries of childbirth and disease. At that point, the veneration of trees reaches its stage of greatest complexity. Societies in both Eastern Europe and the South Pacific presented ceremonial offerings to trees in the hopes that they would furnish rain and sunshine. Women who hoped to bear children might be instructed to embrace special trees thought to give fertility. The appearance of these beliefs, in which the fruitfulness of trees suggests the fruitfulness of harvests and family-building, indicates that a society has made its first steps toward symbolic and abstract thinking.

More Available

11. According to paragraph 5 of the passage, ancient peoples saw special meaning in

(A)   the ability of trees to bear fruit

(B)   the three stages in the life cycle of a tree

(C)   trees that required little rain and sun

(D)   the raising of trees by women

Paragraph 5 is marked with an arrow [➤]

The Veneration of Trees

In *The Golden Bough,* his classic catalog of mythologies, Sir James George Frazer extensively documents the significance of trees in world religion. His chapters on tree spirits roam from Northern Europe to the Eastern Seaboard of what is now the United States to the islands of the Pacific. Despite the lack of contact among these regions, the veneration of trees united them. The woods that covered large areas of Europe and North America, in particular, were difficult to penetrate and dangerous to cross. It was not a great mental leap for people to see the trees that populated them as embodiments of the natural forces that governed their lives.

On the basis of Frazer's classification, one can derive three loose stages of tree worship. In the first, a society sees the tree as the physical body of the spirit that inhabits it, much as the human body can be seen as housing the mind. It is known that both the Celtic and the Germanic tribes that inhabited ancient Northern Europe regarded certain trees as sacred, setting them apart by species (as the Druids worshipped oaks) or by location (the way certain natural groves were regarded as natural temples or sacred spaces in what is now Germany). Early on, each of these trees was regarded as an animate being with both spirit and body. It had a distinct identity, like an individual person. This suggests that it was believed to have the same impulses and reactions as the people who venerated it.

Accordingly, ancient peoples had elaborate taboos designed to avoid causing offense to trees. These taboos were taken very seriously. In some places, one could be punished severely for injuring the bark of a tree or stealing its fruit. Before a tree was felled for human use, woodcutters in many world cultures would offer it both apologies and thanks for the resources it was about to provide them. This was necessary to avoid insulting the tree and inviting bad fortune. It was also the case, however, that injuries were said to cause suffering to trees as they did to people. In some societies, it was claimed that trees cry out in pain when struck or cut into. A tree's spirit and body are considered inseparable in this first stage.

A society makes a leap in sophistication and reaches Frazer's second stage when it begins to regard them as separate. That is, the spirit exists independently of the physical tree, even if it chooses to dwell there most of the time. The same spirit may thus take up residence in any tree of a forest; it is not killed when an individual tree is cut down. It is not bound to a single tree but rather stands for a group. The distinction may seem small, but it is a significant first step toward symbolic thinking. A forest, after all, is more than the sum of its parts. It encompasses not only its trees but also the animals and brush that flourish among them. The dangers of the forest are hidden; a traveler may or may not encounter them on a given journey. To think about a tree spirit identified with the forest as a whole, therefore, people had to think about phenomena that were removed from them in time and space—ideas rather than things. Such a tree spirit represented the potential and abstract rather than the concrete and immediate.

➤That transition is completed in the third stage. Liberated from each other, trees and their spirits can begin to be seen as symbols and embodiments of other natural processes of significance to primitive life: the power of weather and seasons to produce good or bad harvests, the mysteries of childbirth and disease. At that point, the veneration of trees reaches its stage of greatest complexity. Societies in both Eastern Europe and the South Pacific presented ceremonial offerings to trees in the hopes that they would furnish rain and sunshine. Women who hoped to bear children might be instructed to embrace special trees thought to give fertility. The appearance of these beliefs, in which the fruitfulness of trees suggests the fruitfulness of harvests and family-building, indicates that a society has made its first steps toward symbolic and abstract thinking.

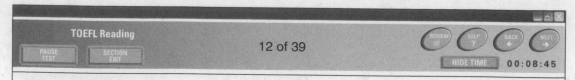

12. **Directions:** An introductory sentence for a brief summary of the passage is provided below. Complete the summary by selecting the THREE answer choices that express the most important ideas in the passage. Some sentences do not belong in the summary because they express ideas that are not presented in the passage or are minor ideas in the passage. *This question is worth 2 points.*

Three basic levels of tree worship can be observed in *The Golden Bough*.

-
-
-

Answer Choices	
It was forbidden to cut down certain trees because they would be seriously offended by an injury.	Ancient Germans believed certain groves were sacred and used them as temples, but Druids venerated the oak tree in particular.
Certain peoples came to believe that tree spirits were independent of individual trees and instead represented a whole forest.	Some societies believed each tree had an individual spirit, the way a human being has a distinct mind.
More is known about the ceremonies of Europe than about the ceremonies of North America and the South Pacific.	A basis for abstract thinking was achieved when tree spirits were believed to control natural forces such as crops and human fertility.

More Available

Daguerreotypes

Only a small number of professional photographers ever had any practical experience as daguerreotypists, those technicians who made photographs through the daguerreotype process. By its strictest definition, the daguerreotype process was common for not more than 20 years in the mid-1800s. Other ways of making photographic images on metal plates, such as tintypes and ferrotypes, were developed rapidly after the advent of the daguerreotype. They quickly eclipsed it in popularity. Today, the surviving photographs produced by these methods are often referred to as daguerreotypes, but that designation is incorrect.

It is not surprising that photography enthusiasts began looking for alternatives to the daguerreotype almost immediately. The materials it required were both expensive—the plates contained silver and one of the developing solutions contained gold—and extremely risky. Strict adherence to proper laboratory procedure was necessary in order to avoid poisoning by noxious gases.

The steps involved in preparing and exposing a daguerreotype were as laborious and frustrating as they were hazardous. Images were recorded on copper plates to which several thin coats of silver had been applied. After being fastened to wooden blocks, the plates were scoured with alcohol and squares of soft flannel. Since even one speck of dust could easily create a deep enough groove to render the final image worthless, they had to be perfectly buffed. The plates were then bathed in solutions of bromine and iodine. The thin layer of bromo-iodine that formed on them made them sensitive to light, at which point they were ready for exposure.

After exposure, the plates were dipped alternately in heated mercury and freezing-cold

More Available

water. The mercury vapors helped fix the images to the plates and developed them. The chilled water kept the plates from breaking up during this critical step. The daguerreotypists next applied hydrosulfate soda to the plate surfaces to dissolve any bromo-iodine that had not been exposed to light and brushed them with a solution of gold and chlorine to brighten the images and sharpen their black-white contrast.

There were difficulties for the daguerreotypists' customers too. The expense of materials and labor was passed on to them in the form of very high prices. Only the rich could easily afford to sit for a daguerreotype portrait. For those of more limited means, a daguerreotype was a once-in-a-lifetime treat. Additionally, daguerreotype plates required long exposures, from 8 to 20 minutes, in order to yield high-quality images. Chairs and tables with special support were designed to help those posing for portraits to remain absolutely still throughout the exposure time. If they did not, the resulting image would be blurred. Not even the cleverest such design, of course, could compensate for the need of the human eye to blink periodically.

For all the disadvantages involved in making daguerreotypes, no one could argue with the finished product when things went well. The process recorded textural detail with a realism that still seems shocking. The sheen of satin and the dull, heavy nap of flannel are easily distinguished. Those posing for daguerreotypes tired after trying to maintain the same facial expression for minutes at a time; the result was that their features often relaxed into an attractive thoughtfulness.

The incentive to develop a photographic process that retained the advantages of the daguerreotype without the disadvantages was thus powerful. The substitute with the most lasting popularity was the ferrotype, or tintype, which used an enamel-coated iron plate.

More Available

Ferrotypes became popular with photographers who set up stalls at street fairs and inexpensive resorts because they could be exposed and developed very quickly. Iron plates were also much less expensive than copper plates, and the resulting photographs were less fragile than daguerreotypes. On the other hand, iron, unlike copper, could rust if not properly stored. Many old ferrotypes were destroyed by long-term display in hot and moist environments.

13. Which of the following can be inferred from paragraph 1 of the passage?

(A) Some photographs are called daguerreotypes inaccurately.

(B) Daguerreotypes were popular for most of the 1800s.

(C) Not all daguerreotypes were made by technicians.

(D) Tintypes and ferrotypes were the first kinds of photographs.

Paragraph 1 is marked with an arrow [➤]

Daguerreotypes

➤ Only a small number of professional photographers ever had any practical experience as daguerreotypists, those technicians who made photographs through the daguerreotype process. By its strictest definition, the daguerreotype process was common for not more than 20 years in the mid-1800s. Other ways of making photographic images on metal plates, such as tintypes and ferrotypes, were developed rapidly after the advent of the daguerreotype. They quickly eclipsed it in popularity. Today, the surviving photographs produced by these methods are often referred to as daguerreotypes, but that designation is incorrect.

It is not surprising that photography enthusiasts began looking for alternatives to the daguerreotype almost immediately. The materials it required were both expensive—the plates contained silver and one of the developing solutions contained gold—and extremely risky. Strict adherence to proper laboratory procedure was necessary in order to avoid poisoning by noxious gases.

The steps involved in preparing and exposing a daguerreotype were as laborious and frustrating as they were hazardous. Images were recorded on copper plates to which several thin coats of silver had been applied. After being fastened to wooden blocks, the plates were scoured with alcohol and squares of soft flannel. Since even one speck of dust could easily create a deep enough groove to render the final image worthless, they had to be perfectly buffed. The plates were then bathed in solutions of bromine and iodine. The thin layer of bromo-iodine that formed on them made them sensitive to light, at which point they were ready for exposure.

After exposure, the plates were dipped alternately in heated mercury and freezing-cold water. The mercury vapors helped fix the images to the plates and developed them. The chilled water kept the plates from breaking up during this critical step. The daguerreotypists next applied hydrosulfate soda to the plate surfaces to dissolve any bromo-iodine that had not been exposed to light and brushed them with a solution of gold and chlorine to brighten the images and sharpen their black-white contrast.

There were difficulties for the daguerreotypists' customers too. The expense of materials and labor was passed on to them in the form of very high prices. Only the rich could easily afford to sit for a daguerreotype portrait. For those of more limited means, a daguerreotype was a once-in-a-lifetime treat. Additionally, daguerreotype plates required long exposures, from 8 to 20 minutes, in order to yield high-quality images. Chairs and tables with special support were designed to help those posing for portraits to remain absolutely still throughout the exposure time. If they did not, the resulting image would be blurred. Not even the cleverest such design, of course, could compensate for the need of the human eye to blink periodically.

For all the disadvantages involved in making daguerreotypes, no one could argue with the finished product when things went well. The process recorded textural detail with a realism that still seems shocking. The sheen of satin and the dull, heavy nap of flannel are easily distinguished. Those posing for daguerreotypes tired after trying to maintain the same facial expression for minutes at a time; the result was that their features often relaxed into an attractive thoughtfulness.

The incentive to develop a photographic process that retained the advantages of the daguerreotype without the disadvantages was thus powerful. The substitute with the most lasting popularity was the ferrotype, or tintype, which used an enamel-coated iron plate. Ferrotypes became popular with photographers who set up stalls at street fairs and inexpensive resorts because they could be exposed and developed very quickly. Iron plates were also much less expensive than copper plates, and the resulting photographs were less fragile than daguerreotypes. On the other hand, iron, unlike copper, could rust if not properly stored. Many old ferrotypes were destroyed by long-term display in hot and moist environments.

More Available

14. The phrase not more than in the passage is closest in meaning to

(A) at first
(B) additionally
(C) at most
(D) historically

Daguerreotypes

Only a small number of professional photographers ever had any practical experience as daguerreotypists, those technicians who made photographs through the daguerreotype process. By its strictest definition, the daguerreotype process was common for not more than 20 years in the mid-1800s. Other ways of making photographic images on metal plates, such as tintypes and ferrotypes, were developed rapidly after the advent of the daguerreotype. They quickly eclipsed it in popularity. Today, the surviving photographs produced by these methods are often referred to as daguerreotypes, but that designation is incorrect.

It is not surprising that photography enthusiasts began looking for alternatives to the daguerreotype almost immediately. The materials it required were both expensive—the plates contained silver and one of the developing solutions contained gold—and extremely risky. Strict adherence to proper laboratory procedure was necessary in order to avoid poisoning by noxious gases.

The steps involved in preparing and exposing a daguerreotype were as laborious and frustrating as they were hazardous. Images were recorded on copper plates to which several thin coats of silver had been applied. After being fastened to wooden blocks, the plates were scoured with alcohol and squares of soft flannel. Since even one speck of dust could easily create a deep enough groove to render the final image worthless, they had to be perfectly buffed. The plates were then bathed in solutions of bromine and iodine. The thin layer of bromo-iodine that formed on them made them sensitive to light, at which point they were ready for exposure.

After exposure, the plates were dipped alternately in heated mercury and freezing-cold water. The mercury vapors helped fix the images to the plates and developed them. The chilled water kept the plates from breaking up during this critical step. The daguerreotypists next applied hydrosulfate soda to the plate surfaces to dissolve any bromo-iodine that had not been exposed to light and brushed them with a solution of gold and chlorine to brighten the images and sharpen their black-white contrast.

There were difficulties for the daguerreotypists' customers too. The expense of materials and labor was passed on to them in the form of very high prices. Only the rich could easily afford to sit for a daguerreotype portrait. For those of more limited means, a daguerreotype was a once-in-a-lifetime treat. Additionally, daguerreotype plates required long exposures, from 8 to 20 minutes, in order to yield high-quality images. Chairs and tables with special support were designed to help those posing for portraits to remain absolutely still throughout the exposure time. If they did not, the resulting image would be blurred. Not even the cleverest such design, of course, could compensate for the need of the human eye to blink periodically.

For all the disadvantages involved in making daguerreotypes, no one could argue with the finished product when things went well. The process recorded textural detail with a realism that still seems shocking. The sheen of satin and the dull, heavy nap of flannel are easily distinguished. Those posing for daguerreotypes tired after trying to maintain the same facial expression for minutes at a time; the result was that their features often relaxed into an attractive thoughtfulness.

The incentive to develop a photographic process that retained the advantages of the daguerreotype without the disadvantages was thus powerful. The substitute with the most lasting popularity was the ferrotype, or tintype, which used an enamel-coated iron plate. Ferrotypes became popular with photographers who set up stalls at street fairs and inexpensive resorts because they could be exposed and developed very quickly. Iron plates were also much less expensive than copper plates, and the resulting photographs were less fragile than daguerreotypes. On the other hand, iron, unlike copper, could rust if not properly stored. Many old ferrotypes were destroyed by long-term display in hot and moist environments.

More Available

15. Why does the author mention proper laboratory procedure?

(A) To contrast daguerreotypists with true scientists

(B) To argue that daguerreotypists influenced other fields

(C) To give an example of an expensive material

(D) To indicate how dangerous daguerreotype making was

Daguerreotypes

Only a small number of professional photographers ever had any practical experience as daguerreotypists, those technicians who made photographs through the daguerreotype process. By its strictest definition, the daguerreotype process was common for not more than 20 years in the mid-1800s. Other ways of making photographic images on metal plates, such as tintypes and ferrotypes, were developed rapidly after the advent of the daguerreotype. They quickly eclipsed it in popularity. Today, the surviving photographs produced by these methods are often referred to as daguerreotypes, but that designation is incorrect.

It is not surprising that photography enthusiasts began looking for alternatives to the daguerreotype almost immediately. The materials it required were both expensive—the plates contained silver and one of the developing solutions contained gold—and extremely risky. Strict adherence to proper laboratory procedure was necessary in order to avoid poisoning by noxious gases.

The steps involved in preparing and exposing a daguerreotype were as laborious and frustrating as they were hazardous. Images were recorded on copper plates to which several thin coats of silver had been applied. After being fastened to wooden blocks, the plates were scoured with alcohol and squares of soft flannel. Since even one speck of dust could easily create a deep enough groove to render the final image worthless, they had to be perfectly buffed. The plates were then bathed in solutions of bromine and iodine. The thin layer of bromo-iodine that formed on them made them sensitive to light, at which point they were ready for exposure.

After exposure, the plates were dipped alternately in heated mercury and freezing-cold water. The mercury vapors helped fix the images to the plates and developed them. The chilled water kept the plates from breaking up during this critical step. The daguerreotypists next applied hydrosulfate soda to the plate surfaces to dissolve any bromo-iodine that had not been exposed to light and brushed them with a solution of gold and chlorine to brighten the images and sharpen their black-white contrast.

There were difficulties for the daguerreotypists' customers too. The expense of materials and labor was passed on to them in the form of very high prices. Only the rich could easily afford to sit for a daguerreotype portrait. For those of more limited means, a daguerreotype was a once-in-a-lifetime treat. Additionally, daguerreotype plates required long exposures, from 8 to 20 minutes, in order to yield high-quality images. Chairs and tables with special support were designed to help those posing for portraits to remain absolutely still throughout the exposure time. If they did not, the resulting image would be blurred. Not even the cleverest such design, of course, could compensate for the need of the human eye to blink periodically.

For all the disadvantages involved in making daguerreotypes, no one could argue with the finished product when things went well. The process recorded textural detail with a realism that still seems shocking. The sheen of satin and the dull, heavy nap of flannel are easily distinguished. Those posing for daguerreotypes tired after trying to maintain the same facial expression for minutes at a time; the result was that their features often relaxed into an attractive thoughtfulness.

The incentive to develop a photographic process that retained the advantages of the daguerreotype without the disadvantages was thus powerful. The substitute with the most lasting popularity was the ferrotype, or tintype, which used an enamel-coated iron plate. Ferrotypes became popular with photographers who set up stalls at street fairs and inexpensive resorts because they could be exposed and developed very quickly. Iron plates were also much less expensive than copper plates, and the resulting photographs were less fragile than daguerreotypes. On the other hand, iron, unlike copper, could rust if not properly stored. Many old ferrotypes were destroyed by long-term display in hot and moist environments.

16. According to paragraph 3, why did daguerreotype plates need to be buffed carefully before exposure?

(A) Dust could harm the plate surfaces.

(B) People preferred highly polished daguerreotypes.

(C) Buffing made the chemicals stick to the copper surface.

(D) A smooth surface was more sensitive to light.

Paragraph 3 is marked with an arrow [➤]

Daguerreotypes

Only a small number of professional photographers ever had any practical experience as daguerreotypists, those technicians who made photographs through the daguerreotype process. By its strictest definition, the daguerreotype process was common for not more than 20 years in the mid-1800s. Other ways of making photographic images on metal plates, such as tintypes and ferrotypes, were developed rapidly after the advent of the daguerreotype. They quickly eclipsed it in popularity. Today, the surviving photographs produced by these methods are often referred to as daguerreotypes, but that designation is incorrect.

It is not surprising that photography enthusiasts began looking for alternatives to the daguerreotype almost immediately. The materials it required were both expensive—the plates contained silver and one of the developing solutions contained gold—and extremely risky. Strict adherence to proper laboratory procedure was necessary in order to avoid poisoning by noxious gases.

➤The steps involved in preparing and exposing a daguerreotype were as laborious and frustrating as they were hazardous. Images were recorded on copper plates to which several thin coats of silver had been applied. After being fastened to wooden blocks, the plates were scoured with alcohol and squares of soft flannel. Since even one speck of dust could easily create a deep enough groove to render the final image worthless, they had to be perfectly buffed. The plates were then bathed in solutions of bromine and iodine. The thin layer of bromo-iodine that formed on them made them sensitive to light, at which point they were ready for exposure.

After exposure, the plates were dipped alternately in heated mercury and freezing-cold water. The mercury vapors helped fix the images to the plates and developed them. The chilled water kept the plates from breaking up during this critical step. The daguerreotypists next applied hydrosulfate soda to the plate surfaces to dissolve any bromo-iodine that had not been exposed to light and brushed them with a solution of gold and chlorine to brighten the images and sharpen their black-white contrast.

There were difficulties for the daguerreotypists' customers too. The expense of materials and labor was passed on to them in the form of very high prices. Only the rich could easily afford to sit for a daguerreotype portrait. For those of more limited means, a daguerreotype was a once-in-a-lifetime treat. Additionally, daguerreotype plates required long exposures, from 8 to 20 minutes, in order to yield high-quality images. Chairs and tables with special support were designed to help those posing for portraits to remain absolutely still throughout the exposure time. If they did not, the resulting image would be blurred. Not even the cleverest such design, of course, could compensate for the need of the human eye to blink periodically.

For all the disadvantages involved in making daguerreotypes, no one could argue with the finished product when things went well. The process recorded textural detail with a realism that still seems shocking. The sheen of satin and the dull, heavy nap of flannel are easily distinguished. Those posing for daguerreotypes tired after trying to maintain the same facial expression for minutes at a time; the result was that their features often relaxed into an attractive thoughtfulness.

The incentive to develop a photographic process that retained the advantages of the daguerreotype without the disadvantages was thus powerful. The substitute with the most lasting popularity was the ferrotype, or tintype, which used an enamel-coated iron plate. Ferrotypes became popular with photographers who set up stalls at street fairs and inexpensive resorts because they could be exposed and developed very quickly. Iron plates were also much less expensive than copper plates, and the resulting photographs were less fragile than daguerreotypes. On the other hand, iron, unlike copper, could rust if not properly stored. Many old ferrotypes were destroyed by long-term display in hot and moist environments.

17. The word fix in the passage is closest in meaning to

(A) correct
(B) cut
(C) brighten
(D) attach

Daguerreotypes

Only a small number of professional photographers ever had any practical experience as daguerreotypists, those technicians who made photographs through the daguerreotype process. By its strictest definition, the daguerreotype process was common for not more than 20 years in the mid-1800s. Other ways of making photographic images on metal plates, such as tintypes and ferrotypes, were developed rapidly after the advent of the daguerreotype. They quickly eclipsed it in popularity. Today, the surviving photographs produced by these methods are often referred to as daguerreotypes, but that designation is incorrect.

It is not surprising that photography enthusiasts began looking for alternatives to the daguerreotype almost immediately. The materials it required were both expensive—the plates contained silver and one of the developing solutions contained gold—and extremely risky. Strict adherence to proper laboratory procedure was necessary in order to avoid poisoning by noxious gases.

The steps involved in preparing and exposing a daguerreotype were as laborious and frustrating as they were hazardous. Images were recorded on copper plates to which several thin coats of silver had been applied. After being fastened to wooden blocks, the plates were scoured with alcohol and squares of soft flannel. Since even one speck of dust could easily create a deep enough groove to render the final image worthless, they had to be perfectly buffed. The plates were then bathed in solutions of bromine and iodine. The thin layer of bromo-iodine that formed on them made them sensitive to light, at which point they were ready for exposure.

After exposure, the plates were dipped alternately in heated mercury and freezing-cold water. The mercury vapors helped fix the images to the plates and developed them. The chilled water kept the plates from breaking up during this critical step. The daguerreotypists next applied hydrosulfate soda to the plate surfaces to dissolve any bromo-iodine that had not been exposed to light and brushed them with a solution of gold and chlorine to brighten the images and sharpen their black-white contrast.

There were difficulties for the daguerreotypists' customers too. The expense of materials and labor was passed on to them in the form of very high prices. Only the rich could easily afford to sit for a daguerreotype portrait. For those of more limited means, a daguerreotype was a once-in-a-lifetime treat. Additionally, daguerreotype plates required long exposures, from 8 to 20 minutes, in order to yield high-quality images. Chairs and tables with special support were designed to help those posing for portraits to remain absolutely still throughout the exposure time. If they did not, the resulting image would be blurred. Not even the cleverest such design, of course, could compensate for the need of the human eye to blink periodically.

For all the disadvantages involved in making daguerreotypes, no one could argue with the finished product when things went well. The process recorded textural detail with a realism that still seems shocking. The sheen of satin and the dull, heavy nap of flannel are easily distinguished. Those posing for daguerreotypes tired after trying to maintain the same facial expression for minutes at a time; the result was that their features often relaxed into an attractive thoughtfulness.

The incentive to develop a photographic process that retained the advantages of the daguerreotype without the disadvantages was thus powerful. The substitute with the most lasting popularity was the ferrotype, or tintype, which used an enamel-coated iron plate. Ferrotypes became popular with photographers who set up stalls at street fairs and inexpensive resorts because they could be exposed and developed very quickly. Iron plates were also much less expensive than copper plates, and the resulting photographs were less fragile than daguerreotypes. On the other hand, iron, unlike copper, could rust if not properly stored. Many old ferrotypes were destroyed by long-term display in hot and moist environments.

More Available

18. The phrase this critical step in the passage refers to

(A)   exposing the plates
(B)   fixing and developing the images
(C)   making sure the water was cold enough
(D)   applying hydrosulfate soda

Daguerreotypes

Only a small number of professional photographers ever had any practical experience as daguerreotypists, those technicians who made photographs through the daguerreotype process. By its strictest definition, the daguerreotype process was common for not more than 20 years in the mid-1800s. Other ways of making photographic images on metal plates, such as tintypes and ferrotypes, were developed rapidly after the advent of the daguerreotype. They quickly eclipsed it in popularity. Today, the surviving photographs produced by these methods are often referred to as daguerreotypes, but that designation is incorrect.

It is not surprising that photography enthusiasts began looking for alternatives to the daguerreotype almost immediately. The materials it required were both expensive—the plates contained silver and one of the developing solutions contained gold—and extremely risky. Strict adherence to proper laboratory procedure was necessary in order to avoid poisoning by noxious gases.

The steps involved in preparing and exposing a daguerreotype were as laborious and frustrating as they were hazardous. Images were recorded on copper plates to which several thin coats of silver had been applied. After being fastened to wooden blocks, the plates were scoured with alcohol and squares of soft flannel. Since even one speck of dust could easily create a deep enough groove to render the final image worthless, they had to be perfectly buffed. The plates were then bathed in solutions of bromine and iodine. The thin layer of bromo-iodine that formed on them made them sensitive to light, at which point they were ready for exposure.

After exposure, the plates were dipped alternately in heated mercury and freezing-cold water. The mercury vapors helped fix the images to the plates and developed them. The chilled water kept the plates from breaking up during this critical step. The daguerreotypists next applied hydrosulfate soda to the plate surfaces to dissolve any bromo-iodine that had not been exposed to light and brushed them with a solution of gold and chlorine to brighten the images and sharpen their black-white contrast.

There were difficulties for the daguerreotypists' customers too. The expense of materials and labor was passed on to them in the form of very high prices. Only the rich could easily afford to sit for a daguerreotype portrait. For those of more limited means, a daguerreotype was a once-in-a-lifetime treat. Additionally, daguerreotype plates required long exposures, from 8 to 20 minutes, in order to yield high-quality images. Chairs and tables with special support were designed to help those posing for portraits to remain absolutely still throughout the exposure time. If they did not, the resulting image would be blurred. Not even the cleverest such design, of course, could compensate for the need of the human eye to blink periodically.

For all the disadvantages involved in making daguerreotypes, no one could argue with the finished product when things went well. The process recorded textural detail with a realism that still seems shocking. The sheen of satin and the dull, heavy nap of flannel are easily distinguished. Those posing for daguerreotypes tired after trying to maintain the same facial expression for minutes at a time; the result was that their features often relaxed into an attractive thoughtfulness.

The incentive to develop a photographic process that retained the advantages of the daguerreotype without the disadvantages was thus powerful. The substitute with the most lasting popularity was the ferrotype, or tintype, which used an enamel-coated iron plate. Ferrotypes became popular with photographers who set up stalls at street fairs and inexpensive resorts because they could be exposed and developed very quickly. Iron plates were also much less expensive than copper plates, and the resulting photographs were less fragile than daguerreotypes. On the other hand, iron, unlike copper, could rust if not properly stored. Many old ferrotypes were destroyed by long-term display in hot and moist environments.

More Available

19. It can be inferred from paragraph 4 that mercury vapors

(A) dissolved any remaining bromo-iodine
(B) could cause the plates to break up
(C) were not noxious
(D) were used before the plates were exposed

Paragraph 4 is marked with an arrow [➤]

Daguerreotypes

Only a small number of professional photographers ever had any practical experience as daguerreotypists, those technicians who made photographs through the daguerreotype process. By its strictest definition, the daguerreotype process was common for not more than 20 years in the mid-1800s. Other ways of making photographic images on metal plates, such as tintypes and ferrotypes, were developed rapidly after the advent of the daguerreotype. They quickly eclipsed it in popularity. Today, the surviving photographs produced by these methods are often referred to as daguerreotypes, but that designation is incorrect.

It is not surprising that photography enthusiasts began looking for alternatives to the daguerreotype almost immediately. The materials it required were both expensive—the plates contained silver and one of the developing solutions contained gold—and extremely risky. Strict adherence to proper laboratory procedure was necessary in order to avoid poisoning by noxious gases.

The steps involved in preparing and exposing a daguerreotype were as laborious and frustrating as they were hazardous. Images were recorded on copper plates to which several thin coats of silver had been applied. After being fastened to wooden blocks, the plates were scoured with alcohol and squares of soft flannel. Since even one speck of dust could easily create a deep enough groove to render the final image worthless, they had to be perfectly buffed. The plates were then bathed in solutions of bromine and iodine. The thin layer of bromo-iodine that formed on them made them sensitive to light, at which point they were ready for exposure.

➤After exposure, the plates were dipped alternately in heated mercury and freezing-cold water. The mercury vapors helped fix the images to the plates and developed them. The chilled water kept the plates from breaking up during this critical step. The daguerreotypists next applied hydrosulfate soda to the plate surfaces to dissolve any bromo-iodine that had not been exposed to light and brushed them with a solution of gold and chlorine to brighten the images and sharpen their black-white contrast.

There were difficulties for the daguerreotypists' customers too. The expense of materials and labor was passed on to them in the form of very high prices. Only the rich could easily afford to sit for a daguerreotype portrait. For those of more limited means, a daguerreotype was a once-in-a-lifetime treat. Additionally, daguerreotype plates required long exposures, from 8 to 20 minutes, in order to yield high-quality images. Chairs and tables with special support were designed to help those posing for portraits to remain absolutely still throughout the exposure time. If they did not, the resulting image would be blurred. Not even the cleverest such design, of course, could compensate for the need of the human eye to blink periodically.

For all the disadvantages involved in making daguerreotypes, no one could argue with the finished product when things went well. The process recorded textural detail with a realism that still seems shocking. The sheen of satin and the dull, heavy nap of flannel are easily distinguished. Those posing for daguerreotypes tired after trying to maintain the same facial expression for minutes at a time; the result was that their features often relaxed into an attractive thoughtfulness.

The incentive to develop a photographic process that retained the advantages of the daguerreotype without the disadvantages was thus powerful. The substitute with the most lasting popularity was the ferrotype, or tintype, which used an enamel-coated iron plate. Ferrotypes became popular with photographers who set up stalls at street fairs and inexpensive resorts because they could be exposed and developed very quickly. Iron plates were also much less expensive than copper plates, and the resulting photographs were less fragile than daguerreotypes. On the other hand, iron, unlike copper, could rust if not properly stored. Many old ferrotypes were destroyed by long-term display in hot and moist environments.

More Available

20. In using the phrase more limited means, the author of the passage is referring to people who

(A) did not have a great deal of money
(B) used inferior photographic equipment
(C) lived far from a daguerreotypist
(D) were satisfied with low-quality images

Daguerreotypes

Only a small number of professional photographers ever had any practical experience as daguerreotypists, those technicians who made photographs through the daguerreotype process. By its strictest definition, the daguerreotype process was common for not more than 20 years in the mid-1800s. Other ways of making photographic images on metal plates, such as tintypes and ferrotypes, were developed rapidly after the advent of the daguerreotype. They quickly eclipsed it in popularity. Today, the surviving photographs produced by these methods are often referred to as daguerreotypes, but that designation is incorrect.

It is not surprising that photography enthusiasts began looking for alternatives to the daguerreotype almost immediately. The materials it required were both expensive—the plates contained silver and one of the developing solutions contained gold—and extremely risky. Strict adherence to proper laboratory procedure was necessary in order to avoid poisoning by noxious gases.

The steps involved in preparing and exposing a daguerreotype were as laborious and frustrating as they were hazardous. Images were recorded on copper plates to which several thin coats of silver had been applied. After being fastened to wooden blocks, the plates were scoured with alcohol and squares of soft flannel. Since even one speck of dust could easily create a deep enough groove to render the final image worthless, they had to be perfectly buffed. The plates were then bathed in solutions of bromine and iodine. The thin layer of bromo-iodine that formed on them made them sensitive to light, at which point they were ready for exposure.

After exposure, the plates were dipped alternately in heated mercury and freezing-cold water. The mercury vapors helped fix the images to the plates and developed them. The chilled water kept the plates from breaking up during this critical step. The daguerreotypists next applied hydrosulfate soda to the plate surfaces to dissolve any bromo-iodine that had not been exposed to light and brushed them with a solution of gold and chlorine to brighten the images and sharpen their black-white contrast.

There were difficulties for the daguerreotypists' customers too. The expense of materials and labor was passed on to them in the form of very high prices. Only the rich could easily afford to sit for a daguerreotype portrait. For those of more limited means, a daguerreotype was a once-in-a-lifetime treat. Additionally, daguerreotype plates required long exposures, from 8 to 20 minutes, in order to yield high-quality images. Chairs and tables with special support were designed to help those posing for portraits to remain absolutely still throughout the exposure time. If they did not, the resulting image would be blurred. Not even the cleverest such design, of course, could compensate for the need of the human eye to blink periodically.

For all the disadvantages involved in making daguerreotypes, no one could argue with the finished product when things went well. The process recorded textural detail with a realism that still seems shocking. The sheen of satin and the dull, heavy nap of flannel are easily distinguished. Those posing for daguerreotypes tired after trying to maintain the same facial expression for minutes at a time; the result was that their features often relaxed into an attractive thoughtfulness.

The incentive to develop a photographic process that retained the advantages of the daguerreotype without the disadvantages was thus powerful. The substitute with the most lasting popularity was the ferrotype, or tintype, which used an enamel-coated iron plate. Ferrotypes became popular with photographers who set up stalls at street fairs and inexpensive resorts because they could be exposed and developed very quickly. Iron plates were also much less expensive than copper plates, and the resulting photographs were less fragile than daguerreotypes. On the other hand, iron, unlike copper, could rust if not properly stored. Many old ferrotypes were destroyed by long-term display in hot and moist environments.

TOEFL Reading

PAUSE TEST

SECTION EXIT

21 of 39

REVIEW

HELP ?

BACK ←

NEXT →

HIDE TIME   00:08:45

More Available

21. According to paragraph 5, how did daguerreotypists prevent the production of blurred images during exposure?

(A) They exposed the plates for shorter lengths of time.

(B) They instructed their customers not to blink.

(C) They had special furniture for their customers to use.

(D) They allowed their customers to take short breaks.

Paragraph 5 is marked with an arrow [➤]

Daguerreotypes

Only a small number of professional photographers ever had any practical experience as daguerreotypists, those technicians who made photographs through the daguerreotype process. By its strictest definition, the daguerreotype process was common for not more than 20 years in the mid-1800s. Other ways of making photographic images on metal plates, such as tintypes and ferrotypes, were developed rapidly after the advent of the daguerreotype. They quickly eclipsed it in popularity. Today, the surviving photographs produced by these methods are often referred to as daguerreotypes, but that designation is incorrect.

It is not surprising that photography enthusiasts began looking for alternatives to the daguerreotype almost immediately. The materials it required were both expensive—the plates contained silver and one of the developing solutions contained gold—and extremely risky. Strict adherence to proper laboratory procedure was necessary in order to avoid poisoning by noxious gases.

The steps involved in preparing and exposing a daguerreotype were as laborious and frustrating as they were hazardous. Images were recorded on copper plates to which several thin coats of silver had been applied. After being fastened to wooden blocks, the plates were scoured with alcohol and squares of soft flannel. Since even one speck of dust could easily create a deep enough groove to render the final image worthless, they had to be perfectly buffed. The plates were then bathed in solutions of bromine and iodine. The thin layer of bromo-iodine that formed on them made them sensitive to light, at which point they were ready for exposure.

After exposure, the plates were dipped alternately in heated mercury and freezing-cold water. The mercury vapors helped fix the images to the plates and developed them. The chilled water kept the plates from breaking up during this critical step. The daguerreotypists next applied hydrosulfate soda to the plate surfaces to dissolve any bromo-iodine that had not been exposed to light and brushed them with a solution of gold and chlorine to brighten the images and sharpen their black-white contrast.

➤There were difficulties for the daguerreotypists' customers too. The expense of materials and labor was passed on to them in the form of very high prices. Only the rich could easily afford to sit for a daguerreotype portrait. For those of more limited means, a daguerreotype was a once-in-a-lifetime treat. Additionally, daguerreotype plates required long exposures, from 8 to 20 minutes, in order to yield high-quality images. Chairs and tables with special support were designed to help those posing for portraits to remain absolutely still throughout the exposure time. If they did not, the resulting image would be blurred. Not even the cleverest such design, of course, could compensate for the need of the human eye to blink periodically.

For all the disadvantages involved in making daguerreotypes, no one could argue with the finished product when things went well. The process recorded textural detail with a realism that still seems shocking. The sheen of satin and the dull, heavy nap of flannel are easily distinguished. Those posing for daguerreotypes tired after trying to maintain the same facial expression for minutes at a time; the result was that their features often relaxed into an attractive thoughtfulness.

The incentive to develop a photographic process that retained the advantages of the daguerreotype without the disadvantages was thus powerful. The substitute with the most lasting popularity was the ferrotype, or tintype, which used an enamel-coated iron plate. Ferrotypes became popular with photographers who set up stalls at street fairs and inexpensive resorts because they could be exposed and developed very quickly. Iron plates were also much less expensive than copper plates, and the resulting photographs were less fragile than daguerreotypes. On the other hand, iron, unlike copper, could rust if not properly stored. Many old ferrotypes were destroyed by long-term display in hot and moist environments.

More Available

22. Which of the following is mentioned in paragraph 6 as a detail recorded realistically in a daguerreotype?

(A) differences in color
(B) degree of luster
(C) how tired the subject was
(D) whether the subject blinked during exposure

Paragraph 6 is marked with an arrow [➤]

Daguerreotypes

Only a small number of professional photographers ever had any practical experience as daguerreotypists, those technicians who made photographs through the daguerreotype process. By its strictest definition, the daguerreotype process was common for not more than 20 years in the mid-1800s. Other ways of making photographic images on metal plates, such as tintypes and ferrotypes, were developed rapidly after the advent of the daguerreotype. They quickly eclipsed it in popularity. Today, the surviving photographs produced by these methods are often referred to as daguerreotypes, but that designation is incorrect.

It is not surprising that photography enthusiasts began looking for alternatives to the daguerreotype almost immediately. The materials it required were both expensive—the plates contained silver and one of the developing solutions contained gold—and extremely risky. Strict adherence to proper laboratory procedure was necessary in order to avoid poisoning by noxious gases.

The steps involved in preparing and exposing a daguerreotype were as laborious and frustrating as they were hazardous. Images were recorded on copper plates to which several thin coats of silver had been applied. After being fastened to wooden blocks, the plates were scoured with alcohol and squares of soft flannel. Since even one speck of dust could easily create a deep enough groove to render the final image worthless, they had to be perfectly buffed. The plates were then bathed in solutions of bromine and iodine. The thin layer of bromo-iodine that formed on them made them sensitive to light, at which point they were ready for exposure.

After exposure, the plates were dipped alternately in heated mercury and freezing-cold water. The mercury vapors helped fix the images to the plates and developed them. The chilled water kept the plates from breaking up during this critical step. The daguerreotypists next applied hydrosulfate soda to the plate surfaces to dissolve any bromo-iodine that had not been exposed to light and brushed them with a solution of gold and chlorine to brighten the images and sharpen their black-white contrast.

There were difficulties for the daguerreotypists' customers too. The expense of materials and labor was passed on to them in the form of very high prices. Only the rich could easily afford to sit for a daguerreotype portrait. For those of more limited means, a daguerreotype was a once-in-a-lifetime treat. Additionally, daguerreotype plates required long exposures, from 8 to 20 minutes, in order to yield high-quality images. Chairs and tables with special support were designed to help those posing for portraits to remain absolutely still throughout the exposure time. If they did not, the resulting image would be blurred. Not even the cleverest such design, of course, could compensate for the need of the human eye to blink periodically.

➤For all the disadvantages involved in making daguerreotypes, no one could argue with the finished product when things went well. The process recorded textural detail with a realism that still seems shocking. The sheen of satin and the dull, heavy nap of flannel are easily distinguished. Those posing for daguerreotypes tired after trying to maintain the same facial expression for minutes at a time; the result was that their features often relaxed into an attractive thoughtfulness.

The incentive to develop a photographic process that retained the advantages of the daguerreotype without the disadvantages was thus powerful. The substitute with the most lasting popularity was the ferrotype, or tintype, which used an enamel-coated iron plate. Ferrotypes became popular with photographers who set up stalls at street fairs and inexpensive resorts because they could be exposed and developed very quickly. Iron plates were also much less expensive than copper plates, and the resulting photographs were less fragile than daguerreotypes. On the other hand, iron, unlike copper, could rust if not properly stored. Many old ferrotypes were destroyed by long-term display in hot and moist environments.

More Available

23. Paragraph 7 mentions each of the following as an advantage of ferrotypes EXCEPT

(A) durability of the images
(B) low cost
(C) speed of developing
(D) resistance to rusting

Paragraph 7 is marked with an arrow [➤]

Daguerreotypes

Only a small number of professional photographers ever had any practical experience as daguerreotypists, those technicians who made photographs through the daguerreotype process. By its strictest definition, the daguerreotype process was common for not more than 20 years in the mid-1800s. Other ways of making photographic images on metal plates, such as tintypes and ferrotypes, were developed rapidly after the advent of the daguerreotype. They quickly eclipsed it in popularity. Today, the surviving photographs produced by these methods are often referred to as daguerreotypes, but that designation is incorrect.

It is not surprising that photography enthusiasts began looking for alternatives to the daguerreotype almost immediately. The materials it required were both expensive—the plates contained silver and one of the developing solutions contained gold—and extremely risky. Strict adherence to proper laboratory procedure was necessary in order to avoid poisoning by noxious gases.

The steps involved in preparing and exposing a daguerreotype were as laborious and frustrating as they were hazardous. Images were recorded on copper plates to which several thin coats of silver had been applied. After being fastened to wooden blocks, the plates were scoured with alcohol and squares of soft flannel. Since even one speck of dust could easily create a deep enough groove to render the final image worthless, they had to be perfectly buffed. The plates were then bathed in solutions of bromine and iodine. The thin layer of bromo-iodine that formed on them made them sensitive to light, at which point they were ready for exposure.

After exposure, the plates were dipped alternately in heated mercury and freezing-cold water. The mercury vapors helped fix the images to the plates and developed them. The chilled water kept the plates from breaking up during this critical step. The daguerreotypists next applied hydrosulfate soda to the plate surfaces to dissolve any bromo-iodine that had not been exposed to light and brushed them with a solution of gold and chlorine to brighten the images and sharpen their black-white contrast.

There were difficulties for the daguerreotypists' customers too. The expense of materials and labor was passed on to them in the form of very high prices. Only the rich could easily afford to sit for a daguerreotype portrait. For those of more limited means, a daguerreotype was a once-in-a-lifetime treat. Additionally, daguerreotype plates required long exposures, from 8 to 20 minutes, in order to yield high-quality images. Chairs and tables with special support were designed to help those posing for portraits to remain absolutely still throughout the exposure time. If they did not, the resulting image would be blurred. Not even the cleverest such design, of course, could compensate for the need of the human eye to blink periodically.

For all the disadvantages involved in making daguerreotypes, no one could argue with the finished product when things went well. The process recorded textural detail with a realism that still seems shocking. The sheen of satin and the dull, heavy nap of flannel are easily distinguished. Those posing for daguerreotypes tired after trying to maintain the same facial expression for minutes at a time; the result was that their features often relaxed into an attractive thoughtfulness.

➤The incentive to develop a photographic process that retained the advantages of the daguerreotype without the disadvantages was thus powerful. The substitute with the most lasting popularity was the ferrotype, or tintype, which used an enamel-coated iron plate. Ferrotypes became popular with photographers who set up stalls at street fairs and inexpensive resorts because they could be exposed and developed very quickly. Iron plates were also much less expensive than copper plates, and the resulting photographs were less fragile than daguerreotypes. On the other hand, iron, unlike copper, could rust if not properly stored. Many old ferrotypes were destroyed by long-term display in hot and moist environments.

More Available

24. The word they in the passage refers to

(A) photographers
(B) stalls
(C) ferrotypes
(D) street fairs and resorts

Daguerreotypes

Only a small number of professional photographers ever had any practical experience as daguerreotypists, those technicians who made photographs through the daguerreotype process. By its strictest definition, the daguerreotype process was common for not more than 20 years in the mid-1800s. Other ways of making photographic images on metal plates, such as tintypes and ferrotypes, were developed rapidly after the advent of the daguerreotype. They quickly eclipsed it in popularity. Today, the surviving photographs produced by these methods are often referred to as daguerreotypes, but that designation is incorrect.

It is not surprising that photography enthusiasts began looking for alternatives to the daguerreotype almost immediately. The materials it required were both expensive—the plates contained silver and one of the developing solutions contained gold—and extremely risky. Strict adherence to proper laboratory procedure was necessary in order to avoid poisoning by noxious gases.

The steps involved in preparing and exposing a daguerreotype were as laborious and frustrating as they were hazardous. Images were recorded on copper plates to which several thin coats of silver had been applied. After being fastened to wooden blocks, the plates were scoured with alcohol and squares of soft flannel. Since even one speck of dust could easily create a deep enough groove to render the final image worthless, they had to be perfectly buffed. The plates were then bathed in solutions of bromine and iodine. The thin layer of bromo-iodine that formed on them made them sensitive to light, at which point they were ready for exposure.

After exposure, the plates were dipped alternately in heated mercury and freezing-cold water. The mercury vapors helped fix the images to the plates and developed them. The chilled water kept the plates from breaking up during this critical step. The daguerreotypists next applied hydrosulfate soda to the plate surfaces to dissolve any bromo-iodine that had not been exposed to light and brushed them with a solution of gold and chlorine to brighten the images and sharpen their black-white contrast.

There were difficulties for the daguerreotypists' customers too. The expense of materials and labor was passed on to them in the form of very high prices. Only the rich could easily afford to sit for a daguerreotype portrait. For those of more limited means, a daguerreotype was a once-in-a-lifetime treat. Additionally, daguerreotype plates required long exposures, from 8 to 20 minutes, in order to yield high-quality images. Chairs and tables with special support were designed to help those posing for portraits to remain absolutely still throughout the exposure time. If they did not, the resulting image would be blurred. Not even the cleverest such design, of course, could compensate for the need of the human eye to blink periodically.

For all the disadvantages involved in making daguerreotypes, no one could argue with the finished product when things went well. The process recorded textural detail with a realism that still seems shocking. The sheen of satin and the dull, heavy nap of flannel are easily distinguished. Those posing for daguerreotypes tired after trying to maintain the same facial expression for minutes at a time; the result was that their features often relaxed into an attractive thoughtfulness.

The incentive to develop a photographic process that retained the advantages of the daguerreotype without the disadvantages was thus powerful. The substitute with the most lasting popularity was the ferrotype, or tintype, which used an enamel-coated iron plate. Ferrotypes became popular with photographers who set up stalls at street fairs and inexpensive resorts because they could be exposed and developed very quickly. Iron plates were also much less expensive than copper plates, and the resulting photographs were less fragile than daguerreotypes. On the other hand, iron, unlike copper, could rust if not properly stored. Many old ferrotypes were destroyed by long-term display in hot and moist environments.

TOEFL Reading

PAUSE TEST

SECTION EXIT

25 of 39

REVIEW

HELP ?

BACK ←

NEXT →

HIDE TIME   00:08:45

More Available

25. It can be inferred from paragraph 7 that storage space for ferrotypes should be

(A) cleaned frequently
(B) cool and dry
(C) brightly lit
(D) coated with enamel

Paragraph 7 is marked with an arrow [➤]

Daguerreotypes

Only a small number of professional photographers ever had any practical experience as daguerreotypists, those technicians who made photographs through the daguerreotype process. By its strictest definition, the daguerreotype process was common for not more than 20 years in the mid-1800s. Other ways of making photographic images on metal plates, such as tintypes and ferrotypes, were developed rapidly after the advent of the daguerreotype. They quickly eclipsed it in popularity. Today, the surviving photographs produced by these methods are often referred to as daguerreotypes, but that designation is incorrect.

It is not surprising that photography enthusiasts began looking for alternatives to the daguerreotype almost immediately. The materials it required were both expensive—the plates contained silver and one of the developing solutions contained gold—and extremely risky. Strict adherence to proper laboratory procedure was necessary in order to avoid poisoning by noxious gases.

The steps involved in preparing and exposing a daguerreotype were as laborious and frustrating as they were hazardous. Images were recorded on copper plates to which several thin coats of silver had been applied. After being fastened to wooden blocks, the plates were scoured with alcohol and squares of soft flannel. Since even one speck of dust could easily create a deep enough groove to render the final image worthless, they had to be perfectly buffed. The plates were then bathed in solutions of bromine and iodine. The thin layer of bromo-iodine that formed on them made them sensitive to light, at which point they were ready for exposure.

After exposure, the plates were dipped alternately in heated mercury and freezing-cold water. The mercury vapors helped fix the images to the plates and developed them. The chilled water kept the plates from breaking up during this critical step. The daguerreotypists next applied hydrosulfate soda to the plate surfaces to dissolve any bromo-iodine that had not been exposed to light and brushed them with a solution of gold and chlorine to brighten the images and sharpen their black-white contrast.

There were difficulties for the daguerreotypists' customers too. The expense of materials and labor was passed on to them in the form of very high prices. Only the rich could easily afford to sit for a daguerreotype portrait. For those of more limited means, a daguerreotype was a once-in-a-lifetime treat. Additionally, daguerreotype plates required long exposures, from 8 to 20 minutes, in order to yield high-quality images. Chairs and tables with special support were designed to help those posing for portraits to remain absolutely still throughout the exposure time. If they did not, the resulting image would be blurred. Not even the cleverest such design, of course, could compensate for the need of the human eye to blink periodically.

For all the disadvantages involved in making daguerreotypes, no one could argue with the finished product when things went well. The process recorded textural detail with a realism that still seems shocking. The sheen of satin and the dull, heavy nap of flannel are easily distinguished. Those posing for daguerreotypes tired after trying to maintain the same facial expression for minutes at a time; the result was that their features often relaxed into an attractive thoughtfulness.

➤The incentive to develop a photographic process that retained the advantages of the daguerreotype without the disadvantages was thus powerful. The substitute with the most lasting popularity was the ferrotype, or tintype, which used an enamel-coated iron plate. Ferrotypes became popular with photographers who set up stalls at street fairs and inexpensive resorts because they could be exposed and developed very quickly. Iron plates were also much less expensive than copper plates, and the resulting photographs were less fragile than daguerreotypes. On the other hand, iron, unlike copper, could rust if not properly stored. Many old ferrotypes were destroyed by long-term display in hot and moist environments.

26. **Directions:** An introductory sentence for a brief summary of the passage is provided below. Complete the summary by selecting the THREE answer choices that express the most important ideas in the passage. Some sentences do not belong in the summary because they express ideas that are not presented in the passage or are minor ideas in the passage. *This question is worth 2 points.*

The daguerreotype was a kind of photography that was briefly popular before being replaced by other methods.

-
-
-

Answer Choices	
Some daguerreotypes have lasted long enough to be enjoyed today.	The ferrotype was less expensive and more durable than the daguerreotype and became a popular substitute.
Daguerreotypes had to be brushed with gold and chlorine to make the images brighter than they would otherwise be.	The daguerreotype process used dangerous chemicals and inconvenienced people posing for pictures.
The images in daguerreotypes were realistic and detailed, so people looked for easier ways to produce them.	Many photographers preferred to continue using the daguerreotype process even after alternatives were introduced.

More Available

Hormones in the Body

Until the beginning of the twentieth century, the nervous system was thought to control all communication within the body and the resulting integration of behavior. Scientists had determined that nerves ran, essentially, on electrical impulses. These impulses were thought to be the engine for thought, emotion, movement, and internal processes such as digestion. However, experiments by William Bayliss and Ernest Starling on the chemical secretin, which is produced in the small intestine when food enters the stomach, eventually challenged that view. From the small intestine, secretin travels through the bloodstream to the pancreas. There, it stimulates the release of digestive chemicals. In this fashion, the intestinal cells that produce secretin ultimately regulate the production of different chemicals in a different organ, the pancreas.

Such a coordination of processes had been thought to require control by the nervous system; Bayliss and Starling showed that it could occur through chemicals alone. This discovery spurred Starling to coin the term *hormone* to refer to secretin, taking it from the Greek word *hormon,* meaning "to excite" or "to set in motion." A hormone is a chemical produced by one tissue to make things happen elsewhere.

As more hormones were discovered, they were categorized, primarily according to the process by which they operated on the body. Some glands (which make up the endocrine system) secrete hormones directly into the bloodstream. Such glands include the thyroid and the pituitary. The exocrine system consists of organs and glands that produce substances that are used outside the bloodstream, primarily for digestion. The pancreas is one such organ, although it

More Available

secretes some chemicals into the blood and thus is also part of the endocrine system.

Much has been learned about hormones since their discovery. Some play such key roles in regulating bodily processes or behavior that their absence would cause immediate death. The most abundant hormones have effects that are less obviously urgent but can be more far-reaching and difficult to track: They modify moods and affect human behavior, even some behavior we normally think of as voluntary. Hormonal systems are very intricate. Even minute amounts of the right chemicals can suppress appetite, calm aggression, and change the attitude of a parent toward a child. Certain hormones accelerate the development of the body, regulating growth and form; others may even define an individual's personality characteristics. **The quantities and proportions of hormones produced change with age, so scientists have given a great deal of study to shifts in the endocrine system over time in the hopes of alleviating ailments associated with aging.**

In fact, some hormone therapies are already very common. ■ **A combination of estrogen and progesterone has been prescribed for decades to women who want to reduce mood swings, sudden changes in body temperature, and other discomforts caused by lower natural levels of those hormones as they enter middle age.** ■ Known as hormone replacement therapy (HRT), the treatment was also believed to prevent weakening of the bones. ■ At least one study has linked HRT with a heightened risk of heart disease and certain types of cancer. **HRT may also increase the likelihood that blood clots—dangerous because they could travel through the bloodstream and block major blood vessels—will form.** Some proponents of HRT have tempered their enthusiasm in the face of this new evidence, recommending it only to

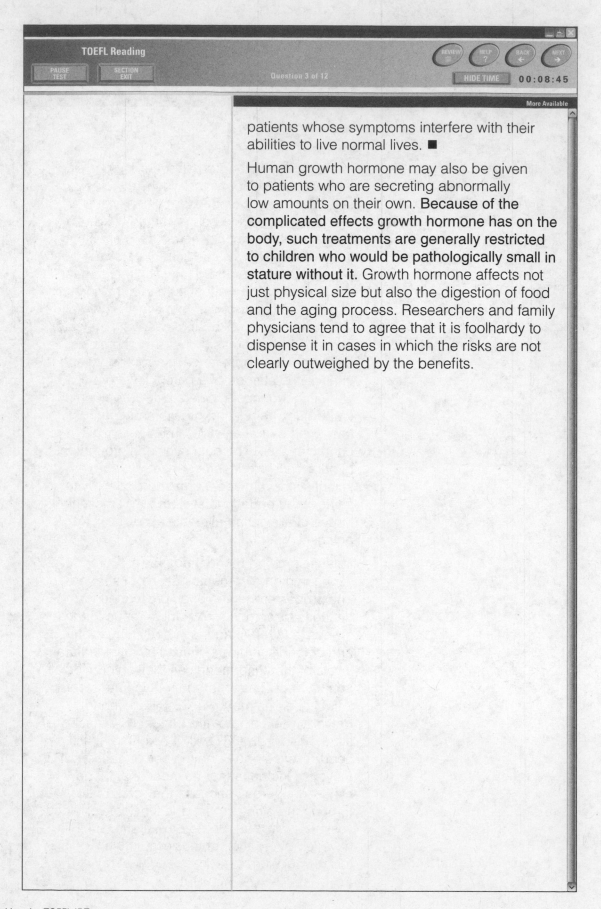

TOEFL Reading

PAUSE TEST

SECTION EXIT

Question 3 of 12

REVIEW

HELP ?

BACK ←

NEXT →

HIDE TIME   00:08:45

More Available

patients whose symptoms interfere with their abilities to live normal lives. ■

Human growth hormone may also be given to patients who are secreting abnormally low amounts on their own. **Because of the complicated effects growth hormone has on the body, such treatments are generally restricted to children who would be pathologically small in stature without it.** Growth hormone affects not just physical size but also the digestion of food and the aging process. Researchers and family physicians tend to agree that it is foolhardy to dispense it in cases in which the risks are not clearly outweighed by the benefits.

More Available

27. The word engine in the passage is closest in meaning to

(A) desire
(B) origin
(C) science
(D) chemical

Hormones in the Body

Until the beginning of the twentieth century, the nervous system was thought to control all communication within the body and the resulting integration of behavior. Scientists had determined that nerves ran, essentially, on electrical impulses. These impulses were thought to be the engine for thought, emotion, movement, and internal processes such as digestion. However, experiments by William Bayliss and Ernest Starling on the chemical secretin, which is produced in the small intestine when food enters the stomach, eventually challenged that view. From the small intestine, secretin travels through the bloodstream to the pancreas. There, it stimulates the release of digestive chemicals. In this fashion, the intestinal cells that produce secretin ultimately regulate the production of different chemicals in a different organ, the pancreas.

Such a coordination of processes had been thought to require control by the nervous system; Bayliss and Starling showed that it could occur through chemicals alone. This discovery spurred Starling to coin the term *hormone* to refer to secretin, taking it from the Greek word *hormon,* meaning "to excite" or "to set in motion." A hormone is a chemical produced by one tissue to make things happen elsewhere.

As more hormones were discovered, they were categorized, primarily according to the process by which they operated on the body. Some glands (which make up the endocrine system) secrete hormones directly into the bloodstream. Such glands include the thyroid and the pituitary. The exocrine system consists of organs and glands that produce substances that are used outside the bloodstream, primarily for digestion. The pancreas is one such organ, although it secretes some chemicals into the blood and thus is also part of the endocrine system.

Much has been learned about hormones since their discovery. Some play such key roles in regulating bodily processes or behavior that their absence would cause immediate death. The most abundant hormones have effects that are less obviously urgent but can be more far-reaching and difficult to track: They modify moods and affect human behavior, even some behavior we normally think of as voluntary. Hormonal systems are very intricate. Even minute amounts of the right chemicals can suppress appetite, calm aggression, and change the attitude of a parent toward a child. Certain hormones accelerate the development of the body, regulating growth and form; others may even define an individual's personality characteristics. **The quantities and proportions of hormones produced change with age, so scientists have given a great deal of study to shifts in the endocrine system over time in the hopes of alleviating ailments associated with aging.**

In fact, some hormone therapies are already very common. ■ **A combination of estrogen and progesterone has been prescribed for decades to women who want to reduce mood swings, sudden changes in body temperature, and other discomforts caused by lower natural levels of those hormones as they enter middle age.** ■ Known as hormone replacement therapy (HRT), the treatment was also believed to prevent weakening of the bones. ■ At least one study has linked HRT with a heightened risk of heart disease and certain types of cancer. **HRT may also increase the likelihood that blood clots—dangerous because they could travel through the bloodstream and block major blood vessels—will form.** Some proponents of HRT have tempered their enthusiasm in the face of this new evidence, recommending it only to patients whose symptoms interfere with their abilities to live normal lives. ■

Human growth hormone may also be given to patients who are secreting abnormally low amounts on their own. **Because of the complicated effects growth hormone has on the body, such treatments are generally restricted to children who would be pathologically small in stature without it.** Growth hormone affects not just physical size but also the digestion of food and the aging process. Researchers and family physicians tend to agree that it is foolhardy to dispense it in cases in which the risks are not clearly outweighed by the benefits.

More Available

28. The word it in the passage refers to

(A) secretin
(B) small intestine
(C) bloodstream
(D) pancreas

Hormones in the Body

Until the beginning of the twentieth century, the nervous system was thought to control all communication within the body and the resulting integration of behavior. Scientists had determined that nerves ran, essentially, on electrical impulses. These impulses were thought to be the engine for thought, emotion, movement, and internal processes such as digestion. However, experiments by William Bayliss and Ernest Starling on the chemical secretin, which is produced in the small intestine when food enters the stomach, eventually challenged that view. From the small intestine, secretin travels through the bloodstream to the pancreas. There, it stimulates the release of digestive chemicals. In this fashion, the intestinal cells that produce secretin ultimately regulate the production of different chemicals in a different organ, the pancreas.

Such a coordination of processes had been thought to require control by the nervous system; Bayliss and Starling showed that it could occur through chemicals alone. This discovery spurred Starling to coin the term *hormone* to refer to secretin, taking it from the Greek word *hormon,* meaning "to excite" or "to set in motion." A hormone is a chemical produced by one tissue to make things happen elsewhere.

As more hormones were discovered, they were categorized, primarily according to the process by which they operated on the body. Some glands (which make up the endocrine system) secrete hormones directly into the bloodstream. Such glands include the thyroid and the pituitary. The exocrine system consists of organs and glands that produce substances that are used outside the bloodstream, primarily for digestion. The pancreas is one such organ, although it secretes some chemicals into the blood and thus is also part of the endocrine system.

Much has been learned about hormones since their discovery. Some play such key roles in regulating bodily processes or behavior that their absence would cause immediate death. The most abundant hormones have effects that are less obviously urgent but can be more far-reaching and difficult to track: They modify moods and affect human behavior, even some behavior we normally think of as voluntary. Hormonal systems are very intricate. Even minute amounts of the right chemicals can suppress appetite, calm aggression, and change the attitude of a parent toward a child. Certain hormones accelerate the development of the body, regulating growth and form; others may even define an individual's personality characteristics. **The quantities and proportions of hormones produced change with age, so scientists have given a great deal of study to shifts in the endocrine system over time in the hopes of alleviating ailments associated with aging.**

In fact, some hormone therapies are already very common. ■ **A combination of estrogen and progesterone has been prescribed for decades to women who want to reduce mood swings, sudden changes in body temperature, and other discomforts caused by lower natural levels of those hormones as they enter middle age.** ■ Known as hormone replacement therapy (HRT), the treatment was also believed to prevent weakening of the bones. ■ At least one study has linked HRT with a heightened risk of heart disease and certain types of cancer. **HRT may also increase the likelihood that blood clots—dangerous because they could travel through the bloodstream and block major blood vessels—will form.** Some proponents of HRT have tempered their enthusiasm in the face of this new evidence, recommending it only to patients whose symptoms interfere with their abilities to live normal lives. ■

Human growth hormone may also be given to patients who are secreting abnormally low amounts on their own. **Because of the complicated effects growth hormone has on the body, such treatments are generally restricted to children who would be pathologically small in stature without it.** Growth hormone affects not just physical size but also the digestion of food and the aging process. Researchers and family physicians tend to agree that it is foolhardy to dispense it in cases in which the risks are not clearly outweighed by the benefits.

More Available

29. The word spurred in the passage is closest in meaning to

(A) remembered
(B) surprised
(C) invented
(D) motivated

Hormones in the Body

Until the beginning of the twentieth century, the nervous system was thought to control all communication within the body and the resulting integration of behavior. Scientists had determined that nerves ran, essentially, on electrical impulses. These impulses were thought to be the engine for thought, emotion, movement, and internal processes such as digestion. However, experiments by William Bayliss and Ernest Starling on the chemical secretin, which is produced in the small intestine when food enters the stomach, eventually challenged that view. From the small intestine, secretin travels through the bloodstream to the pancreas. There, it stimulates the release of digestive chemicals. In this fashion, the intestinal cells that produce secretin ultimately regulate the production of different chemicals in a different organ, the pancreas.

Such a coordination of processes had been thought to require control by the nervous system; Bayliss and Starling showed that it could occur through chemicals alone. This discovery spurred Starling to coin the term *hormone* to refer to secretin, taking it from the Greek word *hormon,* meaning "to excite" or "to set in motion." A hormone is a chemical produced by one tissue to make things happen elsewhere.

As more hormones were discovered, they were categorized, primarily according to the process by which they operated on the body. Some glands (which make up the endocrine system) secrete hormones directly into the bloodstream. Such glands include the thyroid and the pituitary. The exocrine system consists of organs and glands that produce substances that are used outside the bloodstream, primarily for digestion. The pancreas is one such organ, although it secretes some chemicals into the blood and thus is also part of the endocrine system.

Much has been learned about hormones since their discovery. Some play such key roles in regulating bodily processes or behavior that their absence would cause immediate death. The most abundant hormones have effects that are less obviously urgent but can be more far-reaching and difficult to track: They modify moods and affect human behavior, even some behavior we normally think of as voluntary. Hormonal systems are very intricate. Even minute amounts of the right chemicals can suppress appetite, calm aggression, and change the attitude of a parent toward a child. Certain hormones accelerate the development of the body, regulating growth and form; others may even define an individual's personality characteristics. **The quantities and proportions of hormones produced change with age, so scientists have given a great deal of study to shifts in the endocrine system over time in the hopes of alleviating ailments associated with aging.**

In fact, some hormone therapies are already very common. ■ **A combination of estrogen and progesterone has been prescribed for decades to women who want to reduce mood swings, sudden changes in body temperature, and other discomforts caused by lower natural levels of those hormones as they enter middle age.** ■ Known as hormone replacement therapy (HRT), the treatment was also believed to prevent weakening of the bones. ■ At least one study has linked HRT with a heightened risk of heart disease and certain types of cancer. **HRT may also increase the likelihood that blood clots—dangerous because they could travel through the bloodstream and block major blood vessels—will form.** Some proponents of HRT have tempered their enthusiasm in the face of this new evidence, recommending it only to patients whose symptoms interfere with their abilities to live normal lives. ■

Human growth hormone may also be given to patients who are secreting abnormally low amounts on their own. **Because of the complicated effects growth hormone has on the body, such treatments are generally restricted to children who would be pathologically small in stature without it.** Growth hormone affects not just physical size but also the digestion of food and the aging process. Researchers and family physicians tend to agree that it is foolhardy to dispense it in cases in which the risks are not clearly outweighed by the benefits.

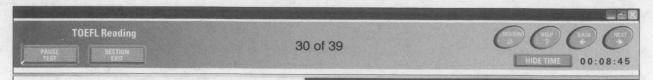

More Available

30. To be considered a hormone, a chemical produced in the body must

(A) be part of the digestive process

(B) influence the operations of the nervous system

(C) affect processes in a different part of the body

(D) regulate attitudes and behavior

Hormones in the Body

Until the beginning of the twentieth century, the nervous system was thought to control all communication within the body and the resulting integration of behavior. Scientists had determined that nerves ran, essentially, on electrical impulses. These impulses were thought to be the engine for thought, emotion, movement, and internal processes such as digestion. However, experiments by William Bayliss and Ernest Starling on the chemical secretin, which is produced in the small intestine when food enters the stomach, eventually challenged that view. From the small intestine, secretin travels through the bloodstream to the pancreas. There, it stimulates the release of digestive chemicals. In this fashion, the intestinal cells that produce secretin ultimately regulate the production of different chemicals in a different organ, the pancreas.

Such a coordination of processes had been thought to require control by the nervous system; Bayliss and Starling showed that it could occur through chemicals alone. This discovery spurred Starling to coin the term *hormone* to refer to secretin, taking it from the Greek word *hormon,* meaning "to excite" or "to set in motion." A hormone is a chemical produced by one tissue to make things happen elsewhere.

As more hormones were discovered, they were categorized, primarily according to the process by which they operated on the body. Some glands (which make up the endocrine system) secrete hormones directly into the bloodstream. Such glands include the thyroid and the pituitary. The exocrine system consists of organs and glands that produce substances that are used outside the bloodstream, primarily for digestion. The pancreas is one such organ, although it secretes some chemicals into the blood and thus is also part of the endocrine system.

Much has been learned about hormones since their discovery. Some play such key roles in regulating bodily processes or behavior that their absence would cause immediate death. The most abundant hormones have effects that are less obviously urgent but can be more far-reaching and difficult to track: They modify moods and affect human behavior, even some behavior we normally think of as voluntary. Hormonal systems are very intricate. Even minute amounts of the right chemicals can suppress appetite, calm aggression, and change the attitude of a parent toward a child. Certain hormones accelerate the development of the body, regulating growth and form; others may even define an individual's personality characteristics. **The quantities and proportions of hormones produced change with age, so scientists have given a great deal of study to shifts in the endocrine system over time in the hopes of alleviating ailments associated with aging.**

In fact, some hormone therapies are already very common. ■ **A combination of estrogen and progesterone has been prescribed for decades to women who want to reduce mood swings, sudden changes in body temperature, and other discomforts caused by lower natural levels of those hormones as they enter middle age.** ■ Known as hormone replacement therapy (HRT), the treatment was also believed to prevent weakening of the bones. ■ At least one study has linked HRT with a heightened risk of heart disease and certain types of cancer. **HRT may also increase the likelihood that blood clots—dangerous because they could travel through the bloodstream and block major blood vessels—will form.** Some proponents of HRT have tempered their enthusiasm in the face of this new evidence, recommending it only to patients whose symptoms interfere with their abilities to live normal lives. ■

Human growth hormone may also be given to patients who are secreting abnormally low amounts on their own. **Because of the complicated effects growth hormone has on the body, such treatments are generally restricted to children who would be pathologically small in stature without it.** Growth hormone affects not just physical size but also the digestion of food and the aging process. Researchers and family physicians tend to agree that it is foolhardy to dispense it in cases in which the risks are not clearly outweighed by the benefits.

TOEFL Reading

31 of 39

REVIEW

HELP ?

BACK

NEXT

PAUSE TEST

SECTION EXIT

HIDE TIME   00:08:45

More Available

31. The glands and organs mentioned in paragraph 3 are categorized according to

(A) whether scientists understand their function

(B) how frequently they release hormones into the body

(C) whether the hormones they secrete influence the aging process

(D) whether they secrete chemicals into the blood

Paragraph 3 is marked with an arrow [➤]

Hormones in the Body

Until the beginning of the twentieth century, the nervous system was thought to control all communication within the body and the resulting integration of behavior. Scientists had determined that nerves ran, essentially, on electrical impulses. These impulses were thought to be the engine for thought, emotion, movement, and internal processes such as digestion. However, experiments by William Bayliss and Ernest Starling on the chemical secretin, which is produced in the small intestine when food enters the stomach, eventually challenged that view. From the small intestine, secretin travels through the bloodstream to the pancreas. There, it stimulates the release of digestive chemicals. In this fashion, the intestinal cells that produce secretin ultimately regulate the production of different chemicals in a different organ, the pancreas.

Such a coordination of processes had been thought to require control by the nervous system; Bayliss and Starling showed that it could occur through chemicals alone. This discovery spurred Starling to coin the term *hormone* to refer to secretin, taking it from the Greek word *hormon,* meaning "to excite" or "to set in motion." A hormone is a chemical produced by one tissue to make things happen elsewhere.

➤As more hormones were discovered, they were categorized, primarily according to the process by which they operated on the body. Some glands (which make up the endocrine system) secrete hormones directly into the bloodstream. Such glands include the thyroid and the pituitary. The exocrine system consists of organs and glands that produce substances that are used outside the bloodstream, primarily for digestion. The pancreas is one such organ, although it secretes some chemicals into the blood and thus is also part of the endocrine system.

Much has been learned about hormones since their discovery. Some play such key roles in regulating bodily processes or behavior that their absence would cause immediate death. The most abundant hormones have effects that are less obviously urgent but can be more far-reaching and difficult to track: They modify moods and affect human behavior, even some behavior we normally think of as voluntary. Hormonal systems are very intricate. Even minute amounts of the right chemicals can suppress appetite, calm aggression, and change the attitude of a parent toward a child. Certain hormones accelerate the development of the body, regulating growth and form; others may even define an individual's personality characteristics. **The quantities and proportions of hormones produced change with age, so scientists have given a great deal of study to shifts in the endocrine system over time in the hopes of alleviating ailments associated with aging.**

In fact, some hormone therapies are already very common. ■ **A combination of estrogen and progesterone has been prescribed for decades to women who want to reduce mood swings, sudden changes in body temperature, and other discomforts caused by lower natural levels of those hormones as they enter middle age.** ■ Known as hormone replacement therapy (HRT), the treatment was also believed to prevent weakening of the bones. ■ At least one study has linked HRT with a heightened risk of heart disease and certain types of cancer. **HRT may also increase the likelihood that blood clots—dangerous because they could travel through the bloodstream and block major blood vessels—will form.** Some proponents of HRT have tempered their enthusiasm in the face of this new evidence, recommending it only to patients whose symptoms interfere with their abilities to live normal lives. ■

Human growth hormone may also be given to patients who are secreting abnormally low amounts on their own. **Because of the complicated effects growth hormone has on the body, such treatments are generally restricted to children who would be pathologically small in stature without it.** Growth hormone affects not just physical size but also the digestion of food and the aging process. Researchers and family physicians tend to agree that it is foolhardy to dispense it in cases in which the risks are not clearly outweighed by the benefits.

32. The word key in the passage is closest in meaning to

(A) misunderstood
(B) precise
(C) significant
(D) simple

More Available

Hormones in the Body

Until the beginning of the twentieth century, the nervous system was thought to control all communication within the body and the resulting integration of behavior. Scientists had determined that nerves ran, essentially, on electrical impulses. These impulses were thought to be the engine for thought, emotion, movement, and internal processes such as digestion. However, experiments by William Bayliss and Ernest Starling on the chemical secretin, which is produced in the small intestine when food enters the stomach, eventually challenged that view. From the small intestine, secretin travels through the bloodstream to the pancreas. There, it stimulates the release of digestive chemicals. In this fashion, the intestinal cells that produce secretin ultimately regulate the production of different chemicals in a different organ, the pancreas.

Such a coordination of processes had been thought to require control by the nervous system; Bayliss and Starling showed that it could occur through chemicals alone. This discovery spurred Starling to coin the term *hormone* to refer to secretin, taking it from the Greek word *hormon,* meaning "to excite" or "to set in motion." A hormone is a chemical produced by one tissue to make things happen elsewhere.

As more hormones were discovered, they were categorized, primarily according to the process by which they operated on the body. Some glands (which make up the endocrine system) secrete hormones directly into the bloodstream. Such glands include the thyroid and the pituitary. The exocrine system consists of organs and glands that produce substances that are used outside the bloodstream, primarily for digestion. The pancreas is one such organ, although it secretes some chemicals into the blood and thus is also part of the endocrine system.

Much has been learned about hormones since their discovery. Some play such key roles in regulating bodily processes or behavior that their absence would cause immediate death. The most abundant hormones have effects that are less obviously urgent but can be more far-reaching and difficult to track: They modify moods and affect human behavior, even some behavior we normally think of as voluntary. Hormonal systems are very intricate. Even minute amounts of the right chemicals can suppress appetite, calm aggression, and change the attitude of a parent toward a child. Certain hormones accelerate the development of the body, regulating growth and form; others may even define an individual's personality characteristics. **The quantities and proportions of hormones produced change with age, so scientists have given a great deal of study to shifts in the endocrine system over time in the hopes of alleviating ailments associated with aging.**

In fact, some hormone therapies are already very common. ■ **A combination of estrogen and progesterone has been prescribed for decades to women who want to reduce mood swings, sudden changes in body temperature, and other discomforts caused by lower natural levels of those hormones as they enter middle age.** ■ Known as hormone replacement therapy (HRT), the treatment was also believed to prevent weakening of the bones. ■ At least one study has linked HRT with a heightened risk of heart disease and certain types of cancer. **HRT may also increase the likelihood that blood clots—dangerous because they could travel through the bloodstream and block major blood vessels—will form.** Some proponents of HRT have tempered their enthusiasm in the face of this new evidence, recommending it only to patients whose symptoms interfere with their abilities to live normal lives. ■

Human growth hormone may also be given to patients who are secreting abnormally low amounts on their own. **Because of the complicated effects growth hormone has on the body, such treatments are generally restricted to children who would be pathologically small in stature without it.** Growth hormone affects not just physical size but also the digestion of food and the aging process. Researchers and family physicians tend to agree that it is foolhardy to dispense it in cases in which the risks are not clearly outweighed by the benefits.

TOEFL Reading

33 of 39

PAUSE TEST   SECTION EXIT

REVIEW   HELP   BACK   NEXT

HIDE TIME   00:08:45

More Available

33. The word minute in the passage is closest in meaning to

(A) sudden
(B) small
(C) seconds
(D) noticeable

Hormones in the Body

Until the beginning of the twentieth century, the nervous system was thought to control all communication within the body and the resulting integration of behavior. Scientists had determined that nerves ran, essentially, on electrical impulses. These impulses were thought to be the engine for thought, emotion, movement, and internal processes such as digestion. However, experiments by William Bayliss and Ernest Starling on the chemical secretin, which is produced in the small intestine when food enters the stomach, eventually challenged that view. From the small intestine, secretin travels through the bloodstream to the pancreas. There, it stimulates the release of digestive chemicals. In this fashion, the intestinal cells that produce secretin ultimately regulate the production of different chemicals in a different organ, the pancreas.

Such a coordination of processes had been thought to require control by the nervous system; Bayliss and Starling showed that it could occur through chemicals alone. This discovery spurred Starling to coin the term *hormone* to refer to secretin, taking it from the Greek word *hormon,* meaning "to excite" or "to set in motion." A hormone is a chemical produced by one tissue to make things happen elsewhere.

As more hormones were discovered, they were categorized, primarily according to the process by which they operated on the body. Some glands (which make up the endocrine system) secrete hormones directly into the bloodstream. Such glands include the thyroid and the pituitary. The exocrine system consists of organs and glands that produce substances that are used outside the bloodstream, primarily for digestion. The pancreas is one such organ, although it secretes some chemicals into the blood and thus is also part of the endocrine system.

Much has been learned about hormones since their discovery. Some play such key roles in regulating bodily processes or behavior that their absence would cause immediate death. The most abundant hormones have effects that are less obviously urgent but can be more far-reaching and difficult to track: They modify moods and affect human behavior, even some behavior we normally think of as voluntary. Hormonal systems are very intricate. Even minute amounts of the right chemicals can suppress appetite, calm aggression, and change the attitude of a parent toward a child. Certain hormones accelerate the development of the body, regulating growth and form; others may even define an individual's personality characteristics. **The quantities and proportions of hormones produced change with age, so scientists have given a great deal of study to shifts in the endocrine system over time in the hopes of alleviating ailments associated with aging.**

In fact, some hormone therapies are already very common. ■ **A combination of estrogen and progesterone has been prescribed for decades to women who want to reduce mood swings, sudden changes in body temperature, and other discomforts caused by lower natural levels of those hormones as they enter middle age.** ■ Known as hormone replacement therapy (HRT), the treatment was also believed to prevent weakening of the bones. ■ At least one study has linked HRT with a heightened risk of heart disease and certain types of cancer. **HRT may also increase the likelihood that blood clots—dangerous because they could travel through the bloodstream and block major blood vessels—will form.** Some proponents of HRT have tempered their enthusiasm in the face of this new evidence, recommending it only to patients whose symptoms interfere with their abilities to live normal lives. ■

Human growth hormone may also be given to patients who are secreting abnormally low amounts on their own. **Because of the complicated effects growth hormone has on the body, such treatments are generally restricted to children who would be pathologically small in stature without it.** Growth hormone affects not just physical size but also the digestion of food and the aging process. Researchers and family physicians tend to agree that it is foolhardy to dispense it in cases in which the risks are not clearly outweighed by the benefits.

More Available

34. Which of the sentences below best expresses the essential information in the highlighted sentence in the passage? *Incorrect* answer choices change the meaning in important ways or leave out essential information.

(A)   Most moods and actions are not voluntary because they are actually produced by the production of hormones in the body.

(B)   Because the effects of hormones are difficult to measure, scientists remain unsure how far-reaching their effects on moods and actions are.

(C)   When the body is not producing enough hormones, urgent treatment may be necessary to avoid psychological damage.

(D)   The influence of many hormones is not easy to measure, but they can affect both people's psychology and actions extensively.

Hormones in the Body

Until the beginning of the twentieth century, the nervous system was thought to control all communication within the body and the resulting integration of behavior. Scientists had determined that nerves ran, essentially, on electrical impulses. These impulses were thought to be the engine for thought, emotion, movement, and internal processes such as digestion. However, experiments by William Bayliss and Ernest Starling on the chemical secretin, which is produced in the small intestine when food enters the stomach, eventually challenged that view. From the small intestine, secretin travels through the bloodstream to the pancreas. There, it stimulates the release of digestive chemicals. In this fashion, the intestinal cells that produce secretin ultimately regulate the production of different chemicals in a different organ, the pancreas.

Such a coordination of processes had been thought to require control by the nervous system; Bayliss and Starling showed that it could occur through chemicals alone. This discovery spurred Starling to coin the term *hormone* to refer to secretin, taking it from the Greek word *hormon,* meaning "to excite" or "to set in motion." A hormone is a chemical produced by one tissue to make things happen elsewhere.

As more hormones were discovered, they were categorized, primarily according to the process by which they operated on the body. Some glands (which make up the endocrine system) secrete hormones directly into the bloodstream. Such glands include the thyroid and the pituitary. The exocrine system consists of organs and glands that produce substances that are used outside the bloodstream, primarily for digestion. The pancreas is one such organ, although it secretes some chemicals into the blood and thus is also part of the endocrine system.

Much has been learned about hormones since their discovery. Some play such key roles in regulating bodily processes or behavior that their absence would cause immediate death. The most abundant hormones have effects that are less obviously urgent but can be more far-reaching and difficult to track: They modify moods and affect human behavior, even some behavior we normally think of as voluntary. Hormonal systems are very intricate. Even minute amounts of the right chemicals can suppress appetite, calm aggression, and change the attitude of a parent toward a child. Certain hormones accelerate the development of the body, regulating growth and form; others may even define an individual's personality characteristics. **The quantities and proportions of hormones produced change with age, so scientists have given a great deal of study to shifts in the endocrine system over time in the hopes of alleviating ailments associated with aging.**

In fact, some hormone therapies are already very common. ■ **A combination of estrogen and progesterone has been prescribed for decades to women who want to reduce mood swings, sudden changes in body temperature, and other discomforts caused by lower natural levels of those hormones as they enter middle age.** ■ Known as hormone replacement therapy (HRT), the treatment was also believed to prevent weakening of the bones. ■ At least one study has linked HRT with a heightened risk of heart disease and certain types of cancer. **HRT may also increase the likelihood that blood clots—dangerous because they could travel through the bloodstream and block major blood vessels—will form.** Some proponents of HRT have tempered their enthusiasm in the face of this new evidence, recommending it only to patients whose symptoms interfere with their abilities to live normal lives. ■

Human growth hormone may also be given to patients who are secreting abnormally low amounts on their own. **Because of the complicated effects growth hormone has on the body, such treatments are generally restricted to children who would be pathologically small in stature without it.** Growth hormone affects not just physical size but also the digestion of food and the aging process. Researchers and family physicians tend to agree that it is foolhardy to dispense it in cases in which the risks are not clearly outweighed by the benefits.

TOEFL Reading

35 of 39

PAUSE TEST   SECTION EXIT

REVIEW   HELP ?   BACK   NEXT

HIDE TIME   00:08:45

More Available

35. The word tempered in the passage is closest in meaning to

(A) decreased
(B) advertised
(C) prescribed
(D) researched

Hormones in the Body

Until the beginning of the twentieth century, the nervous system was thought to control all communication within the body and the resulting integration of behavior. Scientists had determined that nerves ran, essentially, on electrical impulses. These impulses were thought to be the engine for thought, emotion, movement, and internal processes such as digestion. However, experiments by William Bayliss and Ernest Starling on the chemical secretin, which is produced in the small intestine when food enters the stomach, eventually challenged that view. From the small intestine, secretin travels through the bloodstream to the pancreas. There, it stimulates the release of digestive chemicals. In this fashion, the intestinal cells that produce secretin ultimately regulate the production of different chemicals in a different organ, the pancreas.

Such a coordination of processes had been thought to require control by the nervous system; Bayliss and Starling showed that it could occur through chemicals alone. This discovery spurred Starling to coin the term *hormone* to refer to secretin, taking it from the Greek word *hormon*, meaning "to excite" or "to set in motion." A hormone is a chemical produced by one tissue to make things happen elsewhere.

As more hormones were discovered, they were categorized, primarily according to the process by which they operated on the body. Some glands (which make up the endocrine system) secrete hormones directly into the bloodstream. Such glands include the thyroid and the pituitary. The exocrine system consists of organs and glands that produce substances that are used outside the bloodstream, primarily for digestion. The pancreas is one such organ, although it secretes some chemicals into the blood and thus is also part of the endocrine system.

Much has been learned about hormones since their discovery. Some play such key roles in regulating bodily processes or behavior that their absence would cause immediate death. The most abundant hormones have effects that are less obviously urgent but can be more far-reaching and difficult to track: They modify moods and affect human behavior, even some behavior we normally think of as voluntary. Hormonal systems are very intricate. Even minute amounts of the right chemicals can suppress appetite, calm aggression, and change the attitude of a parent toward a child. Certain hormones accelerate the development of the body, regulating growth and form; others may even define an individual's personality characteristics. **The quantities and proportions of hormones produced change with age, so scientists have given a great deal of study to shifts in the endocrine system over time in the hopes of alleviating ailments associated with aging.**

In fact, some hormone therapies are already very common. ■ **A combination of estrogen and progesterone has been prescribed for decades to women who want to reduce mood swings, sudden changes in body temperature, and other discomforts caused by lower natural levels of those hormones as they enter middle age.** ■ Known as hormone replacement therapy (HRT), the treatment was also believed to prevent weakening of the bones. ■ At least one study has linked HRT with a heightened risk of heart disease and certain types of cancer. **HRT may also increase the likelihood that blood clots—dangerous because they could travel through the bloodstream and block major blood vessels—will form.** Some proponents of HRT have tempered their enthusiasm in the face of this new evidence, recommending it only to patients whose symptoms interfere with their abilities to live normal lives. ■

Human growth hormone may also be given to patients who are secreting abnormally low amounts on their own. **Because of the complicated effects growth hormone has on the body, such treatments are generally restricted to children who would be pathologically small in stature without it.** Growth hormone affects not just physical size but also the digestion of food and the aging process. Researchers and family physicians tend to agree that it is foolhardy to dispense it in cases in which the risks are not clearly outweighed by the benefits.

36. Which patients are usually treated with growth hormone?

(A) Adults of smaller stature than normal

(B) Adults with strong digestive systems

(C) Children who are not at risk from the treatment

(D) Children who may remain abnormally small

More Available

Hormones in the Body

Until the beginning of the twentieth century, the nervous system was thought to control all communication within the body and the resulting integration of behavior. Scientists had determined that nerves ran, essentially, on electrical impulses. These impulses were thought to be the engine for thought, emotion, movement, and internal processes such as digestion. However, experiments by William Bayliss and Ernest Starling on the chemical secretin, which is produced in the small intestine when food enters the stomach, eventually challenged that view. From the small intestine, secretin travels through the bloodstream to the pancreas. There, it stimulates the release of digestive chemicals. In this fashion, the intestinal cells that produce secretin ultimately regulate the production of different chemicals in a different organ, the pancreas.

Such a coordination of processes had been thought to require control by the nervous system; Bayliss and Starling showed that it could occur through chemicals alone. This discovery spurred Starling to coin the term *hormone* to refer to secretin, taking it from the Greek word *hormon*, meaning "to excite" or "to set in motion." A hormone is a chemical produced by one tissue to make things happen elsewhere.

As more hormones were discovered, they were categorized, primarily according to the process by which they operated on the body. Some glands (which make up the endocrine system) secrete hormones directly into the bloodstream. Such glands include the thyroid and the pituitary. The exocrine system consists of organs and glands that produce substances that are used outside the bloodstream, primarily for digestion. The pancreas is one such organ, although it secretes some chemicals into the blood and thus is also part of the endocrine system.

Much has been learned about hormones since their discovery. Some play such key roles in regulating bodily processes or behavior that their absence would cause immediate death. The most abundant hormones have effects that are less obviously urgent but can be more far-reaching and difficult to track: They modify moods and affect human behavior, even some behavior we normally think of as voluntary. Hormonal systems are very intricate. Even minute amounts of the right chemicals can suppress appetite, calm aggression, and change the attitude of a parent toward a child. Certain hormones accelerate the development of the body, regulating growth and form; others may even define an individual's personality characteristics. **The quantities and proportions of hormones produced change with age, so scientists have given a great deal of study to shifts in the endocrine system over time in the hopes of alleviating ailments associated with aging.**

In fact, some hormone therapies are already very common. ■ **A combination of estrogen and progesterone has been prescribed for decades to women who want to reduce mood swings, sudden changes in body temperature, and other discomforts caused by lower natural levels of those hormones as they enter middle age.** ■ Known as hormone replacement therapy (HRT), the treatment was also believed to prevent weakening of the bones. ■ At least one study has linked HRT with a heightened risk of heart disease and certain types of cancer. **HRT may also increase the likelihood that blood clots—dangerous because they could travel through the bloodstream and block major blood vessels—will form.** Some proponents of HRT have tempered their enthusiasm in the face of this new evidence, recommending it only to patients whose symptoms interfere with their abilities to live normal lives. ■

Human growth hormone may also be given to patients who are secreting abnormally low amounts on their own. **Because of the complicated effects growth hormone has on the body, such treatments are generally restricted to children who would be pathologically small in stature without it.** Growth hormone affects not just physical size but also the digestion of food and the aging process. Researchers and family physicians tend to agree that it is foolhardy to dispense it in cases in which the risks are not clearly outweighed by the benefits.

More Available

37. Click on the highlighted sentence (in bold text in the passage and repeated below) in the passage where the author explains the primary goal of hormone replacement therapy.

(A)   The quantities and proportions of hormones produced change with age, so scientists have given a great deal of study to shifts in the endocrine system over time in the hopes of alleviating ailments associated with aging.

(B)   A combination of estrogen and progesterone has been prescribed for decades to women who want to reduce mood swings, sudden changes in body temperature, and other discomforts caused by lower natural levels of those hormones as they enter middle age.

(C)   HRT may also increase the likelihood that blood clots—dangerous because they could travel through the bloodstream and block major blood vessels—will form.

(D)   Because of the complicated effects growth hormone has on the body, such treatments are generally restricted to children who would be pathologically small in stature without it.

Hormones in the Body

Until the beginning of the twentieth century, the nervous system was thought to control all communication within the body and the resulting integration of behavior. Scientists had determined that nerves ran, essentially, on electrical impulses. These impulses were thought to be the engine for thought, emotion, movement, and internal processes such as digestion. However, experiments by William Bayliss and Ernest Starling on the chemical secretin, which is produced in the small intestine when food enters the stomach, eventually challenged that view. From the small intestine, secretin travels through the bloodstream to the pancreas. There, it stimulates the release of digestive chemicals. In this fashion, the intestinal cells that produce secretin ultimately regulate the production of different chemicals in a different organ, the pancreas.

Such a coordination of processes had been thought to require control by the nervous system; Bayliss and Starling showed that it could occur through chemicals alone. This discovery spurred Starling to coin the term *hormone* to refer to secretin, taking it from the Greek word *hormon,* meaning "to excite" or "to set in motion." A hormone is a chemical produced by one tissue to make things happen elsewhere.

As more hormones were discovered, they were categorized, primarily according to the process by which they operated on the body. Some glands (which make up the endocrine system) secrete hormones directly into the bloodstream. Such glands include the thyroid and the pituitary. The exocrine system consists of organs and glands that produce substances that are used outside the bloodstream, primarily for digestion. The pancreas is one such organ, although it secretes some chemicals into the blood and thus is also part of the endocrine system.

Much has been learned about hormones since their discovery. Some play such key roles in regulating bodily processes or behavior that their absence would cause immediate death. The most abundant hormones have effects that are less obviously urgent but can be more far-reaching and difficult to track: They modify moods and affect human behavior, even some behavior we normally think of as voluntary. Hormonal systems are very intricate. Even minute amounts of the right chemicals can suppress appetite, calm aggression, and change the attitude of a parent toward a child. Certain hormones accelerate the development of the body, regulating growth and form; others may even define an individual's personality characteristics. **The quantities and proportions of hormones produced change with age, so scientists have given a great deal of study to shifts in the endocrine system over time in the hopes of alleviating ailments associated with aging.**

In fact, some hormone therapies are already very common. ■ **A combination of estrogen and progesterone has been prescribed for decades to women who want to reduce mood swings, sudden changes in body temperature, and other discomforts caused by lower natural levels of those hormones as they enter middle age.** ■ Known as hormone replacement therapy (HRT), the treatment was also believed to prevent weakening of the bones. ■ At least one study has linked HRT with a heightened risk of heart disease and certain types of cancer. **HRT may also increase the likelihood that blood clots—dangerous because they could travel through the bloodstream and block major blood vessels—will form.** Some proponents of HRT have tempered their enthusiasm in the face of this new evidence, recommending it only to patients whose symptoms interfere with their abilities to live normal lives. ■

Human growth hormone may also be given to patients who are secreting abnormally low amounts on their own. **Because of the complicated effects growth hormone has on the body, such treatments are generally restricted to children who would be pathologically small in stature without it.** Growth hormone affects not just physical size but also the digestion of food and the aging process. Researchers and family physicians tend to agree that it is foolhardy to dispense it in cases in which the risks are not clearly outweighed by the benefits.

TOEFL Reading

PAUSE TEST   SECTION EXIT

38 of 39

REVIEW   HELP   BACK   NEXT

HIDE TIME   00:08:45

More Available

38. Look at the four squares [■] that indicate where the following sentence could be added to the passage.

The body is a complex machine, however, and recent studies have called into question the wisdom of essentially trying to fool its systems into believing they aren't aging.

Where would the sentence best fit?

Click on a square [■] to add the sentence to the passage.

[Here, on this practice test, circle your answer below.]

(A) Square 1
(B) Square 2
(C) Square 3
(D) Square 4

Hormones in the Body

Until the beginning of the twentieth century, the nervous system was thought to control all communication within the body and the resulting integration of behavior. Scientists had determined that nerves ran, essentially, on electrical impulses. These impulses were thought to be the engine for thought, emotion, movement, and internal processes such as digestion. However, experiments by William Bayliss and Ernest Starling on the chemical secretin, which is produced in the small intestine when food enters the stomach, eventually challenged that view. From the small intestine, secretin travels through the bloodstream to the pancreas. There, it stimulates the release of digestive chemicals. In this fashion, the intestinal cells that produce secretin ultimately regulate the production of different chemicals in a different organ, the pancreas.

Such a coordination of processes had been thought to require control by the nervous system; Bayliss and Starling showed that it could occur through chemicals alone. This discovery spurred Starling to coin the term *hormone* to refer to secretin, taking it from the Greek word *hormon,* meaning "to excite" or "to set in motion." A hormone is a chemical produced by one tissue to make things happen elsewhere.

As more hormones were discovered, they were categorized, primarily according to the process by which they operated on the body. Some glands (which make up the endocrine system) secrete hormones directly into the bloodstream. Such glands include the thyroid and the pituitary. The exocrine system consists of organs and glands that produce substances that are used outside the bloodstream, primarily for digestion. The pancreas is one such organ, although it secretes some chemicals into the blood and thus is also part of the endocrine system.

Much has been learned about hormones since their discovery. Some play such key roles in regulating bodily processes or behavior that their absence would cause immediate death. The most abundant hormones have effects that are less obviously urgent but can be more far-reaching and difficult to track: They modify moods and affect human behavior, even some behavior we normally think of as voluntary. Hormonal systems are very intricate. Even minute amounts of the right chemicals can suppress appetite, calm aggression, and change the attitude of a parent toward a child. Certain hormones accelerate the development of the body, regulating growth and form; others may even define an individual's personality characteristics. **The quantities and proportions of hormones produced change with age, so scientists have given a great deal of study to shifts in the endocrine system over time in the hopes of alleviating ailments associated with aging.**

In fact, some hormone therapies are already very common. ■ **A combination of estrogen and progesterone has been prescribed for decades to women who want to reduce mood swings, sudden changes in body temperature, and other discomforts caused by lower natural levels of those hormones as they enter middle age.** ■ Known as hormone replacement therapy (HRT), the treatment was also believed to prevent weakening of the bones. ■ At least one study has linked HRT with a heightened risk of heart disease and certain types of cancer. **HRT may also increase the likelihood that blood clots—dangerous because they could travel through the bloodstream and block major blood vessels—will form.** Some proponents of HRT have tempered their enthusiasm in the face of this new evidence, recommending it only to patients whose symptoms interfere with their abilities to live normal lives. ■

Human growth hormone may also be given to patients who are secreting abnormally low amounts on their own. **Because of the complicated effects growth hormone has on the body, such treatments are generally restricted to children who would be pathologically small in stature without it.** Growth hormone affects not just physical size but also the digestion of food and the aging process. Researchers and family physicians tend to agree that it is foolhardy to dispense it in cases in which the risks are not clearly outweighed by the benefits.

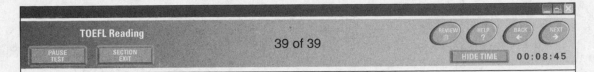
39. **Directions**: An introductory sentence for a brief summary of the passage is provided below. Complete the summary by selecting the THREE answer choices that express the most important ideas in the passage. Some sentences do not belong in the summary because they express ideas that are not presented in the passage or are minor ideas in the passage. *This question is worth 2 points.*

> The class of chemicals called hormones was discovered by two researchers studying a substance produced in the small intestine.

- •
- •
- •

Answer Choices	
The term hormone is based on a Greek word that means "to excite" or "to set in motion."	Researchers are looking for ways to decrease the dangers of treatments with growth hormone so that more patients can benefit from it.
Hormones can be given artificially, but such treatments have risks and must be used carefully.	Hormones can affect not only life processes such as growth but also behavior and emotion.
Scientists have discovered that not only the nervous system but also certain chemicals can affect bodily processes far from their points of origin.	Hormone replacement therapy (HRT) may increase the risk of blood clots and heart disease in middle-age women.

THE LISTENING SECTION

This section measures your ability to understand lectures and conversations in English. You will hear each selection only once. Each lecture or conversation will be followed by a series of questions, typically about the main idea and supporting details. Answer the questions in the order they appear. You may not skip a question and return to it. You may take notes while you listen and use your notes to help you answer the questions.

On the actual test, you will have 20 minutes to answer the questions. The time will not run down while you are listening to the test material. You will see screens similar to the ones shown in the next pages to introduce questions or provide instructions, such as "listen again to."

To most closely simulate the actual test conditions, listen to the CD and then set a timer or ask a friend to time you for 20 minutes. You will need to pause the CD after each question, but remember, give yourself only 20 minutes to finish the entire section. Begin now.

Listening 1

Please play Track 24 of the accompanying CD.

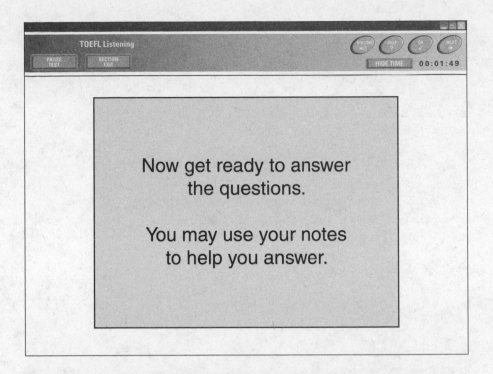

Now get ready to answer
the questions.

You may use your notes
to help you answer.

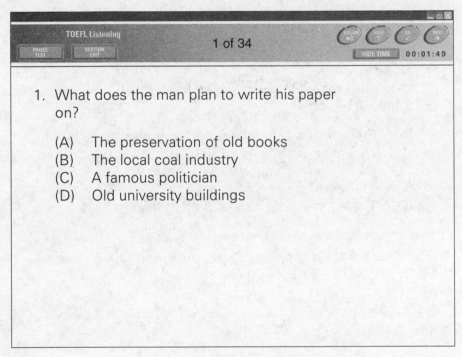

1. What does the man plan to write his paper on?

(A)   The preservation of old books
(B)   The local coal industry
(C)   A famous politician
(D)   Old university buildings

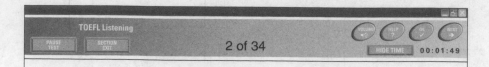

2. What security procedures does the librarian
    tell the man he must follow?

    Click on 2 answers.

    (A) Show her his note cards before leaving
    (B) Allow his ID card to be copied
    (C) Submit a deposit of five dollars
    (D) Sign in and out of the archives room

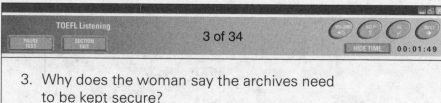

3. Why does the woman say the archives need
    to be kept secure?

    (A) Students from other universities frequently use the
         collection.
    (B) Some items are worth a lot of money.
    (C) Many items cannot be replaced.
    (D) There have been several thefts recently.

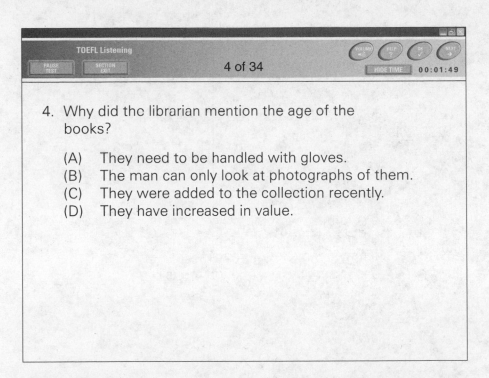

4. Why did the librarian mention the age of the books?

(A) They need to be handled with gloves.
(B) The man can only look at photographs of them.
(C) They were added to the collection recently.
(D) They have increased in value.

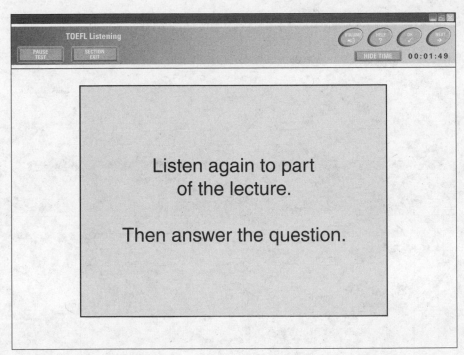

Listen again to part of the lecture.

Then answer the question.

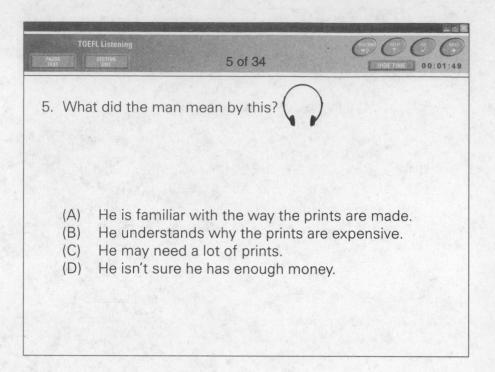

5. What did the man mean by this?

(A) He is familiar with the way the prints are made.
(B) He understands why the prints are expensive.
(C) He may need a lot of prints.
(D) He isn't sure he has enough money.

Listening 2

Please play Track 25 on the accompanying CD.

Pause the CD after each question.

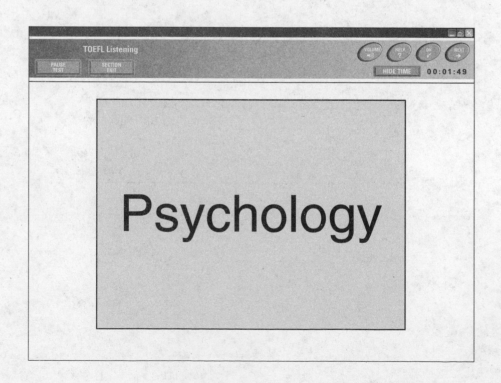

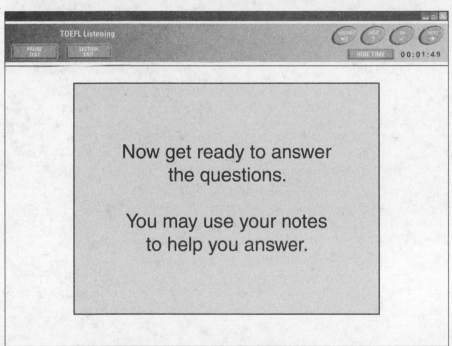

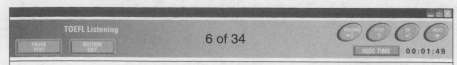

6. What is the lecture mainly about?

    (A) Why some events are more memorable than others
    (B) The process by which memories form in the brain
    (C) Research on animals that may help explain human memory
    (D) Ways students can strengthen their abilities to remember things

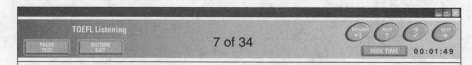

7. Why does the professor say Walter Freeman mentioned two types of crowds?

    (A) People can be taught to recall information that has fallen into disuse.
    (B) Scientists are studying why some people have a better sense of direction than others.
    (C) Impulses in the brain may follow a pattern researchers don't yet understand.
    (D) Each individual person has a unique way of remembering things.

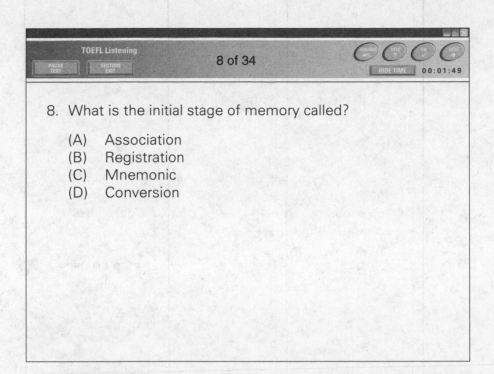

8. What is the initial stage of memory called?

(A) Association
(B) Registration
(C) Mnemonic
(D) Conversion

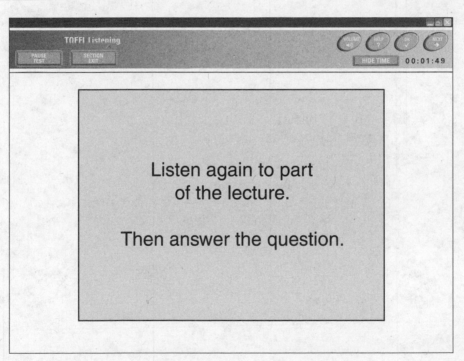

Listen again to part
of the lecture.

Then answer the question.

9. What is the professor trying to illustrate?

(A) People have an easier time remembering unusual images.
(B) The most memorable images come from nature.
(C) Some people have names with few easy associations.
(D) Large objects are easier to remember than small objects.

10. What does the professor imply about a memory that has passed through the long-term retention stage?

(A) It usually takes a long time to recall.
(B) It could still be lost if not used frequently.
(C) It can be recalled even if the brain is injured.
(D) It often comes back suddenly in old age.

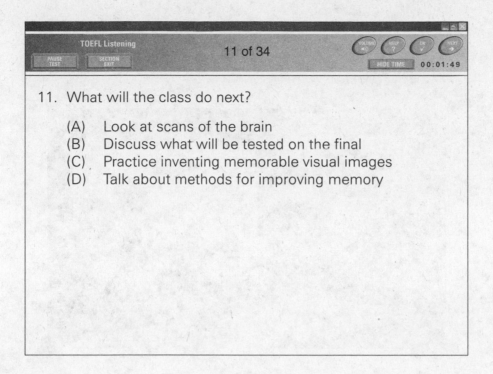

11. What will the class do next?

    (A)   Look at scans of the brain
    (B)   Discuss what will be tested on the final
    (C)   Practice inventing memorable visual images
    (D)   Talk about methods for improving memory

Listening 3

Please play Track 26 on the accompanying CD.

Pause the CD after each question.

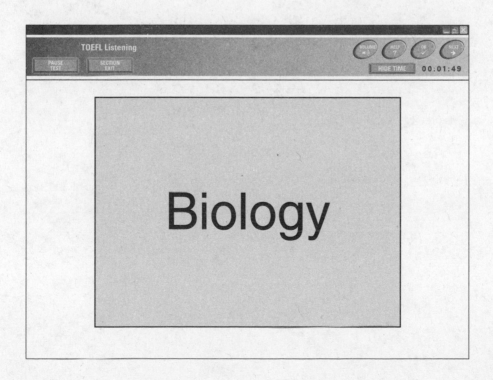

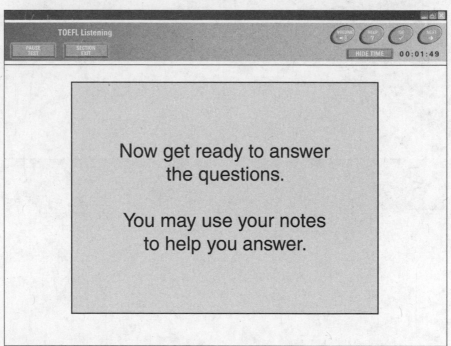

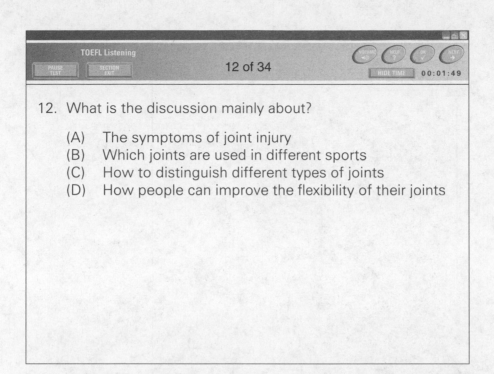

12. What is the discussion mainly about?

(A) The symptoms of joint injury
(B) Which joints are used in different sports
(C) How to distinguish different types of joints
(D) How people can improve the flexibility of their joints

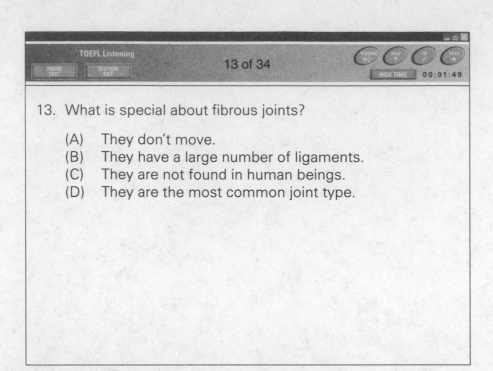

13. What is special about fibrous joints?

    (A) They don't move.
    (B) They have a large number of ligaments.
    (C) They are not found in human beings.
    (D) They are the most common joint type.

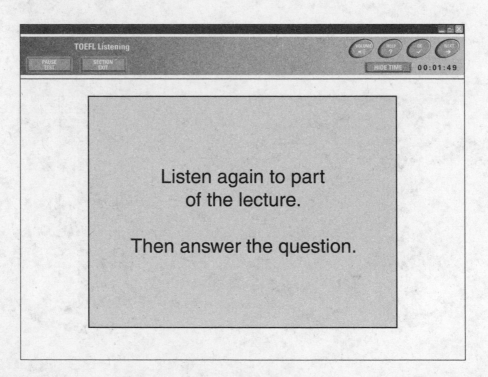

Listen again to part
of the lecture.

Then answer the question.

14. What does the professor say about the jaw?

(A)   She has already discussed its joint type.
(B)   It is the best example of a fibrous joint.
(C)   It does not have the type of joint she is describing.
(D)   She almost forgot to mention it.

15. According to the professor, what is an example of a hinge joint?

(A)   The hip
(B)   The knuckles
(C)   The shoulder
(D)   The neck

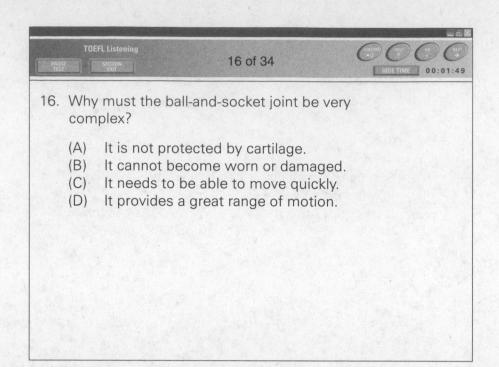

16. Why must the ball-and-socket joint be very complex?

(A) It is not protected by cartilage.
(B) It cannot become worn or damaged.
(C) It needs to be able to move quickly.
(D) It provides a great range of motion.

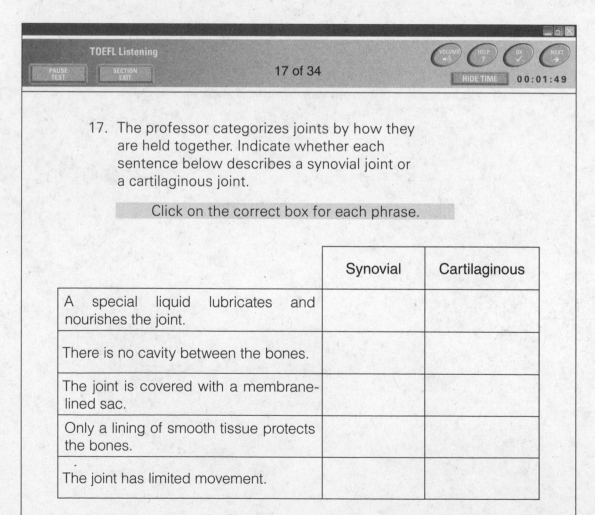

17. The professor categorizes joints by how they are held together. Indicate whether each sentence below describes a synovial joint or a cartilaginous joint.

Click on the correct box for each phrase.

	Synovial	Cartilaginous
A special liquid lubricates and nourishes the joint.		
There is no cavity between the bones.		
The joint is covered with a membrane-lined sac.		
Only a lining of smooth tissue protects the bones.		
The joint has limited movement.		

Listening 4

Please play Track 27 on the accompanying CD.

Pause the CD after each question.

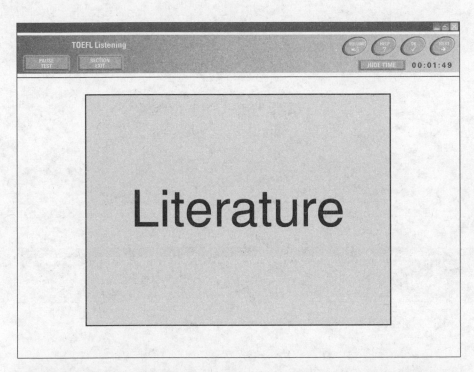

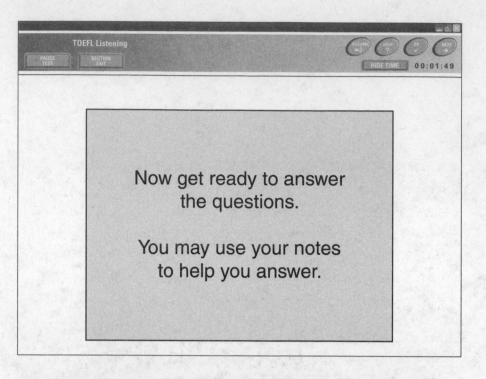

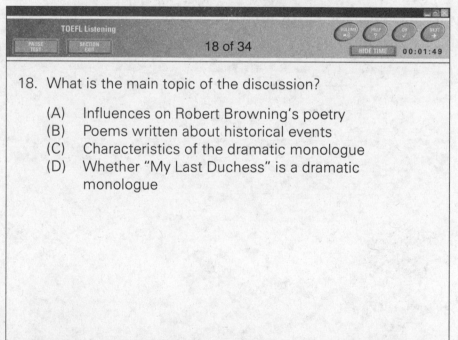

18. What is the main topic of the discussion?

   (A) Influences on Robert Browning's poetry
   (B) Poems written about historical events
   (C) Characteristics of the dramatic monologue
   (D) Whether "My Last Duchess" is a dramatic monologue

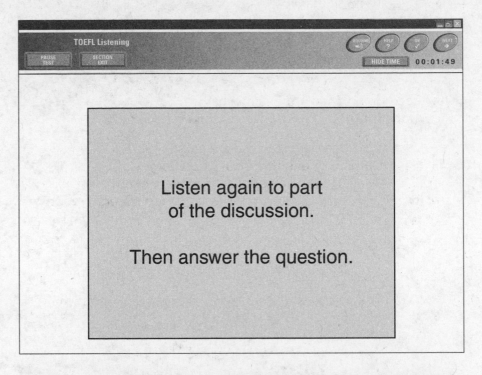

Listen again to part
of the discussion.

Then answer the question.

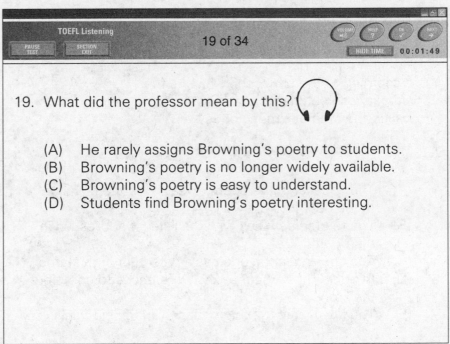

19. What did the professor mean by this?

(A) He rarely assigns Browning's poetry to students.
(B) Browning's poetry is no longer widely available.
(C) Browning's poetry is easy to understand.
(D) Students find Browning's poetry interesting.

20. According to the professor, what is a monologue?

    (A)   A speech given by a single person
    (B)   A profile of one historical character
    (C)   A description of a specific historical event
    (D)   A poet who writes in the voice of a different person

21. According to the professor, what are the primary characteristics of the poetic form called the dramatic monologue?

Click on 3 answers.

    (A)   The speaker in the poem reveals what he plans to do in the near future.
    (B)   The reader identifies with the listener addressed in the poem.
    (C)   The speaker in the poem is a person of high status.
    (D)   Readers must use their own inferences to complete the story.
    (E)   The speaker in the poem tries to justify his thinking.

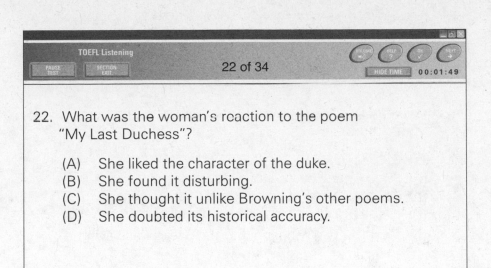

22. What was the woman's reaction to the poem
"My Last Duchess"?

    (A)   She liked the character of the duke.
    (B)   She found it disturbing.
    (C)   She thought it unlike Browning's other poems.
    (D)   She doubted its historical accuracy.

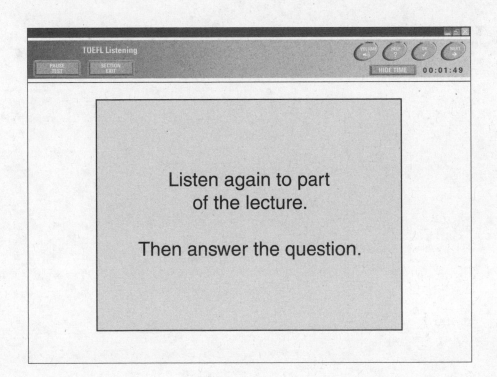

Listen again to part
of the lecture.

Then answer the question.

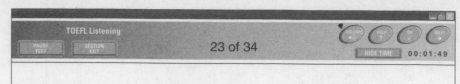

23. What does the professor ask the woman to do?

(A) Consider a different interpretation
(B) Allow her classmates to give their opinions
(C) Wait until later to talk about the poem
(D) Explain what she thought the poem was saying

Listening 5

Please play Track 28 on the accompanying CD.

Pause the CD after each question.

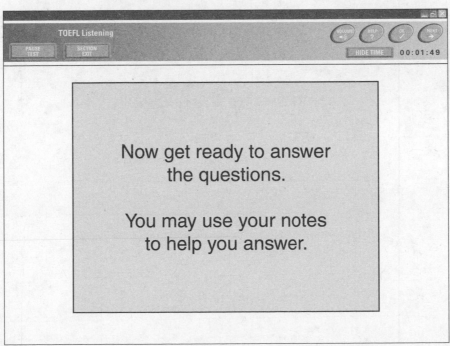

Now get ready to answer
the questions.

You may use your notes
to help you answer.

24. What will the woman spend the evening doing?

(A) Catching up on her math homework
(B) Having dinner with the man
(C) Seeing a tutor about one of her classes
(D) Helping high school students with their studies

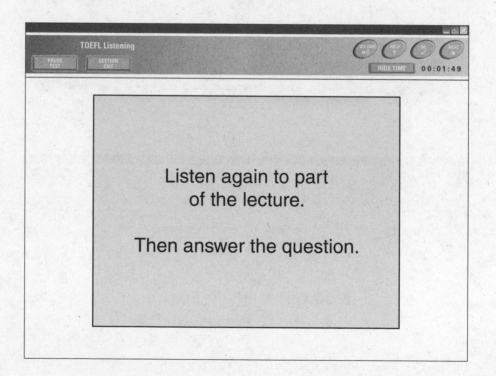

Listen again to part of the lecture.

Then answer the question.

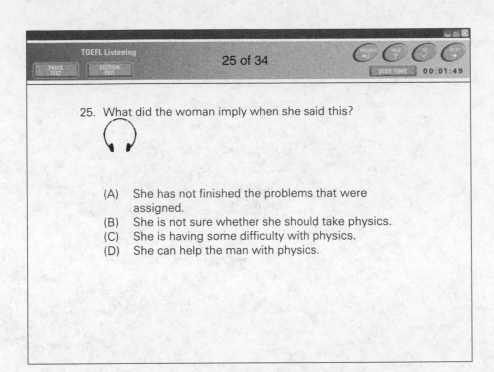

25. What did the woman imply when she said this?

(A) She has not finished the problems that were assigned.
(B) She is not sure whether she should take physics.
(C) She is having some difficulty with physics.
(D) She can help the man with physics.

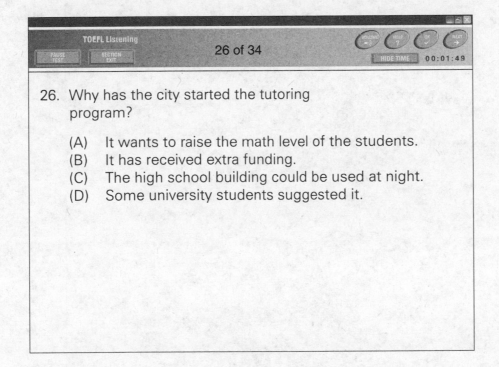

26. Why has the city started the tutoring program?

(A) It wants to raise the math level of the students.
(B) It has received extra funding.
(C) The high school building could be used at night.
(D) Some university students suggested it.

27. What does the education department like
    about the tutors?

   (A)   Most of them have taught students before.
   (B)   The tutors are available in the afternoon.
   (C)   Most of them went to the city high school.
   (D)   It doesn't have to pay them.

28. What does the woman think tutoring will
    prepare her for?

   (A)   Her upcoming math tests
   (B)   Her duties as a graduate student
   (C)   A job as a high school teacher
   (D)   A job at the City Department of Education

Listening 6

Please play Track 29 on the accompanying CD.

Pause the CD after each question.

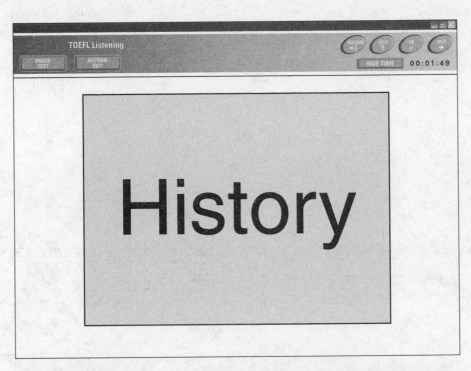

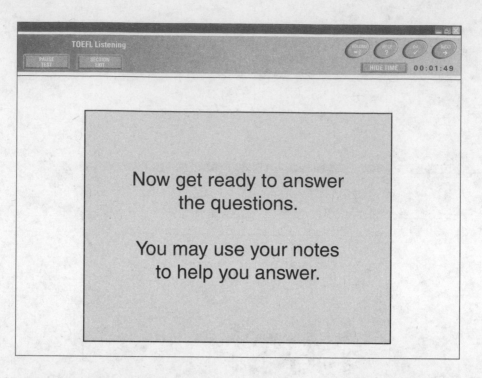

29. What did the professor mainly discuss?

(A) Types of goods traded in the colonies
(B) Major wars of the colonial period
(C) How the colonists defeated new tax laws
(D) How the British increased the flow of money to the colonies

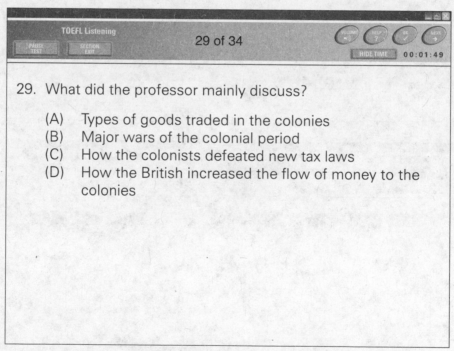

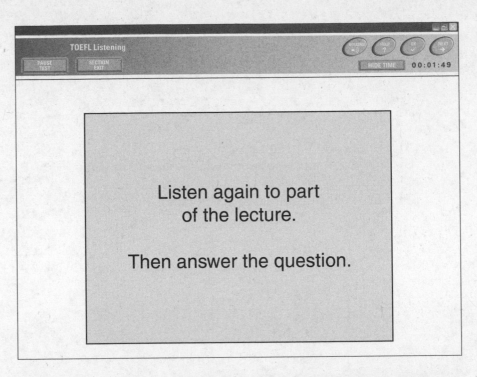

Listen again to part
of the lecture.

Then answer the question.

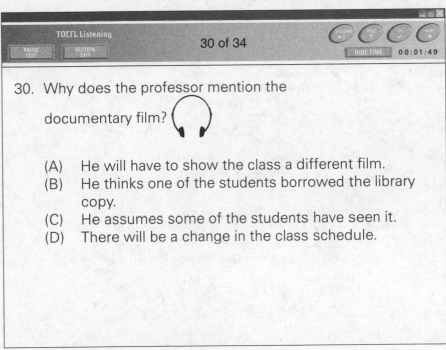

30. Why does the professor mention the documentary film?

- (A) He will have to show the class a different film.
- (B) He thinks one of the students borrowed the library copy.
- (C) He assumes some of the students have seen it.
- (D) There will be a change in the class schedule.

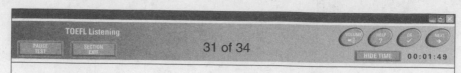

31. Why did Britain want to receive more money from the American colonies?

    (A)   It had just finished a costly war.
    (B)   Colonial paper currency had increased in value.
    (C)   The colonies were producing more sugar.
    (D)   Taxes in Britain had been lowered.

32. Which of the following did the professor mention as changes that accompanied the Sugar Act?

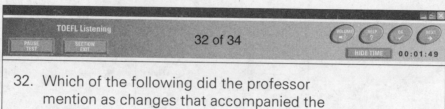

Click on 2 answers.

    (A)   A greater number of commodities were taxed.
    (B)   The taxes were collected more carefully.
    (C)   The tax on sugar replaced the tax on coffee and wines.
    (D)   The Stamp Act was no longer necessary.

33. Why does the professor say the colonists developed their own paper currency?

(A) They needed more money to pay the sugar tax.
(B) Their British currency was used to pay for British goods.
(C) Property could be bought only with paper currency.
(D) Paper currency was easier for laborers to transport.

34. According to the professor, why did the Stamp Act affect both merchants and laborers in the colonies?

(A) It outlawed newspapers read by both groups.
(B) Many colonists had fought in the French and Indian War.
(C) Many everyday activities were taxed.
(D) Both groups consumed large amounts of sugar.

THE SPEAKING SECTION

In this section, you will demonstrate your ability to speak about various topics. You will answer eight questions. Answer each question as completely as possible.

Questions 1 and 2 will ask you about familiar topics. For questions 3 and 4, you will first read a short text. Next, you will listen to a lecture on the same topic. You will then be asked a question about what you have read and heard. Questions 5 and 6 require you to listen to a short piece and a conversation between two students giving their reactions. Questions 7 and 8 require you to listen to a lecture first. You will then be asked two questions about what you just heard. You may take notes while you read and listen. You may use your notes to help you prepare.

For each task, you will be given a short period of time to prepare your response; to most closely simulate actual test conditions, you will need to pause and restart the audio CD as instructed in the following pages.

Note to students: If possible, record your responses or have someone proficient in English listen to your response. Compare your responses with the samples at the end of the test.

Speaking 1

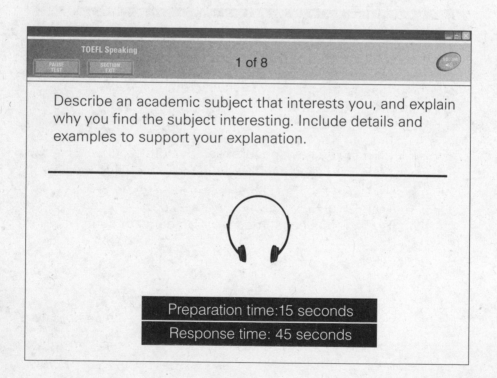

TOEFL Speaking

PAUSE TEST   SECTION EXIT

1 of 8

Describe an academic subject that interests you, and explain why you find the subject interesting. Include details and examples to support your explanation.

Preparation time: 15 seconds
Response time: 45 seconds

Speaking 2

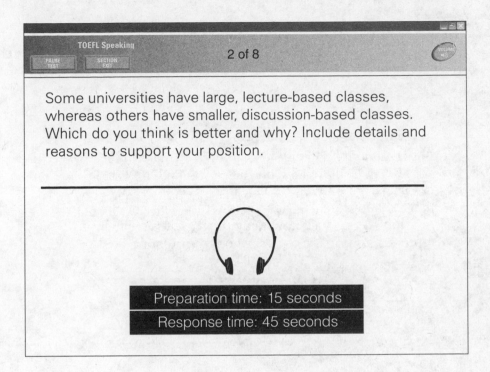

Some universities have large, lecture-based classes, whereas others have smaller, discussion-based classes. Which do you think is better and why? Include details and reasons to support your position.

Preparation time: 15 seconds
Response time: 45 seconds

Speaking 3

Please play Track 30 on the accompanying CD.

Narrator: Now read the passage about birds of prey. You have 45 seconds to read the passage. Begin reading now.

[Stop CD for 45 seconds]

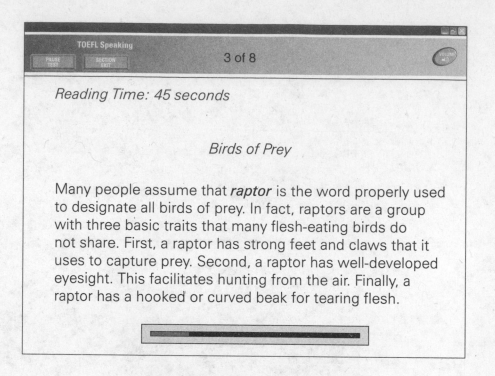

Reading Time: 45 seconds

Birds of Prey

Many people assume that ***raptor*** is the word properly used to designate all birds of prey. In fact, raptors are a group with three basic traits that many flesh-eating birds do not share. First, a raptor has strong feet and claws that it uses to capture prey. Second, a raptor has well-developed eyesight. This facilitates hunting from the air. Finally, a raptor has a hooked or curved beak for tearing flesh.

[Restart audio CD.]

Narrator: Now listen to part of a lecture on this topic given in a biology class.

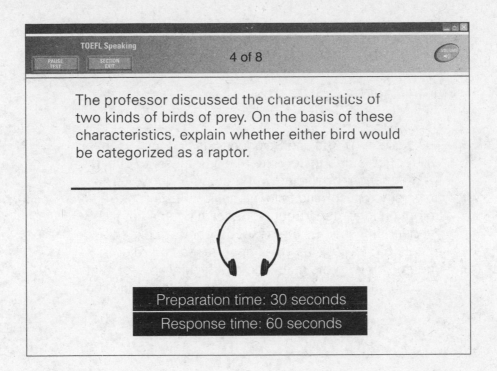

The professor discussed the characteristics of two kinds of birds of prey. On the basis of these characteristics, explain whether either bird would be categorized as a raptor.

Preparation time: 30 seconds

Response time: 60 seconds

Speaking 4

Please play Track 31 on the accompanying CD.

Narrator: The College of Arts and Sciences at Eastern University has decided to add a senior project to its existing graduation requirements. The campus newspaper printed the following report about the announcement of the new requirement. You have 45 seconds to read the report. Begin reading now.

[Stop CD for 45 seconds.]

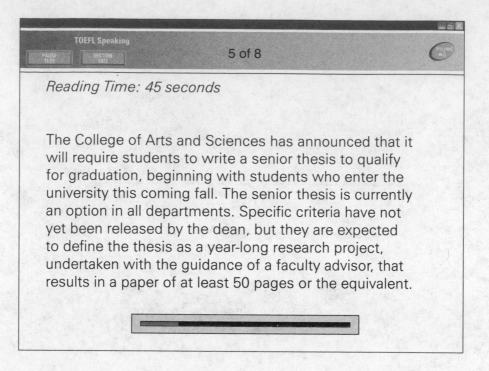

Reading Time: 45 seconds

The College of Arts and Sciences has announced that it will require students to write a senior thesis to qualify for graduation, beginning with students who enter the university this coming fall. The senior thesis is currently an option in all departments. Specific criteria have not yet been released by the dean, but they are expected to define the thesis as a year-long research project, undertaken with the guidance of a faculty advisor, that results in a paper of at least 50 pages or the equivalent.

[Restart audio CD.] 🎧

Narrator: Now listen to two students as they discuss the report.

The woman explains her opinion of the announcement made by the College of Arts and Sciences. State her opinion, and explain the reasons she gives for holding that opinion.

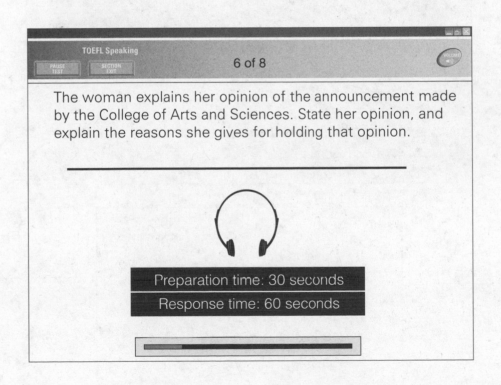

Preparation time: 30 seconds

Response time: 60 seconds

Speaking 5

Please play Track 32 on the accompanying CD.

Narrator: Now listen to a conversation between two students.

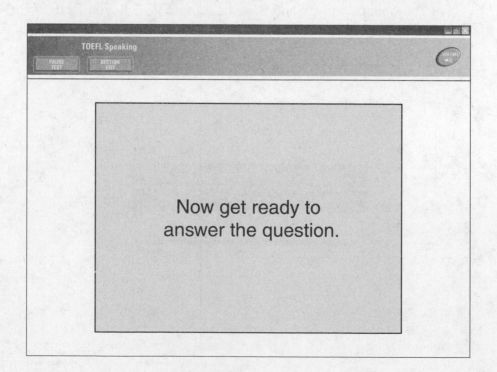

Now get ready to
answer the question.

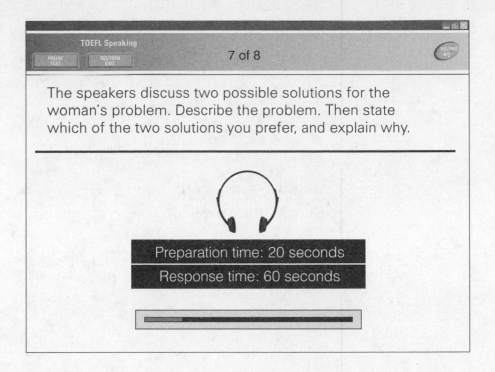

The speakers discuss two possible solutions for the woman's problem. Describe the problem. Then state which of the two solutions you prefer, and explain why.

Preparation time: 20 seconds
Response time: 60 seconds

Speaking 6

Please play Track 33 on the accompanying CD.

Narrator: Now listen to part of a lecture in a history class.

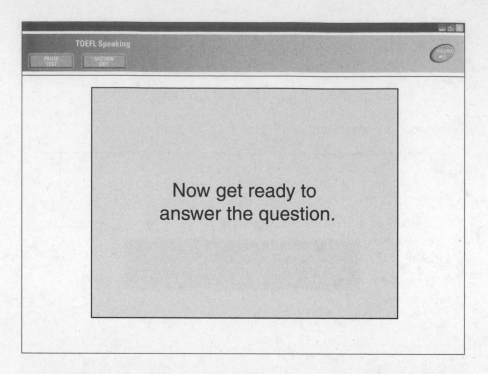

Now get ready to
answer the question.

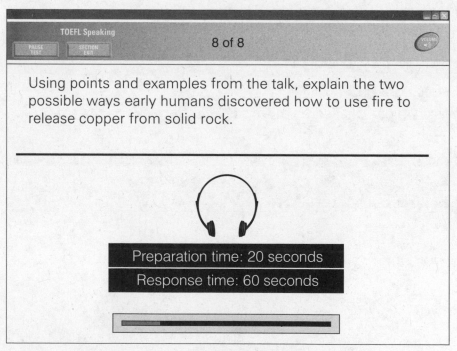

Using points and examples from the talk, explain the two possible ways early humans discovered how to use fire to release copper from solid rock.

Preparation time: 20 seconds

Response time: 60 seconds

THE WRITING SECTION

This section measures your ability to communicate in an academic environment. There are two writing tasks. The first task asks you to read a passage, listen to a lecture, and respond. You will answer the second question based on your own knowledge and experience. To most closely simulate actual test conditions, you will need to pause and restart the audio CD as instructed throughout this section.

Writing 1

Directions: You will have 20 minutes to plan and write your response. The break between the reading and lecture is not timed on the CD, because some students may need to practice untimed. Therefore, you will need to stop the CD for the duration of the break. You have three minutes to read the selection.

Please play Track 34 on the accompanying CD.

> *Narrator:* Now read the passage about the suppression of forest fires. You have three minutes to read the passage. Begin reading now.

[Stop CD for 3 minutes.]

Wilderness management has advanced greatly over the last century, due in part to such practices as the suppression of forest fires and limitations on the clear-cutting of trees. Monitoring forests for small brushfires is easier with aircraft, as is the use of large amounts of water and sophisticated chemical fire extinguishers to prevent fires from spreading.

The goals of decreasing the amount of destruction by fires and cutting are wide- ranging. One is simply the longer lives and improved health of trees. In some areas of hickory and oak forest on the Eastern Seaboard, fire suppression has allowed the maturation of so many trees that the treetops form a continuous canopy.

There is evidence of the healthful effects of fire suppression closer to the ground as well. Vines and low bushes that would be burned out in a forest fire can flourish when fires are suppressed, of course, but there is a more indirect way fires harm plant life. Chemical tests on areas that have recently experienced forest fires demonstrate that burning decreases the overall amount of nutrients in the soil. Suppressing fires prevents such a decrease. Ferns, wildflowers, and herbs grow without disturbance.

Finally, wildlife can benefit. In the eastern hickory and oak forests, the suppression of fires has meant that forest animals—ranging from small insects and birds to large deer and bears—are not burned to death. Deer populations, in particular, have increased notably.

Narrator: Now listen to part of a lecture on the topic you just read about.

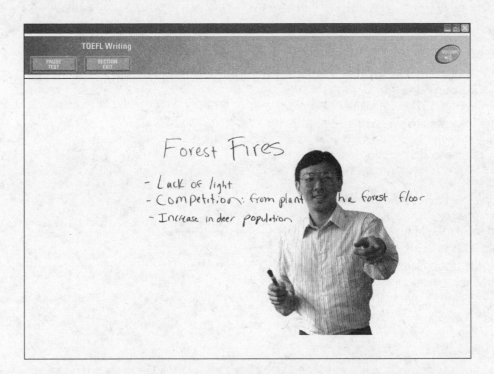

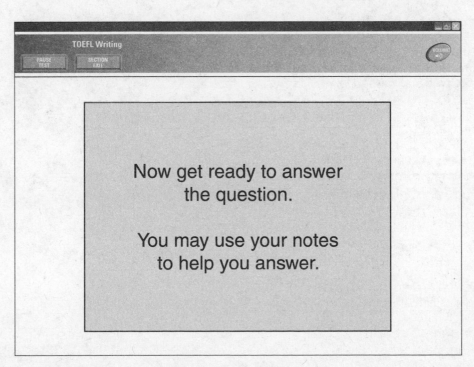

Directions: You have 20 minutes to plan and write your response. Your response will be graded on the quality of your writing and on how well your response presents the points in the lecture and their relationship to the reading passage. Typically, an effective response will be 150 to 225 words.

Question: Summarize the points made in the lecture you just heard, explaining how they cast doubt on the contents of reading. You may refer to the passage as you write.

Copy   Cut   Paste   Word Count: 0

Wilderness management has advanced greatly over the last century, due in part to such practices as the suppression of forest fires and limitations on the clear-cutting of trees. Monitoring forests for small brushfires is easier with aircraft, as is the use of large amounts of water and sophisticated chemical fire extinguishers to prevent fires from spreading.

The goals of decreasing the amount of destruction by fires and cutting are wide-ranging. One is simply the longer lives and improved health of trees. In some areas of hickory and oak forest on the Eastern Seaboard, fire suppression has allowed the maturation of so many trees that the treetops form a continuous canopy.

There is evidence of the healthful effects of fire suppression closer to the ground as well. Vines and low bushes that would be burned out in a forest fire can flourish when fires are suppressed, of course, but there is a more indirect way fires harm plant life. Chemical tests on areas that have recently experienced forest fires demonstrate that burning decreases the overall amount of nutrients in the soil. Suppressing fires prevents such a decrease. Ferns, wildflowers, and herbs grow without disturbance.

Finally, wildlife can benefit. In the eastern hickory and oak forests, the suppression of fires has meant that forest animals—ranging from small insects and birds to large deer and bears—are not burned to death. Deer populations, in particular, have increased notably.

Writing 2

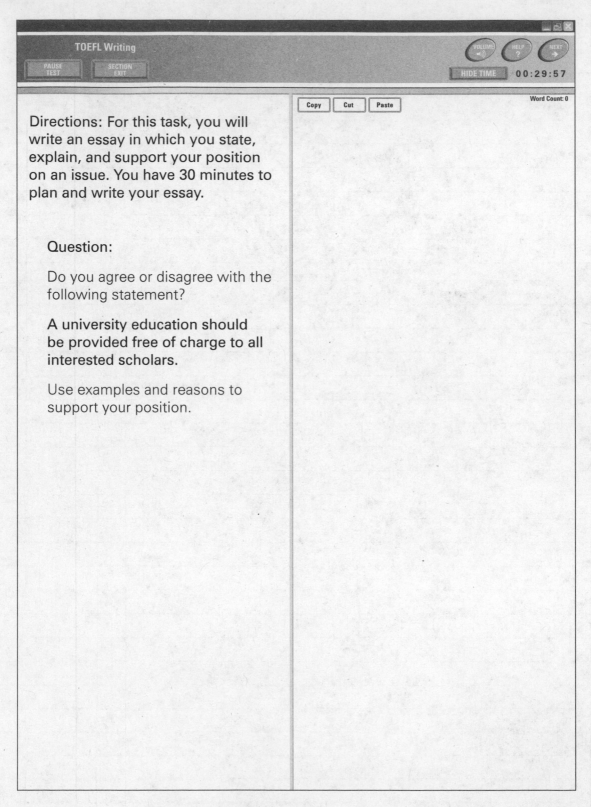

Directions: For this task, you will write an essay in which you state, explain, and support your position on an issue. You have 30 minutes to plan and write your essay.

Question:

Do you agree or disagree with the following statement?

A university education should be provided free of charge to all interested scholars.

Use examples and reasons to support your position.

Chapter 19
Answer Key

READING

1. C
2. A
3. C
4. B
5. D
6. D
7. A
8. C
9. D
10. B
11. A
12. See explanations
13. A
14. C
15. D
16. A
17. D
18. B
19. B
20. A
21. C
22. B
23. D
24. C
25. B
26. See explanations
27. B
28. A
29. D
30. C
31. D
32. C
33. B
34. D
35. A
36. D
37. A, See explanations
38. See explanations
39. See explanations

LISTENING

1. B
2. B, D
3. C
4. A
5. B
6. B
7. C
8. B
9. A
10. B
11. D
12. C
13. A
14. C
15. B
16. D
17. See explanations
18. C
19. D
20. A
21. B, D, E
22. B
23. C
24. D
25. C
26. A
27. D
28. B
29. D
30. D
31. A
32. A, B
33. B
34. C

Because the Speaking and Writing section questions are not multiple choice, see the explanations in the next chapter for how these questions may be answered.

Chapter 20
Answers and
Explanations

THE READING SECTION

Reading Passage #1: The Veneration of Trees

1.   **C**   Refer back to the first paragraph for the answer to this question. The text says

> It was not a great mental leap for people to see the trees that populated them as embodiments of the natural forces that governed their lives.

Answer choice (C) is the only choice close in meaning to these lines. Here's why the other choices are incorrect.

- Fortunately, neither (A) nor (B) is mentioned at all in this paragraph.
- Answer choice (D) is a trap. Although the paragraph does say that the veneration of trees united people, this is not how people viewed the trees.

2.   **A**   Here is the line in question.

> The woods that covered large areas of Europe and North America, particularly, were difficult to _____ and dangerous to cross.

We should look for an answer that refers to woods that are "dangerous to cross." *Enter* is closest in meaning to "cross." The other answer choices are not close in meaning to the word *cross*.

3.   **C**   This question asks us, *Why does the author mention Druids?* Go back to the second paragraph and read the lines about Druids.

> It is known that both the Celtic and the Germanic tribes that inhabited ancient Northern Europe regarded certain trees as sacred, setting them apart by species (as the Druids worshipped oaks)…

These lines tell us that the Druids "worshipped oaks," which is what choice (C) states. Here's why the other answer choices are incorrect.

- Eliminate choice (A) because the author has not introduced the other two stages yet.
- And (B) and (D) are not mentioned in relationship to Druids.

4.   **B**   Let's look at the lines referred to in the question for a clue to the answer.

> These taboos were taken very seriously. In some places, one could be punished _____ for injuring the bark of a tree or stealing its fruit.

According to these lines, the taboos were taken "seriously." Therefore, the word we need in the blank should mean "seriously." Answer choice (B) is best. Here's why the other answer choices are incorrect.

- There is no mention of how often the punishment took place, so eliminate (A) and (C), both of which pertain to time.
- Also, the lines do not say that the punishment was "secret," so eliminate (D).

5. **D** For a NOT question, return to the passage and look for evidence for each answer. If you're having trouble figuring out where to look, remember that the questions appear roughly in the sequence of the passage. Here's each answer choice, with the corresponding lines of text that contradict each choice, thereby eliminating them.

    (A) "Before a tree was felled for human use, woodcutters in many world cultures would offer it both apologies and thanks for the resources it was about to provide them."

    (B) "In some places, one could be punished severely for injuring the bark of a tree or stealing its fruit."

    (C) "In some societies, it was claimed that trees cry out in pain when struck or cut into."

    (D) This is not in the passage, so this is the correct answer.

6. **D** This question asks, *What is the distinction in the second stage of tree worship?* That means the answer is where the passage discusses the "second stage of tree worship." Here are the lines we need.

    > It is not bound to a single tree but rather stands for a group. The distinction may seem small, but it is a significant first step toward symbolic thinking.

    These lines say that the distinction is not a "single tree" but a "group," which is a paraphrase of (D). The other choices are not mentioned as a distinction in the paragraph.

7. **A** Once again, we need to look at the lines around the shaded word and look for a clue to its meaning. Take a look at these lines.

    > The same spirit may thus take up residence in any tree of a forest; it is not killed when an individual tree is cut down. It is not bound to a single tree but rather stands for a group.

    These lines say that the spirit does not take up "residence" in a "single" tree. This is the type of word we need for our answer. Therefore, "limited to," choice (A), makes sense with a "single" tree. Here's why the other choices are incorrect.

    - Although answer (B) may be tempting, it's a trap. The lines do not say that the spirit is "hidden" inside the tree.
    - Answers (C) and (D) do not have this meaning, so eliminate them.

8. **C** The question asks us, *Why does the author use this phrase?* Return to the passage to see these lines.

    > To think about a tree spirit identified with the forest as a whole, therefore, people had to think about phenomena that were removed from them in time and space—ideas rather than things. Such a tree spirit represented the potential and abstract rather than the concrete and immediate.

    These lines tell us that people had to think of things that were "removed from them in time and space." The spirits also represent "the potential and abstract." Both these lines point to choice (C) as the answer. Here's why the other choices are incorrect.

    - These lines do not mention danger, so eliminate answer (A).
    - Similarly, these lines do not say the people stopped fearing the forest, so answer (B) is incorrect.
    - Answer (D) is extreme and also not mentioned.

9. **D** This is an *inference* question, asking us about the "most complex" phase of tree worship. We should look in the last paragraph, where the author talks about "complexity." Here are the appropriate lines.

> Liberated from each other, trees and their spirits can begin to be seen as symbols and embodiments of other natural processes of significance to primitive life: the power of weather and seasons to produce good or bad harvests, the mysteries of child-birth and disease. At that point, the veneration of trees reaches its stage of greatest complexity.

Also, later in the paragraph, it states: "The appearance of these beliefs…indicates that a society has made its first steps toward symbolic and abstract thinking." Thus, answer choice (D), which talks of trees as "symbols" is best. Here's why the other choices are incorrect.

- Eliminate (A) because it is extreme—there is no information about "all" trees provided.
- Male and female tree spirits are not mentioned, so answer choice (B) must be wrong.
- And no evidence is offered about different "ceremonies" for different seasons, so eliminate choice (C).

10. **B** Read the following sentence for the clue to this question:

> Societies in both Eastern Europe and the South Pacific presented ceremonial offerings to trees in the hopes that they would furnish rain and sunshine.

This says that the societies "presented offerings" to the trees. Thus, we should look for a word that is similar in meaning to this. The best match is answer choice (B). Here's why the other choices are incorrect.

- Answer choice (A) doesn't make sense in this sentence.
- Answers (C) and (D) are the opposite of what we need.

11. **A** Return to paragraph five for the answer to this question. It may be best to use POE on the answer choices.

- The second answer refers to the "three stages" of a tree. But the paragraph is about the third stage of the *people's beliefs,* not *the tree.* So eliminate (B).
- Answer choice (C) talks about trees that required "little" rain or sun. But the only mention of rain and sunshine states that people asked trees to provide rain and sunshine. Therefore, choice (C) is wrong.
- The final answer choice mentions trees "raised by women." The paragraph says that women "embraced" trees, but it doesn't say they "raised" them.
- Thus, answer choice (A) is the correct choice.

12. From the previous question and any active reading you've done, you may have noted that the main idea of the passage is the three stages of tree veneration. Here's the correctly completed chart.

> Three basic levels of tree worship can be observed in *The Golden Bough*.

- Some societies believed each tree had an individual spirit, the way a human being has a distinct mind.

- Certain peoples came to believe that tree spirits were independent of individual trees and instead represented a whole forest.
- A basis for abstract thinking was achieved when tree spirits were believed to control natural forces such as crops and human fertility.

Here's why the other choices are incorrect.
- "It was forbidden to cut down certain trees because they would be seriously offended by an injury" is wrong because it only mentions a detail about one of the stages.
- "More is known about the ceremonies of Europe than about the ceremonies of North America and the South Pacific" is wrong because it talks about ceremonies, not stages of belief.
- "Ancient Germans believed certain groves were sacred and used them as temples, but Druids venerated the oak tree in particular" is also a specific detail that is mentioned only once in the passage.

Reading Passage #2: Daguerreotypes

13. **A** This is an *inference* question. Feel free to skip it and do any easier questions first and come back to it later. The answer to this question is in the following lines:

> Today, the surviving photographs produced by these methods are often referred to as daguerreotypes, but that designation is incorrect.

Answer choice (A) is correct because it refers to this inaccuracy. Here's why the other choices are incorrect.
- Eliminate choices (B) and (D) because they use the extreme words *most* and *first*.
- It is not clear from the paragraph whether (C) is true or not, so eliminate it. Remember that the answer to an inference question must be true.

14. **C** This question is a bit tougher than some of the others we've seen. Here are the lines we need.

> By its strictest definition, the daguerreotype process was common for not more than 20 years in the mid-1800s. Other ways of making photographic images on metal plates, such as tintypes and ferrotypes, were developed rapidly after the advent of the daguerreotype.

These lines say that the daguerreotype process was "common for…20 years" and that "other ways… developed rapidly." So we need a word that means the daguerreotype process didn't last a long time. Choice (C) is closest in meaning. None of the other answers fits, and watch out for answer choice (D), it is a trap.

15. **D** To answer this question, we need to go to the following lines:

> The materials it required were both expensive—the plates contained silver and one of the developing solutions contained gold—and extremely risky. Strict adherence to proper laboratory procedure was necessary in order to avoid poisoning by noxious gases.

According to the lines above, the materials were "extremely risky" and could cause "poisoning by noxious gases." Therefore, the author must be referring to choice (D), the dangers of daguerreotype making. Here's why the other choices are incorrect.
- There are no "true scientists" mentioned, so eliminate choice (A).
- Nor does the author talk about "other fields," so choice (B) is wrong.
- Answer choice (C) is wrong because the "laboratory procedure" is not an example of an "expensive material."

16. **A** Look back at the third paragraph, focusing on the part about "dust." It says

> Since even one speck of dust could easily create a deep enough groove to render the final image worthless, they had to be perfectly buffed.

The author says the dust can make the final image "worthless." That makes choice (A) correct. Here's why the other choices are incorrect.
- What people prefer is not mentioned, so eliminate choice (B).
- The lines do not talk about making chemicals "stick" to the surface, which means that choice (C) is incorrect.
- Finally, the paragraph states that the layer of bromo-iodine makes the plates more sensitive, not the buffing. Thus, choice (D) is wrong.

17. **D** Here are the lines we need for this question.

> After exposure, the plates were dipped alternately in heated mercury and freezing-cold water. The mercury vapors helped fix the images to the plates and developed them.

We need a word that describes what happens "after exposure" and before the pictures are "developed." The only answer that makes sense is choice (D). This is also a good question on which to use POE.
- Choice (A) is a trap answer because a different meaning of "fix" is synonymous with "correct," but this is not the meaning of "fix" that is used in this passage. The lines discuss the initial process, not repairing the pictures.
- There is no support for "cut" or "brighten" either.

18. **B** Treat this question just like the *vocabulary in context* questions at which we've looked. Go back to the following lines:

> The mercury vapors helped fix the images to the plates and developed them. The chilled water kept the plates from breaking up during _____.

The author is describing the process. What step is being detailed? The "fixing and developing" part. That is our answer. Here's why the other choices are incorrect.
- Choices (A) and (C) are not part of the process described.
- The hydrosulfate soda appears "next" in the process, so eliminate choice (D).

19. **B** This is another *inference* question. Go back to the paragraph, and look for what the author says about "mercury." The passage states

After exposure, the plates were dipped alternately in heated mercury and freezing-cold water. The mercury vapors helped fix the images to the plates and developed them. The chilled water kept the plates from breaking up during this critical step.

These are the only lines about mercury, so the answer must be here. The only answer choice that matches is (B). Here's why the other choices are incorrect.

- These lines do not mention "bromo-iodine," so eliminate (A).
- The author talked about "noxious" vapors in the *previous* paragraph, not here. That means (C) is wrong.
- Choice (D) is contradicted in the passage because it states that the mercury is used "after exposure."

20. **A** This question asks you to figure out to whom the author is referring. The passage says

Only the rich could easily afford to sit for a daguerreotype portrait. For those of _____, a daguerreotype was a once-in-a-lifetime treat.

The clue here is "only the rich could…afford…a daguerreotype." Therefore, the answer should refer to people who are not rich. Only choice (A) refers to these people. None of the other answers is mentioned.

21. **C** Here are the lines that answer this question.

Chairs and tables with special support were designed to help those posing for portraits to remain absolutely still throughout the exposure time. If they did not, the resulting image would be blurred.

Here's why the other choices are incorrect.

- Answer choices (A) and (B) are contradicted by the passage, which states that the exposure time was long and that there was no way to stop people from blinking.
- And choice (D) is not mentioned at all.

22. **B** If you're not sure of the vocabulary in this question save the choices with words you don't know and use POE to get rid of as many as possible. The paragraph states

The process recorded textural detail with a realism that still seems shocking. The sheen of satin and the dull, heavy nap of flannel are easily distinguished.

Here's how to use POE.

- These lines do not mention color, so (A) is eliminated.
- Choices (C) and (D) refer to people, not satin and flannel, so eliminate them.
- That leaves only (B).

23. **D** Go to paragraph seven, and use the answer choices as a checklist.
    (A)   "…and the resulting photographs were less fragile than daguerreotypes." *Less fragile* pertains to *durability*.
    (B)   "Iron plates were also much less expensive than copper plates…." *Less expensive* is synonymous with *low cost*.

(C) "…they could be exposed and developed very quickly." Obviously, *very quickly* pertains to *speed*.

(D) This is not mentioned in the paragraph, so this is the correct answer: This is the exception.

24. **C** Return to the passage, and look at the following:

> Ferrotypes became popular with photographers who set up stalls at street fairs and inexpensive resorts because _____ could be exposed and developed very quickly.

What is it that can be "exposed and developed very quickly?" Let's use POE.
- Hopefully, it is not photographers, so eliminate (A).
- Choices (B) and (D) don't make any sense: They pertain to *where* the exposures were done, but not to *what* is being exposed, which is what the question is asking.

25. **B** This question asks about the type of storage space for ferrotypes. Here are the lines we need.

> On the other hand, iron, unlike copper, could rust if not properly stored. Many old ferrotypes were destroyed by long-term display in hot and moist environments.

These lines say that "hot and moist" places destroy ferrotypes. Thus, we want the opposite. This is answer choice (B). The other choices do not work because they have nothing to do with the *temperature* of the environments.

26. Use your understanding of the main idea and the previous questions to answer this one. The passage describes daguerreotypes, gives some of their problems, and states that they were replaced. Here are the correct answers.

> The daguerreotype was a kind of photography that was briefly popular before being replaced by other methods.
>
> - The daguerreotype process used dangerous chemicals and inconvenienced people posing for pictures.
> - The images in daguerreotypes were realistic and detailed, so people looked for easier ways to produce them.
> - The ferrotype was less expensive and more durable than the daguerreotype and became a popular substitute.

These answers match pretty well with the summary above. Here's why the other choices are incorrect.
- "Some daguerreotypes have lasted long enough to be enjoyed today" is wrong because it doesn't fit with the main idea of daguerreotypes eventually being replaced. It also refers to only "some" daguerreotypes, meaning it is a fairly *minor detail.*
- "Daguerreotypes had to be brushed with gold and chlorine to make the images brighter than they would otherwise be" gives a specific *detail* about the process, but it doesn't fit into *the main idea*. It simply explains how daguerreotypes are processed.
- "Many photographers preferred to continue using the daguerreotype process even after alternatives were introduced" also *contradicts the main idea*. The point is that the daguerreotype was eventually replaced by other types.

Reading Passage #3: Hormones in the Body

27.　**B**　This *vocabulary in context* question refers to the lines below.

> Until the beginning of the twentieth century, the nervous system was thought to control all communication within the body and the resulting integration of behavior...These impulses were thought to be the engine for thought, emotion, movement, and internal processes such as digestion.

These lines make it clear that the nervous system was believed to "control all communication." We need a word that shows that all things are *connected* to the nervous system. Choice (B) is the only match. Here's why the other choices are incorrect.
- Choices (A) and (C) don't make sense.
- Choice (D) is contradicted by the lines stating that the nervous system is *electrical,* not chemical.

28.　**A**　Look at the following lines:

> From the small intestine, secretin travels through the bloodstream to the pancreas. There, _____ stimulates the release of digestive chemicals.

The shaded word refers to the noun that "stimulates the release of...chemicals." That can only be secretin, answer choice (A). Here's why the other answer choices are incorrect.
- The small intestine, choice (B), doesn't "stimulate the release of...chemicals."
- Nor does the pancreas, choice (D).
- The secretin does travel through the bloodstream, choice (C), but the bloodstream doesn't release chemicals.

29.　**D**　This is another *vocabulary in context* question. These are the key lines.

> Bayliss and Starling showed that it could occur through chemicals alone. This discovery _____ Starling to coin the term *hormone* to refer to secretin...

Try to put in your own word for the blank. The discovery "resulted" in a new word. This makes (D) the best choice. Here's why the other choices are incorrect.
- There is nothing in the sentence about memory, so eliminate choice (A).
- The lines do not say that Starling was "surprised," so (B) is out.
- "Invented" in choice (C) may refer to the new word (*hormone*), but the blank is referring to what Starling did.

30.　**C**　Use the word "hormone" to lead you to the correct answer. The author states

> This discovery spurred Starling to coin the term *hormone* to refer to secretin, taking it from the Greek word *hormon,* meaning "to excite" or "to set in motion." A hormone is a chemical produced by one tissue to make things happen elsewhere.

Thus, a hormone is something that "makes things happen elsewhere," which means the same thing as answer choice (C). Here's why the other choices are incorrect.

- Answer choice (A) is not part of the definition of a hormone.
- Choice (B) is partially correct, but the problem is that it only refers to the "nervous system."
- These lines do not mention attitudes and behavior, so (D) is wrong.

31. **D** This question wants to know how the hormones are categorized. The answer is in the following lines:

> As more hormones were discovered, they were categorized, primarily according to the process by which they operated on the body. Some glands (which make up the endocrine system) secrete hormones directly into the bloodstream…The exocrine system consists of organs and glands that produce substances that are used outside the bloodstream, primarily for digestion.

It appears that the main difference is whether the hormones are dispensed into the bloodstream or not, which is what choice (D) states. Here's why the other choices are incorrect.
- The issue is not whether scientists understand the function or not, as in choice (A).
- The passage doesn't talk about how frequently the hormones work, so (B) is wrong.
- The aging process, the subject of choice (C), is not mentioned at all.

32. **C** We need to look at these lines to answer this question.

> Some play such _____ roles in regulating bodily processes or behavior that their absence would cause immediate death.

It says that without the hormones, the result could be "immediate death." That means the hormones are very important. Answer (C) is the best match, whereas none of the other choices is close.

33. **B** This question is tougher because you have to pay attention to a trigger word. The passage states

> Even _____ amounts of the right chemicals can suppress appetite, calm aggression, and change the attitude of a parent toward a child.

The sentence describes some very powerful effects—calming aggression, changing attitudes—and the word *even* means that we need something opposite of these major changes; choice (B), *small* comes closest to the opposite of *major*. Here's why the other choices are incorrect.
- Answer choice (A), *sudden* is not the opposite of *major* or *powerful*.
- Nor is choice (C), *seconds*. This is a trap answer; if you didn't read the lines in the passage, you might think that *minute* was referring to a unit of time.
- Answer choice (D) is the opposite of what we're looking for because *noticeable* is somewhat similar to *major*.

34. **D** This is a paraphrase question. Remember to trim the fat.

> …hormones have effects that are less…urgent but can be…far-reaching and difficult to track: They modify moods and affect human behavior…

The basic idea is that hormones can have a strong effect on human behavior. So let's use POE.
- Eliminate (A) because it has the wrong subject. The sentence is not about moods and behavior; it's about "hormones."
- Answer choice (B) also wrongly focuses on "scientists" when it should focus on "hormones."

- Choice (C) introduces "psychological damage," which is not part of the original sentence.
- Thus, (D) is the best choice.

35. **A** The answer to this question is in the following lines:

> Some proponents of HRT have _____ their enthusiasm in the face of this new evidence, recommending it only to patients whose symptoms interfere with their abilities to live normal lives.

If the proponents now recommend HRT "only" to a small group of patients, their enthusiasm for it must have decreased. This makes (A) the best choice. Here's why the other choices are incorrect.
- There is no mention of advertising, so (B) is wrong.
- And the shaded word refers to "enthusiasm," not HRT, so choices (C) and (D) make no sense.

36. **D** To answer this question, we need to look at the final paragraph. It states that

> Because of the complicated effects growth hormone has on the body, such treatments are generally restricted to children who would be pathologically small in stature without it.

Now use POE.
- Because the treatment is for children, eliminate answers (A) and (B), which pertain to adults only.
- And eliminate (C) because it contradicts the passage, which states that the treatment is risky no matter who the patient is.
- Thus, (D) is correct.

37. **A** This question asks us to find the purpose of hormone therapy. Here are the choices.

> The quantities and proportions of hormones produced change with age, so scientists have given a great deal of study to shifts in the endocrine system over time in the **hopes of alleviating ailments associated with aging.**

This is the correct answer because the purpose is to "alleviate ailments associated with aging."

Here's why the other choices are incorrect.

> A combination of estrogen and progesterone has been prescribed for decades to women who want to reduce mood swings, sudden changes in body temperature, and other discomforts caused by lower natural levels of those hormones as they enter middle age.

This answer is incorrect because it refers to a *specific type* of hormone treatment (estrogen and progesterone), not the overall *purpose* of the therapy.

> HRT may also increase the likelihood that blood clots—dangerous because they could travel through the bloodstream and block major blood vessels—will form.

This answer also refers to only one type of hormone. Furthermore, it describes the *problems* with it, again, not the purpose of hormone therapy.

- • Because of the complicated effects growth hormone has on the body, such treatments are generally restricted to children who would be pathologically small in stature without it.

This answer also talks about *problems* with the therapy, again, rather than the purpose of hormone therapy.

38. **C** This sentence should be inserted here.

Known as hormone replacement therapy (HRT), the treatment was also believed to prevent weakening of the bones. **The body is a complex machine, however, and recent studies have called into question the wisdom of essentially trying to fool its systems into believing they aren't aging.** At least one study has linked HRT with a heightened risk of heart disease and certain types of cancer.

This is the best place because the new sentence talks about "recent studies," which are mentioned in the next sentence. It also uses the word *however* to indicate a transition from the first sentence, which discusses a positive aspect of the treatment, to the other sentence, which mentions a negative.

39. This passage focuses on the discovery of hormones, what they do, and what new medical techniques may result from them. This corresponds to the following correct answers:

The class of chemicals called *hormones* was discovered by two researchers studying a substance produced in the small intestine.

- • Scientists have discovered that not only the nervous system but also certain chemicals can affect bodily processes far from their points of origin.
- • Hormones can affect not only life processes such as growth but also behavior and emotion.
- • Researchers are looking for ways to decrease the dangers of treatments with growth hormone so that more patients can benefit from it.

Here's why the other choices are incorrect.
- • The first wrong answer is "The term *hormone* is based on a Greek word that means 'to excite' or 'to set in motion.'" This choice is wrong because it only details the origin of the word; it has nothing to do with hormones or how they work.
- • "Hormones can be given artificially, but such treatments have risks and must be used carefully" is wrong because it is too specific. It mentions hormone treatment, but it focuses on the risks.
- • "Hormone replacement therapy (HRT) may increase the risk of blood clots and heart disease in middle-age women" is wrong because it mentions problems for only one small group of people, a detail that doesn't belong in the main idea.

THE LISTENING SECTION

Listening 1

Here is a transcript of the conversation (Track 24 on the accompanying CD). Pay attention to the structure and main idea/purpose.

N: Listen to part of a conversation at a university library.

M: Hi. May I speak to the...uh, the archives librarian?

W: I'm the archives librarian. What can I help you with?

M: Well, actually, I'm not a student here. I'm studying history at State U. across town, but there's a collection of—

W: Oh, wait. Are you the...sorry, I don't remember your name, but the librarian over there asked me about giving someone access to the Jacobson collection. Is that you?

M: Yes, that's right. See, my paper is on the development of the coal-mining industry here in the city, and the Jacobson collection has a lot of information about John Jacobson...like, when he founded the company and things, right?

W: Yes, it does. More than you'll be able to fit into a paper, I'd bet. Did your librarian explain what our system is here?

M: A little. She told me to make sure I brought my college ID so I could get in the door.

W: Yes, well, I'll need to take a copy of it too. Even our own students who look at items from our archive collections have to leave a copy of their ID with us. You'll also have to sign into the archives room whenever you enter and sign out whenever you leave. There's a desk. You know, for security.

M: Wow. So a lot of this stuff is valuable?

W: Hmm. Well, I don't know whether you'd get much money for it, but a lot of it is one-of-a-kind, so if it were taken...that's it. It'd be gone.

M: I'll be careful.

W: Thank you. The other thing is, the things in the Jacobson collection are more than 100 years old, so I'll have to ask you to wear special gloves while handling the books. Also, I'm afraid you won't be able to photocopy anything.

M: I figured that. I ought to...I mean, I can probably get everything I need on note cards, but suppose there's a page or two I really want a copy of? Can I...I don't know, take a picture, or something?

W: Well, I can't let you take a picture. But we have scans...images...of all the pages in the collection. You can buy a print of any page you want, but they're expensive—five dollars a piece. So be sure you know which pages you want before you ask for them.

M: Five dollars! Well, I guess given how rare these things are... Okay, so you want a copy of my ID, and then can you tell me how to get to the archives room so I can get started?

1. **B** The man states the topic of his paper in his third statement. Here's why the other choices are incorrect.
    *   If you were unsure and had to guess, choice (A) would be a good choice to avoid because it is a trap—the student needs to *use* old books for his paper, but the paper isn't *about* old books.
    *   Eliminate answers (C) and (D). These two subjects were not mentioned at all in the discussion.

2. **B** and **D**

    The librarian tells the man "I'll need to take a copy of it [his ID]" and at the end of the conversation, she tells him he'll have to sign in and out of the archives room. Here's why the other choices are incorrect.
    *   Choice (A) is incorrect because the woman never said that the man has to show her his notes.
    *   The five-dollar fee was for copying images, not entering the room, which is why choice (C) is incorrect.

3. **C** The librarian says "a lot of it [the archival material] is one-of-a-kind, so if it were taken...that's it. It'd be gone." Here's why the other choices are incorrect.
    *   Answer choice (B) is the opposite of what the woman said: "Well, I don't know if you'd get much money for it..."
    *   Choices (A) and (D) were not mentioned in the conversation.

4. **A** The librarian mentions the age of the books to explain why the student needs to wear gloves to handle them. Here's why the other choices are incorrect.
    *   Eliminate answer choice (B) because it is extreme; it says that the man can "only" look at photographs, whereas he can actually buy a print of any page he wants.
    *   Answer choice (D), again, is the opposite of what the woman said about the value of the books (see the explanation of question 3).

5. **B** This question asks you to listen again to the following part of the conversation and to determine what the man meant in part of it (highlighted below):

    W: Well, I can't let you take a picture. But we have scans...images...of all the pages in the collection. You can buy a print of any page you want, but they're expensive—five dollars a piece. So be sure you know which pages you want before you ask for them.

    M: Five dollars! **Well, I guess given how rare these things are...**

Choice B is correct because the man admits "...given how rare these things are..." Here's why the other choices are incorrect.

- Eliminate answer choices (A) and (C) because they have nothing to do with money.
- Answer choice (D) is not mentioned by the man.

Listening 2

Here is a transcript of the lecture (Track 25 on the accompanying CD).

N: Listen to a professor lecture on the process of memory.

P: A popular saying goes, "An elephant never forgets." But how about people? Have you ever forgotten the name of someone you just met at a party? Sure, we all have. This is because our memories are complex processes.

We're not going to be able to talk much about the physiology of memory here...both because, well, it's not our subject, and because there's a lot we still need to learn about how the brain stores things. One thing we do know is that the mechanism isn't simple. When researchers scan the brain as a memory is forming, parts seem to light up—by "light up" I mean, you know, become active—in random, scattered formations. But of course they can't be random because memory produces very orderly results.

One researcher...this is Walter Freeman of the University of California at Berkeley... compares it to two kinds of crowds. The impulses in the brain look completely random, like the movement of a mob of people who are frightened. You know, they just keep moving, and they're not really going anywhere, and there's no pattern to their movement. That's the way impulses in the brain look at first. But since memory does, in fact, work, the impulses must be moving more like people in a crowded train station. You know, if you've got people running in and out and from one train line to another, it seems like complete confusion. But really they all know where they're going. They're following a set of instructions—the timetable for the trains, the board that tells which track is for which train, all that stuff. So you have to look carefully to see that there's actually organization, a system, involved. That's how memory impulses must function. Freeman figures we just haven't figured out what the timetable and track numbers are!

So we'll leave the physiology there; we're going to talk about the psychology of memory... the actual process. Psychologists divide memory into three stages: registration, long-term retention, and recall.

In the initial stage, registration, information is perceived and understood, like when you first hear a name or address. This information is then retained in the short-term memory system. Unfortunately, the short-term memory is limited in the amount of material it can store at one time. And, unless refreshed by constant repetition, the new contents are lost within minutes when replaced by even newer information. To solve this dilemma, the information needs to be transformed into the second stage, long-term retention.

The conversion to the long-term retention stage is most easily accomplished using what the research team labeled association. Associating the new information with the visual imagery evoked by it gives the individual a sort of "memory" crutch to rely on. For example, let's say you're at a party, and you've just met a woman named Lily. To remember her name, visualize it in connection to the flower, the lily. Oh, and be sure to make it outlandish...kind of silly, even. Those images are most memorable. Picture her with a big basket of lilies, or wearing a hat with a lily on it, or even sitting inside a giant lily.

The third stage, recall, is when the information stored—stored through long-term retention—at an unconscious level is then deliberately brought into the conscious mind. However, this final stage primarily depends on how well the material was stored in stage two. Of course, there are disturbances that may affect the recall stage—age, for example. The older a person gets, the less new information he can recall. Disuse is another example. Here, forgetting occurs because stored information is not used and, therefore, is lost. Memory loss can also be physiological. If a person receives an injury to the head, he may experience what is known as *amnesia*, the failure to remember certain or even all events preceding the accident.

Of course, many self-help books on how to improve your memory have been published, and many other mnemonic methods have been tried and tested. Let's take a closer look at some of the more widely accepted approaches to memory enhancement. Perhaps you may even incorporate some of them into your study habits as you prepare for the upcoming finals.

6. **B** Here's why the other choices are incorrect.
   - And choice (A) wrongly focuses on "events" instead of memory.
   - Answer (C) is also a good candidate for POE because animals are not the main focus.
   - Eliminate answer choice (D) because the professor doesn't mention this topic (of how to strengthen memory) until the very end of the lecture.

7. **C** Here's why the other choices are incorrect.
   - You may have recalled that the information in choice (A) doesn't appear until later in the lecture.
   - For this question, answer choice (B) is not related to the main idea, so eliminate it—this idea of "direction" was used only in the crowded train station analogy.
   - Answer choice (D) is extreme; it says that each person has a "unique" way of remembering things.

8. **B** This is a question in which there isn't much you can do if you missed the part of the lecture that gives the definition. (The three stages were "registration, long-term retention, and recall" and were first introduced, then each stage was discussed in detail.) If you did miss this, just guess and move on.

9. **A** This question asks you to listen again to the following part of the lecture:

   For example, let's say you've just met a woman named Lily. To remember her name, visualize it in connection to the flower, the lily. Oh, and be sure to make it outlandish... kind of silly, even. Those images are most memorable. Picture her with a big basket of lilies, or wearing a hat with a lily on it, or even sitting inside a giant lily.

Here's why the other choices are incorrect.

- Choice (B) is extreme; eliminate it: The "lily" example was exactly that—an example, not a recommendation of how to help one's memory by thinking of something from nature.
- Answer choice (C) wrongly focuses on the specifies of the example rather than the point of the professor's illustration.
- Answer choice (D) has nothing to do with remembering a person's name.

10. **B** Toward the end of the lecture, the professor talks about the "disturbances" that may affect the recall of stored memories. He says: "Disuse.... Here forgetting occurs because stored information is not used and, therefore, is lost," which supports answer choice (B). Here's why the other choices are incorrect.

- Choices (A) and (C) are not mentioned by the professor (note that brain injury, the topic of (C) *is* mentioned, but only in the context of amnesia).
- Answer choice (D) is the opposite of what is stated in the lecture. ("The older a person gets, the less new information he or she can recall.")

11. **D** The professor ends the lecture with these words: "Let's take a closer look at some of the more widely accepted approaches to memory enhancement. Perhaps you may even incorporate some of them into your study habits as you prepare for the upcoming finals."

Here's why the other choices are incorrect.

- Choices (A) and (C) are not mentioned.
- Eliminate choice (B) because it has nothing to do with the main idea.

Listening 3

Here is a transcript of the class discussion (Track 26 on the accompanying CD).

N: Listen to part of a class discussion on the different types of joints.

P: Now, I know that most of you are healthy individuals who participate in some sort of physical activity pretty regularly. Some of you jog, others bicycle, you might throw around the Frisbee with your friends, or Rollerblade. Our movements are so easy and fluid that you may not have stopped to think that the system of joints that makes them possible is highly complex. A joint is the place where two or more bones connect, and because that's the technical definition, it actually includes some places that don't move. Since it's movement that we're interested in, I won't spend much time on the immovable joints. They're called fibrous joints. The reason is that...uh, well, they're joined together by bone fibers. It's kind of like welding or soldering two pieces of metal together. **There are fibrous joints, for example, between the different bones that make up the top part of your skull. The bones don't move, right? I'm talking about the top of your head—forget your jaw for a second. If your jaw had a fibrous joint, you couldn't talk!** The round dome of the skull is made of several bone plates with fibers holding them together.

Okay, so those are the fibrous joints. The other joints, the ones we're interested in, are movable. In a movable joint, the bones aren't fused to each other. They're held together with ligaments. Ligaments are long and flexible; they're kind of like ropes or cables. But because the bones have to slide or rub over each other when the joint moves, it also needs to be cushioned against abrasion. These joints are categorized by the types of tissues used to keep them working smoothly.

Cartilaginous joints have a tough, smooth lining over the parts of the bone. It's like a pad or cushion; it protects the bone from friction that could wear it down or cause it to splinter. And, in fact, if this cartilage—the protective tissue is called cartilage—if it becomes worn or damaged, joint movement may be painful or severely restricted because now you have bone hitting bone. That's because cartilaginous joints are tight; the bones fit very closely together—for example, the bones in your spine.

Some joints require more movement. They're called synovial joints. There has to be a space between the bones, a joint cavity. Those more mobile joints, in addition to being padded with cartilage, are lubricated with liquid that flows through the cavity. The knuckles of your fingers are examples of synovial joints. Of course, the fluid has to be held in place, otherwise it'll seep into the surrounding tissues and be absorbed back into the body, and what holds it in place is a little membrane-lined sac called a bursa. So the joint is encased in this membrane, and the membrane is a pocket for that lubricating fluid. By the way, the fluid also keeps the joint nourished—it doesn't have an independent blood supply in adults, so the fluid absorbs nutrients from the blood through the joint's outer membrane. That's a synovial joint.

Tony, do you have a question?

M: Yeah, I'm kind of confused. When we learned about the joints in high school, I don't remember talking about them this way. I thought we talked about them more like machines...uh, like, the directions in which they moved.

P: Uh-huh, we're getting to that. Okay, now that we have joints categorized by how their surfaces are put together—fibrous, synovial, and cartilaginous—we can talk about how the movable joints actually move. I mentioned your knuckles a few minutes ago, and they're good examples of hinge joints. They work kind of like the hinge on a door, so the joint can flex and extend in one direction only. But hinge joints aren't the only movable joints in the body. The hip, as well as the shoulder, is an example of the ball-and-socket joint. The ball-and-socket joint allows the greatest range of movement, and therefore, it has to be the most anatomically complex. In a ball-and-socket, one bone has a rounded knob at the end, and it fits snugly into the socket, a round cavity, of another bone. The ball-and-socket joint is a type characteristically found in more evolved creatures, such as apes and us humans. It allows you to move through 360 degrees of motion, the way you can wind your arm back before you throw a ball.

While we're at it, can anyone think of another type of joint?

W: Well, I know that when I Rollerblade, I have to turn my head constantly to make sure I don't crash into anyone. But the neck doesn't seem to be an example of either a hinge joint or a ball-and-socket joint.

P: Good example, Louise. The neck is actually a type of pivot joint. Pivot joints permit rotation, the way you can twist your head around. Well, it doesn't go all the way around, but it moves around your neck. It pivots on an axis.

12. **C** Here's why the other choices are incorrect.
    - There is no mention of injuries, so (A) is wrong.
    - Eliminate answer choice (B) because sports are mentioned only at the very beginning of the lecture, as a way of introducing the main topic.
    - Flexibility, choice (D), is not mentioned either.

13. **A** Here's why the other choices are incorrect.
    - Choice (B) regarding ligaments, pertains to the *other* type of joint: movable joints, not fibrous joints.
    - Of the choices, answer (C) is the best candidate for POE. The entire lecture talked about humans, so it wouldn't make sense for (C) to be correct.
    - You can also eliminate choice (D) because of the word "most."

14. **C** This question asks you to listen again to the following part of the discussion:

    There are fibrous joints, for example, between the different bones that make up the top part of your skull. The bones don't move, right? I'm talking about the top of your head—forget your jaw for a second. If your jaw had a fibrous joint, you couldn't talk!

    Here's why the other choices are incorrect.
    - Choice (B) is extreme; it uses the word *best*.
    - Answer (D) is a good trap because the instructor said "forget your jaw…" However, if you're unsure of the correct answer and one choice seems too easy, it's probably a trap.

15. **B** This is a question in which POE doesn't help much. If you didn't quite catch the part of the lecture, take your best guess and move on. If you remember that shoulders and hips are the same type of joint, you can eliminate both of them because you can only choose one answer.

16. **D** The professor stated this at the end of the lecture. Here's why the other choices are incorrect.
    - Cartilage was mentioned earlier in the talk, so eliminate (A).
    - Eliminate (B) because it is too strong—it is unlikely that the joint "cannot" be damaged at all.
    - Eliminate (C) because the professor never says that ball-and-socket joints need to move quickly. He says they allow for the "greatest range of motion."

17. This one's tough. The completed chart is on the next page.

	Synovial	Cartilaginous
A special liquid lubricates and nourishes the joint.	×	
There is no cavity between the bones.		×
The joint is covered with a membrane-lined sac.	×	
Only a lining of smooth tissue protects the bones.		×
The joint has limited movement.		×

Listening 4

Here is a transcript of the class discussion (Track 27 on the accompanying CD).

N: Listen to part of a discussion in a class on English literature.

P: Everyone here? Okay, I hope that you all did the readings for this week. I know it's midterm time, and you're all busy, but Robert Browning is one of the most important poets in the history of English literature. He deserves all your attention. Actually, it's usually not hard to sell Browning on my students, I find—his poetry really draws people in. Uh, so, what did you all think?

W: Well, you're certainly right that it draws you in, but I have to say, it really confused me at first.

P: What was it that confused you?

W: Well, I mean, the poems we've read so far have been—it's like, the poet is just kind of writing the poem. The poems we read by this Browning guy...it took me a few minutes to realize that he was using the voice of some historical character. It was supposed to be someone else speaking.

P: Sure. The reason I assigned this particular set of poems by Browning was so you could see what his most famous style was. He perfected a style called the *dramatic monologue*. And its major features are what you saw in the readings. It's called dramatic because a poem of this type takes place at some sort of dramatic moment in the middle of a story. And a monologue is a long speech given by an individual, right? And so are these poems. You have Browning writing as if he were a different person, usually someone from history, speaking at length. And he talks about something that's happening to him when the poem takes place.

M: Professor, I kind of cheated and looked up information about Browning when I did the readings—I was like Karen; I was really confused at first. It seemed strange that this form of poetry, you know, the dramatic monologue, is so new. Browning only lived in the nineteenth century. Was he really the first person to develop a kind of poetry where he pretended to be someone from history giving a speech? It surprised me to read that.

P: Well, you see, the dramatic monologue is actually a more complex style of poetry than it might seem to be at first. For one thing, a lot of poems are addressed to the world in general, sort of; but a dramatic monologue isn't. The speaker in a dramatic monologue is addressing a particular person involved in the story. So for example in the poem "My Last Duchess," the duke is doing the speaking...and he's specifically speaking to a servant of his future father-in-law. That's important. A lot of the poem doesn't make sense unless you bear in mind that he's trying to give a message to the father of his new wife.

W: It took me a while to figure that out. And then, when I realized what was going on, it really creeped me out. I mean, did I read it right? He seemed to be admitting—

P: Karen, why don't we hold off on analyzing the poem too much for right now. I don't want to shut you down, but I do want to stick to the general structure of the poems for a bit.

I will say that when Karen talks about finding the poem a little spooky, part of that probably comes from the fact that...well, you figure, within the poem, the speaker is talking to someone in particular. So when you read the poem, you kind of take that person's role—the role of the person being addressed. That's one chief characteristic of the dramatic monologue.

Now, obviously, the other thing Karen was probably unsettled by, in the case of "My Last Duchess," is that the duke doesn't sound like a very nice character! We know that because of another key element of the dramatic monologue. What the speaker says is designed to make an argument—he's trying to persuade the listener...and you the reader by extension...that what he did was right, or that his viewpoint is correct, or whatever. He makes a case, kind of like a lawyer with a judge or jury, and in the process he reveals his way of thinking, something of his psychology. And you have to decide whether you believe him.

M: It's kind of hard because—I felt like a lot of the story was missing. The speaker in the poem only told his side of things, and you got the feeling that there had to be more going on, but it was all just guesswork.

P: Now you see why I said the form was complex, huh? Sure. You have to fill in the back story yourself. And that's the third big characteristic of a dramatic monologue. Now, with those things in mind, let's look at the actual poems you read for this week.

18. **C** This term was emphasized by the professor early on in the lecture. Here's why the other choices are incorrect.
- Choice (A) is wrong because the discussion is about Browning, not his influences.
- Answer choice (B) is too broad. Make sure your choice reflects the topic of the discussion.
- Eliminate (D) because the professor doesn't mention "My Last Duchess" until halfway through the lecture.

19. **D** This question asks you to listen again to the following part of the discussion and to determine what the professor meant in part of it (highlighted below):

> Okay, I hope that you all did the readings for this week. I know it's midterm time, and you're all busy, but Robert Browning is one of the most important poets in the history of English literature. He deserves all your attention. **Actually, it's usually not hard to sell Browning on my students, I find—his poetry really draws people in.**

Here's why the other choices are incorrect.
- Answer choices (A) and (B) don't make sense; the professor stated that Browning is very popular.
- Answer choice (C) is pretty much contradicted by the fact that both students say they were "confused" and the professor says "the dramatic monologue is actually a *more complex* [emphasis added] style of poetry" and thus, not "easy to understand."

20. **A** The professor says, "a monologue is a long speech given by an individual, right?" Here's why the other choices are incorrect.
- And the discussion is all about poems and people, not historical characters (choice (B)) or events (choice (C)).
- For this question, answer choice (D) is obviously out because a monologue is not a person.

21. **B, D, & E**

Here's why the other choices are incorrect.
- And answer choice (A) is not stated.
- Answer choice (C) is not mentioned. Although "My Last Duchess" may be about a duke, it doesn't mean that all poems of this sort are about people of high status.

22. **B** The student says, "...when I realized what was going on, it really creeped me out." Here's why the other choices are incorrect.
- Answer (A) is the opposite of what the woman felt.
- Answer choice (C) should be eliminated because no other poems are mentioned.
- The woman says she had trouble realizing that Browning was "using the voice of some historical character." She never questions the historical accuracy of the poem. Eliminate choice (D).

23. **C** This question asks you to listen again to the following part of the discussion:

> *W:* It took me a while to figure that out. And then, when I realized what was going on, it really creeped me out. I mean, did I read it right? He seemed to be admitting—

> *P:* Karen, why don't we hold off on analyzing the poem too much for right now. I don't want to shut you down, but I do want to stick to the general structure of the poems for a bit.

The professor said, "why don't we hold off on analyzing the poem too much for right now," meaning that he didn't want to talk about the specifics. Here's why the other choices are incorrect.
- Answer choice (D) is the opposite meaning of the sentence above. Choices (A) and (B) also invite further discussion, which is not what the professor is doing at this point.

Listening 5

Here is a transcript of the conversation (Track 28 on the accompanying CD).

N: Listen to a conversation on a college campus.

M: Amy, a bunch of us are probably going to ditch the dining hall and go for pizza tonight. If you're free, you can meet us at the east gate at seven.

W: You know, I'd love to, but I have tutoring tonight.

M: **Tutoring? I can't imagine you needing help with a class.**

W: **The tutoring I'm talking about is tutoring I'm doing for someone else—though, now that you mention it, physics has been giving me more problems than usual this semester.**

M: I find that hard to believe. Uh, so are you tutoring one of the lower-classmen, or something?

W: Actually, no, I go downtown to tutor a few students at the high school.

M: High school kids? Wow. In math or something?

W: Right. You've probably read about this in the paper, but the city's trying to raise the standards for its math classes. The problem is, a lot of the kids are behind when they get to junior high school.

M: So you help them get caught up?

W: Basically. I have three students for forty-five minutes each on Wednesday night. So I'm there from 6:00 to 8:30 or so.

M: Isn't that late for kids to be still at school?

W: Well, they'd be doing homework at that hour if they were home, anyway. The thing is, most of the tutors are students here at the university, so our classes aren't over until late afternoon. And the city education department likes us. We're good at what we do, but we volunteer, so the program doesn't cost a lot beyond, you know, the heat and electricity to keep the high school open at night.

M: Can you afford to take that much time away from your own studying?

W: Some weeks it's kind of hard, but, I mean, when I go to grad school, I'm going to have to start teaching physics to students as a professor's assistant, anyway. I may as well get used to teaching with easier material and just one student at a time.

M: And it must be nice to help people.

W: Definitely. That goes without saying. Forty-five minutes a week isn't much time, but all three of my students have improved in the months we've worked together. It's really inspiring.

M: Cool.

W: So, anyway, sorry about dinner. It sounds like fun, and if it were any other night—

M: Hey, I understand. Have fun, and I guess I'll see you in class tomorrow morning.

24. **D** This is the main idea of the conversation. The other choices are not part of the conversation.

25. **C** This question asks you to listen again to the following part of the conversation and to determine what the woman meant in part of it (highlighted below):

M: Tutoring? I can't imagine you needing help with a class.

W: The tutoring I'm talking about is tutoring I'm doing for someone else—**Though, now that you mention it, physics has been giving me more problems than usual this semester.**

The woman says "physics has been giving me more problems than usual this semester." Here's why the other choices are incorrect.
- And choice (A) isn't correct because the only mention of physics is the general comment that the class is giving her problems; there's no specific mention about any particular assignment.
- Choice (B) doesn't make sense because she wouldn't have problems with physics if she weren't taking it.
- She is not referring to the man, so eliminate choice (D).

26. **A** Here's the statement from the conversation: "...the city's trying to raise the standards for its math classes." Here's why the other choices are incorrect.
- Answer choice (B) is the opposite of what the woman states about the program; she says it doesn't have a lot of money.
- Answer choice (C) doesn't answer the question of "why" the program was started.
- Answer choice (D) doesn't work because there's no mention that the university students *initiated* or *suggested* the tutoring, just that they're doing it.

27. **D** Here's the statement from the conversation: "...the city education department likes us. We're good at what we do, but we volunteer, so the program doesn't cost a lot..." Here's why the other choices are incorrect.
- Eliminate choices (A) and (C) because of the word *most*, which is an extreme word. Remember to avoid these.
- Answer choice (B) is the opposite of what the woman says—she tutors at night.

28. **B** Here's the statement from the conversation: "...when I go to grad school, I'm going to have to start teaching physics to students...anyway. I may as well get used to teaching..." Here's why the other choices are incorrect.

- Answer choice (A) doesn't make sense: The woman is not being tutored; instead, she is tutoring other students.
- The jobs mentioned in answers (C) and (D) are not mentioned by the woman. She only mentions her future teaching duties as a grad student.

Listening 6

Here is a transcript of the lecture (Track 29 on the accompanying CD).

N: Listen to part of a lecture on events leading up to the American Revolution.

P: Okay, while I think of it, on Tuesday, I was originally going to show you a documentary film about a town in New England that was founded in the colonial period...uh, but it looks like we had a mix-up at the library, and they lent it out to someone, so I won't be able to show it until Thursday's class. So, instead of what I told you before, do the readings over the weekend and be prepared to discuss them on Tuesday. Hope that doesn't inconvenience you.

Okay, we're going to be talking about the American Revolution—what we often call the Revolutionary War—and we'll talk about two or three laws—the Sugar Act, the Currency Act, and the Stamp Act. They were all enacted soon after the French and Indian War ended in 1763. The British had won the war and, as a consequence, gained a lot of territory. But there was a downside to their victory: The war had cost a lot of money. So, British Parliament looked for ways to make sure that trade money from the American colonies came back to Britain. The increased money would help pay for the war. The way the British decided to get that money was to put taxes on certain purchases and to put limits on what kinds of goods the colonists could buy and sell, and that's where the trouble started.

The Sugar Act was passed in 1764. It was actually a revised version of an old tax on sugar by-products like molasses, and it had two big effects. One, Parliament lowered the tax on molasses but increased the tax on sugar and certain kinds of cloth, coffee, some wines, and fruits from the tropics. Second, it made sure the taxes were collected—the old tax on molasses hadn't been enforced very well. Now, what this did was, mostly, it made it more difficult for rich people—they were the ones buying the wines and tropical fruits and refined sugar, as you might imagine—to get things they wanted.

Now, that same year, Parliament passed the Currency Act. The colonists had to buy most of their goods from home, from England; that took up most of their British currency. So, what happened, of course, was that when they wanted to trade with each other within the colonies, they didn't have any money left over to use. That gave them an incentive to come up with their own paper currency. Some was backed by—meaning, its value was based on—people's property. It was useless for buying things from England, but it was very useful for workers with a little farmland who wanted to pay off their debts quickly. They could use the paper notes and then try to earn back the real value in produce from their farms. What did the Currency Act do? It invalidated all these colonial forms of paper currency. The colonists were told they couldn't use them anymore. So now you have the rich merchants, the traders, angered by the Sugar Act, and you have the laborers in debt who need to rely on paper money, and they're angered by the Currency Act.

Okay, so now the third law: the Stamp Act. The Sugar Act put a tax on sugar, so you might think the Stamp Act put a tax on stamps, but that wasn't the idea. The idea was that there would now be a tax on all sorts of official documents the colonists used to get for free: marriage licenses, newspapers, even playing cards. Well, these were the kinds of things people needed for everyday life, so everyone—merchants and laborers alike— was outraged.

Now, I'm leaving out some things in the sequence of events—such as that the British government adjusted some of the provisions of these laws when the colonists complained. But the main point I'm trying to make is, these laws were meant to get more money, more revenue, for the British government to pay for the French and Indian War, but the effect they had on the colonists was to make them feel as if they were being pushed around by a bunch of people in Parliament on the other side of the ocean. Up until this point, the taxes in the colonies had been administered by local governments in the colonies themselves. For the first time, Britain not only imposed taxes on the colonists but showed that it would use force to collect them. And this was the origin of the famous slogan "Taxation Without Representation," and it stoked the movement among the colonists to be free of British rule.

29. **D** Here's why the other choices are incorrect.
   - Answer choice (A) is not related to the main idea.
   - Choice (B) is far too broad.
   - No mention is made of choice (C).

30. **D** This question asks you to listen again to the following part of the lecture:

   P: Okay, while I think of it, on Tuesday, I was originally going to show you a documentary film about a town in New England that was founded in the colonial period...uh, but it looks like we had a mix-up at the library, and they lent it out to someone, so I won't be able to show it until Thursday's class. So instead of what I told you before, do the readings over the weekend and be prepared to discuss them on Tuesday. Hope that doesn't inconvenience you.

   The other choices are not correct because they are not mentioned at all. There's no further discussion of the film except to say that it's not available.

31. **A** This information is given in the professor's introduction: "They [the tax acts described in the rest of the lecture] were all enacted soon after the French and Indian War ended in 1763...the war had cost a lot of money." Here's why the other choices are incorrect.
   - Answers (B) and (C) are related to the actual taxes, but they do not answer the question of "why" the British needed money.
   - Choice (D) is incorrect because there's no mention of taxes in Britain, only in the American colonies.

32. **A & B**

Here's why the other choices are incorrect.

- Choice (C) is a little tricky because the lecture does say that the Sugar Act was "a *revised* version of an old tax on sugar by-products," [emphasis added] and it *does* mention taxes on coffee and wines, but not that they were *replaced*; instead, it says the Sugar Act "*increased* the tax on sugar and...coffee, some wines..." [again, emphasis added.]
- Of the choices, answer choice (D) is the best candidate for POE because it contradicts the main idea of the lecture, which is that there were too many taxes on the colonists.

33. **B** Here's the statement in the lecture: "The colonists had to buy most of their goods from home, from England; that took up most of their British currency." Here's why the other choices are incorrect.

- Eliminate choice (A) because although the colonists *did* need more money to pay the higher Sugar Tax, this is not the reason they developed their own paper currency; instead, the reason is that "they wanted to trade with each other within the colonies, [and] they didn't have any money [i.e., British currency] left over to use. That gave them an incentive to come up with their own paper currency."
- Eliminate choice (C) because it is extreme.
- There is no mention of answer choice (D) in the lecture.

34. **C** Here's why the other choices are incorrect.

- Answer choice (A) is wrong because newspapers are mentioned, but only because the Stamp Act taxed them and other "official documents"; reading them isn't mentioned at all.
- Also, eliminate answer choice (B) because the war was mentioned in a different part of the lecture.
- Answer choice (D) refers to the wrong act, so eliminate it.

THE SPEAKING SECTION: SAMPLE RESPONSES

Compare your responses with the samples below. All the samples are of high-scoring responses. Try to copy the style and structure of the sample responses.

Speaking 1

Describe an academic subject that interests you, and explain why you find the subject interesting. Include details and examples to support your explanation.

Here's one way you could have answered this question.

State personal preference	One of my favorite subjects is biology. I find it interesting for many reasons.
Reason #1	The first reason I find biology interesting is that I enjoy working with living things.
Specific detail for reason #1	Studying biology gives me the opportunity to work with plants, insects, and different kinds of animals.
Reason #2	Another reason I find biology interesting is the strange facts I have discovered.
Specific detail for reason #2	For example, there are some animals that have no mouths and some that live for only one day.
Reason #3	Finally, I find biology interesting because I will need it for my future career.
Specific detail for reason #3	I hope one day to be a doctor, and biology will be very useful to me.

Speaking 2

Narrator: Some universities have large, lecture-based classes while others have smaller, discussion-based classes. Which do think is better and why? Include details and reasons to support your position.

Here's one way you could have answered this question.

State option	I believe that small classes are better than larger ones.
Reason #1	I think it is important for students to be able to talk about ideas.
Specific detail for reason #1	If you are in a large class, you will not be heard and will not be able to interact with the teacher.
Reason #2	Also, a small class is better because the student will get to know the professor.
Specific detail for reason #2	The student will have a better experience if he or she knows the professor well. The student will get more out of the class.
Reason #3	Finally, I prefer small classes because they are more interesting.
Specific detail for reason #3	It is easy to become distracted or lost during a lecture. But during a talk, you are more involved.

Speaking 3

Here is a transcript of the passage (Track 30 on the accompanying CD).

Narrator: Now read the passage about birds of prey. You have 45 seconds to read the passage. Begin reading now.

Birds of Prey

Many people assume that *raptor* is the word properly used to designate all birds of prey. In fact, raptors are a group with three basic traits that many flesh-eating birds do not share. First, a raptor has strong feet and claws that it uses to capture prey. Second, a raptor has well-developed eyesight. This facilitates hunting from the air. Finally, a raptor has a hooked or curved beak for tearing flesh.

N: Now listen to part of a lecture on this topic given in a biology class.

P: There are two bird species found in our local area that I think do a good job of exemplifying the range of ways birds of prey can adapt. One is the bald eagle, and the other is the great blue heron. They both feed largely on fish, and they're both large. But the more closely you observe them, the more the differences show.

The bald eagle is always on the lookout for dead fish at the side of a river or lake or for fish that it can grab from close to the surface of the water. That's because it has very sharp eyesight and strong talons. It can swoop down, grab a fish in its claws, and start eating it midair. Its beak curves; it has sort of a hook at the end so it can start pulling food into its mouth.

The great blue heron might eat those same fish, but it would have to go about it differently. The heron does have good eyesight—it'd be hard to see prey otherwise, right? But its claws aren't as strong as the eagle's, so it usually attacks by diving into the water headfirst. The heron has a long, straight beak that it can use either like a spear to impale a fish or like tongs to grab it.

N: The professor discussed the characteristics of two kinds of birds of prey. On the basis of these characteristics, explain whether either bird would be categorized as a raptor.

Here's one way you could have answered this question.

Main response	According to the reading, a raptor has several characteristics. The eagle is a raptor but the heron isn't.
Characteristic #1 from reading	First, a raptor has claws on its feet. It uses its claws to capture food.
Detail #1 from lecture	The eagle mentioned in the lecture has these types of claws. However, the heron uses its beak to capture food.
Characteristic #2 from reading	Another quality of the raptor is strong eyesight. Its eyesight helps the bird hunt.
Detail #2 from lecture	The professor said that the eagle has strong eyesight. The heron does as well.
Characteristic #3 from reading	The last thing about a raptor is a hooked beak.
Detail #3 from lecture	The eagle has this, but the heron doesn't.

Speaking 4

Here is a transcript of the discussion (Track 31 on the accompanying CD).

N: The College of Arts and Sciences at Eastern University has decided to add a senior project to its existing graduation requirements. The campus newspaper printed the following report about the announcement of the new requirement. You have 45 seconds to read the report. Begin reading now.

The College of Arts and Sciences has announced that it will require students to write a senior thesis to qualify for graduation, beginning with students who enter the university this coming fall. The senior thesis is currently an option in all departments. Specific criteria have not yet been released by the dean, but they are expected to define the thesis as a year-long research project, undertaken with the guidance of a faculty advisor, that results in a paper of at least 50 pages or the equivalent.

N: Now listen to two students as they discuss the report.

W: Wow, look at this. The dean seems to be serious about tightening graduation requirements—they'll be forcing students to write a senior thesis in order to graduate.

M: Yeah, you know, I read that at breakfast. It seems a little weird.

W: Weird? Haven't you seen all those reports about how graduates with poor writing skills are having trouble finding jobs? Companies don't want to hire them.

M: Uh-huh.

W: And the ones that want to apply to graduate school—if they can't write, they can't present their research ideas effectively in their essays.

M: I guess I'm more thinking about the science people—biology, physics. I mean, it seems strange to give them this big paper to do.

W: Maybe. On the other hand, the paper—see here?—it says you have to write a paper "or equivalent." So presumably, you can do a project that ends up as a lot of data and stuff... maybe make it a presentation instead of a paper. But even so, I mean, don't biologists have to learn how to write up their research in order to get it published? It seems to me that having a writing requirement is long overdue.

N: The woman explains her opinion of the announcement made by the College of Arts and Sciences. State her opinion, and explain the reasons she gives for holding that opinion.

Here's how you could have answered this question.

State opinion	The woman states that the senior thesis is a good idea.
Reason #1	She thinks this is a good idea because students should know how to write.
Detail for reason #1	The woman says that companies don't want to hire people who are bad writers.
Reason #2	The woman also agrees with the idea because of graduate school.
Detail for reason #2	According to the woman, students need to write well in order to succeed in graduate school.

Speaking 5
Here is a transcript of the conversation (Track 32 on the accompanying CD).

N: Now listen to a conversation between two students.

W: The walls of my dorm room are so thin, I can hear everything my neighbors do.

M: Oh yeah, you live in one of the newer dorms, huh?

W: Yup. Their voices and music come right through, even when they're trying to be quiet. I really can't study there anymore.

M: Well, it's the middle of the semester, and the housing office has some odd rooms no one's in. They'll let you move if you ask.

W: I guess. It'd be a big project.

M: Yeah, but if it's affecting your ability to study. There must be somewhere quieter than your room now.

W: Right.

M: Or what about studying at a quiet place in the library?

W: I know a lot of people do that. I've just always studied in my room because it's more convenient than dragging all my textbooks and notes and things across campus.

M: Sure, but you also don't have your TV and stereo with you. I find it much less easy to get distracted when I use the library.

W: I can see that.

M: Right? I find my work gets done much faster—and I remember what I've read better—when I study in the library. And the lighting's probably better for your eyes than the lamp in your room.

N: The speakers discuss two possible solutions for the woman's problem. Describe the problem. Then state which of the two solutions you prefer, and explain why.

Here's how you may have answered this question.

State the problem	The problem is that it is too loud in the student's room to study.
State the solutions	The friend offers two solutions. One is to move, and the other is to study in the library.
State your preference	I think the best option would be to study in the library.
Reason #1	The library is a good place to study because it is quiet.
Detail for reason #1	The student will not have to worry about music or loud conversations at the library.
Reason #2	I also think the library is better because the student won't be distracted there.
Detail for reason #2	It is very easy to focus on work when at the library.

Speaking 6

Here is the transcript of the lecture (Track 33 on the accompanying CD).

N: Now listen to part of a lecture in a history class.

P: The discovery of copper was a great advance for civilization, but no one is quite sure how it happened. Of course, in nature, metal like copper is usually buried in rock. Early humans must have accidentally discovered that heating the rock melted the metal and released it. There are two interesting ways that might have happened.

One relates to the use of primitive campfires. Once humans figured out how to control fire for light and heat, they knew that they needed to keep their fires confined. One of the ways they did this was to take stones and cover the fire with them partially. That kept the fire enclosed, and it also made sure it didn't burn too fast and use up the fuel. Now, what do you think might have happened? Some of those stones contained copper, and before the fire died down, it was hot enough to melt the copper out of the stones. When people went back to the fire after it had burned out, they discovered small pieces of shiny metal that had melted out and cooled.

There's a second possibility that relates to pottery. Early humans discovered how to make pottery before they learned how to use copper. Of course, to make pottery, you have to bake it in an oven, right? Well, some societies got into the habit of decorating their containers with colored stones before baking them. One of those stones is a mineral called *malachite,* and malachite contains...that's right: copper. The hot temperature inside the oven released the copper metal from the other ingredients. When the people took their pottery out of the oven, they found pieces of copper at the bottom.

N: Using points and examples from the talk, explain the two possible ways early humans discovered how to use fire to release copper from solid rock.

Here's how you may have answered this question.

State main idea	The professor states that it was an accident that humans discovered copper.
Reason #1	Humans may have discovered copper by using campfires.
Detail for reason #1	Copper is stuck inside rocks, and people used rocks to contain their fires.
Link between reason #1 and main idea	If the fire was hot enough, the people would have noticed pieces of copper in their fires.
Reason #2	Another way people could have discovered copper was through pottery.
Detail for reason #2	Sometimes the people put stones in the oven with the pottery.
Link between reason #2 and main idea	The heat caused the copper to melt and come out, and the people could have discovered it that way.

THE WRITING SECTION: SAMPLE RESPONSES

Look over your written responses. Make sure they answer the question effectively, are of the appropriate length, and are well organized. Use the following responses as guides.

Writing 1

Narrator: Now read the passage about the suppression of forest fires. You have three minutes to read the passage. Begin reading now.

Wilderness management has advanced greatly over the last century, due in part to such practices as the suppression of forest fires and limitations on the clear-cutting of trees. Monitoring forests for small brushfires is easier with aircraft, as is the use of large amounts of water and sophisticated chemical fire extinguishers to prevent fires from spreading.

The goals of decreasing the amount of destruction by fires and cutting are wide-ranging. One is simply the longer lives and improved health of trees. In some areas of hickory and oak forest on the Eastern Seaboard, fire suppression has allowed the maturation of so many trees that the treetops form a continuous canopy.

There is evidence of the healthful effects of fire suppression closer to the ground as well. Vines and low bushes that would be burned out in a forest fire can flourish when fires are suppressed, of course, but there is a more indirect way fires harm plant life. Chemical tests on areas that have recently experienced forest fires demonstrate that burning decreases the overall amount of nutrients in the soil. Suppressing fires prevents such a decrease. Ferns, wildflowers, and herbs grow without disturbance.

Finally, wildlife can benefit. In the eastern hickory and oak forests, the suppression of fires has meant that forest animals—ranging from small insects and birds to large deer and bears—are not burned to death. Deer populations, in particular, have increased notably.

Here is a transcript of the lecture (Track 34 on the accompanying CD).

N: Now listen to part of a lecture on the topic you just read about.

P: For years, forest fires were regarded as uniformly destructive, and forest managers put a lot of effort into preventing them. But it turns out that fire suppression may have destructive long-term effects on the forests it's supposed to protect.

For instance, mature oaks have grown so thickly in some places that little light reaches the forest floor. But young oak trees need light in order to grow properly. The lack of light has meant that new oaks aren't maturing rapidly enough to replace the older oaks. It also means that other tree species that don't need so much light, such as maples, are invading oak and hickory forests and competing for resources.

There are competition problems at ground level too. What forest fires, both natural and artificial, used to do is burn off some of the plants on the forest floor before they could grow into huge thickets. Now they run wild over the ground—and again, that means it's hard for young trees and other native plants to grow.

Then there's the increase in the deer population—this partially results from the lack of forest fires and partially from limitations on hunting—but the thing is, deer like to eat the leaves off oak saplings. So if one of those oak seedlings somehow does manage to get a good start, despite the shade and all the other plants competing for nutrients, it's likely to be killed by having its leaves eaten.

Oh, and one other thing: Scientists are now finding that forest fires release nutrients from the plants and animals that are burned. That means that, even though the total amount of nutrients is decreased, there can actually be more nutrients available on the soil surface for plants that are trying to grow back afterward.

N: Summarize the points made in the lecture you just heard, explaining how they challenge specific claims made in the reading passage. You may refer to the passage as you write.

Sample High-Scoring Response

In the lecture, the professor made several points about the effects of forest fires. The professor argues that forest fires can actually be good for the forests, not bad. The talk by the professor however, is different from the reading. According to the reading, forest fires are harmful to the land and should be stopped. But the professor casts doubt on that view with several points.

The first point the teacher makes is that if there are too many trees, it is hard for some trees to get light and nutrition. This means that the trees are not healthy. The professor's point is different from the reading. The reading states that it is good to have a lot of trees in the forest. But the lecture shows that too many trees is actually bad for the forest.

Another point made by the professor is that burning a forest actually puts more nutrients into the land. This is not what the reading says. The reading says that fires take nutrients out of the soil. However, the professor says there are more nutrients at the top for plants to use.

In conclusion, the professor challenges the claims made in the reading by showing that forest fires are sometimes needed for a healthy forest.

Writing 2

Directions: For this task, you will write an essay in which you state, explain, and support your position on an issue. You have 30 minutes to plan and write your essay.

Question:

Do you agree or disagree with the following statement?

A university education should be provided free of charge to all interested scholars.

Use examples and reasons to support your position.

Sample High-Scoring Response

The issue stated by the topic is whether or not a university education should be provided free to all that are interested. This is a very important issue because the cost of education is rising and because education is very important. However, I believe that universities should not give an education for free.

I do not think that university education should be free because who is going to pay for it if the students do not? If the government has to pay for it then that means taxes are raised. This is not fair to the people because if they have to pay higher taxes they might not want to go to the university. That means they are paying for something they won't even use, which is not fair.

Furthermore, I don't think university education should be free because universities that have more money can give better education. The only way for the universities to get more money is to charge the students. If the education is free, how will the universities get money to buy computers, books, and hire good professors to teach? For this reason, we should not have a free university.

Finally, I think the university should not be free because there are many schools available and they have different prices. Poor students can go to a school that doesn't cost as much and still learn a lot. Also, many universities give aid or scholarships so a student can attend even if they don't have money. So there is no need to make a university education free.

In conclusion, university education should not be made free. I believe this because the colleges need the money to make them better. If the universities are free, taxes will be raised and people will have to pay for things they might not use. Since there are many schools available with scholarships and aid, university should not be made free.

NOTES

NOTES

NOTES

NOTES

AP Exams

Cracking the AP Biology Exam, 2009 Edition
978-0-375-42884-5 • $18.00/C$21.00

Cracking the AP Calculus AB & BC Exams, 2009 Edition
978-0-375-42885-2 • $19.00/C$22.00

Cracking the AP Chemistry Exam, 2009 Edition
978-0-375-42886-9 • $18.00/C$22.00

Cracking the AP Computer Science A & AB, 2006–2007
978-0-375-76528-5 • $19.00/C$27.00

Cracking the AP Economics Macro & Micro Exams, 2009 Edition
978-0-375-42887-6 • $18.00/C$21.00

Cracking the AP English Language & Composition Exam, 2009 Edition
978-0-375-42888-3 • $18.00/C$21.00

Cracking the AP English Literature & Composition Exam, 2009 Edition
978-0-375-42889-0 • $18.00/C$21.00

Cracking the AP Environmental Science Exam, 2009 Edition
978-0-375-42890-6 • $18.00/C$21.00

Cracking the AP European History Exam, 2009 Edition
978-0-375-42891-3 • $18.00/C$21.00

Cracking the AP Physics B Exam, 2009 Edition
978-0-375-42892-0 • $18.00/C$21.00

Cracking the AP Physics C Exam, 2009 Edition
978-0-375-42893-7 • $18.00/C$21.00

Cracking the AP Psychology Exam, 2009 Edition
978-0-375-42894-4 • $18.00/C$21.00

Cracking the AP Spanish Exam, with Audio CD, 2009 Edition
978-0-375-76530-8 • $24.95/$27.95

Cracking the AP Statistics Exam, 2009 Edition
978-0-375-42848-7 • $19.00/C$22.00

Cracking the AP U.S. Government and Politics Exam, 2009 Edition
978-0-375-42896-8 • $18.00/C$21.00

Cracking the AP U.S. History Exam, 2009 Edition
978-0-375-42897-5 • $18.00/C$21.00

Cracking the AP World History Exam, 2009 Edition
978-0-375-42898-2 • $18.00/C$21.00

SAT Subject Tests

Cracking the SAT Biology E/M Subject Test, 2009–2010 Edition
978-0-375-42905-7 • $19.00/C$22.00

Cracking the SAT Chemistry Subject Test, 2009–2010 Edition
978-0-375-42906-4 • $19.00/C$22.00

Cracking the SAT French Subject Test, 2009–2010 Edition
978-0-375-42907-1 • $19.00/C$22.00

Cracking the SAT U.S. & World History Subject Tests, 2009–2010 Edition
978-0-375-42908-8 • $19.00/C$22.00

Cracking the SAT Literature Subject Test, 2009–2010 Edition
978-0-375-42909-5 • $19.00/C$22.00

Cracking the SAT Math 1 & 2 Subject Tests, 2009–2010 Edition
978-0-375-42910-1 • $19.00/C$22.00

Cracking the SAT Physics Subject Test, 2009–2010 Edition
978-0-375-42911-8 • $19.00/C$22.00

Cracking the SAT Spanish Subject Test, 2009–2010 Edition
978-0-375-42912-5 • $19.00/C$22.00